# GLOBALIZATION AND DEVELOPMENT

The Oxford India Handbooks are an important new initiative in academic publishing. Each volume offers a comprehensive survey of research in a critical subject area and provides facts, figure, and analyses for a well-grounded perspective. The series intends to provide scholars, students, and policy planners with a well-rounded understanding of wide range of issues in the social sciences.

*Other Titles in the Series*

HANDBOOK OF HUMAN DEVELOPMENT
Sakiko Fukuda-Parr and A.K. Shiva kumar (Editors)

HANDBOOK OF URBANIZATION IN INDIA (OIP)
K.C. Shivaramakrishnan, Amitabh Kundu, and B.N. Singh

HANDBOOK OF HUMAN RIGHTS AND CRIMINAL JUSTICE IN INDIA
*The System and Procedure* (Second Edition)
South Asia Human Rights Documentation Centre

HANDBOOK OF WATER RESOURCES IN INDIA
The World Bank

HANDBOOK OF AGRICULTURE IN INDIA
Shovan Ray (Editor)

HANDBOOK OF INTERNATIONAL HUMANITARIAN LAW IN SOUTH ASIA
V.S. Mani (Editor)

HANDBOOK OF INDIAN SOCIOLOGY (OIP)
Veena Das (Editor)

MAKING NEWS
*Handbook of the Media in Contemporary India* (OIP)
Uday Sahay (Editor)

HANDBOOK OF POVERTY IN INDIA
*Perspectives, Policies, and Programmes*
R. Radhakrishna and Shovan Ray (Editors)

MANAGING BUSINESS IN THE 21ST CENTURY
*A Handbook* (OIP)
Anindya Sen and P.K. Sett (Editors)

HANDBOOK OF ENERGY AND THE ENVIRONMENT
Bani P. Banerjee

# GLOBALIZATION AND DEVELOPMENT

## A Handbook of New Perspectives

Edited by
Ashwini Deshpande

OXFORD
UNIVERSITY PRESS

**OXFORD**
UNIVERSITY PRESS

Oxford University Press is a department of the University of Oxford.
It furthers the University's objective of excellence in research, scholarship,
and education by publishing worldwide. Oxford is a registered trademark of
Oxford University Press in the UK and in certain other countries

Published in India by
Oxford University Press
2/11 Ground Floor, Ansari Road, Daryaganj, New Delhi 110 002, India



First Edition published in 2008
Oxford India Paperbacks 2010



ISBN-13: 978-0-19-806910-2
ISBN-10: 0-19-806910-3

Typeset in Dante MT 11/13
by Eleven Arts, Keshav Puram, New Delhi 110 035
Printed in India by Repro Knowledgecast Limited, Thane

# Contents

# Tables

## APPENDIX TABLES

# Figures

## APPENDIX FIGURES

# Abbreviations

| | |
|---|---|
| ACDC | Annual Conference on Development and Change |
| ACE | Association of Caribbean Economists |
| ACP | Africa Caribbean Pacific |
| ADF | Augmented Dickey–Fuller |
| AMIS | Annual manufacturing Industry Statistics |
| ATC | Agreement on Textiles & Clothing |
| BDL | Banque du Liban |
| BSL | Banque du Syrie and du Liban |
| BWI | Bretton Woods Institution |
| CA | Cotonou Agreement |
| CAPORDE | Cambridge Advanced Programme on Rethinking Development Economics |
| CEEC | Central and East European Countries |
| CIFIT | China International Fair for Investment and Trade |
| CVI | composite vulnerability index |
| EBA | Everything but Arms |
| EC | Enabling Clause |
| EGA | Employment Guarantee Act |
| EGA | Employment Guarantee Act |
| EPA | Economic Partnership Agreement |
| EPZ | export processing zone |
| EU | European Union |
| FC | foreign currency |
| FDI | foreign direct investment |
| FTA | free trade agreement |
| FTAA | Free Trade Agreement of the Americas |
| GATT | General Agreement on Tariffs and Trade |
| GCSE/CGSE | Consultative Committee on Smaller Economies |

| | |
|---|---|
| GEM | Gender and Macroeconomics Programme |
| GSP | Generalized System of references |
| GVC | global value chain |
| IFI | International financial institutions |
| IFP | indicators of financial position |
| IMF | International Monetary Fund |
| IPA | investment promotion agency |
| I-S | import-substitution |
| ISI | Import Substitution Industrialization |
| ITCS | International Trade in Commodities Statistics |
| JV | Joint venture |
| LBP | Lebanese Pound |
| LD | liability dollarization |
| LDC | less developed country |
| LTA | Long-term arrangement |
| LTFR | Less than full reciprocity |
| MFA | multi fibre agreement |
| MIA | Multilateral Investment Agreement |
| MNC | multinational corporation |
| NAC | National Advisory Council |
| NAFTA | North American Free Trade Agreement |
| NAMA | Non-agricultural market access |
| NCMP | National Common Minimum Programme |
| NFWP | National Food for Work Programme |
| NGO | Non-governmental Organization |
| NIEO | New International Economic Order |
| NREGA | National Rural Employment Guarantee Act |
| NTB | Non-tariff Barrier |
| OAP | offshore Assembly Processing |
| OPT | Outward Processing Trade |
| PRC | People's Republic of China |
| RCAI | Revealed Comparative Advantage Index |
| S&D | special and differential treatment |
| SAARC | South Asian Association for Regional Co-operation |
| SAI | State Administrative Tribunal |
| SAP | Structural Adjustment Programme |
| SEATINI | Southern & Eastern African Trade Information and Negotiations Institute |
| SEZ | special Economic Zone |
| SIDS | Small Island developing states |
| SIS | State Institute of Statistics |
| SME | Small and medium enterprise |
| SOE | state-owned enterprise |

| | |
|---|---|
| SPIVs | social, political, and institutional variables |
| T&C | textiles and clothing |
| TINA | there is no alternative |
| TNC | Trade Negotiation Committee |
| UNCTAD | United Nations Conference on Trade and Development |
| UNDP | United Nations Development Programme |
| UPA | United progressive Alliance |
| UR | Uruguay Round |
| VAR | vector autoregression |
| VAT | Value added tax |
| VII | vulnerability impact index |
| WTO | World Trade Organization |

# Contributors

P.L. Beena is Lecturer at the Centre for Development Studies, Thiruvanthapuram.

Mario Biggeri is Associate Professor of development economics at the University of Florence, Italy.

Miguel Ceara-Hatton is Economist at the Centro de Investigación Económica para el Caribe (CIECA).

Ha-joon Chang is Reader of Economics, University of Cambridge.

R.H.J. de Kadt is Head of the School of Politics at the University of KwaZulu-Natal.

Ashwini Deshpande is Professor of Economics at the Delhi School of Economics, University of Delhi. Her recent publications include *Capital Without Borders: Challenges to Development*, 2010.

Jean Drèze is Professor, Centre for Development Economics at the Delhi School of Economics.

Johannes Fedderke is Professor of economics at the University of Cape Town, and the Director of Economic Research Southern Africa.

Pável Isa Contreras is President of CIECA and advisor on trade and fiscal policies for the Technical Secretariat of the Presidency of the Dominican Republic.

Burça Kizilirmak is Assistant Professor of economics at Ankara University, Turkey.

Gilberto A. Libanio is Professor of economics at Federal University of Minas Gerais

J.M. Luiz is Dean of the Faculty of Management at the University of Johannesburg.

Emel Memis, completed her PhD in Economics at the University of UTAH. She was formerly a consultant for Asia-Pacific Trade and Investment Initiative at UNDP Regional Centre in Colombo.

Martín P. Abeles is Director of the Economics Working Group in the Argentina Observatory, New School University and faculty member at the Graduate Program in International Affairs, New School University.

ARMEN V. PAPAZIAN is Research Associate at the Judge Business School, University of Cambridge, and a Senior Consultant at the Dubai International Financial Exchange, UAE.

FIONA TREGENNA is Associate Professor in the Department of Economics and Econometrics at the University of Johannesburg, South Africa.

RAMAA VASUDEVAN is Assistant Professor at Colorado State University, Fort Collins.

JINKANG ZHANG is Associate Professor of economics at Yunnan University of Finance and Economics, China.

# Acknowledgements

The Annual Conference on Development and Change as a platform for young, heterodox scholars is primarily the product of the vision and imagination of Manuel Montes who, at the time, was with the Ford Foundation in New York. He persuaded me to take this project on and supported it in myriad ways. All the members of the first steering committee of the Conference were from successive batches of CAPORDE (Cambridge Advanced Programme on Rethinking Development Economics) which, at the time of going to press, has completed its sixth session of training young scholars and practitioners from all over the globe. The programme is conducted annually under the able chairmanship of Ha-Joon Chang at the University of Cambridge. One of the outcomes of the first conference was that we were successfully able to build firm partnerships with other global initiatives and expand the steering committee for the second conference to reflect these synergies. The Carnegie Council of Ethics and International Affairs, New York, and Nadia Roumani in particular, supported the ACDC efficiently by housing the project and by providing other kinds of logistical help. Homagni Choudhary from Delhi University provided competent assistance in a variety of tasks related to the Conference. All the paper presenters, panelists, and discussants, not to mention the exquisite environment of Neemrana, contributed to make the first Conference a very exciting experience. Two anonymous referees gave helpful suggestions. Editors at the Oxford University Press was encouraging all along and accommodated my erratic schedule without any complaints and supervised the production of the book. This volume, thus, represents the combined efforts of several individuals; especially, the fantastic teamwork of the first steering committee: Keith Nurse, Luiz Niemeyer, Codrina Rada, Peter Jacobs, and Nadia Roumani.

Ashwini Deshpande
Delhi School of Economics

# Preface to the Paperback Edition

In less than three years of its first publication, the fact that this handbook is being reprinted as a paperback is testimony to the enduring relevance of the concerns articulated in this volume. At the time of the first Annual Conference for Development and Change (ACDC) in 2005, which resulted in this book, most of the participants had voiced their sense of disquiet about the financial fragility of the US economy and about the sustainability of the predominant model of economic growth that not only disregarded the interests of the majority of the poor and the working masses in the developing countries, but also reduced the 'policy space' for developing countries as a whole. At the time, any advocacy, for instance, of industrial or sectoral policies to remedy deep-seated imbalances in patterns of development was seen as conservative, old-fashioned, anti-market and therefore, anti-development.

The momentous events in the global economy over the last three years have shifted the terms of discourse such that many 'old-fashioned' concepts are back in circulation. Sub-prime housing loans were once seen as the logical market solutions to the housing needs of the poorer sections of the US population, and thus considered highly desirable. However, they resulted in a housing bubble that raised property prices way beyond their 'market' price and once the bubble burst, it hurt the same poor much more than it hurt the rich. Innovations in financial markets that were being championed for having heralded a new era of technical complexity, as well as new opportunities to suit all kinds of investor 'needs', suddenly lost their gloss and sheen, as it turned out that despite the window dressing, the recipe for financial market stability cannot ignore the old-fashioned prudential lending considerations. Even the International Monetary Fund, with its rigid and ahistorical approach to development, and strict aversion to government intervention, is now starting to acknowledge the desirability of limited financial market regulation.

As banks and financial markets collapsed in rapid succession since 2008, the global economy's worst crisis since the Great Depression of the 1930s created massive unemployment through lay-offs and closures, and resulted in wage freezes for those lucky enough with jobs, and thus hurt not only the poor, but made large sections of the middle and the elite classes—who had ridden high on the roller-coaster of the bubble years—extremely vulnerable. The wheel of policy discourse has now turned a full circle since the 1950s: now the leaders of several developed countries, not to mention World Bank economists, advocate the use of industrial policy as an effective instrument to battle serious unemployment in the developed countries as well to bring about the badly needed structural change in developing countries.

Just as there was talk in the US economy about whether the 'green shoots of recovery' could be seen and whether the world had seen the worst of it, European economies were hit by a massive debt crisis, spearheaded by the collapse of banks in Greece and Iceland, leading to a serious recession. The efforts to save the euro have resulted in the announcement of the largest bail-out package. While the bail-out is seen as inevitable and welcomed by some, it has to be matched by an austerity package which will have serious adverse effects on the lives of the working classes. In a tragic repeat of history, mirroring the 1980s developing countries' debt crisis, the working populations of the crisis-ridden countries have to tighten their belts and pay the price for the profligacy of the banking and financial sector.

These events, underscore, once again, the need for reorienting economic policies to serve the interests of the working people, rather than the interests of the dominant vested interests. For developing countries, this question is additionally complicated by the shrinking policy space that is discussed in chapter 2 of this book. Within a country, an example of how policy space can be reclaimed in the interests of the poor and working masses was included in the first edition of this volume via discussion on India's National Rural Employment Guarantee Act (NREGA). Between 2005 and now, when the essay on 'India's Employment Guarantee Act: Reclaiming Policy Space' was written by Jean Drèze—the NREGA has expanded to cover all the 600 districts of the country. It has also been accompanied by the Right to Information Act that aims to make policies and policymakers' actions more transparent. However, the challenges in the implementation of both these pieces of legislation demonstrate the vicious grip of power and the not-so-inconsiderable ability of the powerful to subvert and undermine moves that might hurt their interests. However, a comprehensive assessment of the implementation of both these Acts presents a mixed picture and the positive aspects need to be seized upon, strengthened, and emulated in other spheres of policy making.

Since its inception in 2005, the ACDC has grown into a vibrant community of young scholars and practitioners all over the world and has forged strong partnerships with other like-minded networks such as GEM (Gender and Macroeconomics at the University of Utah), ACE (Association of Caribbean Economists), and APORDE (African Program on Rethinking Development Economics). After the first conference in Neemrana, we have had conferences in Sao Paulo, Cape Town, and Johannesburg. We hope to continue growing, despite financial difficulties, and hope to expand as a platform for young heterodox scholars to showcase their rigorous policy oriented research aimed at promoting development in a globalized world.

July 2010

Ashwini Deshpande
Chairperson, ACDC

# 1

# Introduction

Ashwini Deshpande

This volume is a collection of some of the papers presented at the first Annual Conference on Development and Change (ACDC), held at Neemrana (India) in December 2005. A size constraint on the final volume dictated the number of papers that could be included in the volume; papers that could not be included due to space constraints are equally informative and insightful as these included. The distinctive feature of the ACDC and, hence, this volume is that it represents active research by younger, not-yet-well-established scholars who are engaged in formulating a critique of the mainstream development policy, as espoused by the Washington Consensus. The conference sessions were interspersed with plenaries that addressed specific themes, where the speakers were relatively senior, well-established scholars. Two of the plenary lectures, by Ha-Joon Chang and Jean Dreze, have been included in the volume, because they provide a fitting start and end to this volume: Ha-Joon Chang's contribution discusses the lack of policy space for developing countries today and Jean Dreze focuses on the creation of the Employment Guarantee Act (EGA) in India, thus suggesting how people's struggles can reclaim, or even create, the vanishing policy space.

Debates about globalization that contain a critique of the orthodox, neo-liberal paradigm abound in the literature;[1] the potential contribution of this volume is that it simultaneously suggests policy alternatives, drawn from a variety of domestic milieus—thus rejecting the claim that there is no alternative to the standard set of policies that the orthodox approach espouses. The alternatives suggested are multiple, are located in the specific contexts of the countries being considered, and thus additionally refute the 'one-size-fits-all' approach. Since each paper focuses on one or more specific countries, the discussion moves from a general critique—that is necessary but not sufficient—to the specific, which needs to be disseminated with urgency. What adds to the specificity is that each of the papers focuses on one particular aspect of policy, thus moving beyond a general,

[1] See, for instance, Bhagwati (2004), Oxfam (2002), Stiglitz (2002), Rodrick (1997) to mention just a few from a huge body of literature.

overall critique of contemporary globalization to a specific examination of particular policies in particular countries.

While the contributions span a number of specific countries, the issues raised are common to most developing countries, thus making the discussion relevant even to readers outside these specific focus countries. Some of the contributions are more technical than others; demonstrating that heterodox critiques need not lack analytical rigour. However, in the relatively technical chapters, the problem and the conclusions are lucidly spelt out and can be followed clearly even by those who prefer to skip the technical details. Therefore, the belief is that this volume will serve as a practically useful handbook to students of development economics and policy, to practitioners, to advocacy groups, and to activists looking to strengthen their arguments by citing concrete examples from countries other than their own.

## THE BACKDROP

While terms such as 'Washington Consensus' are widely used, it is useful to spell them out at the very beginning. The reference is to a particular consensus on development that is espoused in the international arena, principally by the International Monetary Fund (IMF) and the World Bank—the two Bretton-Woods institutions (BWIs). This view believes that the primary route out of underdevelopment is by minimizing the role of the state in economic activity; privatizing state-owned enterprises and services; liberalizing all markets; reducing tariffs and regulations to trade in goods and services (eliminating protectionism); gradually eliminating restrictions on movements of capital (capital account convertibility); and completely integrating with the global economy. Since the same set of prescriptions is advocated for all countries at all times, it constitutes an orthodoxy. However, this orthodoxy has a very large number of adherents among economists, decision makers within national governments as well as in international bodies, as well as the media—a huge international community believes in the infallibility of these prescriptions. These are seen as the magic cure to the problem of low growth and persistent underdevelopment and when countries do not perform as well as they are supposed to, the blame is laid on incomplete adherence to the whole package, rather than on its possible inappropriateness.

The policies advanced by the Washington Consensus have had a dubious effect on rates of growth in most cases; they have vastly improved the living standards and opportunities for a small elite in developing countries, while increasing the insecurities and vulnerabilities for the vast majority of working people. Since these institutions recognize that this could exacerbate social tensions, they, particularly the World Bank, offer a palliative in the form of 'social safety nets'.

Over the last several years, a number of initiatives have emerged across the globe that have questioned and challenged the established orthodoxy that dominates development economics and dictates the prescriptions that are imposed on a large number of countries in the name of development. These initiatives, such as the Cambridge Advanced Programme on Rethinking Development Economics (CAPORDE), Association of Caribbean Economists (ACE), Gender and Macroeconomics Programme at the University of Utah (GEM), Southern and Eastern African Trade Information and Negotiations Institute (SEATINI), initiatives of the United Nations Development Programme (UNDP), and several others, train several young scholars, mostly economists, every year. This growing community of heterodox thinkers is actively engaged in research that substantiates the concerns of all those who are worried about the immiserizing impact of contemporary globalization on the vast majority of working people across the world.

Several critics of the mainstream approach ultimately defend it on the grounds of TINA (there is no alternative). Thus, they recognize that the mainstream prescriptions might be inappropriate in certain contexts, but support them nevertheless on the grounds that there are no other feasible alternatives, particularly in the face of the collapse of the socialist system.

Thus, busting the TINA myth is as important as highlighting the problems inherent in the mainstream approach. For us, it was equally imperative that the synergies between these networks was tapped, and their research consolidated and showcased in a way that concrete policy alternatives could be offered and widely disseminated. The ACDC was started with precisely these objectives. This volume represents a small fraction from a very large pool of research that is motivated by the belief that real development must mean an improvement in the lives of the poor and the working people in all countries.

## SHRINKING POLICY SPACE

In the opening chapter, Ha-Joon Chang discusses how the 'policy space' available to the developing countries has shrunk over the last quarter of a century so much that their sovereignty in the realm of economic policy is vanishing. He traces the current shrinkage of policy space to the late 1980s when the IMF and the World Bank, in the aftermath of the debt crisis, increased the scope of the structural adjustment programmes and the conditionalities attached to their loans. Thus, he shows how the BWI conditionalities, earlier concerned with budget deficits, privatization, and trade liberalization, in a gradual 'mission creep', moved into other areas, so much so that 'these days there is virtually no area on which the Bank and the Fund do not have (often very strong influence)—democracy, judicial reform, corporate governance, health, education and what not'. He argues that the shrinkage in policy space has been the most acute in the realm of trade and industrial policies. The paper traces the evolution of the World Trade Organization (WTO) from the General Agreement on Trade and Tariffs and persuasively demonstrates how the issues currently under the purview of the latter, were earlier policy variables of independent governments. Lest this be thought of as an inevitable consequence of globalization, he shows how developed countries continue to retain their right to decide on economic polices that are best suited to their interests, and how these often run contrary to their own advice on 'best' policies. Chang's earlier work very convincingly demonstrates how the present-day developed countries themselves followed 'bad' policies when they were at similar stages of development as the developing countries are today. He thus accuses them of 'kicking away the ladder' in a provocative book by this title. This suggests that the current orthodoxy really stems from the needs of certain global vested interests.

## TRADE REGIMES

If, as Chang argues, policy space is shrinking, particularly in the realm of trade and industrial policies, then it is crucial that we examine the working of the contemporary trade regime, responsible for this shrinkage, in all its complexity to see how 'the rules of the game' have been changing. Pável Isa–Contreras and Miguel Ceara-Halton explain how, measures for special and differential treatment (SDT), which helped the smaller and developing countries in early stages of their development, have been substantially weakened at the multilateral level by the introduction of far-reaching mandatory commitments. This dismantling or weakening of SDT provisions is taking place in the name of the presumably undisputed positive effects of trade liberalization. The authors argue that this has seriously impeded the ability of smaller countries to pursue an independent development agenda without the promised benefits of higher rates of growth and poverty reduction. On the contrary, there is some evidence that this might have exacerbated structural deficiencies and worsened income distribution, as smaller countries have not been fully able to adapt to the new global trade regime. Small countries need the SDT provisions particularly due to the several disadvantages that arise due to their size—narrowness of the natural resource base; lack of economies of scale; export concentration and economic vulnerability arising from a high degree of openness. These problems are further exacerbated in the case of the small island developing states (SIDS). The record of the WTO with respect to the SDT treatment has been disappointing but the authors suggest that the proposed Economic Partnership Agreement (EPA) between Africa Caribbean Pacific (ACP) countries and the European Union (EU) as delineated in the Cotonou Agreement (CA) provides some hope that more comprehensive, deeper and sustained commitments will be adopted. Isa's paper indicates how regional co-operation between like-minded countries with a common goal can bring about small changes, even when the larger apparatus (the WTO) remains unresponsive to the needs of the small countries.

That trade liberalization has not benefited the small countries unambiguously is hardly surprising in view of the experience of some of the larger nations. P.L. Beena examines the limits to universal trade liberalization in the context of textile and clothing (T&C) exports from South Asia particularly in the period after the Agreement on Textile and Clothing (ATC), under the WTO. The ATC completely dismantled the extensive network of bilateral quotas on 31 December 2004. The duplicity of the developed countries that Chang's work documents more than adequately, can be seen in Beena's account as well, since the ATC removes quota restrictions as a part of the WTO's trade liberalization mantra, but retains non-quota provisions such as tariff and non-tariff barriers that can be, and are being, used as tools to protect the domestic producers of the developed countries. Beena's description shows how, in fact, the growth of world trade in T&C during the post-ATC period is actually *lower* than the earlier period, suggesting that instead of trade liberalization acting as a boost to trade, it might actually be depressing it. South Asia, particularly, has felt the brunt, as during 1985–2003 (the pre-ATC phase), the growth of T&C exports from this region was higher than the world average whereas the post-ATC phase has seen a decline in the rate of growth. Thus, at least in this sector, the presumed benefits of export-led industrialization have not yielded the desired returns to South Asian countries. Beena's paper, therefore, underscores the need for formulating selective, country-specific industrial and trade policies rather than adopting a universal trade liberalization policy.

## FINANCIAL FRAGILITY, CURRENCY CONVERTIBILITY, AND MONETARY POLICY

Capital and financial flows are perhaps the area where the dominance of the developed countries, particularly that of the USA, is most obviously. Ramaa Vasudevan's contribution on financial intermediation and fragility focuses on global imbalances in financial flows and her analysis of the US deficit (and how it is being sustained) illustrates how the pressure on developing countries to adopt capital account convertibility can be very simply understood in terms of the imperatives of sustaining the US deficit. She argues that a distinctive feature of today's international economy is that the leading 'hegemonic' country of the world—whose currency enjoys the status of 'international money'—has a large and mounting external deficit which it finances by issuing debt in its own currency, while absorbing savings and capital from the rest of the world. She develops a triangular model that demonstrates how the open financial markets of the developing countries have provided a safety valve for the US dollar by sustaining the growing US deficits and hence, the hegemony of the dollar itself. She contends that the US is at the apex of a pattern of triangular payments with large and growing deficits with major trade partners such as Japan and China and surpluses with debtor countries, in what can be termed as the periphery of open liberalized countries, for example, those in Latin America. The model suggests that by precipitating a shift from assets denominated in domestic currency to those denominated in dollars, capital flight from these countries allows the US to maintain its deficit. Thus, Beena claims, that instead of addressing the basic causes of the US deficit, the international monetary system has developed a readjustment mechanism that exacerbates these finances, and any 'meaningful' reform of the international financial system needs to take this into account.

Martin Abeles looks at Argentina's 2001 crisis in terms of Minsky's analytical framework that distinguishes between hedged, speculative, and Ponzi financing positions. Abeles develops a set of financial indicators and investigates the state of corporate balance sheets between 1998 and 2001 for Argentina's 500 largest non-financial firms. To recap, a hedged unit is one whose assets are expected to produce a cash flow from operating projects that exceeds financing costs and operating expense, including dividends to shareholders by a sufficient margin of safety capable of absorbing any unforeseen changes in cash inflows and outflows. A firm engages in speculative finance as its margin of safety declines and the probability of it being unable to meet pending financial commitments increases, so that at some point over the life of the loan the firm may require an extension from its creditors or a reduction in the amount of dividends normally paid out to shareholders. In an open economy, firms in a speculative financial position are also allowed to borrow foreign funds and are, therefore, also exposed to unexpected changes in exchange rates. Finally, a Ponzi position is where the 'margin of safety' of the firm is nil, when shortfalls are likely to occur almost throughout the entire maturing phase of the project, so that the firm needs to borrow additional funds just to meet interest payments.

According to Minsky, an economy is financially fragile if the bankruptcy of one firm can set off a chain reaction of bankruptcies of other firms, giving way to a recursive negative spiral. Hence, the likelihood of a systemic breakdown depends on the distribution of firms' financial positions along a line that goes from more robust (hedged) to more fragile (Ponzi). With this apparatus, Abeles uses data from Argentina to provide a different explanation than the mainstream one (that focuses on fiscal imbalances alone) to explain the build-up of the crisis. In fact, he argues that 'diminishing corporate cash flows may have themselves had an effect on fiscal revenues, and not the other way round'. He finds that foreign firms moved more quickly into financially fragile positions as compared to domestic firms. Thus, he suggests that 'private foreign over-indebtedness' gave way to momentous defaults after the 2002 currency devaluation, in conjunction with the public sector's (more notorious) defaults.

Armen Papazian's interesting contribution explains the persistence of high ratios of deposit and liability dollarization in Lebanon in terms of a 'market imposed monetary condition, a response to the unfree and co-opted nature of the state'. Most studies on dollarization have focused on Latin America. Papazian's study is one of the rare studies that focuses on Lebanon. Again, the mainstream approach favours full dollarization as the least bad alternative, in that it would protect domestic consumers from local wealth destroying policies. However, Papazian, using a political economy perspective, very persuasively argues that since it is the lack of trust in the state that has led to dollarization, it essentially reflects 'local institutional and leadership weaknesses'. Thus, de-dollarization needs to be advocated, not only because dollarization leads to losses in terms of loss of seignorage revenue, loss of independent monetary policy, loss of central bank's role as the lender of last resort, more exposure to shocks experienced by the anchor currency, but also more fundamentally, as a means of reclaiming economic identity. Thus, de-dollarization would reflect a 'fundamental expression of societal trust'. There are other critiques of dollarization that argue how, while dollarization is being advocated for emerging markets, there is no evidence that it actually works. Dollarization removes the money printing powers of the state but no real evidence exists that it guarantees financial discipline. Papazian goes beyond a critique to outline, concretely, how a new Lebanese Lira could provide the required incentives and inspire the much needed trust.

Loss of an independent monetary policy is a critical concern, even in countries that are not dollarized. When developing countries with liberalized capital accounts and flexible exchange rates are asked to focus on inflation targeting as the desired goal of monetary policy, the economies could experience negative real effects, contrary to mainstream wisdom. Gilberto Libanio's paper looks at the implications of 'good governance' in monetary policy for three countries: Brazil, Chile, and Mexico. Libanio argues that in practice, central banks under inflation targeting tend to place an increased focus on inflation and tend to be less concerned with output fluctuations. In fact, as Libanio points out, most of the discussion about monetary policy under inflation targeting does not even refer explicitly to real outcomes, except for recognizing that an increase in interest rates may cause a decline in aggregate demand in the short run, this being one of the channels through which inflation may be affected. Studies on the effects of inflation targeting show that these countries were able to reduce inflation volatility at the expense of an increase in output volatility. This, as the author demonstrates, is especially likely to happen in emerging market economies with liberalized capital accounts. His empirical results show that for the period 1999–2005, monetary policy has been pro-cyclical in Brazil and Chile and counter-cyclical in Mexico and that it has reacted asymmetrically to GDP growth rates in Brazil, Chile, and Mexico in different ways. Thus, he concludes that inflation targeting has not only increased output volatility but is also likely to result in negative effects on growth rates in the long run.

## LABOUR AND EMPLOYMENT

This section directly addresses the impact of policies directed by globalization on the lives of the working people. Fiona Tregenna's paper looks at changes in the manufacturing employment in South Africa during 1970 and 2004. Unemployment is a very serious concern as levels of employment have been stagnant, and the labour force has been growing rapidly, resulting in a situation where 'broad' unemployment currently stands at 40 per cent, while 'narrow' unemployment (excluding discouraged job seekers) is close to 27 per cent. The author looks at the relationships between capital stock, capacity utilization, relative factor utilization, and employment in order to understand the factors that are blocking employment growth. Her most striking finding is in terms of relative factor utilization, with a dramatic and almost continuous fall in the ratio of labour employed to utilized capital. The drop in labour intensity of production accounts for an overwhelmingly negative change in labour demand in manufacturing. While this paper examines trends in the manufacturing sector, other work by the author has examined different sectors and similar results obtain. Her contribution then presents an extremely critical result for other developing countries grappling with stagnating employment or with jobless growth: capital investment alone is insufficient for employment creation. In fact, particular types of capital investment may actually reduce employment. Tregenna's research suggests that much of the investment that has occurred in South African manufacturing has been the labour displacing kind, rather than the labour absorbing kind.

This result radically questions the conventional wisdom on foreign direct investment (FDI) and its presumed employment generating and, hence, livelihood enhancing effect. As Tregenna reminds us, it is not merely the overall quantity of capital stock but also the 'quality' that determines its impact on the economy. Quality has several dimensions, and one very important dimension is, or ought to be, its labour absorbing capacity. This conclusion can be used to argue that developing countries ought to be able to receive or reject FDI evaluated on this criterion, rather than be forced to accept all kinds of FDI.

Emel Memis empirically examines the pattern of inter-industry wage differentials in Turkish manufacturing by using a clustering method—one of the newer methods used in economics. Turkey adopted the structural adjustment programme in 1980 and has become fully liberalized since. Memis asks the question: given the widening wage differentials across clusters during the liberalization period, what can we learn from cluster composition of exports over the period? It turns out that commodities using low technology are exported, as standard theory predicts. However, employees in these industries kept earning lower wages, contrary to conventional wisdom. Also, all the clusters that author considers reveal a negative annual average growth rate in wage share, suggesting a steady change in income distribution in favour of profits vis-à-vis wages since the start of liberalization.

Additionally, the domestic terms of trade between agriculture and manufacturing shifted against manufacturing, which resulted in sections of the agricultural population moving to low-paid, low-technology sectors. Privatization also had a similar impact on employment and wages; the employees of state-owned enterprises (SOE) who were re-employed in the private sector typically earned only 33 per cent of their SOE earnings. These new jobs were not only worse in terms of wages, but also in terms of fringe benefits and lower labour standards. Thus, Memis' study presents solid evidence against the argument that wage structure is stable and neutral to policy changes.

When labour markets do not provide satisfactory outcomes, particularly to marginalized groups such as women, self-employment is offered as the panacea. The World Bank particularly has been pushing micro-credit and financing of self help groups as methods to enhance the economic independence of women, especially as an alternate route to that of wage employment. As the previous two contributions in this section show, there are no guarantees that wage employment will expand as a result of a liberalized policy and even if it does, it might result in very low wages, thus not contributing much to economic independence. While the micro-credit route can work for small groups in certain contexts, it is problematic to see it as an alternative to wage employment.

Structural changes in the economy are typically not gender-neutral in their impact. In a study of labour market participation decisions of married women in Turkey, A. Burca Kizilirmak points out that contrary to the trends in many other countries, female labour force participation has been decreasing in Turkey in the last decades. One of the reasons is higher enrollment in education but the other important reason is a structural shift away from agriculture and women who are released from agriculture typically are not able to find employment in industry or services due to lack of skills or qualifications. The specific contribution of this paper is to look at women's labour supply decisions as a function of their husbands' economic status. The author finds evidence of the 'added worker effect': wives decided to participate in the labour force in order to compensate for the loss of income due to the husband's unemployment. Wives of unemployed husbands tend to get permanent wage employment rather than temporary employment or self employment. But she also finds evidence of this being dominated by the 'discouraged worker effect' as the unemployment crisis intensifies: a wife's search for work decreases due to unfavourable labour market conditions facing the whole family. Women thus continue to be secondary workers in the liberalized and globalized Turkey, suggesting that greater market orientation does not necessarily reduce inter-group disparities.

## ISSUES IN CROSS-NATIONAL GROWTH COMPARISONS

Mainstream explanations of persistent underdevelopment prefer to focus on internal or domestic factors in poor countries, suggesting some sort of endogeneity to the lack of development, so that attention shifts away from structural constraints of the international economy that exacerbates inequality between the developed and the developing world.

Thus, cross-country, cross-section growth equations with all kinds of explanatory variables are often estimated to explain the differentials in growth rates. The analytical power of these cross-country regressions is often dubious. Fedderke, Luiz, and Kadt examine the use of 'fractionalization indices' (that measure ethnic fractionalization) to explain growth performance with a particular focus on the African growth experience. The standard prediction is that polarized societies will be prone to competitive rent-seeking that impedes agreement about the provision of public goods and creates possible incentives for growth-reducing policies. However as the authors point out, a limitation of these studies is that they do not provide a basis for exploring how growth interacts with ethno-linguistic diversity. Also, they ask the other very important question: how legitimate is it to view ethno-linguistic fractionalization as constant over time? Growth itself may impact fractionalization, and the direction and causes of this impact would have to be elucidated, not assumed.

The authors, therefore, argue for a time-series study while admitting to several ambiguities with the concept of fractionalization itself. For instance, in a country with several possible group identities (religion, caste, language, and so forth), there is no easy basis for settling on one and rejecting another as an explanation for growth. Also, some of these indices suffer from a 'grouping problem' in which umbrella categories sometimes subsume groups that are clearly distinct and often highly antagonistic. For instance, the Rwanda measure collapses the Hutus and the Tutsis into a monolithic category! Also, most of the time, these measures do not assign political weights to ethnic groups, and are thus unable to capture the differential impact that these groups typically have on the country's polity.

The time series analysis by Fedderke et al. finds that the measure of fractionalization is not static but changes strongly over time. The more dramatic finding is that it is not rising, but falling, racial fractionalization that appears to be associated with rising political instability. Thus, the association between fractionalization and distributional conflict is more non-linear than the mainstream literature assumes. While studies of fractionalization and ethnic conflict are vital, their ability to explain inter-country growth experiences may be severely limited.

## LESSONS FROM CHINA

If we could identify one country that has made a dramatic transition in its economic status in recent times, it would undisputedly be China. As the country makes a transition from socialism to capitalism under the leadership of the communist party, it remains one of the most enigmatic development experiences in history. Indeed, it probably defies all kinds of stereotypes. While an entire conference (and more) could be dedicated to the study of Chinese development, here we reproduce two papers. Jinkang Zhang discusses the role of the targeted FDI promotion strategy that intends to draw the 'right kind of FDI' that best promotes the goals of Chinese development. She discusses the role of several factors that contributed to the right kind of FDI: gradual opening up, tax policies, investment promotion, FDI management agencies, sectoral division of policies, and so forth. She believes that the 'Beijing Consensus' can provide a model for the rest of the developing countries to emulate that would help them to avoid indiscriminate and unwanted FDI inflows.

Mario Biggeri attempts to put China in perspective by suggesting that we look beyond the economic miracle to the impact on human development. He points to low wages, sectoral imbalances, inequalities between regions and sectors, and a reduction in government investment in rural areas that have adverse implications for wages and employment and so forth as the multifarious problems of human development that have accompanied the dramatic economic development. He argues that China needs to emphasize long-term human development and poverty reduction as one of its goals. His analysis yet again points out that high rates of economic development can co-exist with large scale human development lacunae or in other words, growth on its own is no guarantee that its benefits will reach the poorest sections.

## CREATING POLICY SPACE

Finally, Jean Dreze's contribution on the Employment Guarantee Act (EGA) in India provides a fitting finale by demonstrating how policies oriented towards improving the lives of ordinary people can be, and are being, created in response to the imperatives of democracy. The strength of the EGA is that it recognizes the right to work as a fundamental right—as a part of the larger set of entitlements to ensure a life of dignity for working people. Moreover, it acknowledges the duty of the state to make 'effective provision' for securing the right to work. In the discourse on globalization, we see plenty of concern about the protection of property rights and the 'rule of law' to ensure smooth sailing for big business, yet, there is remarkably little concern about other, equally (if not more) important rights of human beings. This disparity in concerns is self-evident in both international and domestic legal structures, where the focus of national governments, BWIs, and the WTO is predominantly on ensuring the legal rights of big business and private property, with minimal attention paid to the human rights of the poor and working people.

Targeted initially at the poorest 200 districts in the country, the EGA aims to provide employment, at the minimum wage, to one adult per household, for 100 days, failing which the state is mandated to provide unemployment allowance. Of course, there are many conceptual and operational complications: How is a household to be defined? Who within the household will get work? How should leakages be prevented? How does one ensure that corruption at all levels does not kill this initiative? These questions are nested in the overarching question about the feasibility of financing this massive and unique policy initiative. Dreze provides a comprehensive introduction to the Act and takes us through the process by which this Act came into being, introducing us to the architects of the Act as well as its detractors. The forceful opposition to the Act, both within the government and outside, which did not succeed in blocking it but did end up diluting it, gives us a glimpse into how the thinking of the Indian ruling classes and 'opinion makers' is firmly aligned with concerns of the elite and with corporate interests.

The journey of the Act is fascinating: something that started off as one of the many points of campaign in the Congress party's electoral manifesto ended up as one of most important pieces of legislation in recent times. This journey was facilitated by the fact that from the very beginning, a variety of individuals and non-governmental organization (NGOs) were involved in consultations—a departure from the usual practice of top-heavy legislation. Dreze also assesses the implementation of the Act one year down the line and shows how it is marked by the expected challenges, but more importantly, by several unexpected bright spots.

The formulation of this Act, and the bright spots in its implementation seen subsequently, have very important lessons and pointers for future legislation in India and elsewhere, as they demonstrate how concrete policy alternatives can be created to ensure a better life for the working people. This focus on concrete policy alternatives is, perhaps, the only feasible way to ensure development in a globalized world.

## REFERENCES

Bhagwati, Jagdish (2004), *In Defense of Globalization*, Oxford University Press, New Delhi.

Oxfam (2002), *Rigged Rules and Double Standards: Trade, Globalisation and the Fight against Poverty*, Oxfam, Oxford.

Stiglitz, Joseph (2002), *Globalisation and Its Discontents*, Norton, New York.

Rodrick, Dani (1997), *Has Globalisation Gone too Far?* Institute for International Economics, Washington DC.

# 2

# Policy Space in Historical Perspective, with special reference to Trade and Industrial Policies

HA-JOON CHANG*

## INTRODUCTION—THE EVER-SHRINKING POLICY SPACE

There is a growing concern that, over the last quarter of a century, the 'policy space' available for the developing countries has shrunk so much so that their ability to achieve economic development is being threatened (see the essays in Gallagher 2005). The current phase of shrinkage in the policy space started in the 1980s, when the World Bank and the IMF massively expanded their 'programme' (as opposed to 'project') loans in the aftermath of the Debt Crisis in 1982 in the form of structural adjustment programmes (SAPs)—and many of its subsequent re-incarnations, which are too numerous to list—and enhanced the scope and strength of the conditionalities attached to their loans.

In the early days, the conditionalities set by the Bank and the Fund were mainly concerned with budget deficits, monetary expansion, privatization, and trade liberalization. However, over time, there has been a constant 'mission creep', so much so that, following the 1997 financial crisis in Korea, the IMF actually ordered the Korean government to grant autonomy to the country's central bank, and, even more amazingly, instructed the Korean private sector companies on how much debt they could have. These days, there is virtually no area on which the Bank and the Fund do not have (often very strong) influence—democracy, judicial reform, corporate governance, health, education, and what not.

Aid policies of the developed countries have also contributed to the shrinking of policy space. In the old days, the main condition attached to aid by the donor countries was that the recipients buy (at least a certain

*An earlier version of the paper was presented at the Queen Elizabeth House 50th Anniversary Conference, 'The Development Threats and Promises', Queen Elizabeth House, University of Oxford, 4–5 July 2005, and at the ACDC, Neemrana, India, 2–4 December 2005. I thank the participants at the two conferences, especially Deepak Nayyar, John Toye, and Jean Dreze, for their comments. I also thank Rammohan Reddy for his comments. This version was published in *Economic and Political Weekly*, 18–24 February 2006, Vol. XLI, No. 7. I thank EPW for allowing reproduction of the article.

portion of) the goods and the services needed for the aid-funded projects from the national companies of the donor countries. However, since the 1980s, the conditions have stretched to include policy recommendations similar to those demanded by the Bank and the Fund on their loans. This is not surprising, when we recall that, after all, the Bank and the Fund are controlled by the countries that are main providers of foreign aid to developing countries.

The shrinkage in policy space has been particularly striking in the area of trade and industrial policies. First, since the 1980s, the BWIs have made trade liberalization—involving tariff cuts, tariffication of quantitative restrictions, and the reduction in non-tariff barriers (NTBs)—a key condition of their loans. The conclusion of the Uruguay Round (UR) of the GATT talks in 1994 and the subsequent launch of the WTO in 1995 have brought hitherto unthinkable issues into the arena of multilateral trade politics—patents (through Trade-related Intellectual Property Rights, TRIPs), regulation of foreign investment (through Trade-related Invested measures, TRIMs), trade in services (through General Agreement on Trade in Service, GATS)—and have also shrunk the space for many of the more 'traditional' areas such as tariffs.

While it is important to recognize that there is still considerable policy space in the WTO (Akyuz et al. 1998, Amsden 2005), it should not be forgotten that there is a constant attempt by the developed countries to reduce this remaining space.

For example, in the run-up to the Cancun ministerial meeting of the WTO in September 2003, the developed countries tried very hard, and failed in the end, to put the multilateral investment agreement (MIA)—which aims to make virtually all restrictions on FDI (and possibly those on portfolio investment) 'illegal'—on the WTO negotiation agenda (for a criticism of the MIA proposal, see Chang and Green 2003; for an analysis of the result of the Cancun meeting, see Chang 2003).

In the Hong Kong ministerial meeting of December 2005, the developed countries tried very hard to radically lower industrial tariffs over the next 10 years or so through the so-called non-agricultural market access (NAMA), negotiations (see Khor and Goh 2004; Akyuz 2005; and Chang 2005, for further details). Even though the 'zero-tariff' proposal made by the USA in December 2002 is considered to be a deliberately radical opening gambit, the core US proposal is to bring average industrial tariffs in developing countries down to 5–7 per cent by 2010, the lowest level since the days of colonialism and unequal treaties when weaker countries were deprived of policy autonomy, especially their right to set tariffs.[1] With very few exceptions, they will be also lower than the rates that prevailed in today's developed countries until the early 1970s (see Tables A2.1 and A2.2).[2]

While the developed countries did not succeed in securing any firm outcome on NAMA in Hong Kong, they managed to get an agreement on the use of the so-called 'Swiss formula', which means steeper tariff cuts for countries with higher industrial tariffs, namely, the developing countries. Although there is a

[1]The EC proposal will bring average industrial tariffs down to 5–15 per cent. The Korean and Indian proposals will bring them down to 10–25 per cent and to 10–50 per cent respectively.

[2]The exceptions are Britain and the Netherlands between the late-19th and the early 20th centuries, Germany in the mid-19th century and Denmark after the Second World War.

possibility that the developing countries may minimize the damage in the April 2006 follow-up meeting in Geneva by securing the use of multiple coefficients in the Swiss formula, it is not clear whether the developed countries will agree to the use of coefficients that will not produce substantial cuts in developing country industrial tariffs.

And it is not just the WTO that restricts developing countries' policy space in trade and industrial policies. The developed countries, especially the USA, have used bilateral and regional free trade agreements (FTAs), and bilateral investment agreements (BITs) to impose restrictions on developing countries that they cannot get accepted in the WTO. And it is not unknown that conditions imposed in some of the FTAs that have nothing to do with trade policies. For example, when it signed the bilateral FTA with the USA, Chile was required to commit itself not to use any capital control in the future.

In addition to these (aid and loan) conditionalities and new international trading rules, the policy space of the developing countries is further limited by the (real and imagined) threat of capital flight in the environment of open capital markets. Fearing 'punishment' by the 'foreign investor' (as if all foreign investors share the same interests and want the same things), developing country governments adopt policies that they think (or that they are told) will please the foreign investor, especially in terms of macroeconomic policy, corporate taxation, labour laws, and environmental regulations. And there are the international media, the credit rating agencies, consulting firms, and various international organizations, which regularly publish material that praises countries doing the 'right' thing and rubbishes those who don't, although they will take a U-turn when it suits them.[3]

At this point, it is important to note that the policy space is also constrained by domestic interest groups with in the developing countries. These are those citizens of developing countries whose interests lie in restricting their own government's policy space. Financiers may want their government to be locked into 'prudent' macroeconomic policies through institutions such as central bank independence, currency board, autonomous revenue agency, deficit rules, and inflation targeting. Some may want their government's freedom to control cross-border capital movements curtailed or hopefully totally taken away, so that they can take money out of the country if and when necessary.[4] Exporters of agricultural products may want to keep their government on the 'narrow and straight path' of free trade through the WTO, bilateral and regional FTAs, and the restraints by the World Bank and other international organizations. And there are those who want their own government's policy space to be restricted for ideological reasons. These days many economists in developing countries are ideologically committed to free

[3]For example, the credit rating agencies started downgrading the Asian countries *after* the outbreak of the 1997 crisis. For another example, the IMF started criticizing Argentina *after* the policy it had recommended to the country led to the 2002 economic collapse.

[4]The Under Secretary of the US Treasury, John Taylor, is reported to have said that free transfer of capital in and out of a country without delay is a 'fundamental right' (testimony on 1 April 2003, before the Subcommittee on domestic and international monetary policy, trade, and technology of the Committee on Financial Services at the US House of Representatives, as cited in Wade 2005, p. 92).

market and want the policy space of their governments to be restricted lest their policies deviate from what (they think) the 'science' of economic says.[5]

## POLICY SPACE IN HISTORICAL PERSPECTIVE

'Policy space' may be a new term, but the phenomenon of shrinking policy space is in fact not new. In the days of imperialism, the stronger countries were able to restrict the policy space of the weaker countries in the most blatant ways (for details and further references see Chang 2002, pp. 51–4). Thus, it may be useful to discuss the historical experiences in order to put the current debate on policy space in an appropriate historical context.

### THE AGE OF IMPERIALISM

#### *Colonies*

Policies towards colonies were, naturally, the most limiting in terms of providing policy space. Typical measures included the following. First, high value-added manufacturing activities were outlawed in the colonies. For example, under Robert Walpole, the British prime minister who is considered the father of British mercantilist policy, the construction of new rolling and slitting steel mills in America was outlawed, which forced Americans to specialize in low value-added pig and bar iron, rather than high value-added steel products.

Second, exports from the colonies that competed with the coloniser's products were banned. For example, the cotton textile industry of India was dealt a heavy blow in the 18th century by the British ban on cotton textile imports from India ('calicoes'), which were superior to the British ones. Another example is the Britain ban on export of woollen cloth from its colonies to other countries, imposed in 1699 (the Wool Act)—which essentially destroyed the Irish woollen industry. This Act also stifled the emergence of the woollen manufacturing industry in the American colonies.

Third, policies were deployed to encourage primary production in the colonies. For example, in the 1720s, Walpole provided export subsidies ('bounties') and abolished import duties on raw materials produced in the American colonies (such as hemp, wood, and timber). This was done in the belief that encouraging the production of raw material would 'divert them from carrying on manufactures which interfered with those of England' (Brisco 1907, p. 157).

Last but not the least, the use of tariffs by colonial authorities was banned; and if tariffs were considered necessary for revenue reasons, they were countered in a number of ways. When, in 1859, the British colonial government in India imposed small import duties on textile goods (3–10 per cent) for purely fiscal reasons, the local producers were taxed to the same magnitude in order to provide a 'level playing field' (Bairoch 1993, p. 89). Even with this 'compensation', the British cotton manufacturers placed constant pressure on the government for the repeal of the duties,

[5]And this ideological commitment makes them believe that anything other than strict free-market policies are irrational, short-sighted, and giving in to populism. For example, several months before the recent Argentinian financial crisis, Domingo Cavallo, the famous free-market finance minister of the country, wrote an article in the *Financial Times*, and argued that the monetary inflexibility accorded by the country's currency board was necessary because of his compatriots' inability to control their spending.

which they finally got in 1882. In the 1890s, when the colonial government in India once again tried to impose tariffs on cotton products—this time in order to protect the Indian cotton industry, rather than for revenue reasons—the cotton textile pressure groups thwarted the attempt. Until 1917, there was no tariff on cotton goods imports into India.

### Semi-Colonies

The weaker countries that were somewhat more fortunate and escaped the fate of colonial occupation were forced into 'unequal treaties' that deprived them of tariff autonomy and their jurisdiction over foreigners ('extra-territoriality') on the ground that their governments were not reliable enough. The deprivation of tariff autonomy involved the imposition of a tariff ceiling, typically at the 5 per cent flat rate.

Britain first used unequal treaties in Latin America, starting with Brazil in 1810, as the countries in the continent acquired political independence. Starting with the Nanking Treaty (1842), which followed the Opium War (1839–42), China was forced to sign a series of unequal treaties over the next couple of decades. These eventually resulted in a complete loss of tariff autonomy, and, very symbolically, a Briton being the head of customs for 55 years—from 1863 to 1908. From 1824 onwards, Thailand (then Siam) signed various unequal treaties, which ended with the most comprehensive one in 1855. Persia signed unequal treaties in 1836 and 1857, and the Ottoman Empire in 1838 and 1861.[6]

Even Japan lost its tariff autonomy following the unequal treaties signed after its opening up in 1853 (see Table A2.1). It was eventually able to end the unequal treaties, but not until 1911 (Johnson 1982, p. 25). In this context, it is also interesting to note that when Japan forcefully opened up Korea in 1876 it imitated the 'Western' countries exactly and forced Korea to sign an unequal treaty that deprived the latter of its tariff autonomy, despite the fact that it did not have tariff autonomy itself.

The larger Latin American countries were able to regain tariff autonomy from the 1880s. Many others regained it only after the First World War, but Turkey had to wait for tariff autonomy until 1923, although it came into effect only in 1929 (the unequal treaty had been signed as early as 1838!) and China until 1929.

It is extremely disconcerting to note that binding of tariff at a low, uniform rate (although not necessarily below 5 per cent) is exactly what modern day, free-trade economists recommend to developing countries. The classic work by Little et al. (1970) argues that the appropriate level of protection is at most 20 per cent for the poorest countries and virtually zero for the more advanced developing countries (pp. 163–4). World Bank (1991) argues that '[e]vidence suggests the merits of phasing out quantitative restrictions rapidly, and reducing tariffs to reasonably *low and uniform* levels, such as a range of 15–25 per cent [emphasis added]' (p. 102). And, most disturbingly, industrial tariffs of developing countries will fall to 5–7 per cent (US proposal) or to 5–15 per cent (EU proposal), if the proposals from the developed countries are adopted at the NAMA negotiations.

## The Post-imperialist Era—Expansion and Contraction of the Policy Space

Having looked at the historical experience, some may point out that the developing

[6] The 1838 Convention of Balta Liman with Turkey (then the Ottoman empire) bound Turkish import duties at 3 per cent (Fielden 1969, p. 91).

countries still have a lot more policy space than they had during the time of imperialism. This is absolutely true.

However, we cannot console ourselves with that knowledge. First, the currently available space is under constant threat. And, more importantly, history shows that things could be better than they are now.

There was a period between the end of the Second World War and the Second Oil Shock when the developing countries were allowed quite a large policy space. The World Bank and the IMF operated with fairly restricted (and still valid today, in theory) mandate—financing of infrastructural development and the provision of liquidity in times of short-term balance-of-payments crises, respectively—and attached few conditions on policies outside these narrow areas. While the developed countries were whittling down many of their tariffs at the GATT during this period, the developing countries were mostly left to do what they saw fit in terms of tariffs and other trade policy matters. There was no 'single undertaking' in the GATT, as is the case with the WTO, so countries could even opt out of some agreements that they were not happy with.

And this is when the developing countries did the best economically, despite the orthodox propaganda that portrays this period as the 'bad old days' of import substitution (the following data are from Chang 2002, p. 4). While the developing countries witnessed minimal, and indeed often negative, growth during the period of colonialism and unequal treaties, they recorded exceptional economic growth during the period of 1950s–1970s.[7] In the 1960s and the 1970s (we are excluding the 1950s, as many developing countries did not gain their independence until the 1960s), per capita income in the developing world grew at 3 per cent, a rate that was two to three times higher than that experienced by the developed countries in the 19th century during their Industrial Revolution (1–1.5 per cent). Some countries grew much faster, making people talk of 'miracle'. Per capita income in countries such as Japan (then still a developing country by any reasonable definition), South Korea, Taiwan, and Singapore grew at 5–6 per cent per year, doubling the income in 12–13 years, as opposed to the 70 years that it would have taken had they grown at 1 per cent per year, as was the case with many European countries during their Industrial Revolutions in the 19th century.

To be sure, the period between the 1950s to the 1970s should not be idealized as some sort of golden age. Aids often came with strings, and a lot of informal influence was exercised by the former colonial masters in the management of the economy in many developing countries. The talk of 'neo-colonialism' was not simply a radical propaganda. Moreover, the episode was not a totally 'innocent' one. There were the Cold War considerations on the part of the USA and other rich capitalist countries, while the developing countries knew and exploited them to the full, often playing the Great Powers against one another. However, compared to the subsequent (and previous) periods, the period certainly qualifies as one when the strong allowed the weak much larger policy space.

[7]Between 1900 and 1950, the Asian developing countries that were colonies or semi-colonies grew extremely slowly. Annual per capita income growth rates were: –0.3 per cent for China, –0.1 per cent for India–Pakistan–Bangladesh and Indonesia, 0.1 per cent for South Korea and Thailand, and 0.4 per cent for Taiwan and the Philippines. The data are from Maddison (1989).

From the 1980s, however, the picture started to change. The 1970s debate surrounding the New International Economic Order (NIEO), where a more equal relationship between the developed and the developing nations was called for by the developing countries, galvanized many developed countries into putting the developing countries in their place. This tendency became quite serious with the election of various neo-liberal governments in the developed countries since the late 1970s, starting with the Thatcher government in the UK in 1979. In the 1980s, the USA became quite aggressive in its dealings with all trading partners, believing that 'unfair' practices by its trading partners (for example, NTBs, lax intellectual property rights laws) were largely to blame for its relative economic decline. And with the end of the Cold War in the 1990s, the developed countries have become much more aggressive in demanding policies from the developing countries that they claim promote development, but in reality hamper it.

It is important to note that, despite adopting 'free trade' and other 'good' policies, the developing countries have been doing much worse in the last quarter of a century than they had in the two decades of supposedly disastrous 'import substitution' industrialization during the 1960s and the 1970s. During the last quarter of a century, per capita incomes in the developing countries have been growing at around half the rate that prevailed in those countries in the 1960s and the 1970s (roughly 3 per cent vs 1.5 per cent). Per capita income in countries in sub-Saharan Africa has actually been shrinking in the last quarter of a century. Income distribution has worsened in the majority of the developing countries, while poverty has increased in many of them. Neo-liberal policies may not be totally responsible for such poor performance, but at the least we can say that these policies failed to deliver on their central promise of accelerated growth.

## POLICY SPACE FOR TRADE AND INDUSTRIAL POLICIES IN THE PRESENT CONTEXT—A CRITICAL LOOK AT SOME KEY UNDERLYING PRINCIPLES

Having put the issue of policy space in its present and historical contexts, I discuss it in more concrete terms, using the case of policy space for trade and industrial policies as an example, with an emphasis on the NAMA negotiation, which is currently the most important issue at the WTO.

The most useful way to do this may be to critically examine some of the key principles that govern the negotiation processes surrounding the international trading system today and expose their internal contradictions and limitations.

### THE 'LEVEL PLAYING FIELD'

In the push for the reduction in policy space for developing countries, the rhetoric of level playing field is usually deployed as the most important justification. The developing countries should 'level the playing field', it is argued, by removing the 'unfair' advantages that they currently enjoy in their competition with the developed countries, such as higher tariffs, weaker protection of intellectual property rights, and more stringent restrictions on foreign investment.

Level playing field is like, as the Americans say, motherhood and apple pie. It is *definitionally* good so that it is difficult to oppose. But it is something that has to be opposed if we are going to build a world trading system that is truly pro-development.

Needless to say, level playing field is the right principle to adopt when the players are equal. However, when the players are unequal, it is the wrong principle to apply. For example, if a team of 13-year old children are playing football against the Brazilian national team, it is only fair that the playing field is not level and that children are allowed to attack from up the hill.

Indeed, in most sports, unequal players are not even allowed to compete against each other. In boxing, wrestling, and many other sports, there are weight classes. A heavyweight boxer such as Muhammad Ali would not have been allowed to box Roberto Duran, the legendary Panamanian boxer, and take away his titles, however likely his victory was.[8]

Weight classes are not the only means to prevent competition on an equal footing among unequal players. In many sports, including football and baseball (the Little League in American baseball), there are age classes—adult teams are not allowed to play against children and juvenile teams. In sports such as golf, there is an explicit system of 'handicaps' that allows weaker players to compete with advantages in (inverse) proportion to their playing skills. And so on.

To take the boxing analogy further, the developed countries seeking a radical tariff reduction, as they are currently doing in the NAMA negotiation, are like a heavyweight boxer who sweet-talks a host of lighter boxers into fighting games with him by promising that they will be allowed to use protective gears and then suddenly turns around and accuses the others of playing foul by arguing that they have 'unfair' protection. And when the heavyweight boxer insists on wearing protective gear for his abdomen (agriculture and textile?) on the ground that it is his weak part, we begin to wonder whether there is any sense of fair play in his mind. Added to this is the fact that the heavyweight boxer almost single-handedly writes the rules of the game, owns the only bank in town (and may refuse to lend money to those boxers who complain about his tactics), and also controls the town newspaper (which will assassinate the characters of boxers who speak up against him); and we begin to see the absurdity of the rhetoric of 'level playing field' in the present world trading system.

## 'Special and Differential Treatment' and 'Less-than-full Reciprocity'

There is, naturally, some unease with the rhetoric of level playing field among the developing countries, which the developed countries cannot totally ignore. This is why we have 'SDT' in the WTO and why the developed countries in the NAMA negotiation say that they happy with 'less than full reciprocity' (LTFR) from the developing countries. However, there are serious problems with these 'concessions' in the forms of SDT and LTFR.

The problem with SDT is the word 'special'. To name something as 'special treatment' implies that the party getting the treatment has an unfair advantage. However, we would not call stair-lifts for wheelchair users or Braille writing for the blind 'special treatments', we should not designate the higher tariffs and other means of protection more extensively (but not exclusively) used by the developing countries as 'special treatments'—they are just differential treatments for countries with differential capabilities and goals.

The notion of LTFR should also be questioned. It implies that developing countries

[8]Duran is one of only four boxers in history to hold four different world titles—lightweight (1972–9), welterweight (1980), junior middleweight (1983), and middleweight (1989–90).

will give less than the developed countries in the NAMA deal. However, the notion of reciprocity cannot be discussed without some reference to the relative positions of the parties involved. We would not say that a poor friend is being 'less than reciprocal' simply because he cannot buy champagne and caviar for his rich friend, as far as he is treating his rich friend often enough and generously enough, *given his means*. Likewise, even a small cut in tariff may be a lot to ask for a developing country that is desperate to preserve jobs, develop industrial capabilities, and collect government revenues, while even a relatively large cut may not be such a big burden on countries with greater wealth and higher industrial capabilities.

So, when the tariff cuts asked from the developing countries are much larger in their impact, due to their greater absolute magnitudes and, more importantly, due to their weaker adjustment capabilities and their greater needs to use the tariffs, it is incorrect to say that these countries are being less than fully reciprocal, even if their tax cuts are lower in proportional terms than those by the developed countries (although even this is not necessarily the case ).[9]

[9]For example, according to calculations by the Indian Government presented in Khor and Goh (2004), the average industrial tariff of Japan will go down from 2.3 per cent to 1.3 per cent (EC formula) or 0.7 per cent (US formula) and that of the USA will go down from 3.2 per cent to 1.7 per cent (EC formula) or 1.0 per cent (US formula). These may be large cuts in proportional terms, but are not larger even in proportional terms than in the case of some developing countries. For instance, the Japanese cut according to the US formula will be about a 70 per cent cut (from 2.3 per cent to 0.7 per cent), whereas the cut for Indonesia will be 82 per cent (from 35.6 per cent to 6.3 per cent) and that for Brazil will be 80 per cent (from 30.8 per cent to 6.2 per cent).

## THE 'ONE-WAY-STREET' VIEW OF FLEXIBILITY

The developed countries have tried to sell certain agreements in the WTO to the developing countries on the ground that they give enough flexibility to the latter—mainly in the form of keeping some sectors away from the agreements. Thus, GATS is said to be flexible because it allows countries to keep some sectors off their market-opening commitments. The same notion of flexibility was bandied about in the (now-dormant) negotiation for the MIA in the run up to the Cancun ministerial meeting in 2003. In NAMA, it is said that there is some flexibility because countries can reserve some sectors from their tariff-binding and tariff-cutting commitments, although the scope for these is supposed to be quite limited.

However, this is a very peculiar notion of flexibility because once a sector is liberalized, there is no going back. Indeed, the whole idea of tariff binding in the WTO is based on this notion. The exercise is based on the belief that there is a tariff rate in a sector above which the tariff should *never* rise.

If there is going to be genuine flexibility, countries should be allowed to unbind and raise their tariffs, if there is a reasonable ground for it. For example, if a country genuinely underestimated the adjustment costs when it made a decision to cut the tariffs in particular industries—as it was in fact case with many developing countries in the UR—it may be reasonable to allow that country to raise tariff ceilings in those particular industries. For another example, a country may have set low tariff ceilings in certain industries because it underestimated the capabilities of domestic producers and did not think any infant industry protection would ever become necessary in those industries. However, it should be allowed to raise tariff ceilings if it later finds that after all there is some hope of viable domestic producers emerging with stronger tariff protection in those industries.

More importantly, it should be recognized that the developing countries, whose economic structures have to evolve a good deal before they can become rich, will need to vary the tariff rates for individual industries in the future to a far greater extent than will the developed countries. As a country climbs up the ladder of international division of labour, tariff protection needs to go down in some of the old infant industries that are now mature, while protection needs to be accorded to new emerging infant industries. If tariffs are cut and bound for each and every industry, as is currently proposed by the developed countries in the NAMA negotiations, this kind of flexibility, which is absolutely crucial for the developing countries, will not exist (see Akyuz 2005 for an elaboration of this point).

## National Autonomy—'The Right to be Wrong'

Many free-trade economists like to present themselves as defenders of the interests of the developing countries. The World Bank, for example, in its famous *East Asian Miracle* report, warned that other developing countries should not try to emulate the interventionist trade and industrial policies of East Asia, because they do not have the administrative capabilities to make these complex policies work (World Bank 1993, for example, p. 26). In doing so, the Bank wants to be seen as protecting the developing countries from harming themselves by employing policies that have little chance of success. Interestingly, Adam Smith was doing the same for the Americans in his *Wealth of Nations*, when he was advising them not to protect manufacturing.[10]

Some would go even further. They would quite explicitly pitch themselves against the ignorant and often corrupt developing-country governments beholden to interest groups, in defence of the 'common men', who would benefit from free trade. For example, right after the collapse of the Cancun ministerial talks of the WTO in September 2003, Willem Buiter, the then chief economist of the European Bank for Reconstruction and Development (EBRD), lamented that 'although the leaders of the developing nations rule countries that are, on average, poor or very poor, it does not follow that these leaders necessarily speak on behalf of the poor and poorest in their countries. Some do; others represent corrupt and repressive elites that feed off the rents created by imposing barriers to trade and other distortions, at the expense of their poorest and most defenceless citizens'.[11]

Thus seen, whichever variant of the free-trade view one takes, the shrinking of policy space for developing country governments in the area of trade and industrial policies is a good thing, as it prevents developing countries

[10] In his *Wealth of Nations*, Adam Smith wrote: 'Were the Americans, either by combination or by any other sort of violence, to stop the importation of European manufactures, and, by thus giving a monopoly to such of their own countrymen as could manufacture the like goods, divert any considerable part of their capital into this employment, they would retard instead of accelerating the further increase in the value of their annual produce, and would obstruct instead of promoting the progress of their country towards real wealth and greatness' (Smith 1973 [1776], pp. 347–8).

[11] 'If anything is rescued from Cancún, politics must take precedence over economics', letter to the editor, *Financial Times*, 16 September 2003.

from making costly policy mistakes, whether out of misguided belief in interventionism (the World Bank version) or due to interest group politics (the Buiter version).

What is curious, however, is that the free-trade economists who display such paternalistic attitude to the developing country policy choice are usually people who would vehemently denounce most government regulations for their underlying paternalism and argue for individual 'freedom to choose'. They would say that governments should not try to restrict people's freedom of choice out of fear that they may make 'wrong' choices, because, after all, the ability to make mistakes and learn from them is the genuine sign of autonomy and free choice.

There is something deeply troubling about this. A consistent free-trade economist who values autonomy and choice for individuals should be willing to do the same for developing countries as independent entities, that is, unless they adopt the Libertarian view and deny the legitimacy of any collective decision. However, if they did that, they would also have to deny the legitimacy of WTO decisions, which they are not doing. If so, they cannot avoid the accusation of employing double standards. They passionately advocate the individual's 'right to be wrong', on the ground of individual autonomy, but they are not willing to respect national autonomy of the developing countries, thus denying them the same 'right to be wrong'.

## CONCLUSION

Policy space is a matter of vital importance. Long-range historical records suggest that it has an enormous influence on a country's ability to achieve economic development. When they were colonies or subject to unequal treaties, the developing countries experienced extremely slow economic growth (and we are not even taking into account the issues of political legitimacy, cultural / racial domination, and social inequity associated with colonialism and imperialism). When they were allowed larger policy space between the 1950s and the 1970s, their growth accelerated beyond expectation. Once the policy space started shrinking from the 1980s onwards, their average growth rate fell to half of what it was in the 'bad old days' of import substitution in the previous period.

Historical comparison shows that the policy space available for today's developing countries is in fact not the smallest by historical standard. However, policy space for developing countries has been constantly shrinking over the last quarter of a century and it is at the risk of shrinking even further, to the point of making the use of any meaningful policy for economic development impossible.

In the chapter, I argued that in order to properly address the issue of policy space, we need to critically re-examine the principles that dominate international negotiations, especially in relation to trade and industrial policies. What pass off in today's international policy negotiations, as principles of level playing field, SDT, LTFR, flexibility, and national autonomy were critically examined and their contradictions and limitations were exposed. I argued that the notion of level playing field needs to be ditched as a fundamentally unfair principle for the weak. The notions of autonomy, reciprocity, and flexibility employed in international policy negotiation, it was argued, need to be rescued from their present Orwellian distortion, where they mean almost the exact opposite of what they normally mean.

Urgent action is needed. If nothing is done, the policy space available for developing countries will shrink to virtually nothing over the next several years, which could spell the end of development. The outcome of the Hong Kong–Geneva meeting could be a watershed in the future of economic development.

## REFERENCES

Akyuz, Y. (2005), 'The WTO Negotiations on Industrial Tariffs: What is at Stake for Developing Countries?', (mimeo), Third World Network, Geneva Office.

Akyuz, Y., H-J. Chang, and R. Kozul-Wright (1998), 'New Perspectives on East Asian Development', *Journal of Development Studies*, Vol. 34, No. 6.

Amsden, A. (2005), 'Promoting Industry under WTO Law', in K. Gallagher (ed.), *Putting Development First—The Importance of Policy Space in the WTO and IFIs*, Zed Press, London.

Bairoch, P. (1993), *Economics and World History—Myths and Paradoxes*, Wheatheaf, Brighton.

Brisco, N. (1907), *The Economic Policy of Robert Walpole*, The Columbia University Press, New York.

Chang, H-J. (2002), *Kicking Away the Ladder—Development Strategy in Historical Perspective*, Anthem Press, London.

—— (2003), 'Future for Trade', *Challenge*, Vol. 46, No. 6.

—— (2005), *Why Developing Countries Need Tariffs—How WTO NAMA Negotiations Could Deny Developing Countries' Right to a Future*, South Centre, Geneva, and Oxfam International, Oxford.

Chang, H-J. and D. Green (2003), *The Northern WTO Agenda on Investment—Do as We Say, Not as We Did*, South Centre, Geneva and CAFOD (Catholic Agency for Overseas Development), London.

Fielden, K. (1969), 'The Rise and Fall of Free Trade', in C. Bartlett (ed.), *Britain Pre-eminent: Studies in British World Influence in the Nineteenth Century*, Macmillan, London.

Gallagher, K. (2005), *Putting Development First—The Importance of Policy Space in the WTO and IFIs*, Zed Press, London.

Johnson, C. (1982), *The MITI and the Japanese Miracle*, Stanford University Press, Stanford.

Khor, M. and C.Y. Goh (2004), 'The WTO Negotiations on Non-Agricultural Market Access: A Development Perspective', Paper presented at the Asia-Pacific Conference on Trade: Contributing to Growth, Poverty Reduction and Human Development, Penang, Malaysia, 22–24 November 2004.

Little, I., T. Scitovsky, and M. Scott (1970), *Industry in Trade in Some Developing Countries—A Comparative Study*, Oxford University Press, London.

Maddison. A. (1989), *The World Economy in the 20th Century*, OECD, Paris.

Panić, M. 1988, *National Management of the International Economy*, Basingstoke, Macmillan Press.

Smith, A. (1973) [1776], *An Inquiry into the Nature and Causes of the Wealth of Nations* (edited, with an introduction, notes, marginal summary, and an enlarged index by Edwin Cannan, with an introduction by Max Lerner), originally published in 1776, Random House, New York.

Wade, R. (2005), 'What Strategies Are Viable for Developing Countries Today?—The World Trade Organisation and the Shrinking of "Development Space"', in K. Gallagher (ed.) *Putting Development First—The Importance of Policy Space in the WTO and IFIs*, Zed Press, London.

World Bank (1991), *World Development Report, 1991—The Development Challenge*, Oxford University Press, New York.

—— (1993), *The East Asian Miracle*, Oxford University Press, New York.

# Part I

# Trade Regimes and Exchange Rate Policies

# 3

# Special and Differential Treatment in Trade Regimes

## A Comparative Analysis of GATT, The WTO, The FTAA, and COTONOU

PÁVEL ISA-CONTRERAS AND MIGUEL CEARA-HATTON*

## INTRODUCTION

A new global trade regime has been emerging since the early 1990s. This has been pushing for dramatic changes in the legal and institutional economic infrastructure and has posed serious challenges for small developing nations, as they face severe limitations in adapting, taking advantages of the opportunities, and making the trade regime work and contributing to a development agenda. Thus, for this group of countries, the trade reform agenda has been forcing undesired restructuring of the economic apparatuses. It has seriously curtailed their ability to pursue development policies and has not fulfilled the promises of higher rates of growth and a reduction in poverty. On the contrary, the perception appears to be that the new regime, and more generally, the globalization process, has exacerbated their structural deficiencies and worsened the income distribution.

This paper argues that the development agenda has been removed from the trade reform agenda by significantly degrading Special and Differential Treatment (SDT) for small developing countries from the multilateral and regional trade regimes. Such degradation has taken place either by making SDT provisions non-mandatory or simply by limiting them to implementation on product-by-product and sector-by-sector bases. The paper provides a comparative analysis of SDT provisions in the WTO, the Free Trade Agreement of the Americas (FTAA) process, and the Economic Parternship Agreements (EPA) as delineated by the Cotonou Agreement (CA). It also discusses the implications of SDT provisions in selected sectors of the Caribbean economies such as manufacturing, financial and health services, focussing on market access and intellectual property rights disciplines.

## SPECIAL AND DIFFERENTIAL TREATMENT IN GATT

There have been three phases in the treatment of problems of developing countries in the

*This paper resulted from a research financed and prepared for the Caribbean NGO's Policy Development Centre (CPDC) / Caribbean Reference Group (CRG).

GATT, the institution preceding the WTO: the pre-Kennedy Round phase, the post-Kennedy Round phase, and the Enabling Clause (EC) phase (after the Tokyo Round).

### The Pre-Kennedy Round phase

The initiative of special trade treatment for developing countries in a multilateral context was introduced as early as 1947 in the so-called Havana Charter, the founding agreement of the GATT. During the first 15 years of the GATT, the treatment of problems and needs of developing countries was limited to Article XVIII. Essentially, this article allowed developing countries to void their commitments, that is, renegotiate their commitments with contracting parties or even withdraw concessions, in cases when: (i) they want to establish an industry 'with the purpose of raising the general standard of living of its people', or (ii) they are experiencing Balance of Payments difficulties as they procure to expand their internal markets.

However, SDT as a concept and as a trade principle is associated with the contributions of Raul Prebisch when he was Secretary General of the United Nations Conference on Trade and Development (UNCTAD). In his report to the First UNCTAD Conference, Prebisch (1964) proposed SDT as a multilateral trade principle in a context where development was associated with industrialization and where protectionism predominated. From the perspective of Prebisch and UNCTAD, SDT was an integral part of the Import Substituting Industrialization (ISI) strategy, in which enhanced access to markets of developed countries by exports from developing countries and protected markets for manufactures in developing countries were essential component for industrialization and modernization. In other words, a key element for industrialization of developing countries was a multilateral trading system that, by recognizing the asymmetries between contracting parties, would provide differential treatment in the form of less stringent demands to, and commitments by, developing countries, as well as non-reciprocity.

This perspective crystallized in the set of agreements reached during the Kennedy Round of negotiations (1962–7). However, even before the beginning of the Kennedy Round, there was a growing consensus on the idea of non-reciprocity from developing countries as a principle for trade agreements.

### The Post-Kennedy Round phase

As a result of the Kennedy Round, Part IV was introduced, which included three key articles. Article XXXVI acknowledged the wide income disparities between developing and developed countries, and stresses on the need for concerted collective efforts to ensure 'a rapid advance in the standards of living in these countries' by means of 'a rapid and sustained expansion of the export earnings of the less-developed contracting parties'. Moreover, this article clearly stated non-reciprocity as a principle: 'the developed contracting parties do not expect reciprocity for commitments made by them in trade negotiations to reduce or remove tariffs and other barriers to the trade of less-developed contracting parties'.

Article XXXVII went further to establish the commitment of developed countries to reduce barriers to imports from less developed countries. The article states 'accord high priority to the reduction and elimination of barriers to products currently or potentially of particular export interest to less-developed contracting parties', and commits developed countries to 'refrain from introducing, or increasing the incidence of, customs duties or non-tariff import barriers on products currently or potentially of particular export interest to less-developed contracting parties.'

Finally, article XXXVIII called for a joint action to further the objectives of article XXXVI through international agreements and other means to increase exports from less developed economies. It also provided the basis to create institutions to advance that agenda, such as the UNCTAD, the GATT's Trade and Development Committee, and the Centre for International Trade in 1964.

## The Tokyo Round (1973–9) and the Enabling Clause

The most important reform regarding the treatment to developing countries during the Tokyo Round was the introduction of the so-called 'Enabling Clause', formally entitled 'Differential and More Favourable Treatment Reciprocity and Fuller Participation of Developing Countries'. This clause formally resolved the contradictions between the Most Favoured Nation principle (Article I of the General Agreement) and differential treatment to developing countries by establishing that countries could provide differentiated and more favourable treatment to developing countries without extending that treatment to the rest of the signing parties (non-reciprocity).

Specifically, the clause referred to four areas, as laid out in Paragraph 2: tariff treatment by developed parties to developing ones; differential and more favourable treatment concerning non-tariff measures; regional or global trade agreements among less developed countries aimed at reducing barriers to trade among themselves; and among developing countries, special treatment to least developed countries in the context of general and specific measures aimed at developing countries in general.

The EC stated that developed countries not only shall not seek reciprocity for developing countries with respect to commitments on tariffs and non-tariffs barriers to trade but also that developing countries shall not be required, in the course of negotiations, to make contributions inconsistent with their development needs, whether they are financial or commercial.

Finally, the EC also introduced, for the first time, the idea that developing countries are expected to gradually improve their capacity to make contributions or to negotiate concessions, in other words, to begin reciprocating, as they develop.

The EC provided the framework within which several preferential trade agreements have been put into place, such as the Generalized System of Preferences (GSP), the Caribbean Basin Initiative, the Lomé Convention and the CA, and the North American Free Trade Agreement (NAFTA) Parity Act. It will also be the framework for the 'Everything But Arms' (EBA) programmes expected to be in place in 2008 by which all Africa–Caribbean–Pacific countries (ACP, signatories of the CA) will by able to export to the EU free of duties.

## Underlying development perspectives in SDT provisions of the GATT

A clear underlying notion of the SDT provisions in GATT was that the international trade regime should provide unequal treatment to unequal parties, as indicated by the non-reciprocity principle introduced by Article XXXVI and the EC. This notion implies an acknowledgment that international trade could in fact widen the income gap between developing and developed countries, and that such a tendency for divergence should be specifically addressed by the introduction and enforcement of differential treatment for developing countries.

In addition, it can be inferred from Article XVIII that both the need to promote the development of productive activities and the need to protect developing countries from external shocks (reduction of vulnerability) are legitimate objectives of trade policies, and that the multilateral trade regime should ensure that developing countries are able to implement specific measures to pursue those objectives. The associated development perspective is that policies towards productive sectors (industrial policies) and trade management rather than plain trade and integration to the world economy have a large responsibility in achieving development goals and reducing international divergence.

In this sense, SDT provisions under GATT sought to provide developing countries with room of manoeuvre to implement development policies while they look to ensure that markets of developed countries open to imports from developing economies. In other words, the specific form that SDT took under GATT was to discipline trade policies of developed countries towards developing economies, while providing relaxed trade policy standards to developing countries.

## GOOD BYE DEVELOPMENT, HELLO TRADE

By the early 1980s, however, the crisis of the ISI strategy coupled with the debt crisis, the persistence of macroeconomic instability along with low income growth in developing economies, created a fertile environment for a strong critique of the ISI strategy. This emphasized its anti-export bias, its 'excessive protectionism', and its 'overall inefficiencies'. As a result, in the medium term, market-driven resource allocation replaced state-led allocation, trade liberalization replaced protection, export orientation replaced import substitution, stabilization replace growth, and opening up of trade and complete integration with the world's goods, services, and financial markets (as opposed to managed trade and capital controls) were prescribed as the right medicine for rapid income growth and development.

In line with the central role that trade liberalization is supposed to play in boosting exports, income, and productivity, the objectives of the international trade regime and the global trade agenda were also changed. Instead of a process that widens the gap between rich and poor countries, international trade was now seen as a force of convergence. Hence, trade liberalization, rather than trade management, is now a key element in promoting investment, growth, and innovation in competitive sectors. Increasing market access thus became the most important goal of international trade negotiations in order to ensure export growth in developing countries, and to increase competition in their domestic markets—which would lead to a more efficient resource allocation as well as productivity gains.

This vision of an unambiguously positive role of international trade in development implied a profound transformation in the international trade regime; one of the most important implications being that SDT has been degraded in both the international trade regime and in regional and plurilateral trade agreements, that trade agenda has been emptied from development content.

## THE URUGUAY ROUND OF THE WTO

The UR represented a dramatic change in both the multilateral trading system and the treatment of development issues in the trade agenda in the following ways. First, although it was not the largest increase in the number of contracting parties,[1] it was the single largest

[1]The largest increase took place in the Tokyo Round with respect to the Kennedy Round when the

increase in the number of developing countries becoming signatories (WTO members, from then on). This implied that GATT was not a club of mostly developed countries any more or a partial plurilateral trade agreement but a global multilateral agreement including the majority of countries.

Second, the scope of the commitments widened substantially, going beyond the traditional trade aspects such as tariff and non-tariff barriers to include a large number of so-called 'trade related issues' which were traditionally domestic matters subject to national sovereignty. These included, for instance, policies related to trade of services, investment regimes, intellectual property rights, and subsidies. Hence, the commitments to the WTO became far-reaching, with serious implications for development policies.

Third, for the first time for developing countries, there were 'hard' trade commitments, with specific targets in a number of areas such as tariffs to imports, export subsidies, and 'tariffication' of NTBs to imports.

Fourth, with the creation of the WTO as an institution responsible for enforcement of the trading rules agreed upon, the multilateral trading system became a complex set of binding agreements whose backbone is the mechanism of settlement of disputes with pre-established procedures to process claims. With the enhancement of that mechanism, the WTO, in fact, turned into an international tribunal on trade and trade-related issues.

In addition, the contracting parties agreed on a number of issues that were of utmost concern to developing countries. Some of them were related to market access to developed countries for key developing country exports: an agreement was reached to progressively dismantle the Multifibre Agreement (MFA) that has supported a highly restrictive trade regime of textiles dominated by import quotas, and to gradually incorporate textiles into the WTO general framework. An agreement was reached to expand access of developing countries agricultural products to developed countries market by reducing domestic and export subsidies to agriculture in the latter, and by replacing import quotas by equivalent tariffs that would be progressively reduced. It was agreed that safeguard measures should be provisional and non-discriminatory, while other measures such as voluntary restrictions to exports were outlawed.

However, for the most part, these agreements, either on their own or due to the way they have been operationalized, have consistently undermined the ability of the multilateral trading system to support development efforts, and in many cases have actually curtailed those efforts by severely restricting governments' room of manoeuvre or by reducing market access for developing countries' exports. In the case of the textile agreement, in very few tariff headings have the import quotas imposed by developed countries been eliminated: 13 out of 750 in the US, 14 out of 219 in the EU, 29 out of 295 in Canada (Khor 2001).

With respect to agricultural products, market access to the US and the EU remains highly restricted. In spite of the substantial reduction in NTBs, tariffs peaks, tariff progressions, specific tariffs, and contingent

number of GATT contracting parties increased from 62 to 102 (including 20 developing countries). At the end of the UR, the number of contracting parties was 128. By 2003, 146 countries had become WTO members (see *http://www.wto.org/english/thewto_e/whatis_e/tif_e/fact4_e.htm*)

tariffs constitute insurmountable and non-transparent barriers to exports for developing countries. In addition, developed countries, specially the US, have increased the use of discriminatory tariffs by resorting to safeguard, antidumping, and countervailing procedures (CEPAL 2003; UNCTAD 1998). Also, the mechanism of settlement dispute has become so costly and complicated that it is prohibitive for small and poor developing countries; while, on the other hand, it has become the means through which developed countries enforce compliance.

Despite all these changes, SDT survived the UR and remained a principle of the multilateral trading system. However, its essence and specific measures changed. From being associated with enhanced market access and non-reciprocity for the developing countries, the focus of SDT changed to facilitate the implementation of WTO discipline in developing countries by providing technical assistance and transition periods (Whalley 1999)

In effect, the WTO has recognized that the majority of the SDT general and specific provisions are non-binding. The total number of SDT provisions is 155. Among these, the WTO Secretariat has identified only 27 articles, paragraphs, or parts of articles and paragraphs which are mandatory, that is, 'shall' is used instead of 'should' (WTO 2001a).

In essence, by diluting SDT provisions, the WTO implicitly assumes that first, the level of development has no relationship with the level of rights and obligation under the multilateral trading system; second, the same policies could be applicable for countries at different levels of development (WTO 2001b); and third, the main problem that developing countries face with respect to the multilateral trading system is that of adaptation, which can be resolved by providing adequate time for transition and technical assistance. This effectively implied a displacement of the development agenda from the trade agenda.

## Pre-Doha, Doha, and post-Doha

After the end of the UR in 1994, countries initiated the process of implementing specific measures in order to comply with their commitments to the WTO that were not restricted to trade barriers and that included countries changing their national legislations to make them compatible with WTO norms.

However, the implementation process created frustrations in many developing countries. Not only were the developed countries not complying, but a number of them also began to address severe criticism of what they perceived as the uneven impact of the liberalization process, especially with regard to intellectual property rights, subsidies and antidumping measures, and the mechanism dispute settlement. The growing criticisms of the so-called 'implementation problems' added to the non-binding character of SDT provisions, and to the lack of institutional, human, and financial capacities of many small and poor countries to implement the agreements and to cope successfully with the consequences (UNDP &TWN 2001).

As a result, while developing countries were insisting on the need for a new agenda for the WTO which would review the results of the UR, developed countries were pushing to start a new round of negotiations where a whole new set of trade-related issues would be negotiated (labour, government procurements, environment, and investment). The failure of the Ministerial Conference in Seattle in 1999 was a result of the inability of the contracting parties to reconcile those two agendas, coupled with the effectiveness of the growing number of civil society organizations—concerned with the implications of the WTO agreements on development—in mobilizing and opposing the agenda of many developed countries.

The failure in Seattle meant that developing countries gained momentum in pushing forward their trade agenda. As a result, the new round of negotiations had to incorporate their concerns. In the context of the debates towards the proposed new round launched in Doha, Qatar, in November 2001, a number of countries in the the so-called 'Like-minded Group' proposed specific elements to bring SDT back to the heart of the multilateral trading system (WTO 2001b). The parties reached a compromise to revise and strengthen SDT provisions:

> We reaffirm that provisions for special and differential treatment are an integral part of the WTO Agreements. We note the concerns expressed regarding their operation in addressing specific constraints faced by developing countries, particularly least-developed countries. In that connection, we also note that some members have proposed a Framework Agreement on Special and Differential Treatment (WT/GC/W/442). We therefore agree that all special and differential treatment provisions shall be reviewed with a view to strengthening them and making them more precise, effective and operational (Paragraph 44, the Doha Ministerial Declaration 2001).

In addition, the WTO members agreed on a number of issues of relevance for developing countries such as an extension of the waiver to provide tax incentives to exports to certain developing countries until 2007, with two years for transition, and a waiver to produce, without licence, certain medicines in the case of national health crises.

At the time, the results from Doha were very positive for developing countries. Nonetheless, the optimism has been vanishing as a number of critical deadlines have passed and no important agreement has been reached.

## SMALLNESS, DEVELOPMENT, AND TRADE

While dramatic changes in the trade and development thinking and policy agenda were taking place, a new concern emerged: the inability of smaller countries to adapt to the new global trade regime and to globalization in general. In terms of the trade regime, that meant the possibility of considering SDT provisions not only based on the criteria of development levels but also on country size.

### MEASURING COUNTRY SIZE

Beginning with Kuznets' *Economic Growth of Small Nations* (1963), the issue of the implication of small country size for development has been abundantly studied. However, how does one define smallness? There are two relevant issues here. First, What is to be measured: territory, population or production? Second, what is the threshold?

Population has been the most popular proxy used to measure country size, particularly because there is a correlation between the size of the population and the economic size (as measured by absolute real gross domestic product, GDP). In addition, many countries with small populations are also geographically small. Several thresholds have been used to consider a country as 'small'. Some have proposed 1.5 million. Others have used 5 million. However, there is no agreement on what 'small' means (WTO 2002a), particularly because each criteria that could be used would group countries with diverse characteristics, and because the thresholds are always arbitrary.

Moreover, this discussion throws up the basic question: Why does size matter? Do small countries have natural disadvantages for growth and development? Based on comparative statistics between small and large countries, many think that it is not the case. Others believe that small countries share specific characteristics that make them particularly weak and vulnerable to swings in the international economy on which they are heavily dependent on, and especially to changes in the world trade regime.

## THE DISADVANTAGES OF SMALL ECONOMIC SIZE

Several arguments have been proposed in the development literature from the 1960s and 1970s that suggest that small country size has negative implications for development.

1. Narrowness of natural resources base. The majority of small economies also have a small territory and little diversity of raw materials and natural resources to support the development of basic industries. Thus, the availability of minerals, for example, and other natural resources largely exceeds domestic demand. Their natural characteristics contribute to making these economies primary product exporters, highly specialized and concentrated, and dependent on a very narrow range of activities (Streeten 1993).

2. Economies of scale. It has been claimed that industrialization might be deterred by small economic size, given that many industrial sectors operate under economies of scale and increasing returns (Briguglio 1998). In addition, given the small size of the market, protective measures necessary to ensure the survival of manufacturing activities might be too large and costly to be justified. Smallness also limits effective domestic competition, making the economies prone to oligopoly and monopoly settings. Hence, smallness imposes serious constraints to efficient import substitution activities (Briguglio 1993). Exports might be a way to overcome that obstacle; however that route carries with it other difficult barriers.

Indivisibilities, economies of scale, and increasing returns in the delivery of public goods is another disadvantage that small economies might face. As these translate into high per capita costs (Alesina and Spolaore 1997) they might have negative consequences for long-term economic performance if private productivity depend on the provision of public goods.

3. Export concentration and economic volatility. Small economies are usually characterized by a high degree of specialization and openness. Usually, they export a small range of products or services (mainly primary products), the share of the exports in the GDP is larger than in larger economies, and their coefficient of openness (exports and imports divided by the GDP) is large. It has been asserted that their high dependence on external trade causes a higher degree of vulnerability to swings in the international economy. Specifically, highly concentrated exports are very likely to imply larger volatility of export proceeds. If in addition, exports represent a large proportion of the GDP, high export volatility would ultimately translate into greater economic instability, which might reduce the long-term rate of growth (Nurske 1958; Lim 1974; Voivodas 1974; Persaud 1989; CS/WB JTF 2000).

Some empirical evidence reveals that small countries face a larger degree of exports and economic instability, although not necessarily a smaller rate of growth (CS/WB JTF 2000; CommRisk ITF 2000; Easterly and Kraay 1999) and that export volatility reduces investment and income growth (Isa 2003).

## VULNERABILITY, OPENNESS, AND ADAPTATION

In the mid-1980s, a new literature emerged on the special problems of small states and the implications of trade liberalization. It was mostly developed or sponsored by the Commonwealth Secretariat[2] but has also received other important contributions such as those by Kaminarides (1989), Briguglio (1993), and CS/WB JTF (2000). As opposed to the contributions of the development camp, the immediate interest of this literature has been on the capacity of small economies to cope with the impacts of a changing international environment.

The first major attempt crystallized in the United Nations Conference on SIDS where a new number of problems that many small countries face were underscored. In particular, the new contributions added three problems associated to small size to the list:

4. Location, remoteness, and transportation costs. If unit costs of transportation decrease with volume, small countries are at a disadvantage in international markets. If, in addition to that, they are landlocked or in remote locations from poles of economic activity, the disadvantage becomes particularly severe because of high transportation costs. This seems to be the case for many islands in the Pacific and some countries in Africa. Insularity and remoteness may also entail discontinuities and irregularities in transportation services, which might give rise to uncertainty in the supply of imports, harm exports, and increase the costs of holding larger stocks (CS/WB JTF 2000; Streeten 1993; Briguglio 1993).

5. Taxation and fiscal deficit. It has also been argued that larger countries rely more heavily on more efficient taxes (that is, income taxes) than smaller ones (that is, tariffs) because of the high set-up costs for the bureaucracy needed to administer more efficient taxes (Easterly and Rebello 1993). In small and/or less developed economies, the share of custom taxes in the total tax revenue is usually large compared to that in larger and more developed ones. If export proceeds and foreign exchange availability in small economies are more volatile than in larger ones, a larger volatility of tax revenue should be expected. This might cause either periodic increases in the fiscal deficit, which may cause inflationary pressures, or sharp fluctuations in public expenditure, most likely public investment, with possible consequences on the level of economic activity, in particular if public and private investment are complementary (crowding-in) rather than rivals (crowding-out). Nonetheless, many LDCs are also small, and it is not clear whether the dependence on foreign trade taxes is a characteristic associated with low per capita income or with economic size.

6. Proneness to natural disasters. It is well-known that SIDS tend to experience much more devastating consequences from natural disasters than other countries. Due to their small size, natural phenomena such as hurricanes and typhoons usually affect the whole agricultural sector and most of the housing and communication infrastructure. Easter (1999) argues that natural disasters are an important factor in explaining growth volatility.

However, the SIDS face a wider range of special problems: the impact of climate change

[2]Some of the most important contributions are Commonwealth Secretariat Advisory Group (1997), Commonwealth Secretariat (1999), Easter (1999), Easterly and Kraay (1999), and Treebhoolhum (1999).

and the rise in sea level, the impact of natural and environmental disasters; the management of waste; the management and preservation of coastal and marine resources, freshwater resources, land resources, energy resources; tourism, biodiversity; national institutions and administrative capacities, and regional institutions and technical co-operation. These issues point towards the unique vulnerabilities and limitations of small islands, and therefore, to the distinctive treatment that these countries should receive.

Through a Joint Task force, the Commonwealth Secretariat and the World Bank launched a second major effort. Concerned with the issue of vulnerability, the Commonwealth developed the composite vulnerability index (CVI) whose aim is to account for the impact of a country's degree of international economic exposure, remoteness, insularity, susceptibility to natural disaster, and resilience.

The key components of the CVI are twofold: the Vulnerability Impact Index (VII) and a proxy for a country's resilience. VII is the predicted value of the output volatility estimated by a weighted least squared regression in which output volatility depends on the susceptibility of natural disasters (measured by the percentage of population affected by the same), the degree of export dependence (measured by the share of exports in the GDP), an indicator of economic diversification (the UNCTAD's diversification index), and an error term. The GDP per capita is used as a proxy for resilience (Easter 1999). It is not surprising that the index of vulnerability is highly correlated with size: the smaller the country the more vulnerable it is and the higher its CVI.

Again, these contributions provide a new rationale for SDT associated not only to the level of development but also to size, and thus provide SDT with an enhanced meaning and purpose.

### The New Consensus: Small is Good

In the late 1990s, country size was decisively incorporated into the development and trade policy debate. However, mirroring the shift of focus in the trade reform agenda, the contemporary debate emptied the conceptualization of the implications of smallness from the development content, and reduced the discussion to the difficulties of small countries to adapt to an environment of liberalized trade. Along these lines, SDT for smaller countries was reduced to assigning transition periods, and assistance to adapt to the new context.

In spite of the contributions above mentioned, by the late 1990s it was clear that the consensus in multilateral organizations was moving in a different direction: instead of adding to and enriching the earlier literature, the consequences of small size were being reconsidered by undermining the arguments put forward by previous contributions.

For instance, an important argument was made about the benefits of smallness: that it allows for near-to-complete international specialization and openness, and that both factors allow small countries to reap substantial productivity gains. The contributions by Easterly and Kraay (1999) and by the CS/WB JTF (2000) are representative of this view: although smallness entails a number of disadvantages, the fact that they tend to be open to trade and foreign investment more than counteracts such disadvantages. Hence, smaller countries do not show lower rates of growth or per capita income than larger ones. Moreover, small states show higher rates of productivity growth. However, Isa (2003) found empirical evidence suggesting that trade openness actually reduces productivity and income growth.

Therefore, the policy recommendation is not to reduce volatility but to integrate with international capital and insurance markets in order to share the risks and distribute them over time. Thus, SDT for small countries should be limited to facilitate their integration with international financial markets, to provide them with longer periods for trade opening (reciprocity) in order to restructure their tax structure (usually heavily dependent on taxes on trade), and to provide them with technical assistance in critical areas. In other words, in this view 'smallness' is not a long-term development problem but a transition problem, and with some 'fine tuning' smaller countries will have the same potential as larger countries to take full advantage of trade liberalization. This view has been conditioning the trade negotiation agenda within the WTO, and, as will be clear in the next section, it has deeply permeated the negotiations of the FTAA.

## SPECIAL AND DIFFERENTIAL TREATMENT IN THE FTAA PROCESS

Since its early stage, the FTAA process recognized the challenges of the development gap between the smaller and poorer countries on the one hand, and larger and richer ones on the other, as well as the obstacles that small size and low income pose in taking full advantage of economic integration with the Hemisphere. However, it was not until San Jose Ministerial Meeting in 1998 that the first steps were taken to address these issues. The Ministers agreed to create a Consultative Committee on Smaller Economies (GCSE) that reports to the Trade Negotiation Committee (TNC).[3] The functions of the GCSE are the following: 'follow the FTAA process, keeping under review the concerns and interests of the smaller economies; and will bring to the attention of the TNC the issues of concern to the smaller economies and make recommendations to address these issues' (San Jose Ministerial Declaration, March 1998).

More than two year later, the Ministerial Meeting in Buenos Aires (April 2001) insisted on the commitment to take into account the differences in the levels of development and size in designing the FTAA to create opportunities for full participation of smaller economies and to increase their level of development. It also reiterated the importance of co-operation to strengthen the productive and competitive capacities of smaller economies, especially through technical assistance and other provisions. The Ministerial Meeting instructed GCSE and the Tripartite Committee[4] to provide guidelines 'on way of applying the treatment of differences in the levels of development

[3]The Declaration stated: 'The TNC will have the responsibility of guiding the work of the negotiating groups and of deciding on the overall architecture of the agreement and institutional issues. The TNC is to take the overall responsibility of ensuring the full participation of all the countries in the FTAA process. *It will also ensure that this issue, in particular the concerns of the smaller economies and concerns related to countries with different levels of development will be dealt with within each negotiating group*'.

[4]The Tripartite Committee is formed by the Inter-American Development Bank (IADB), the Economic Commission for Latin America and the Caribbean (ECLAC), and the Organization of Americas States (OAS) and has the mission to provide technical assistance to the FTAA process.

and size of economies', and mandated incorporation of the inputs from the GCSE in all substantive negotiating areas.

Based on that mandate, several proposals were put forward by countries and groups of countries.[5] The following is a list of proposed principles and specific measures to implement SDT in the FTAA (Ceara-Hatton 2001): SDT in the FTAA should be WTO+; Implementation of SDT measures should be flexible as to fit the needs of specific countries, issues, and sectors; SDT measures should be considered in each negotiating group; in some cases, SDT measures could be implemented on a 'case by case' basis; duration of SDT measures should be determined on a 'case by case' basis; certain SDT measures in certain areas of negotiation should be applied by group of countries; SDT measure require a Hemispheric Co-operation Plan; and SDT measures should be mandatory.

The specific measures are: provisions to enhance trade opportunities (access to technology, information, etc.); flexibility in the application of SDT measures; lower requirements for smaller economies; longer periods for implementation of commitments; exceptions granted in certain areas; facilitating access to the mechanism of dispute settlement for smaller economies; technical assistance and training during the negotiation period and during the phase of implementation; special Balance of Payments safeguard measures; special safeguard measures for specific needs of smaller economies; allowing the existence of special fiscal regimes such as export processing zones (EPZs); and allowing special investment incentives.

In a document agreed on most points by all countries, the CGSE proposed a framework to implement SDT treatment in the FTAA. The proposal picked many of the suggestions put forward by countries, groups of countries, and institutions. In this list of principles and measures for implementing SDT, there are at least three aspects that deserve be underscored. First, there was a consensus that SDT in FTAA should be WTO+. A reasonable interpretation of this is that proponents (countries, institutions, and the CGSE) believe that SDT provisions as stipulated and implemented within the WTO are insufficient to address the needs of small developing countries.

Second, some proposals insisted on the need for mandatory provisions for SDT rather than non-binding ones. In essence, some smaller developing countries called for rules and enforcement, just as developed countries demand full compliance with the commitments and use the available mechanisms effectively to enforce them.

Third, some of the proposals imply that SDT needs are not limited to specific areas of negotiation (which may point towards a 'treatment of exception') but are needs associated to the 'general condition' of being a small developing country and the characteristics that the condition entails. In other words, SDT should be both specific and transversal to all areas of negotiation.

However, the TNC agreements reached at the ninth meeting in Managua in September 2001 watered down the proposals put forward by countries and even by the CGSE on SDT. In effect, in that meeting the TNC prepared a document entitled 'Guidelines for the Treatment of Differences in the Levels of Development and Size of the Economies'

[5]The countries, groups of countries, and institutions that presented specific proposals were: the Association of Caribbean States (ACS), the Caribbean Community (CARICOM), the Andean Community, El Salvador and Honduras, the Dominican Republic, the United States of America, and Canada.

(FTAA.TNC/18, September 28, 2001) whose proposals for SDT are as follows: SDT measures should provide a flexible framework that addresses the needs of each country participating in the negotiating process; SDT measures should be transparent, simple, and easily implemented, recognizing the degree of heterogeneity of countries; SDT measures should be determined within each negotiating group; when the treatment goes beyond a negotiating group (transversal), the TNC should determine the same; measures should be decided on a 'case by case' basis; SDT could include transition measures that would be coupled with technical co-operation programmes; special measures should take into account the access market conditions for smaller economies in the hemisphere; SDT measures could consider longer periods for compliance; and a Hemispherical Technical Co-operation Programme should accompany the SDT measures.

In the TNC guidelines, there are neither general principles for SDT, nor mandatory measures (or enforcement for that matter). SDT was limited to the provision of longer transition periods and technical support, and was specified to be provided on a 'case by case' basis.

In summary, for all intentions and purposes in the case of the FTAA, the development agenda was, once more, removed from the trade agenda. Despite the rhetoric, trade liberalization was placed as the ultimate goal.

## PROSPECTS FOR SPECIAL AND DIFFERENTIAL TREATMENT IN THE EPAs

In spite of the poor record of the WTO on SDT for small developing countries, and the concrete decisions taken with respect to the FTAA process on this matter, the proposed EPA between ACP countries and the EU as delineated in the CA appears to provide some hope that more comprehensive, deeper, and sustained commitments will be adopted.

Notwithstanding the ultimate concrete goal of the EPA, viz, to replace the current non-reciprocal market access preferences to the EU by a reciprocal treaty by January 2008 through a process which will involve 'essentially all areas relevant to trade' (Article 36.1 of the CA), the objectives and principles of economic and trade co-operation between the EU and the ACP provide a strong framework for the adoption of specific and mandatory measures for SDT under the EPA (Articles 34 through 38 of the CA).They advocate smooth and gradual integration of ACP states into the world economy, thus contributing to poverty eradication and sustainable development; creating a new trading dynamic between the EU and ACP states; enhancing ACP states' capacities to handle all trade related issues; implementing measures to increase competitive capacities in ACP states. The new partnership will build on existing regional integration schemes as they are considered vital to development efforts and to the reinsertion of smaller developing countries into the global economy.

The modalities and procedures are also very relevant to the implementation of SDT treatment. Article 37.5 of the agreement stipulates that negotiations with ACP countries will be undertaken by countries 'which consider themselves in a position to do so, at the level they consider appropriate'. Moreover, it states that the procedures for negotiations will be agreed by the ACP group, and will take into account regional integration processes (Article 37.7) insofar as 'integration is a key instrument for integrating ACP countries intro the world economy' (CA, Article 35.2) and as 'regional integration and cooperation within the ACP regions is the launching pad for enhancing ACP competitiveness' (ACP Procedural Guidelines for the Preparation and Negotiation of New Trade Arrangements, December 2001, hereafter, the ACP Guidelines or simply the Guidelines). In short, negotiations will be started by ACP countries whch feel prepared, in the way they consider adequate, and by groups, thus providing them with more negotiating power.

Following the lines of the CA, the 'Guidelines' stated that negotiations for the EPAs should be founded on development objectives—poverty reduction, income growth, and increased participation in the world economy—and should be compatible with specific development agendas and country priorities:

> Before deciding whether or not they should engage in negotiations, each ACP country should as a first step define and prioritise its own development agenda. It should then define how its external trade policy could be applied to negotiate an arrangement that positively contributes to the development objectives that have already been spelled out. Therefore EPAs/NTAs should be made (to) be compatible with development objectives of each single ACP country (ACP Guidelines 2001, pp. 6–7).

Furthermore, the Guidelines listed specific objectives of the EPAs: enhancing productive capacities in the main sectors; enhancing supply and trading capacity of ACP; increasing competitiveness of a large part of the export sector; attracting greater volumes of investment and technology in the key sectors; diversifying export markets and products; hard and soft infrastructure development; enhancing capacity in human resources; building the required institutions and confidence in the multilateral trading system; carrying out structural transformation of the economies, which includes strengthening and deepening domestic policy reform to regain the share of the world trade they have lost and to gain flexibility to adjust to the pace of globalization (ACP Procedural Guidelines 2001, p. 3).

The Guidelines also underscore the role of regional integration and remind the Doha Ministerial Declaration of the commitment of WTO members to clarify and improve disciplines and procedures applying to regional trade agreements where members agreed that 'the negotiations shall take into account the development aspects of regional trade agreements'.

With respect to market access measures from the EU, identified as key for SDT treatment in the WTO, the Guidelines treat the reform of the EU's Common Agricultural Policy (CAP) and the EBA initiative for less developed countries (LDCs) as factors influencing the negotiating position of the ACP.

Finally, in the Guidelines, the ACP Group explicitly introduced the SDT treatment as part of its negotiating principles:

> Negotiating principles should reaffirm those stated in article 35 of the CA and should include, *inter alia*, policy objectives in all areas of negotiations and Special and differential treatment that recognize asymmetry in terms of different time frame, product coverage, vulnerability, small economies, level of obligations, and reciprocity based on the achievement of development threshold (ACP Guidelines 2001, p. 11).

In this regard, contrary to the decisions made in the FTAA process, the ACP Group recognizes not only product specific issues that should be dealt with, but also crosscutting, and region-specific trade issues. This is, in fact, an acknowledgment that SDT is not related only to specific products but to development problems which are common to all developing countries, and some of them specific to regions (ACP Guidelines 2001, p. 11).

The ACP Mandate for the Negotiations of Economic Partnership Agreements of June 2002 (hereafter, the Mandate) goes further to provide principles and strategic and specific objectives of ACP countries in negotiating the EPAs, with more specific proposals seeking SDT. With respect to the principles, the ACP Mandate cites the following: EPAs should be development-oriented; unity and solidarity should guide the negotiations; EPAs should preserve, build upon, and improve the comprehensive approach reached in the previous ACP–EU Conventions, specially improving market access to the EU for ACP countries, safeguarding the benefits from the commodity protocols, and reciprocity from ACP States should not by accepted a *priori*. An overriding principle with respect to WTO-compatibility is that WTO rules are inherently unbalanced against the development needs of ACP countries; hence, ACP states should not make further commitments until these pending issues in the WTO are properly resolved; recognizing their different levels of development, provisions for SDT to ACP countries must be essential to the EPAs, specially to LDCs, small vulnerable islands, and landlocked countries as well. Acknowledging the differentiated levels of development, the EU should be as flexible as possible towards the ACPs during negotiations; such flexibility should also be included in the WTO rules; EPAs should be sustainable by maximizing benefits and minimizing costs. Sustainability should be viewed in the light of adjustment costs, social and political implications, institutional and human capacities of ACP states, and governability. ACP states must maintain overall coherent and consistent positions in the various negotiations in which they are involved (WTO, EPAs, regional, sub-regional and bilateral agreements, with the IMF, the World Bank, or regional development banks). As far as sequencing is concerned, regional integration should take priority and/or precede EPAs; moreover, EPAs should support the integration processes; EPAs should have legitimacy in the ACP states; public support, public scrutiny, transparent negotiation procedures, and clear dispute settlement procedures should be essential components of the process; and resources for adjustment should be available (ACP Mandate 2002, pp. 5–8)

Some strategic objectives outlined by the ACP Mandate are even more specific to the development agenda: to reduce dependence of ACP's on primary products and natural resource-based sectors through diversification; to promote structural transformation of ACP states so as to foster knowledge-based competitive economies capable of exploiting new market access in the EU and in the world at large; and to address the obstacles to exports of ACP goods, specially the constraints associated with physical infrastructure, communications, and legal and administrative trade regimes (ACP Mandate 2002, p. 9).

With respect to safeguards, the Mandate explicitly mentions the objective of SDT treatment for ACP countries. In competition policy, a sustainable industrialization process is an objective, as well as reaching an agreement that does not destabilize ACP firms. On the negotiations on intellectual property rights, ACP countries will seek that the agreement ensures equitable benefits for owners and receivers of technology, that the agreement promotes technological innovation conducive to meeting public and social objectives, that ACP states are able to take advantage of technological transfers, and that they are able to protect sources and allow disclosure of the sources of traditional knowledge and genetic resources.

Finally, the Mandate presents a number of development-related issues as specific objectives of the EPAs including: tackling supply side constraints that prevent ACPs from taking full advantage of market access facilities (such as unreliable provision of public utilities, poor infrastructure, weak institutional and policy frameworks, and low labour productivity), and measures to address adjustment costs of the EPAs such as fiscal measures, addressing the external debt burden, labour reallocation needs as a result of trade opening and the associated productive restructuring, the promotion of investment and technology transfer, and support to industrial development, research, and innovation.

## CONCLUSIONS

This paper traces the development of SDT provisions in the international trading system. A clear underlying notion behind the SDT provisions in GATT was that international trade could in fact widen the income gap between developing and developed countries, and that such divergence tendency should be addressed by introducing and enforcing differential treatment for developing countries, and that developing countries should be allowed to implement measures to pursue development objectives such as industrial policies and trade management—in short, that the international trade regime should provide unequal treatment to unequal parties. However, by the early 1980s, there were apparent cracks in the dominant development perspective. In contrast with the past, it was assumed that international trade is a force of convergence, that trade liberalization is a key element in promoting growth, and that increasing global market access should be the most important goal of international trade negotiations.

Thus, the UR agenda also changed, resulting in a widening of the scope of the commitments to include a number of 'trade related issues' which were traditionally domestic matters subject to national sovereignty (services, investment, intellectual property rights, and subsidies), limiting the ability of members to implement development policies. In addition, the WTO became the institution responsible for enforcing the rules of trade, a complex set of binding agreements, turning it into an international tribunal on trade and trade-related issues.

Perhaps the single most important result of the UR was that there was a de facto degradation of SDT and an emptying of the trade agenda from its development content. In effect, most of the general and specific SDT provisions are non-binding. In the 1990s, small country size was incorporated in the development and trade policy debate as an additional reason for SDT in trade negotiations. However, in line with the dominant view, it was argued that SDT for small countries should be limited to facilitate their integration to the international financial markets, to provide them with longer periods for trade opening, and to the provide them with technical assistance in critical areas.

This is the context in which the FTAA process is analysed. The paper shows that despite recognizing the problem correctly, so far it has provided neither general principles for SDT, nor any mandatory measures. In spite of the poor record of the WTO on SDT for small developing countries, and the concrete decisions taken with respect to the FTAA process on this matter, the proposed EPA between the ACP and the EU, as delineated in the CA appears to provide some hope that more comprehensive, deeper, and sustained commitments will be adopted in that specific case.

## REFERENCES


ACP (2001), ACP Procedural Guidelines for Preparation and Negotiation of New Trade Agreements, Draft, Brussels, 4 December, ACP/61/057/01, Rev. 4. B.

____ (2002), Mandate for the Negotiations of Economic Partnership Agreements (2002), Draft, Brussels, 3 June, ACP/61/056/02.

Alesina, Alberto and Enrico Spolaore (1997), 'On the Number and Size of Nations', *The Quarterly Journal of Economics*, November.

Briguglio, Lino (1993), 'Small Island Developing States and Their Economic Vulnerabilities', *World Development*, Vol. 23, No. 9, pp. 1615–32.

____ (1998), 'Small Country Size and Returns to Scale in Manufacturing', *World Development*, Vol. 26, No. 3, pp. 507–15.

Ceara-Hatton, Miguel (2001), 'Pequeñas Economías y Trato Especial y Diferenciado en el ALCA', Trinidad and Tobago (mimeo).

Centro de Comercio Internacional, Commonwealth Secretariat (2000), *Guía para la Comunidad Empresarial: El sistema mundial de comercio*, Segunda Edición, London.

CEPAL (2003), 'Panorama de la Inserción Internacional de América Latina y el Caribe, 2001–2002', Capítulo IV. División de Comercio Internacional e Integración, *www.eclac.cl*.

Commodity Risk Management in Developing Countries—Comm Risk (2000), 'A Proposed Market-Based Approach and its Relevance for Small States', Paper presented at the Global conference on the Development Agenda for Small States, London, 17–18 February.

Commonwealth Secretariat Advisory Group (1997), 'A Future for Small States. Overcoming Vulnerability'. Commonwealth Secretariat, London.

Commonwealth Secretariat (1999), 'Small States: A Composite Vulnerability Index', Paper presented at the Conference on Small States, St. Lucia, 17–19 February.

Commonwealth Secretariat and Quaker Peace and Service, 'TRIPs, BIODIVERSITY AND COMMONWEALTH COUNTRIES: capacity building priorities for the 1999 review of TRIPs Article 27.3 (b)', A discussion paper, Available at *http://www.ukabc.org/TRIPs/trips99.pdf*

Comunicación de Argentina, Australia, Canadá, Chile, El Salvador, Estados Unidos, Filipinas, Guatemala, Nueva Zelandia, Paraguay, República Dominicana y Taipei Chino. *Implicaciones de la Ampliación del Ámbito del Artículo 23*. IP/C/W/386, 8 de noviembre de 2002.

Cotonou Agreement (2000),

CS/WB JTF Commonwealth Secretariat/World Bank Joint Task Force on Small States (2000), 'Small States: Meeting Challenges in the Global Economy', *http://www.worldbank.org/html/extdr/smallstates*.

Easter, Christopher (1999), 'Small States Development: A Commonwealth Vulnerability Index', The Round Table, 351, pp. 403–22.

Easterly, William and Aart Kraay (1999), 'Small States, Small Problems?', Paper presented at the Conference on Small States, St. Lucia, 17–19 February.

Easterly, William and Sergio Rebello (1993), 'Fiscal Policy and Economic Growth: An Empirical Investigation', *Quarterly Journal of Economics*, Vol. 32, pp. 417–57.

Erb, Guy and Salvatore Schiavo-Campos (1969), 'Export Instability, Level of Development and Economic Size of Less Developed Countries', *Oxford Bulletin of Economics*, Vol. 31, No. 4.

FTAA (2000), TNC/18, September 28.

General Agreement on Tariffs and Trade (GATT) (1947 1967, and 1979).

Isa, Pável (2003), 'Economic Size and Long Term Growth. An empirical analysis of the consequences of small economic size on investment, productivity and income growth', Ph.D. Dissertation Proceedings, University of Massachusetts Amherst.

Joint Communication from the African Group (2003), Taking forward the review of article 27.3(B) of the TRIP'S Agreement, IP/C/W/404, 26 June.

Kaminarides, J. (1989), 'The Small Developing Countries: An Introduction', in Kaminarides, J., L. Briguglio, and H. Hoogendonk (eds), *The Economic Development of Small Countries: Problems, Strategies and Policies*, Eburon Publishing, The Netherlands, pp. 15–26.

Kathuria, Sanjay and Anjali Bhardwaj (1998), 'Export Quotas and Policy Constraints in the Indian Textile and Garment Industries, *Policy Research Working Paper*, The World Bank.

Khor, Martin (2001), 'On the Multilateral Trading System', Statement presented to the Group of 15 Meeting of Trade and Economics Ministers. Jakarta, 27 May, *www.tedtebba.org*.

Kuznets, Simon (1963), 'Economic Growth of Small Nations', in E. A. G. Robinson (ed.), *Economic Consequences of the Size of Nations*, MacMillan, London, pp. 14–32.

Lim, David (1974), 'Export Instability and Economic Development: The Example of West Malaysia', *Oxford Economic Papers*, March.

Mollet, Montserrat (2001), *La regulación del comercio internacional: del GATT a la OMC*, Edición electrónica disponible en Internet: *www.estudios.lacaixa.es*, Servicio de Estudios Colección Estudios Económicos. Núm. 24, Barcelona.

Nurkse, Ragnar (1958), 'Trade Fluctuations and Buffer Policies of Low-Income Countries', Kyklos, Vol. XI, Fasc. 2, pp. 141–4.

OMC (2001a), Declaración Ministerial. Conferencia Ministerial, Doha, 9–14 Noviembre, WT/MIN(01)/DEC/W/1.

—— (2001b), Declaración Relativa al Acuerdo Sobre los ADPIC y la Salud Pública. Conferencia Ministerial. Doha, 9–14 Noviembre, WT/MIN(01)/DEC/W/2.

—— (2001c). *Comunicación del Grupo Africano, Barbados, Bolivia, Brasil, Cuba, República Dominicana, Ecuador, Honduras, India, Indonesia, Jamaica, Pakistán, Paraguay, Filipinas, Perú, Sri lanka, Tailandia y Venezuela*. Consejo de los Aspectos de los Derechos de Propiedad Intelectual relacionados con el Comercio. IP/C/W/296. 29 de junio.

—— (2001d), Con el comercio hacia el futuro. Introducción a la OMC, 2a edición, revisada, *www.wto.org*

—— (2002), *Información Disponible Sobre la Capacidad para Fabricar Medicamentos*. Consejo de los Aspectos de los Derechos de Propiedad Intelectual relacionados con el Comercio, IP/C/W/345. 24 de mayo.

Persaud, B. (1989), 'Small States: Economic problems and Prospects', in J., Kaminarides, Lino Briguglio, and H. Hoogendonk (eds), *The Economic Development of Small Countries. Problems, Strategies and Policies*, Eburon Publishers, The Netherlands, pp. 15–26.

Prebisch, Raul (1964), 'La Nueva Política Comercial para el Desarrollo', Informe preparado para la I Conferencia de las Naciones Unidas sobre Comercio y Desarrollo (Ginebra, 1964), En Adolfo Gurrieri, 'La Obra de Prebisch en la CEPAL', Lecturas del Fondo # 46, Tomo II, Mexico 1982.

Report of the Commission on Intellectual Property Rights (2002), Integrating Intellectual Property Rights and Development Policy, Commission on Intellectual Property Rights, London, September.

Streeten, Paul (1993), 'The Special Problems of Small Countries', *World Development*, Vol. 21, No. 2, pp. 197–202.

Treebhoolhum, Nikhil (1999), 'The Mauritanian Experience', Paper presented at the Conference on Small States, St. Lucia, 17–19 February.

UNCTAD (1998), 'The Least Developed Countries 1998 Report, Overview by the Secretary General', *www.unctad.org*

UNDP and TWN (Third World Network) (2001), 'The Multilateral Trading System: A Development Perspective', Third World Network, New York, December.

Voivodas, C. S. (1974), 'The Effect of Foreign Exchange Instability on Growth', *Review of Economics and Statistics*, August.

Whalley, John (1999), 'Special and Differential Treatment in the Millennium Round', CSGR Working Paper No. 30/99.

WTO (2001a), Implementation of Special and Differential Treatment Provisions in WTO Agreements and Decisions, 21 September 2001, WT/COMTD/W/77/Rev.1

—— (2001b), 'Preparations for the Fourth Session of the Ministerial Conference. Proposal for a Framework Agreement on Special and Differential Treatment', Communication from Cuba, Dominican Republic, Honduras, India, Indonesia, Kenya, Malaysia, Pakistan, Sri Lanka, Tanzania, Uganda and Zimbabwe, WT/GC/W/442.

—— (2002a), 'Small Economies: A Literature Review', World Trade Organization, WT/COMTD/W/4.

—— (2002b), 'Trade and Economic Performance: The Role of Economic Size', WT/COMTD/W/5.

# 4

# Limits to Universal Trade Liberalization Experience of South Asia in Textiles and Clothing Sector

P.L. Beena*

## INTRODUCTION

This paper looks at the impact of trade liberalization on the export performance of textiles and clothing (T&C) sector in five[1] major countries of South Asia in the light of the major theoretical debates regarding the relevance of outward looking/export-oriented strategies over the inward looking/import-substitution (I-S) strategies. One of the main criticisms of the I-S strategies (Prebisch 1959) was with regard to their limitations in building up diversified industrial structures and diversifying exports (Hirschman 1992). Another important criticism was with respect to the infant industry protection (List 1856) adopted by countries as part of the industrialization process. It was argued that universal trade liberalization would make industries more competent and an FDI-driven, export-led industrialization policy was recommended (Little et al. 1970; Bhagwati 1978; Krueger 1978; and Balassa 1980). However, the opposing argument is that historically the developed countries themselves had taken recourse to protective policies of industrialization, which are now being denied to the DCs under the paradigm of universal trade liberalization (Amsden 2001; Chang 2002; Chandrasekhar and Ghosh 2005; Shafaeddin 2005).

The T&C sector has served as an engine of growth for most South Asian countries in terms of value addition, employment generation, and foreign exchange earnings.[2] The

*I have benefited from discussions with V.R. Panchamukhi, Biswajit Dhar, C.P. Chandrasekhar, and Aditya Bhattacharjea. I thank D. Narayana, K.J. Joseph, Vineetha Menon, Gilbert Sebastian and an anonymous referee for their valuable comments. Finally, I thank Barbara Harriss-White for introducing me to the school of Heterodox Economics. However, I own up responsibility for any persisting error or omission.

[1]We have taken up the study of only five major countries in South Asia, namely, India, Pakistan, Bangladesh, Sri Lanka, and Nepal and have left out of our purview Bhutan and Maldives, particularly because of the non-availability of data on these two small economies.

[2]The exports by South Asian Countries to the EU and the US were governed by quota restrictions under the MFA (in operation since 1974). In fact, T&C sector falls into an important labour-intensive product

quotas imposed by developed countries had a determining effect on the export expansion of this sector.[3] The developing countries had agreed to the inclusion of Textile trade under GATT on grounds that the exports of this sector from developing countries to developed countries would be greater without an MFA[4] (UNCTAD 1994). The new Agreement on T&C under WTO dismantled the extensive network of bilateral quotas on 31 December 2004. While the new agreement aimed at removing quota restrictions, it has other non-quota provisions such as tariff and non-tariff barriers, which can be used as tools to protect the domestic producers of the developed countries. Restrictions through NTBs may be introduced in the form of rules of origin, anti-dumping duties and safeguard provisions, as well as labour and environment standards. Moreover, the rising expectations of retailers in terms of suppliers' service capabilities and locational proximity, and changes in the international regulatory context of the Clothing sector, are likely to increase barriers to the entry of new suppliers from developing countries into the Clothing global value chains (GVCs) (Palpacuer, Gibbon, and Thomsen 2005). Existing literature on this sector in South Asia can be grouped into country-specific studies as well as region-specific studies. Most of the work focused mainly on the supply-related reasons for the poor performance of the growth of this sector and questions related to demand constraints (that is, market access or the question of tariff and non-tariff barriers in particular) imposed by developed countries. There is, however, no analysis of the export performance of South Asian countries during the post-1995 period *vis-à-vis* the global trends. This paper aims to fill this gap—drawing comparisons with the earlier phase (that is 1985–95) and mainly focusing on the issue of sustainability of export growth of T&C in South Asian countries, particularly in the context of universal trade liberalization. It also seeks to explore the various factors that determine the pattern of export growth registered by the South Asian countries—demand factors such as the emergence of powerful new competitors and shrinkage in demand growth on the world-scale, and supply factors such as the nature of the industrial structure in these countries. We further explore how the removal of quota restrictions would have a differential impact on various countries in South Asia. Accordingly, this paper is divided into six sections.

In the next section we try to situate the pattern of world trade in the T&C sector during 1985–2008. The export competitiveness of this sector in South Asia is examined in the third section. The market potential of the T&C sector in South Asian countries vis-á-vis two major destinations that is, the EU and the US and the relative strengths and weaknesses in various product categories (at HS 6-digit level) has been analysed in the fourth section. The fifth section provides an overview of

category, which accounts for about 60 per cent of the total exports of manufactured goods from developing countries (Shafaeddin 2005, p.183).

[3]The rapid expansion of cotton textile exports from LDCs during the late 1950s, threatened not only the exports, but also the domestic markets of North American and West European countries. This prompted the developed countries to negotiate a trading arrangement with the less developed exporting countries, in order to regulate the expansion of trade in cotton textiles (Nayyar 1976, p. 64).

[4]This meant the end of MFA that was in operation since 1974. A study by the United States International Trade Commission estimated that the value of exports of currently constrained suppliers to the US market would rise by 20.5 per cent for textiles and 36.5 per cent for clothing or an average of 35 per cent in both product groups (UNCTAD 1994, p. 108).

agreements on T&C initiated since the 1960s and the constraints that have arisen as a consequence of the same. In this section, we also seek to analyse the extent of use of the quota system, the phasing out of an MFA regime, tariff and non-tariff barriers their results. The sixth section discusses supply-side factors such as the structure of T&C industries in South Asian countries and the last section draws up major findings and policy implications.

## SITUATING THE T&C SECTOR

Our analysis of the overall international trading patterns of T&C sector during the period 1985–2008 shows that the world trade has been increasing at an annual average growth of 7.59 per cent (see Table 4.1). Interestingly, the overall trade in Clothing has increased much faster than that in Textiles, indicating that the countries may be shifting to higher value addition activities.

As far as the developing countries as a whole are concerned, an expansion of Clothing exports had begun in the 1960s, partly because the exports of cotton manufactures and clothing did not fall under the long term arrangement (LTA) (Chandrasekhar 1981) and partly because this sector has vast differences in comparative advantage across countries (arising to a substantial extent from labour costs), thus offering large opportunities for international trade flows (EXIM Bank 1995). Special tariff provisions such as offshore assembly processing (OAP) and outward processing trade (OPT) also speeded up the globalization of apparel trade. Further the evidence shows that the total exports of T&C in the world grew much faster during 1985–95 as compared to 1995–2008. The annual average growth for the former period was 11.53 per cent whereas the latter period recorded only 4.65 per cent growth.

A similar trend is observed when we analyse the growth patterns for Textiles and Clothing separately. However, China's average export growth during the 1995–2008 is 19 per cent, which is much higher than the world growth during the corresponding period. Apparently, high growth rates and entry into the WTO regime on 1 December 2001, have contributed to the present status of China in T&C exports.

It can be seen that China, which was in the eighth position in terms of share in world exports in both Textiles and in Clothing during 1980, has now overtaken every other country in the world in T&C exports (Tables 4.2 and 4.3). One of the factors contributing to China's emergence as a major exporter may be the increased labour cost per hour in Hong Kong and South Korea during the 1990s as compared to that in the 1970s. However, the corresponding

Table 4.1: Growth Pattern of T&C Trade at the World Level

*(per cent)*

| Items | 1985–90 | 1985–95 | 1995–2005 | 2005–2008 | 1995–2008 | 1985–2008 |
|---|---|---|---|---|---|---|
| Textile Fibre and Waste (26) | 7.29 | 6.85 | –3.10 | 8.18 | –0.61 | 2.57 |
| Textile Yarns, Fabrics etc. (65) | 14.62 | 11.22 | 2.79 | 9.64 | 4.33 | 6.64 |
| Clothing and Accessories (84) | 18.13 | 13.18 | 5.21 | 12.92 | 6.94 | 9.17 |
| Total T&C | 15.11 | 11.53 | 3.28 | 9.37 | 4.65(19.02) | 7.59 |

*Note*: *The figure in brackets is the growth rate for China.
*Source*: Data Compiled from UNCOMTRADE Statistics.

Table 4.2: Leading Textiles Exporters in the World (Top 15) during 1980–2007

| | Share in World Exports | | | | |
|---|---|---|---|---|---|
| Countries | 2007 | 2003 | 1998 | 1993 | 1980 |
| Germany | NL | NA | 8.78 (1) | 10.53 (1) | 11.4 (1) |
| Italy | NL | NA | 8.63 (2) | 8.85 (2) | 7.60 (3) |
| China | 23.5 | 15.9 | 8.49 (3) | 7.70 (4) | 4.60 (8) |
| Korea, Republic of | 4.4 | 6 | 7.47 (4) | 7.96 (3) | 4.0 (9) |
| Chinese Taipei | 4.1 | 5.5 | 7.30 (5) | 7.26 (5) | 3.20 (10) |
| Top 5 | 42.8 | NA | 40.67 | 42.3 | 30.80 |
| Top 15 | 91.4 | NA | 68.76 | 79.82 | 85 |
| Total world exports | 100 | 100 | 100 | 100 | 100 |

*Note*: Figures in brackets indicate ranking of countries. NA stands for 'not available'. NL stands for 'not listed' in the Top 15 leading exporting countries.
*Source*: WTO, *International Trade Statistics*, Various Issues.

Table 4.3: Leading Clothing Exporters in the World (Top 15) during 1980–2007

| | Share in World Exports | | | | |
|---|---|---|---|---|---|
| Countries | 2007 | 2003 | 1998 | 1993 | 1980 |
| China | 33.4(1) | 23 | 16.69 (1) | 14.38 (1) | 4 (8) |
| Italy | NL | NA | 8.19 (2) | 9.22 (2) | 11.3 (2) |
| Hong Kong, (Dome exports) | 8.3(2) | 3.6 | 5.37 (3) | 7.27 (3) | 11.5 (1) |
| United States | 1.2(10) | 2.5 | 4.88 (4) | 3.91 (6) | 3.1 (9) |
| Germany | NL | NA | 4.27 (5) | 5.23 (4) | 7.1 (4) |
| Top 5 | 51.5 | NA | 39.4 | 40.94 | 43.2 |
| Top 15 | 86.3 | NA | 65.82 | 71.25 | 85.8 |
| Total world exports | 100 | 100 | 100 | 100 | 100 |

*Note*: Figures in brackets indicate the ranking of countries; NA stands for 'not available'. NL stands for 'not listed' in the Top 15 leading exporting countries.
*Source*: WTO, *International Trade Statistics*, various issues.

cost per hour for China is quite low during the 1990s as compared to the level prevailing in the 1970s (Ramaswamy and Gereffi 2000; Texcon 1997; Chandra 1999). However, the changes in growth rate cannot be explained by the cost comparative advantage in terms of wage rate alone. For instance, labour cost for the Apparel industry in South Asian countries (US$ 0.7 per hour for India; US$ 0.6 per hour for Sri Lanka; US$ 0.2 per hour for Pakistan; and US$ 0.2 per hour for Bangladesh) is much lower than that in China (US $ 0.9 per hour) (ILO 2003). Thus, there is a need to seek other explanations for the better performance of China's exports in this sector.[5] An attempt

[5]It is found that China's export growth was not restricted under MFA, by the quotas imposed by the

has been made in this paper to analyse, in detail, the export performance of this sector in South Asian countries.

## EXPORT COMPETITIVENESS OF SOUTH ASIAN COUNTRIES

Export performance of South Asian countries is analysed here in terms of the relative strength of the T&C sector in their total exports, share of T&C exports in world exports, and the revealed comparative advantage indices. With an export level of the US $ 23.27 billion in 2008, India was far ahead of other South Asian countries, with Pakistan at US $ 11.28 billion, Bangladesh at US $ 10.73 billion, Sri Lanka at US $ 3.67 billion, and Nepal at US $ 0.3 billion.

Total exports of T&C have been growing continuously since 1985 in Sri Lanka, Bangladesh, and Nepal, although the growth has been from a much smaller base in comparison to India or Pakistan. It is further evident that the overall exports of T&C during 1985–2008 in all South Asian countries grew faster than the world exports from this sector (see Table 4.4). A similar trend is observed in the case of exports of Clothing whereas, the export of Textile yarns and Fabrics in Bangladesh was quite low as compared to the world trend. Our analysis further reveals that the total exports of T&C in South Asia grew much faster during 1985–95 as compared to the tardy growth in the post-1995 period. A similar trend has been seen for Textile yarn and fabrics and Clothing. The possible reasons for the stagnation in exports of T&C during the post-1995 period could be the slow growth in world trade during this period and also the emergence of powerful competitors.

Although the countries studied here have a meagre share in global trade in T&C, the sector is important for the individual countries as it has a significant share in the total exports of the economies in question (Table 4.5). It is, however, interesting to note that the export share of T&C only in the case of India and Bangladesh, showed an increasing trend in world exports throughout our study period (see Table 4.6).

From the above exercise, we can conclude that the growth of exports of T&C in South Asian countries was quite high during 1985–2008 as compared to the growth at the global level. However, there is a declining trend during the period 1995–2008 for all countries, which coincides with the world trend. We may be able to account for the better performance of Nepal by considering its exports to a major non-quota market—Japan. As for Sri Lanka, the industry was dominated by foreign multinationals and their already existing demand–supply chain at the international level might account for the country's better performance. Bangladesh, being a least developed country, had better market access to the EU under the GSP and that might be an explanation for its better performance.

The revealed comparative advantage for a country in a particular product is measured by the product's share in the country's exports relative to its share in world trade. Thus the Revealed Comparative Advantage Index (RCAI) would indicate the advantage of the country in that product. It has sometimes been argued that under the quota system, comparative advantage is created artificially. However, it may be noted that even countries

US and the EU, as these were not the main destinations for China's exports. It is estimated that there were 100 joint ventures and wholly Japanese companies manufacturing garments to be shipped to Japan (Koshy 1997). Chinese expatriates from Hong Kong, Taiwan, Europe, and the US have played a very constructive role of 'market makers' as well as producers with factories in China (see Chandra 1999, p. M-22, for details).

Table 4.4: Growth of Total Exports of T&C in South Asian Countries

| Items Code | Period | India | Bangladesh | Sri Lanka | Pakistan | Nepal |
|---|---|---|---|---|---|---|
| Textile Fibre and Waste (26) | 1985–95 | 16.02 | –4.28 | 2.66 | –5.83 | –3.39 |
| | 1995–2008 | 27.17 | 12.29 | 9.43 | –1.80 | –34.63 |
| | 1985–2008 | 16.21 | 4.76 | 6.31 | –3.57 | –18.79 |
| Textile Yarns, Fabrics etc. (65) | 1985–95 | 15.44 | 1.66 | 25.65 | 15.92 | 19.43 |
| | 1995–2008 | 6.89 | 6.51 | 1.84 | 4.11 | –5.28 |
| | 1985–2008 | 10.53 | 4.37 | 10.49 | 9.09 | 7.74 |
| Clothing and Accessories (84) | 1985–95 | 16.26 | 27.94 | 20.39 | 20.60 | 14.98 |
| | 1995–2008 | 7.86 | 12.77 | 6.27 | 6.82 | 9.23 |
| | 1985–2008 | 10.93 | 19.13 | 11.29 | 12.46 | 12.39 |
| Total T & C | 1985–95 | 15.58 | 14.21 | 20.18 | 13.90 | 16.97 |
| | 1995–2008 | 8.02 | 11.92 | 6.41 | 4.76 | 2.25 |
| | 1985–2008 | 11.24 | 12.91 | 11.30 | 8.64 | 10.18 |

*Source:* UNCOMTRADE Statistics. Data for Nepal is available only up to the year 2003.

Table 4.5: Export Share of T&C in Total Exports of South Asian Economies

| Item Code | Country | 1985 | 1996 | 2003 | 2008 |
|---|---|---|---|---|---|
| Textile Fibre and Waste (26) | India | 0.71 | 1.42 | 0.48 | 1.16 |
| | Pakistan | 16.41 | 2.04 | 1.88 | 0.96 |
| | Bangladesh | 12.64 | 2.08 | 1.94 | 2.73 |
| | Sri Lanka | 1.32 | 0.67 | 0.66 | 0.84 |
| | Nepal | 1.98 | 0.51 | 0.01 | NA |
| | World | 0.87 | 0.6 | 0.30 | 0.20 |
| Textile Yarns, Fabrics etc. (65) | India | 11.53 | 14.75 | 10.88 | 5.70 |
| | Pakistan | 35.48 | 52.86 | 47.49 | 35.44 |
| | Bangladesh | 37.66 | 12.57 | 7.33 | 7.46 |
| | Sri Lanka | 1.33 | 4.14 | 3.31 | 2.06 |
| | Nepal | 21.84 | 46.85 | 16.46 | NA |
| | World | 2.85 | 2.97 | 2.55 | 1.67 |
| Clothing and Accessories (84) | India | 10.17 | 12.64 | 10.54 | 6.03 |
| | Pakistan | 9.34 | 21.66 | 17.78 | 19.26 |
| | Bangladesh | 17.21 | 62.69 | 75.93 | 71.46 |
| | Sri Lanka | 2.19 | 46.24 | 51.69 | 42.04 |
| | Nepal | 21.47 | 31.48 | 34.60 | NA |
| | World | 2.41 | 3.14 | 3.32 | 2.41 |

*(contd...)*

*(Table 4.5 continued)*

| Item Code | Country | 1985 | 1996 | 2003 | 2008 |
|---|---|---|---|---|---|
| Total T & C | India | 22.41 | 28.81 | 21.89 | 12.85 |
| | Pakistan | 61.23 | 78.75 | 66.47 | 51.65 |
| | Bangladesh | 65.50 | 77.35 | 85.19 | 81.65 |
| | Sri Lanka | 24.56 | 51.05 | 55.67 | 44.94 |
| | Nepal | 45.29 | 78.84 | 51.07 | NA |
| | World | 6.14 | 6.71 | 6.16 | 4.28 |

*Source:* UNCOMTRADE Statistics. Data for Nepal is available only up to the year 2003.

Table 4.6: Export Share of South Asian Countries in the World Trade in T&C Sector

| Code | Country | 1985 | 1996 | 2003 | 2008 |
|---|---|---|---|---|---|
| Textile Fibre and Waste (26) | India | 0.37 | 1.44 | 1.49 | 6.62 |
| | Pakistan | 2.62 | 0.53 | 0.74 | 0.63 |
| | Bangladesh | 0.71 | 0.22 | 0.45 | 1.14 |
| | Sri Lanka | 0.09 | 0.07 | 0.16 | 0.23 |
| | Nepal | 0.01 | 0.005 | 0.0003 | NA |
| Textile Yarns, Fabrics etc. (65) | India | 1.85 | 3.03 | 3.99 | 4.11 |
| | Pakistan | 1.74 | 2.73 | 1.31 | 1.55 |
| | Bangladesh | 0.65 | 0.27 | 0.20 | 0.40 |
| | Sri Lanka | 0.03 | 0.09 | 0.094 | 0.07 |
| | Nepal | 0.05 | 0.10 | 0.06 | NA |
| Clothing and Accessories (84) | India | 1.93 | 2.45 | 2.97 | 3.01 |
| | Pakistan | 0.54 | 0.98 | 1.01 | 1.07 |
| | Bangladesh | 0.35 | 1.28 | 1.62 | 2.64 |
| | Sri Lanka | 0.59 | 0.99 | 1.12 | 0.94 |
| | Nepal | 0.05 | 0.06 | 0.10 | NA |
| Total T & C | India | 4.16 | 6.93 | 8.47 | 13.74 |
| | Pakistan | 4.91 | 4.25 | 3.06 | 3.76 |
| | Bangladesh | 1.73 | 1.78 | 2.27 | 4.18 |
| | Sri Lanka | 0.72 | 1.2 | 1.37 | 1.24 |
| | Nepal | 0.05 | 0.08 | 0.16 | NA |

*Source:* UNCOMTRADE Statistics. Data for Nepal is available only up to the year 2003.

that benefited from the quota system had to maintain competitiveness in terms of price, quality etc. vis-a-vis their counterparts. Thus, we maintain that RCA is a reliable indicator for measuring competitiveness.

On the basis of product category-wise RCA indices, a consistent improvement is observed in the case of Clothing for Nepal, Sri Lanka, and Bangladesh, although the same has declined in the case of India and Pakistan during 1985–2003. The RCA for Textiles in Pakistan and Sri Lanka, to some extent, showed consistent improvement, while Bangladesh and Nepal lost their position in 2003. The index for Textiles is quite high for Pakistan and Nepal as compared to that for the other countries (see Beena 2006 for more details). In the next section, we look at the export performance of these countries[6] in their two major export destinations, EU and the US, during the 1990s.

## RELATIVE STRENGTH OF SOUTH ASIAN T&C EXPORTS IN THE US AND EU MARKETS

The three big suppliers of Textiles in the US market in 1981 were Japan, China, and India. However, Japan lost its position by 2008. The major gainers in 2008 were China, India, Canada, and Pakistan (WTO 2009). Similarly, in the case of Clothing, Hong Kong, Chinese Taipei, and Korea were the major suppliers to the US market in 1981. In 2008, however, there are more countries exporting Clothing to the US. China has become major import suppliers of the US. It is also evident that regional trade arrangements such as NAFTA and the OAP provisions led to the rapid growth of non-Asian supplies to the US Clothing market.

While analysing the distribution of exports to the US market from South Asian countries, we find that a relatively large percentage of T&C products had less than 10 per cent export share in the US market in 1993 as well as in 1997.

Further, we observe that in the case of most South Asian countries, more than one-third of the total number of T&C products[7] exported to the US market showed a decreasing trend in their export shares during 1997. But the scenario is encouraging for Pakistan, which showed an increase of 73 per cent (see Table 4.7).

In the case of Textiles, European Unioin itself controls the production in the major import supplying countries of Textiles to the EU. China and Turkey emerged as major import suppliers of Textiles in 1998 pushing Switzerland and Austria down (WTO 2000). In addition to China and Turkey, India and Pakistan have emerged as major import suppliers among non-EU suppliers by 2008 (WTO 2009). Similarly, in the case of Clothing, European Union countries themselves control the major share of imports of the EU. China and Turkey have emerged as major import suppliers of Clothing to the EU in 1998 pushing down Hong Kong and the Republic of Korea and the similar trend continued even in 2003 and 2008 (WTO 2004; WTO 2009).

Turkey's joining the EU Customs Union and the bilateral agreement of the EU with Central and East European Countries (CEECs) had a major role in bringing about these

[6]We could not include Nepal for this analysis because of the non-availability of data on this country.

[7]The analysis focuses on those items, which registered more than 10 per cent export share either in the EU or the US markets in any of the years between 1993 and 1997.

Table 4.7: Growth Distribution of Exported T&C items to the US from South Asia, 1993–7

| | Increased | | Decreased | | Total Exported |
|---|---|---|---|---|---|
| | No. | Per cent Share to Total No. | No. | Per cent Share to Total No. | T&C items* |
| India | 54 | 51.92 | 50 | 48.08 | 104(385) |
| Pakistan | 63 | 73.26 | 23 | 26.74 | 86(291) |
| Bangladesh | 15 | 53.57 | 13 | 46.43 | 28(162) |
| Sri Lanka | 16 | 59.26 | 11 | 40.74 | 27(203) |

*Note*: *The figures in brackets represent the total number of items imported in to the US market.
*Source*: Data extracted from TRAINS, UN Database. The total imports from South Asian countries have been considered as the total exports of South Asian countries.

Table 4.8: Growth Distribution of Exported T&C Items to the EU from South Asia, 1993–7

| | Increased | | Decreased | | Total Exported |
|---|---|---|---|---|---|
| | No. | Per cent Share to Total No. | No. | Per cent Share to Total No. | T&C items* |
| India | 138 | 63.89 | 78 | 36.11 | 216(652) |
| Pakistan | 61 | 57.55 | 45 | 42.55 | 106(411) |
| Bangladesh | 16 | 72.73 | 6 | 27.27 | 22(229) |
| Sri Lanka | 9 | 47.37 | 10 | 52.63 | 19(310) |

*Note*: *Figures in brackets represent the total number of items imported into the EU market.
*Source*: Data extracted from TRAINS, UN Database. The total imports from South Asian countries have been considered as the total exports of South Asian countries.

structural changes. It has been argued elsewhere that the declining trend in trade between Asia and Eastern Europe could be attributed to the significant expansion of Clothing production in Eastern Europe, especially in Bulgaria and Romania (UNCTAD 2000, p. 82).

It is further noticed that as in the case of the US market, a large share of T&C items exported from South Asian countries to the EU had less than 10 per cent market share. However, a relatively large share of these items from India and Pakistan had more than 10 per cent market share in the EU market. This is not true in the case of Bangladesh and Sri Lanka. As in the case of the US market, more than one-third of the items exported from South Asian countries to the EU showed a declining trend (Table 4.8). This is mostly steady or sharp, which is quite discouraging (see Beena 2006 for more details). Further it is worth noting that South Asian countries lack product diversification in T&C exports to EU and US.[8]

[8]Our analysis reveals that the top 30 items in terms of total value in 1997, contributed more than two-thirds of the total exports of South Asian countries to the US market. A similar trend is noticed even in the case of South Asian exports to the EU except in the case of India. For India, the top 30 products accounted for two-

Evidence reveals that China is the major competitor of South Asian countries in the US and the EU markets. The ability to make almost any type of Clothing of any quality at competitive prices has helped China to become a leading world exporter in this sector (Palpacuer, Gibbon, and Thomsen 2005, p. 412). Moreover, China's exports are more diversified and less dependent on quota countries such as the US and the EU and more dependent on non-quota countries such as Japan. We now look at how the export markets of T&C in South Asia are constrained by the tariff and non-tariff barriers imposed by the quota countries, particularly the US and the EU.

## AGREEMENT ON THE T&C SECTOR AND THE ISSUES ON IMPLEMENTATION

The policies pursued in developing countries during the 1950s had a major role to play in the T&C trade performance. A large number of developing countries had emerged as exporters of T&C since the 1950s due to their comparative advantage in terms of low production costs, especially in the wage component. But this had adversely affected the growth of investment and employment in Textile production in developed countries. With the aim of restructuring industries in the developed countries, agreements on Textiles began to be signed, starting in 1961.[9]

Thus, discriminatory restraints such as the short-term Cotton Arrangement in 1961 and the long-term Cotton Arrangement during 1962–73 were introduced to control international trade in cotton textiles. The most important objectives of these transitional arrangements were: to significantly increase access to restricted markets; to maintain orderly access to markets; and to secure restraints on exporting countries to avoid disruption. Numerous changes were adopted in the operation of the arrangements during the period, 1974–94. The restraints under the MFA were negotiated in case of unilateral actions at short intervals. By 1994, bilateral quotas from the EU and the US handicapped almost all developing countries, which constituted the largest set of exporters of Textiles (Bagchi 1998). It was argued that the existence of export quota restrictions acted as a disincentive for developing countries in adopting new technology with comparative ease in the Clothing sector.[10] This caused a diversion of FDI to the T&C sectors of those countries, which were less restricted under the quota system. The quota system under the MFA encouraged economies such as Hong Kong to continue production in spite of a relatively low comparative advantage in the labour-intensive Clothing sector (Kathuria et al. 2000).

A formal decision to phase out the three and a half-decade long quota trade in T&C was taken at the end of the UR negotiations. The prescribed obligation for each WTO member was to integrate products accounting for 16 per cent of imports at the beginning of the first stage (that is, January 1995), 17 per cent at the beginning of the second stage (January 1998), and 18 per cent at the beginning of the third stage (January 2002). The rest of

thirds of the total exports in 1993 and this share has declined to the level of around 34 per cent during 1997.

[9]In fact, during the post-War period, the developed countries had adopted such restrictions in order to ease their balance of payments crises.

[10]The handloom exports that were previously exempt from the purview of quotas under the MFA that had come into existence in 1974, became subject to greater export restrictions in the US and the EU markets after 1977 (Chatterjee and Mohan 1993).

Table 4.9: Number of Items to be Integrated

| Countries | Stage I | | Stage II | | Total Imported Items | |
|---|---|---|---|---|---|---|
| | US | EU | US | EU | US | EU |
| India | 79(32) | 28(12) | 154(38) | 130(28) | 385(104) | 652(216) |
| Bangladesh | 27(9) | 10(5) | 69(13) | 70(0) | 162(28) | 229(22) |
| Pakistan | 48(4) | 13(2) | 92(5) | 112(19) | 291(86) | 411(106) |
| Sri Lanka | 24(6) | 11(0) | 80(12) | 81(0) | 203(27) | 310(19) |

*Note*: Figures in brackets represent the number of items, which had more than 10 per cent export share in the US market.
*Source*: TRAINS DATA and WTO, Geneva.

the 49 per cent was integrated on the expiry of the ATC, that is, on 1 January 2005.

An examination of the actual implementation of the removal of provisions relating to trade barriers (namely, phasing out quotas, tariff and non-tariff barriers) and the extent to which this has facilitated market access to the South Asian countries is fruitful. With regard to the implementation of the phasing out of quotas (from the review carried out by the Council for Trade in Goods), it is observed that the proportion of integrated trade relating to products that were under restraint was in the range of 0 to 3 per cent of the 1990 imports of products covered by the ATC (GOI 2000). It is also argued elsewhere (Bagchi 1998) that the EU and the US removed quotas on imports, accounting for merely 3.15 per cent and 1.3 per cent, respectively at the beginning of the second stage in early 1998. Further, integration of Clothing, which involved higher value added and was subject to higher protection (tariff peaks), was left to the final stage of the phasing-out (Shafaeddin 2005; p. 184). It was also seen that the international trade regime in T&C continued to impose a distortionary tax on Indian exports (Kathuria 1998). In fact, the US lags behind the EU in terms of reduction of restrictions of the quota regime.

A detailed analysis on the implementation of quota integration in stages I and II in the US and the EU and the significance of these for the export performance of South Asian countries shows that the list earmarked for integration in the two stages by the EU and the US markets did not include those products, which had a significant presence, that is, more than 10 per cent export share from South Asian countries (Table 4.9). Moreover, there is a discrepancy in the EU proposal for integration under stages I and II. None of the items under stage I were integrated during that period, whereas, four items that had been earmarked for stage II were integrated during stage I (1995–8).[11] Considering the integration process so far, the argument that it has been a 'win–win game' for both the developed and the developing countries does not hold ground.

With regard to the proposed tariff cuts that were actually achieved, it is seen that the

[11]These are synthetic yarn, synthetic staple fibre, artificial staple fibre, and handkerchiefs, other than knitted or crocheted. Thus the evidence shows that the targeted phasing out of quotas was not effectively implemented.

tariff cut on textile items during the post-UR period in all developed countries was only 22 per cent whereas it was 40 per cent on industrial items in all developed countries (Ahmed 1997). The average tariff on Textile products in all developed countries was 12 per cent during the post-UR period—three times higher than an average of 3.9 per cent on industrial goods. The tariff rate on T&C sector in the US was 14.6 per cent, which is still higher than the rate for developed countries as a whole (Ahmed 1997). It is important to note that these rates are higher in developed countries and were reduced to a lesser extent in the course of UR negotiations as compared to those in developing countries.

Turning to the issue of anti-dumping, WTO allows anti-dumping measures to be used by member countries to protect their respective national interests and to ensure a 'level playing field' among all countries. Its traditional users such as the EU, the US, Canada, Australia, etc. are now being joined by a number of developing countries such as Argentina, Mexico, India, Brazil, Turkey, and South Africa, etc. However, it is the developing countries that are most often found to be at the receiving end of anti-dumping initiations. India faced its first anti-dumping case initiated by the EU on the exports of synthetic fibre in 1990 (Baruah 2005). Of the nearly 175 anti-dumping cases related to Textile products (which account for 7 per cent of all anti-dumping cases) initiated by all countries during 1995–2004, Textiles and Textile articles accounted for 13 per cent of all anti-dumping cases against India during 1995–2004. In the case of Pakistan, Textiles accounted for 78 per cent of all the anti-dumping cases initiated by all countries during 1995–2004 (WTO Anti-dumping database). India and Pakistan faced a relatively larger share of anti-dumping cases against Textile articles, initiated by the EU.

With reference to the Rules of Origin, according to the new US proposals, countries specializing in processing operations such as dyeing, printing, etc. will be denied originating status. The origin of yarn and fabrics—regardless of dyeing, printing, and many other processing operations taking place elsewhere—would be traced back to the country of spinning and weaving. Thus the new proposal gives a discriminatory advantage to domestic producers vis-á vis foreign sources of yarn and fabrics (Harilal and Beena 2005). Such upstream protection proposed by the US through new rules of origin will not only protect its own T&C industries but also lead to a failure to attract foreign investment to this sector in the South Asian region.

Similarly, the rules of origin under the EU–GSP scheme stipulate value addition criteria for non-textile related exports to the EU and a processing criterion for T&C products (BEI 2004, p. 25). While the processing criterion is intended to encourage backward integration in the domestic economy, the existing stringent rules of origin do not allow Bangladesh and other LDCs to access the benefits permitted under the preferential regime as there is clear evidence that the expansion of backward integration has been very slow (BEI 2004). The low level of EU–GSP utilization (that is, 35–40 per cent) suggests that the stringent rules of origin provisions act as constraining factors in expanding Bangladesh's exports to the EU (BEI 2004, p. 25). Further, it is also argued that the criteria proposed by the EU rules of origin could result in the relocation of textile mills from Pakistan to Sri Lanka and Bangladesh which would have an adverse impact on the Pakistan economy (Rana 2005).

Other forms of barriers, namely, environmental and labour standards are also significant as emphasis on ecology and labour practices can be used as impediments for the growth of T&C exports from South Asia. For instance, the readymade garment industry in Bangladesh faces stringent regulations in the European market regarding dyes and chemicals used in the fabrics. Germany particularly prohibits apparels containing Azo dyes. Given this situation, garment exporters in Bangladesh are obliged to comply with the requirements of environmental standards put forward by other agreements. Similarly, the Customs Department of Germany has stopped the import of certain products from India on the grounds that their production involved the use of child labour (Apparel Online 2000).[12] The new agreement, which had been designed to encourage more fair and open trading was, in short, not effectively implemented. The question of market access for developing countries may now have more to do with NTBs. Anti-dumping measures, rules of origin, and other forms of NTBs could gain popularity when liberalization of the trade regime takes place (Spinanger 1999; Edwards 1996; Bagchi 1998).

## STRUCTURE OF THE T&C INDUSTRY IN SOUTH ASIAN COUNTRIES

This section dwells on the country-specific, supply-side factors, including the respective industrial structures of the South Asian countries. T&C industries have played a crucial role in the economies of the South Asian countries in terms of employment generation,[13] export earnings, and contribution to the GDP. However, during the 1990s, the traditionally important textile mills in India, Pakistan, and Sri Lanka faced closure, resulting in major retrenchment of labour particularly due to the restructuring of this industry (see Beena 2006 for more details). On the other hand, there has been a tremendous growth in total employment in Bangladesh. The estimated employment generation in Bangladesh—approximately at 2 million by 2003 with almost 90 per cent women—is striking in comparison to the employment loss in India, Pakistan, and Sri Lanka. Bangladesh has been fairly successful in attracting FDI to its EPZs particularly in the readymade garments sector (ESCAP 1998 as cited in Sobhan and Zaman 2004, p. 158). The pattern of FDI inflow into the T&C sector in South Asia is quite insignificant as compared to the pattern of FDI use in regions

[12]Although labour and environment issues are of serious concern, application of trade barriers on these counts could only lead these countries into a vicious cycle of further marginalization and faltering on these issues yet again.

[13]This sector in Bangladesh accounts for 37 per cent of the total industrial production and 80 per cent of total foreign exchange earnings (GTO 2003 as cited in BEI 2004). At present the T&C sector accounts for about 4 per cent of the GDP, 14 per cent of industrial production, 20 per cent of the total labour force[13] and 21 per cent of the export earnings in the Indian economy (GOI 2005). In the case of Nepal, this sector accounts for 34 per cent of the total industrial production and 40 per cent of the total export earnings. It employs more than one lakh persons directly and accounts for more than five per cent of the total employment of the manufacturing sector (Ministry of Commerce, Nepal 2000). The T&C sector in Pakistan accounts for 27 per cent share in the value added of the manufacturing sector, 8.5 per cent of the GDP, a whopping 60 per cent of total export earnings and employs 38 per cent of the workforce in the manufacturing sector (*www.pakboi.gov.pk*). The garment industry in Sri Lanka accounts for 6 per cent of GDP, 39 per cent of the industrial production, 33 per cent of the manufacturing employment, and 52 per cent of total export earnings of the country (Kelegama 2005).

such as East Asia. Although the quota system under MFA has apparently helped Bangladesh, Sri Lanka, and Nepal to develop their export-oriented Clothing industry, these countries faced the problem of an absence of sufficient backward linkages for this sector. The export-oriented, readymade garments industry in Bangladesh uses less than 15 per cent of its fabric from domestic sources (Bakht 2000). In the case of Sri Lanka, 65 per cent of the raw materials are imported (Kelegama and Foley 1999). Similarly, Nepal imports textiles for the production of export clothing[14] as also for domestic consumption. While these countries have the disadvantage of the absence of backward linkages, Pakistan has the disadvantage of absence of sufficient forward linkages for its Textiles sector (Din and Abbas 2000).[15] In comparison India is the only country with better forward–backward linkages, holding out better prospects for the T&C industries. A significant characteristic of the Indian garment industry is that it subcontracted production to the extent of 74 per cent of its output, while the corresponding figure for a country like China is only 18 per cent (Khanna 2000).[16] Nevertheless, the viability of the industrial structure of Indian T&C cannot be attributed to FDI-driven, export-led industrialization policies. Even though many factors—such as firm's strategies in product design and marketing, new entrants from low labour cost countries, enforcement of NTBs, etc.—have their specific impact on competitiveness, many of these appear to be closely related to technology (Kell and Richtering 1991). Therefore, these countries need to build their capabilities to face the challenges that are emerging in the new international trade regime. It must be borne in mind that even the US Textile industry, that was rarely competitive at world prices during the 200 years spanning 1800 to 2000 (Amsden 2001, p. 49), has historically adopted a protective industrial policy regime. The resistance shown by the US on the first-quarter surge in textile exports to the US from China, prompted even countries in the EU (such as France and Italy) to follow suit by demanding greater protection for their textile production (Chandrasekhar and Ghosh 2005). A recent survey reveals that the South Asian manufacturers in the T&C sector are not well prepared to face the competition that is emerging after the phasing out of MFA (Das 2004). In the light of these issues, we would argue that the governments of all the disadvantaged countries like those in South Asia should creatively intervene in providing at least promotional support to this industry, keeping in view their own respective national interests.

[14] The development of the clothing sector in Nepal began with the initiative of Indian entrepreneurs who were heavily restricted by quotas in the major developed country markets. The export of yarns and fabrics is quite small in volume terms. Of all the export destinations, the US is the most important market with a share of 83 per cent in the total exports in 1996–7. The current bilateral agreement contains quotas on nine categories. Seven categories belong to the clothing group and there are two quotas on made-up products. The EU does not apply bilateral restraint but has placed a tariff quota under its GSP (Ministry of Commerce, Nepal 2000).

[15] Pakistan's T&C sector experienced low level of quota utilization rates. Although Pakistan was among the top five cotton-producing countries in the world, its share in world exports of textiles is only about 3 per cent, that is less than half the share of Korea (8.6 per cent) (WTO 1997 as cited in Din and Abbas 2000).

[16] Further it is seen that the productivity of the Indian garment (clothing) industry is quite low as compared to its major competitors (Verma 2002; Hashim 2005).

## CONCLUSION

Although South Asian countries in general do not figure among the leading T&C exporters in the world, except for India and Pakistan to some extent, this sector is significant for these countries in terms of export earning, contribution to employment, and GDP. However, the performance of the T&C industry in South Asia has been rather unsatisfactory and many units have been closing down in India, Sri Lanka, and Pakistan. The export shares of T&C in world trade for all South Asian countries, except for Pakistan, have increased consistently during 1985–2008. The export growth in South Asian countries in the T&C sector during 1985–2008 is quite high as compared to their overall trade growth at the global level. However, their growth as compared to the pre-1995 period is much lower in the post-1995 period. And this lower growth rate may be considered as coinciding with the trends in international trade for this sector.

The emergence of China as an immensely powerful competitor and others such as Bulgaria, Romania, and Turkey, and the mismatch between excess capacity in T&C on the world level, on the one hand and the shrinking demand growth on the other are crucial factors that underlie the low growth pattern of the T&C sector in South Asian countries during the post-1995 period. As for the shrinkage in demand growth, more than one-third of the products, which had more than 10 per cent export share, showed a decreasing pattern in their exports to the EU and the US markets during 1993–7. This is mostly steady or sharp, which is quite discouraging. Evidence reveals that China is the major competitor of South Asian countries in the US and EU markets. Our evidence further supports the argument made by some other studies that a significant level of protectionism is still present in both the US and the EU. Therefore, we argue that besides 'kicking away the ladder', the developed countries are also designing a protective shell around themselves, so as to deny market access to the developing countries.

Coming to the supply factors, we recommend that the South Asian countries should also adopt the specific tactics of industrial policy that have been adopted by successful countries, not only on the production-related aspects of improving R&D and productivity but also engaging in more effective promotional activities such as developing brands, delivery on time, etc. With regard to the country-wise industrial structure, we observe that Pakistan has a clear advantage in the textile sector, whereas Bangladesh and Sri Lanka show a relatively better advantage in the clothing sector. While Pakistan faces a lack of forward linkages in the textile industry, Sri Lanka, Bangladesh, and Nepal face a lack of backward linkages in the clothing industry. India is the only country with relatively better forward–backward linkages in the T&C industries and therefore it is in a better position to tap the benefits under the new dispensation. Apparently, if conscious steps are adopted to rectify the lopsidedness of the industrial structure, Pakistan does have the potential to develop forward linkages. Pakistan has a relatively well-developed textiles sector and does not have to be import-dependent to develop its clothing industry.

In the ultimate analysis, our case study of the T&C sector shows that the proposed export-led industrialization has not yielded the desired returns to the South Asian countries. There is a long way to go before these countries tap their potential in the export performance of T&C and gear up to face the future challenges. For the sake of the sustainability of this sector in South Asian countries, we stress on the need to draw up selective, country-specific industrial policies rather than adopting a universal trade liberalization policy or proposals for integration into South Asian Association for Regional Co-operation (SAARC).

## REFERENCES


Amsden, A.H. (2001), *The Rise of 'The Rest': Challenges to the West from Late-Industrializing Economies,* Oxford University Press, Oxford.

Ahmed, Munir (1997), 'Is Free Global Textiles Trade A Myth?', in *World Textiles: Challenges Ahead* (Proceedings), An International Conference on Textiles &Clothing, 14–16 December, CII, Ahmedabad, Texcon 1997.

Apparel Online (2000), 1–15 March.

Balassa, B. (1980), 'The Prospects of Industrial Development and Alternative Development Strategies', World Bank Staff Working Paper, No. 438, Washington, DC.

Bagchi, Sanjoy (1998), 'Will There Be Free Trade in Textiles?', *Economic and Political Weekly*, 4 July.

Bakht, Zaid (2000), 'Impact on Enhancing Environmental Standards on International Trade of South Asian Countries', Country Paper on South Asia Workshop on Trade and Environment, RIS, New Delhi.

Baruah, Nandana (2005), 'Anti Dumping Duty as a Measure of Contingent Protection: An Analysis of Indian Experience', Working Paper No. 377, Centre for Development Studies, Trivandrum.

Beena, P.L (2006), 'Limits to Universal Trade Liberalization: The Contemporary Scenario for Textiles and Clothing Sector in South Asia', Working Paper 379, Centre for Development Studies, Trivandrum.

BEI (2004), *A Review of History, Doha Mandate and Stage of Current Negotiations Agreement on T&C,* Bangladesh Enterprise Institute, Dhaka, *www.bei-bd.org.*

Bhagwati, J. (1978), *Foreign Trade Regimes and Economic Development, Anatomy and Consequences of Exchange Control Regimes*, Ballinger Publishing Company, Cambridge.

Chandrasekhar, C.P. (1981), 'Growth and Technical Change in the Indian Cotton-mill Industry:1947–77', Unpublished PhD thesis submitted to the Jawaharlal Nehru University, New Delhi.

Chandrasekhar, C. P. and Jayati Ghosh (2005), 'The Chinese Bogeyman in US Clothing' at *http://www.networkideas.org.*

Chandra, Pankaj (1999), 'Competing through Capabilities Strategies for Global Competitiveness of Indian Textile Industry', *Economic and Political Weekly*, 27 February.

Chang, H. (2002), *Kicking Away the Ladder: Development Strategy in Historical Perspective,* Anthem Press, London.

Chang, Ha-Joon (ed.) (2003), *Rethinking Development Economics*, Anthem Press, London.

Chatterjee, Somnath and Rakesh Mohan (1993), 'India's Garment Exports' (mimeo), Ministry of Industry, Government of India, New Delhi, February.

Das, Ram Upendra (2004), 'Industrial Restructuring and Export Competitiveness of the Textiles and Clothing Sector in SAARC in the context of MFA Phase-out', Research Information System—Discussion Paper 85.

Din, Musleh-Ud and Kalbe Abbas (2000), 'The Uruguay Round Agreement and Pakistan's Trade in Textiles and Clothing', *South Asia Economic Journal,* Vol. 1, No.1.

Edwards, Chris (1996), 'The Uruguay Round and MFA Quotas: The Textiles and Garment Industries in Sri Lanka—The next 10 Years', Research Studies, Industrialization Series No. 4, IPS, Sri Lanka.

EXIM Bank (1995), 'Indian Garment Exports: Implications of the MFA Phase-Out', *Occasional Paper*, No. 34, EXIM Bank of India, Mumbai.

*Financial Express* (2001), 3 September.

GOI (Government of India) (2000), 'WTO Agreement on Textiles and Clothing: An Explanatory Note', Ministry of Industry, Textiles Division, Government of India, New Delhi.

—— (2002–03), 'Directorate General of Anti-dumping and Allied Duties', Ministry of Commerce and Industry, New Delhi.

____ (2005), Annual Report, Ministry of Textiles, New Delhi.

Government of Pakistan, 'Textile Sector Profile', at *www.pakboi.gov.pk/Policies/textile_sector_profile_.html.*

Harilal, K.N. and P.L. Beena (2005), 'Reining in Rules of Origin Based Protectionism: A Critique of WTO Initiatives', *Economic and Political Weekly*, Vol. 40, No. 51, 17–25 December.

Hashim, Danish A. (2005), 'Post MFA: Making the Textile and Garment Industry Competitive', *Economic and Political Weekly*, Vol. 40, No. 2, 8–14 January.

Hirschman, A.O. (1992), 'Industrialization and its Manifold Discontents: West, East and South', *World Development*, Vol. 20, No. 9, pp.1225–32.

United Nations (Various Years), *International Trade Statistics Yearbook*, Volumes I and II, New York.

ILO (2003), (Reprinted, Original 2002), *Garment Industry in South Asia: Rags or Riches?* International Labour Organization.

Kathuria, Sanjay, Martin Will, and Anjali Bhardwaj (2000), 'Implications of MFA Abolition for South Asian Countries', Paper presented at the NCAER-World Bank–WTO 2000 South Asia Workshop, 20–21 December, New Delhi.

Kelegama, Saman (2005), 'Readymade Garment Industry in Sri Lanka: Preparing to Face the Global Challenges', *Asia-Pacific Trade and Investment Review*, Vol. 1, No. 1.

Kelegama, Saman and Fritz Foley (1999), 'Impediments to Promoting Backward Linkages from the Garment Industry in Sri Lanka', *World Development*, Vol. 27, No. 8, pp. 1445–60.

Kell, George and Jurgen Richtering (1991), 'Technology and Competitiveness in the Textile Industry', UNCTAD Working Paper No. 42.

Khanna, R. (2000), 'Competitive Challanges before Indian Textile and Clothing Industry', National Seminar Bachground Papers, NIFT, 25–6 February.

Koshy, Darlie O. (1997), *Garment Exports: Winning Strategies*, Prentice Hall of India Private Limited, New Delhi.

Krueger, A.O. (1978), *Foreign Trade Regimes and Economic Development: Liberalization Attempts and Consequences*, NBER, New York.

Kumar, Ajit V. (2001), 'Textile Stocks rise 20 per cent as mills shut shop', *Financial Express*, Coimbatore, 3 September.

List, F. (1856), *The National System of Political Economy* (translated by G.A. Mattile), J.B. Lippincott & Co., Philadelphia.

Little, I.M.D., T. Scitovsky, and M. Scott (1970), *Industry and Trade in some Developing Countries*, Oxford University Press, Oxford.

Ministry of Commerce, Nepal (2000), *Nepal's Accession to World Trade Organisation: Project Status Review Preparatory Assistance Phase*, January 1997–June 1999, Kathmandu.

Nayyar, Deepak (1976), *India's Exports and Export Policies in the 1960*, Cambridge University Press, Cambridge.

Narula, Manoj (1999), 'Living in Fantasyland', *Business India*, 29 November–12 December.

Prebisch, R. (1959), 'Commercial Policy in the Underdeveloped Countries', *American Economic Review*, Papers and Proceedings, May, pp. 251–73.

Palpacuer, Florence, Peter Gibbon, and Lotte Thomson (2005), 'New Challenges for Developing Country Suppliers in Global Clothing Chains: A Comparative European Perspective', *World Development*, Vol. 33, No. 3, pp. 409–30.

Ramaswamy, K.V. and Gereffi Gary (2000), 'India's Apparel Exports: The Challenge of Global Markets', *The Developing Economies*, Vol. 38, No. 2, pp. 186–210.

Rana, P. I. (2005), 'New EU Rules of Origin to Hit the Textile Industry', *DAWN-Business*, 6 July, at *http:DAWN.com*.

Shafaeddin, M. (2005), *Trade Policy at the Crossroads: The Recent Experience of Developing Countries*, Palgrave, Houndmills, New York.

Sobhan, Farooq and Riffat Zaman (2004), 'Trade and Investment in South Asia', Chapter 11 in Ramesh Thakur and Oddny Wiggen (eds), *South*

*Asia in the World: Problem Solving Perspectives on Security, Sustainable Development and Good Governance*, UNU Press, Bookwell, New Delhi.

Spinanger, Dean (1999), 'Faking Liberalization and Finagling Protectionism: The ATC at its Best', *Background Paper*, Kiel Institute of World Economics, Washington, DC.

Tewari, Meena (2005), 'Post-MFA Adjustments in India's Textile and Apparel Industry: Emerging Issues and Trends', Working Paper No. 167, ICRIER, New Delhi.

Texcon (1997), An International Conference on Textile and Clothing, 14–16 December, Ahmedabad.

UNCTAD (1988), *Responding to the New Global Environment, The Least Developed Countries*, UN, New York.

____ (1994), 'Agreement on Textiles and Clothing: The Outcome of the Uruguay Round: An Initial Assessment', Supporting Papers to the Trade and Development Report, UN, New York.

____ (2000), 'Competitveness Challenge: Transnational Corporations and Industrial Restructuring', UN, New York.

Verma, S. (2002), 'Export Competitiveness of the Indian Textile and Garment Industry', Working Paper, No. 94, ICRIER, New Delhi.

Weerakoon, Dushni and Janaka Vijayasiri (1999), *Textiles and Clothing Sector in Sri Lanka*, Institute of Policy Studies, Colombo.

World Bank (1987), *Promoting Higher Growth and Human Development, Country Studies*, Bangladesh and Washington, DC, U S A.

WTO (World Trade Organization) (2000), *International Trade Statistics*, Volume II.

____ (2004), *International Trade Statistics*, Volume II.

____ (2009), *International Trade Statistics*, WTO Publications, Switzerland.

# Part II

# Financial Fragility, Currency Convertibility, and Monetary Policy

# 5

# Core–Periphery Asymmetry, Triangular Adjustment Patterns, and the Export of Fragility

## A Stock-Flow Consistent Model

RAMAA VASUDEVAN*

## INTRODUCTION

The proliferation of finance is one of the defining characteristics of the recent phase of capitalist development. Given the magnitude of capital and financial flows, internationally, it is evident that attempts to comprehend the global mechanisms of 'uneven development' and imperialism in today's world would have to address this dimension. The first generation of North–South trade models, inspired by the work of Singer, Prebisch, and the Structuralist school, focused primarily on the implications of terms of trade for the developing south. Different institutional constraints as well as specifications of closure conditions for the North and the South were incorporated into the trade model in order to investigate the implications of trade for accumulation in the South.[1] Later models relaxed the assumption of balanced trade to specifically explore the impact of capital flows.[2] The spate of currency crises in the last two decades since the opening and liberalization of financial markets in developing countries in Asia and Latin America has brought to the fore the dimension of growing debt burdens and financial fragility in developing countries and emerging markets.[3]

On the one hand, mainstream explanations of currency crises in emerging markets have focused on weak fundamentals, moral hazard, and weak financial institutions as the proximate causes of crisis. More heterodox readings (Taylor 1998; Erturk 2006), on the other hand, have highlighted the role of private investors chasing quick speculative profits. The massive influx of capital flows in the wake of financial liberalization is, in this heterodox view, the precursor to the asset bubble and the consequent currency crisis. Capital inflows arise in the context of specific conjunctures and historical factors that create wide financial spreads between returns to assets in emerging

*I am grateful to Lance Taylor and Duncan Foley for extensive discussions and comments on this paper. The implications for the sustainability of, and mechanisms of, adjustment to global imbalances are addressed in Vasudevan (2006b).

[1]Taylor (1981) and Dutt (1989). Patnaik (1997) develops a macroeconomic model that focuses on how downward flexibility of wages in the periphery ensures stable growth in the core.

[2]Blecker (1996).

[3]Kregel (2004a, 2004b).

markets and the borrowing rate abroad (Taylor 1998). Within this framework, the present paper takes the argument a step further in highlighting the structural roots of the 'credit boom' that precipitates financial fragility in the periphery. These roots lie in the institutional mechanisms of financial intermediation in the US—where international liquidity is generated by the US by incurring dollar-denominated short-term debt. Thus, the global imbalance that has arisen from the growing deficit of the US has been transmitted to the emerging markets in the periphery. Countries in the periphery perform a critical role in absorbing the brunt of deflationary adjustment, and enabling the hegemonic country to sustain its debts and deficits.[4]

It is in this sense that the financial arrangements of the last two decades are not so much a 'Revived Bretton Woods System' (Dooley et al. 2004), as they are a refashioning of the triangular adjustment patterns that underlay the workings of the International Gold Standard. Britain was able to preserve the status of the pound through a triangular pattern of settlements, recycling the surpluses of creditor (peripheral) countries such as India and Japan (placed as sterling deposits at the disposal of the Bank of England), to the 'emerging markets' in Latin America and Australia.[5] In an analogous manner, contemporary international settlements are based on the recycling of surpluses from creditor countries such as Japan and China which invest heavily in US treasury bills and the liberalized emerging markets in Latin America or South East Asia. In both periods, private capital flows to the periphery came to perform a crucial role in stabilizing the core, and these emerging markets came to bear the brunt of adjustment in the form of currency crises in the 1990s. In fact, in both the gold standard period, and after the collapse of the Bretton Woods, the incidence is disproportionately larger in the 'periphery' as compared to the core (see Table 5.1).

The paper sets out a highly simplified, three country 'closed system model' of the world, based on consistent accounts, that illustrates the channels through which peripheral adjustment might stabilize the hegemonic centre. The focus of this paper is on how the open financial markets of developing countries have provided a safety valve for the dollar in the post-Bretton Woods world.

## THE FRAMEWORK

The modeling framework developed here seeks to explore the implications of financial intermediation and specifically the relationship between the US and countries in the periphery.[6] These constitute a triangular pattern of

[4]This critical connection between deflationary adjustment in the periphery and the preservation of stability in the centre has been argued by Patnaik (2002a, 2002b). Kregel (2004a) argues that the need to finance the growing deficit of the US engenders a proliferation of dollar denominated capital flows, with implications for the volatility of exchange rates in developing countries in the periphery. The net resource transfer from developing countries to the US has been seen to reflect the exploitative dynamic centre–periphery relations, alongside the autonomous growth of indebtedness of economies in the periphery (Boratav 2004).

[5]This argument is elaborated in Vasudevan (2006a, chaper 2), through a comparative-historical analysis of the two monetary systems.

[6]The analysis draws heavily on the two country analysis in Taylor (2004b), Godley (1999, 2006), Godley and Lavoie (2003, 2004, 2006) which is extended to a three country framework along with some simplifying assumptions. See also Izurieta (2003, 2005). Gray and Gray (1989) also analyse international payments by developing a flow of funds matrix for the world, identifying constraints and interdependencies which characterize the 'closed global system'.

payments, encompassing surplus and debtor countries in the periphery, that sustains dollar hegemony and US deficits (Figure 5.1). Other advanced countries and most importantly the EU are ignored.

The international economy is represented as three interdependent blocs.

1. USA, the hegemon with its trade deficit (A).
2. 'trade account' countries in the periphery (earlier Japan, but more recently China) which have a current account surplus that are financing the bulk of the US deficit through active intervention and reserve accumulation that seeks to preserve the dollar exchange rate in support of an export-led strategy of industrialization (B).
3. debtor 'capital account countries' with liberalized capital markets (Latin America, South East Asia) (C).

Table 5.1: Financial Crises in the Core and Periphery

| Market | Year | Banking | Currency | Twin Crises | All Crises |
|---|---|---|---|---|---|
| Industrial Countries | 1880–1913 | 4 | 2 | 1 | 7 |
| | 1919–39 | 11 | 13 | 12 | 36 |
| | 1945–71 | 0 | 21 | 0 | 21 |
| | 1973–97 | 9 | 29 | 6 | 44 |
| Emerging Markets | 1880–1913 | 11 | 6 | 8 | 25 |
| | 1919–39 | 7 | 3 | 3 | 13 |
| | 1945–71 | 0 | 16 | 1 | 17 |
| | 1973–97 | 17 | 57 | 21 | 95 |

*Source*: Bordo and Eichengreen (2002), Table 6.

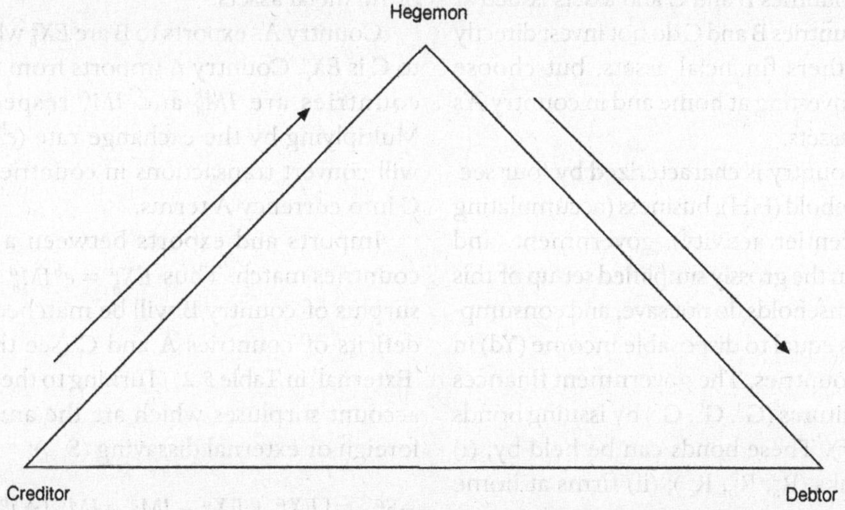


Figure 5.1: Triangular Adjustment Patterns

An open economy social accounting matrix, presenting the world economy as a closed system with no 'black holes', is set out, showing both transactions (flows) and the corresponding balance sheets (stocks) in Table 5.2 and 5.3. In the social accounting matrix in Table 5.2, the basic accounting constraint is that the rows and columns sum to zero. Cross-border transactions are mediated by an 'exchange conversion' and inflows into a country are matched by corresponding outflows from another country.

The US is the 'hegemon' and its currency is the sole international reserve.[7] All trade is undertaken in the currency of the hegemonic country. $e^b$and $e^c$ are the exchange rates of countries B and C in terms of country A's currency (the dollar), and the exchange rate of country C in terms of country B's currency $e^{cb} = e^c / e^b$. The hegemonic character of the country A is captured by the assumption that banks in B and C hold country A treasury bills in addition to domestic bills as reserves while A only holds its own bills as reserves. The hegemon can substitute between the financial assets of countries B and C and assets issued at home. Countries B and C do not invest directly in each others financial assets, but choose between investing at home and in country A's financial assets.

Each country is characterized by four sectors: household (HH), business (accumulating through rentier activity), government, and Banking. In the grossly simplified set-up of this model, households do not save, and consumption (C), is equal to disposable income (Yd) in all three countries. The government finances its expenditures ($G^a$, $G^b$, $G^c$) by issuing bonds ($B^a$, $B^b$, $B^c$). These bonds can be held by: (i) home banks ($R^a_a$, $R^b_b$, $R^c_c$); (ii) firms at home ($B^a_a$, $B^c_c$, $B^b_b$ ) or abroad ($B^a_b$, $B^a_c$, $B^c_c$ $B^a_a$, $B^b_b$, $B^c_c$), and (iii) foreign banks as reserves ($R^a_b$, $R^a_c$). Private accumulation of financial assets is undertaken by firms and banks, either as cash ($H^a$, $H^b$, $H^c$) or bonds . The superscripts denote the country of origin of the assets and the subscripts the country where the assets are held.

The balance sheets in Table 5.2 represent the pattern of accumulation of stocks of financial assets in the three countries. Changes in the financial position of any one sector affect the other sectors and are intrinsically linked. Accounting consistency demands that the accumulation of financial wealth generates stocks of wealth and debt that in turn regulate macroeconomic behaviour. The banking system is assumed to have a net worth of zero. The government finances its expenditures ($G^a$, $G^b$, $G^c$) by issuing bonds ($B^a$, $B^b$, $B^c$). This model ignores investment and abstracts from the important real financial linkages in order to highlight the financial flows. Thus, savings are used to accumulate financial assets alone. Private business investors are responsible for all the private accumulation of financial assets.

Country A's exports to B are $EX^a_b$ while that to C is $EX^a_c$. Country A imports from the two countries are $IM^b_a$ and $IM^c_a$ respectively. Multiplying by the exchange rate ($e^b$ and $e^c$) will convert transactions in countries B and C into currency A terms.

Imports and exports between a pair of countries match. Thus $EX^a_b = e^b IM^a_b$ and the surplus of country B will be matched by the deficits of countries A and C (see the rows 'External' in Table 5.2). Turning to the current account surpluses which are the amount of foreign or external dissaving ($S_{ext}$):

$$-S^a_{ext} = [EX^a_b + EX^a_c - IM^b_a - IM^c_a] + i^b e^b B^b_a + i^c e^c B^c_a - i^a (B^a_b + B^a_c + R^a_b + R^a_c) \qquad (5.1)$$

[7]See in this context D'arista (2004).

## Table 5.2: Social Accounts Matrix for the 'Closed System' of Three Countries

| | Hegemon A($) | | | | | Surplus (B) | | | | | Periphery (C) | | | | |
|---|---|---|---|---|---|---|---|---|---|---|---|---|---|---|---|
| | HH | Firms | Bank | Govt | | HH | Firms | Bank | Govt | | HH | Firms | Bank | Govt | |
| Income Expenditure | | | | | | | | | | | | | | | |
| Consumption | $-C^a$ | $C^a$ | | | | $-C^b$ | $C^b$ | | | | $-C^c$ | $C^c$ | | | 0 |
| Government | | $G^a$ | | $-G^a$ | | | $G^b$ | | $-G^b$ | | | $G^c$ | | $-G^c$ | 0 |
| External | | $EX_b{}^a$ | | | | | $-IM_b{}^a/e^b$ | | | | | | | | 0 |
| | | $EX_c{}^a$ | | | $*e^b$ | | | | | $*e^c$ | | $-IM_c{}^a/e^c$ | | | 0 |
| | | $-IM_a{}^b.e^b$ | | | | | $EX_a{}^b$ | | | | | | | | 0 |
| | | $-IM_a{}^c.e^c$ | | | | | | | | | | $EX_a{}^c$ | | | 0 |
| | | | | | | | $-IM_b{}^c.e^{bc}$ | | | | $EX_b{}^c$ | | | | 0 |
| | | | | | | | $EX_b{}^a$ | | | | | $-IM_b{}^a/e^{bc}$ | | | 0 |
| Disposable Income | $Yd^a$ | $-Yd^a$ | | | | $Yd^b$ | $-Yd^b$ | | | | $Yd^c$ | $-Yd^c$ | | | 0 |
| Interest Payments | | $i^a.B_a{}^a$ | $i^a.R_a{}^a$ | $-i^a.B^a$ | | | $i^a.B_b{}^a/e^b$ | $i^a.R_b{}^a/e^b$ | | $i^a.B_c{}^a/e^c$ | $i^a.R_c{}^a/e^c$ | | | | 0 |
| | | $i^bB_b{}^a.e^b$ | | | | | $i^b.B_b{}^b$ | $i^b.R_b{}^b$ | $-i^b.B^b$ | | | | | | 0 |
| | | $i^c.B_c{}^a.e^c$ | | | | | | | | | | $I^c.B_c{}^c$ | $I^c.R_c{}^c$ | $-i^c.B^c$ | 0 |
| Balances | | $-S_p{}^a$ | $-Sf^a$ | $-S_g{}^a$ | | $-S_p{}^b$ | $-S_f{}^b$ | $-S_g{}^b$ | | | | $-S_p{}^c$ | $-S_f{}^c$ | $-S_g{}^c$ | 0 |
| | | 0 | 0 | 0 | | | 0 | 0 | 0 | | 0 | 0 | 0 | 0 | |
| Flow of Funds | | | | | | | | | | | | | | | |
| Balances | | $S_f^a+S_b{}^a$ | | $S_g{}^a$ | $*e^b$ | | $S_f^b+S_b{}^b$ | | $S_g{}^a$ | $*e^c$ | | $S_p{}^c+S_f^c$ | | $S_g{}^c$ | 0 |
| Cash | | $-\Delta H^a$ | $\Delta H^a$ | | | | $-\Delta H^b$ | $\Delta H^b$ | | | | $-\Delta H^c$ | $\Delta H^c$ | | 0 |
| $ Bills | | $-\Delta B_a{}^a$ | $-\Delta R_a{}^a$ | $\Delta B^a$ | | | $-\Delta B_b{}^a.e^b$ | $-\Delta B_b{}^a.e^b$ | | $-\Delta B_c{}^a.e^b$ | $-\Delta B_c{}^a.e^b$ | | | | 0 |
| # Bills | | $-\Delta B_a{}^b.e^b$ | | | | | $-\Delta B_b{}^b$ | $-\Delta R_b{}^b$ | $\Delta B^b$ | | | | | | 0 |
| ¥ Bills | | $-\Delta B_a{}^c.e^c$ | | | | | | | | | | $-\Delta B_c{}^c$ | $-\Delta R_c{}^c$ | $\Delta B^c$ | 0 |
| | 0 | 0 | 0 | 0 | | 0 | 0 | 0 | 0 | | 0 | 0 | 0 | 0 | |

*Note*: Multiplying the cells for countries B and C by their exchange rate would yield sum totals in A's currency A.

Table 5.3: Financial Balance Sheets for the Three Countries

| | Hegemon(A) | | | | Surplus (B) | | | | Periphery (C) | | |
|---|---|---|---|---|---|---|---|---|---|---|---|
| | Firms | Bank | Govt | | Firms | Bank | Govt | | Firms | Bank | Govt |
| Cash | $H^a$ | $-H^a$ | | $*e^b$ | $H^b$ | $-H^b$ | | $*e^c$ | $H^c$ | –Hc | |
| A Bills | $B^a a$ | $R^a$ | $-B^a$ | | $B^a_b/e¥$ | $R^a_b/e¥$ | | | $B^a_c/e\#$ | $R^a_c e\#$ | |
| B Bills | $B^b_a e^b$ | | | | $B^b_b$ | $R^a_b$ | $-B^b$ | | | | |
| C Bills | $B^c_a.e^c$ | | – | | | | | | $B^c_c$ | $R^c_c$ | $-B^c$ |
| Net Worth | $-\Omega^a$ | | $-B^a$ | | $-\Omega^b$ | | $-B^b$ | | $-\Omega^c$ | | $-B^c$ |

$$-S^b_{ext} = [EX^b_a + EX^c_a - IM^a_b / e^b - IM^c_b / e^{cb}]$$
$$+i^a(B^a_b + R^a_b)/e^b - i^a B^b_a \qquad (5.2)$$

$$-S^b_{ext} = [EX^c_a + EX^c_b - IM^a_c / e^c - IM^b_c \cdot e^{cb}]$$
$$+i^a(B^a_c + R^a_c)/e^c - i^a B^c_a \qquad (5.3)$$

From a global perspective, the current account balance must sum to zero so that the surplus must be exactly matched by deficits, that is,

$$S^a_{ext} + e^b S^a_{ext} + e^c S^c_{ext} = 0$$

Turning to the Capital Account, the net foreign assets (N) relations for the three countries can be represented as follows:

$$N^a = e^b B^b_a + e^c B^c_a - B^a_b - B^a_c - R^a_b - R^a_c \qquad (5.4)$$
$$N^b = (B^a_b + R^a_b)/e^b - B^b_a \qquad (5.5)$$
$$N^c = (B^a_c + R^a_c)/e^c - B^c_a \qquad (5.6)$$

The net foreign asset relation is the accumulation rule for net foreign assets, and serves as a binding constraint on macroeconomic adjustment (Taylor 2004a, 2004b). Current account balances are equal to the net change/accumulation of foreign assets ($\Delta$N).

$$-S^a_{ext} = \Delta N^a = e_b \Delta B^b_a + e^c \Delta B^c_a - \Delta B^a_b$$
$$-\Delta B^a_c - \Delta R^a_b - \Delta R^a_c \qquad (5.7)$$

$$-S^a_{ext} = \Delta N^b = (\Delta B^a_b + \Delta R^a_b)/e^b - \Delta B^b_a \qquad (5.8)$$

$$-S^a_{ext} = \Delta N^c = (\Delta B^a_c + \Delta R^a_c)/e^c - \Delta B^c_a \qquad (5.9)$$

Also, in the closed system with total global balances summing to zero,

$$\Delta N^a + e^b \Delta N^b + e^b \Delta N^c = 0 \qquad (5.10)$$

It can be shown that the net worth in each country ($\Omega^a$, $\Omega^b$, $\Omega^c$) is the sum of its government debt and net foreign assets:

$$\Omega^a = B^a + N^a \qquad (5.11)$$
$$\Omega^b = B^b + N^b \qquad (5.12)$$
$$\Omega^c = B^c + N^c \qquad (5.13)$$

Global net worth ($\Omega^g$) is equal to the total debt of the government sector in the three countries.

$$\Omega^g = B^a + e^b B^b + e^c B^c$$

## ACCUMULATION OF FINANCIAL ASSETS

Our focus here is solely on the accumulation of financial assets. Turning to the determination of demand for assets (money and bills) we have, from very simplified Tobinesque formulations, the following:

In country A

$$H^a = \lambda_1 \Omega^a \qquad (5.14.1.1)$$
$$B^a_a = \lambda_2 \Omega^a \qquad (5.14.1.2)$$
$$e^b B^b_a = \lambda_3 \Omega^a \qquad (5.14.1.3)$$

$$e^c B_a^c = \lambda_4 \Omega^a \quad (514.1.4)$$

Such that $\lambda_1 + \lambda_2 + \lambda_3 + \lambda_4 = 1$.

Money market equilibrium in A is given by:

$$R_a^a = H^a \quad (5.14.2)$$

Bond market equilibrium in A is given by:

$$B^a = B_a^a + B_b^a + B_c^a + R_a^a + R_b^a + R_c^a \quad (5.14.3)$$

In country B

$$H^b = \mu_1 \Omega^b \quad (5.15.1)$$

$$B_b^b = \mu_2 \Omega^b \quad (5.15.2)$$

$$B_b^a / e^b = \mu_3 \Omega^b \quad (5.15.3)$$

Such that $\mu_1 + \mu_2 + \mu_3 = 1$.

Money market equilibrium in B is given by:

$$R_b^b + R_b^a / e^b = H^b \quad (5.16.1)$$

Bond market equilibrium is given by:

$$B^b = B_b^b + e^b B_a^b + +R_b^b \quad (5.16.2)$$

In country C

$$H^c = \eta_1 \Omega^c \quad (5.17.1)$$

$$B_c^c = \eta_2 \Omega^c \quad (5.17.2)$$

$$B_c^a / e^c = \eta_3 \Omega^c \quad (5.17.3)$$

Such that $\eta_1 + \eta_2 + \eta_3 = 1$.

Money market equilibrium is given by:

$$R_c^c + R_c^a / e^c = H^c \quad (5.18.1)$$

Bond market equilibrium in B is given by:

$$B^c = B_c^c + e^c B_a^c + R_c^c \quad (5.18.2)$$

Note the coefficients, $\lambda_i$, $\mu_i$, $\eta_i$ would vary with interest rates and exchange rates.

From the balance sheets we can see that net worth in the three countries ($\Omega^a$, $\Omega^b$, $\Omega^{ac}$) is the sum of its government debt and net foreign assets, given by:

$$\Omega^a = B^a + N^a \quad (5.19)$$

$$\Omega^b = B^b + N^b \quad (5.20)$$

$$\Omega^c = B^c + N^c \quad (5.21)$$

## DEPENDENCE OF THE ASSET MARKETS

Taylor (2004a, 2004b) has demonstrated that the equations for equilibrium for money and financial assets are not independent for a two-country closed system. It is easy to show that this dependence holds for a three-country setting as well.

From 5.14.2 and 5.14.1 in equilibrium,

$$R_a^a + \lambda_1 \Omega^a \quad (5.22)$$

$$B^a = B_a^a + B_b^a + B_c^a + R_a^a + R_b^a + R_c^a$$

$$B^a - R_a^a - R_b^a - R_c^a = \lambda_2 \Omega^a + e^b \mu_2 \Omega^b + e^c \eta_2 \Omega^c$$

Substituting for $R_b^a$ and $R_c^a$ from the net foreign asset condition (5.4),

$$B^a - R_a^a + N^a - e^b B_a^b - e^c B_a^c + B_b^a + B_c^a = \lambda_2 \Omega^a + e^b \mu_2 \Omega^b + e^c \eta_2 \Omega^c$$

On rearranging and substituting from the asset demand equations, and the equation for net worth (5.19) we get:

$$B^a + N^a - \lambda_2 \Omega^a - \lambda_3 \Omega^a - \lambda_4 \Omega^a = R_a^a$$

$$\lambda_1 \Omega^a = R_a^a$$

Thus the condition for equilibrium in country A's bond market and the net foreign asset constraint together ensure that the money market in A is also in equilibrium. This dependence can also be demonstrated for the two financial markets in countries B and C. Thus, of the six equations for financial asset equilibrium (5.14.2, 5.14.3, 5.16.1, 5.16.2, 5.18.1, 5.18.2) only three are independent. If interest rates in the three countries are assumed to clear the three bond markets (or alternatively the money markets), then this dependence leaves no asset market-clearing role for the exchange rate (Taylor 2004a, 2005b). Alternatively, interest rates could be assumed to be exogenously fixed by Central Bank policy with the exchange rate and reserve holdings adjusting to clear the markets (Godley and Lavoie 2006). However, in our three country setting, with a hegemonic country fulfilling the task of financial intermediation we can explore a different closure. Country A fixes its interest rate and the central bank in B buys up US bonds to the extent necessary to keep the exchange rate at a stable level, then the interest rate in B and C ($i^b$, $i^c$) and $e^c$ can be endogenously determined.

## INTERMEDIATION: ROLE OF PRIVATE CAPITAL MARKETS

In this section we elaborate the accounting identities in order to trace the implications for financial intermediation. Specifically, the accounts are animated by the different structural positions of B and C. This reflects in the basic asymmetry between the country with a structural surplus (earning reserves through export earnings) and the debtor country that accumulates reserves largely through borrowing.

For the hegemon A, in equilibrium, the net foreign assets relation (5.4) would imply that:

$$N^a = l_3\Omega^a + l_4\Omega^a - e^b\mu_3\Omega^b - e^c\eta_3\Omega^c$$
$$-R_b^a - R_c^a$$

Country B's central bank adjusts its holdings of A's bonds to cover its current account surplus in order maintain its exchange rate. From Country B's net foreign asset constraint, this would imply that:

$$R_b^a = e^b N^b - e^b\mu_3\Omega^b + \lambda_3\Omega^a \qquad (5.23)$$

Substituting the value of $R_b^a$ from (5.21), in the equation for country A's net foreign asset relation:

$$N^a = \lambda_3\Omega^a + \lambda_4\Omega^a - e^b\mu_3\Omega^b - e^c\eta_3\Omega^c$$
$$-e^b N^b + e^b\mu_3\Omega^b - \lambda_3\Omega^a - R_c^a$$
$$N^a = \lambda_4\Omega^a - e^c\eta_3\Omega^c - e^b N^b - R_c^a$$

In a three country model of the world treated as a closed system (with $e^b N^b = -N^a - e^c N^c$), the above equation can be rewritten as:

$$N^a = \lambda_4\Omega^a + e^c\eta_3\Omega^c - R_c^a + e^c N^c + N^a$$

Substituting country C's net foreign asset constraint (5.6) into the above equation and rearranging we get:

$$eN^c = B_c^a + R_c^a - e^c B_a^c = e^c\eta_3\Omega^c - \lambda_4\Omega^a + R_c^a$$

From the above we get

$$\lambda_4\Omega^a - e^c B_a^c = e^c\eta_3\Omega^c - B_c^a \qquad (5.24)$$

Country A's role in financial intermediation is in essence captured by Equation 5.24, which highlights the role played by private capital markets in the debtor emerging market countries in the adjustment mechanisms of the international monetary system. Thus equilibrium in the market for country A's bonds in our model of financial intermediation—once we incorporate the net foreign asset constraint conditions—is residually determined by conditions in the market for country C's bonds in country A. Country A's excess demand for country C's bonds is matched by country C's excess demand of bonds in A.[8]

It is possible to generate symmetric results with capital markets of B in terms of pure

[8]The bond market would, of course, be in balance if these two excess demands were equal to zero. But what is being stressed is that the overall market for A's bonds could still balance despite an excess demand for these bonds by C's private investors. It would be matched by excess demand for C's bonds by country A investors, which would, through the net foreign asset constraint, translate into an excess supply of country A reserve holdings by C's central bank.

accounting manipulations; however, the economic logic of the above elaboration rests on the different positions and roles of countries B and C with respect to the structure of financial intermediation.

## Adjustment Dynamics in the Debtor Country

Consider the growing current account deficit of the hegemon. The financing of this deficit hinges on its ability to find a market for its bonds, either among official holders in foreign central banks or in the private capital market. Suppose there is a shortfall in demand for country A bonds, or an excess supply of country A bills, because the central bank in B decides not to continue financing the trade deficit with A by piling up reserves. Country A would then have to raise its interest rate or devalue its currency in response to an excess supply of its home bonds. Adjustment, in this story, would be brought about by a slowing down of output and a consequent contraction of the current account imbalance.

However, A's role in financial intermediation (Equation 5.24) suggests another path to adjustment. An overall excess supply of A's bonds (LHS > RHS in 5.24), would imply an excess demand for C's bonds held by private investors in A.[9]

$$\lambda_4 \Omega^a - e^c B_a^c > e^c \eta_2 \Omega^c - B_c^a$$

Instead of raising $i^a$, adjustment could be brought about by transferring the burden of adjustment of country A's bond markets to the financial markets in country C. As the 'international financial intermediary', A can draw on the surpluses of B, while transmitting the burden of adjustment to the capital markets in C. Financial liberalization and unfettered capital mobility are integral to this mechanism.

The implicit overvaluation of country C's currency, that the relative excess demand for country C assets reflects, would pave the way for destabilizing speculation in a liberalized regime.[10] The net inflow of capital consequent to the excess demand for C's bonds, would lead to the appreciation of C's currency, that is, $e^c$ would fall. As country C's external liabilities increase, external assets would also have to rise to fulfill the net foreign asset constraint, and central bank holdings of A bonds would increase, fuelling a credit boom.

The interest rate spread between A and C is given by:

$$\sigma^c = i^c - i^a - \hat{e^c}$$

From C's net foreign asset constraint (5.6), ignoring interest receipts on central bank holdings of bonds, and holdings gains due to exchange rate movements, we have:

$$R_c^a = -e^c TD^c - (e^c i^c B_a^c - i^a B_c^a)$$
$$- e^c \eta_2 \Omega^c + \lambda_4 \Omega^a$$
$$\dot{R}_c^a = e^c N^c - e^c \eta_2 \Omega^c + \lambda_4 \Omega^a$$

Reserves rise at a faster rate with net private capital inflows $(\lambda_4 \Omega^a - e^c \eta_2 \Omega^c)$ and are eroded by deficits and net interest payments. The credit boom following an increase in reserves would lead to a worsening trade deficit, consequently eroding reserves.

$$\frac{\delta \dot{R}_c^a}{\delta R_c^a} < 0$$

An increase in $\sigma^c$ would increase inflows and reduce net interest payments to C. Assuming that the former effect dominates:

[9] If the sub-market for A's bonds in Country C is balanced (LHS in 5.24 is zero), it implies an excess demand of C's bonds among country A's private investors.

[10] The argument is based on Frenkel's model as presented in Taylor (1998, 2004b).

$$\frac{\delta R_c^a}{\delta \sigma} > 0$$

So that,

$$R_c^a = R_c(R_c^a, \sigma^c) \quad (5.25)$$

The spread is likely to fall with rising reserves, but there is a feedback effect of speculative behaviour so that a rise in the spread leads to an increased perception of risk.

$$\frac{\delta \sigma^c}{\delta R_c^a} < 0, \frac{\delta \sigma^c}{\delta \sigma} > 0$$

$$\sigma^c = \sigma^c(R_c^a, \sigma^c) \quad (5.26)$$

The expected appreciation of C's currency, and the opening of the interest rate spread ($\sigma_c > 0$), propels an increase in country A demand for C's bonds ($\lambda_4$ increases). The capital inflow leads to an increase in reserves, slowing down the increase in the spread, and leading to an appreciation of C's currency. As the trade deficit rises, the reserves start eroding, pushing up the interest rate spread. For the emerging market country, the increasing fragility of its financial system is compounded by the currency mismatch between its assets (denominated in local currency) and its liabilities (denominated in dollars). At some point, speculative expectations about the overvaluation of the currency come into play, thus, precipitating capital flight (Taylor 2004b).

Formulating the dynamic system given by (5.25) and (5.26) in a simple linear, first-order form:

$$\dot{R}_c^a = -aR_c^a + b\sigma^c$$

$$\dot{\sigma}^c = -cR_c^a + d\sigma^c$$

With a strong speculative feedback effect, $d > a$, and the trace of the Jacobian would be positive—giving rise to instability. Thus, capital inflows consequent to the emergence of currency overvaluation and high interest rates give rise to a credit boom and a growing current account deficit. With the emergence of increasingly speculative positions and a growing currency mismatch in the balance sheets, there is an unwinding with capital flight and sharp devaluations of C's currency. This implies that the excess supply of country A bonds could be reversed, even without an increase in the interest rate in A, as a consequence of the Minskian debt deflation cycle that unfolds in the debtor periphery. As long as there is no alternative 'international money', A can sustain its growing external debt and continue to find buyers for its bonds in the international market. The adjustment to shortfalls in demand for its bonds can precipitate financial crises in country C with a sharp rise in $e^c$.

## Adjustment Dynamics in the Creditor Country

To complete the story we need to trace the mechanisms of adjustment with respect to B. Changes in reserves holdings by the central bank in B are given by:

$$\dot{R}_b^a = e^b \dot{N}^b - e^b \mu_2 \dot{\Omega}^b + \lambda_3 \dot{\Omega}^b$$

$$\dot{R}_b^a = e^b TS^b - (i^b B_a^b - i^a B_b^a) - e^b \mu_2 \dot{\Omega}^c + \lambda_3 \dot{\Omega}^a \quad (5.27)$$

Reserves accumulate more rapidly with an increase in the trade surplus and a net inflow of interest payments and net private capital inflows. Appreciation of B's currency would also erode reserve accumulation through its impact on reducing the trade surplus and interest payments.[11] Further, if the imbalance created by growing surpluses with A and the

[11]Note that we are not basing the argument on the rigid maintenance of fixed pegs. However, we do assume that private capital flows between A and C are less responsive to changes in the exchange rate.

consequent overhang of reserve accumulation is displaced through the above-mentioned mechanisms to the private capital markets in C, then the feedback effect of reserve accumulation in B would tend to be stabilizing.

$$\frac{\delta \dot{R}_b^a}{\delta R_b^a} < 0,$$

The spread is given by:

$$\sigma^b = i^a - i^b + \hat{e^b} \tag{5.28}$$

As the spread increases, net capital outflows would increase along with net interest payments to B, reducing reserves. Thus:

$$\frac{\delta \dot{R}_b^a}{\delta \sigma^b} < 0$$

The spread is likely to increase with rising reserves, because of expected depreciation of A's currency. However, the feedback effect of speculative behaviour may be muted. The liabilities of country A are denominated in its own currency, so that expected depreciation would in fact increase A's net worth through valuation gains. This is the fundamental difference between the debtor positions of C and A. The signs for the partial derivatives for the spread are:

$$\frac{\delta \dot{\sigma}^b}{\delta R_b^a} > 0,$$

$$\frac{\delta \dot{\sigma}^b}{\delta \sigma^b} > 0 \text{ (but not significantly large)}$$

The dynamics of adjustment can be illustrated by formulating the dynamic system given by 5.27 and 5.28 in a simple, linear, first-order form.

$$\dot{R}_b^a = -aR_b^a - b\sigma^b$$

$$\dot{\sigma}^c = cR_b^a + d\sigma^a$$

The trace of the Jacobian is likely to be negative, as long as $a > d$. The determinant ($bc - ad$) would be positive for a small speculative feedback effect of $\sigma^c$ (a small d) leading to stable dynamics. The adjustment mechanisms are thus likely to be more stable than those between countries C and A.

## CONTRASTING DYNAMICS IN THE HEGEMON AND THE PERIPHERAL DEBTOR COUNTRY

Another way of thinking through the mechanism of adjustments is by focusing on the asymmetry of the impact of imbalance. In B, imbalances reflect policy decisions determining the extent to which the central bank is willing to accumulate reserves to maintain its currency peg with A. Suppose there is a shortfall in the reserve accumulation by country B (that is, the reserve holdings by the central bank in B do not entirely accommodate the trade deficit of A) denoted by β.

The exchange rate would respond to this shortfall, and B's currency would appreciate with an increase in this shortfall.

$$\dot{e^b} = e^b(\beta);\ f'(\beta) < 0$$

An appreciation of B's currency would erode the trade surplus, and increase net interest payments, so that the shortfall, β responds positively to changes in $e^b$.

$$\beta = \beta(e^b);\ \beta'(e^b) > 0$$

This implies a negative feedback effect on the exchange rate, imparting stability to the adjustment

$$\frac{\delta \dot{e^b}}{\delta e^b} < 0$$

However, as argued above, the imbalance in A's bond markets spills over into an imbalance in the private market for C's bond in the form of the net excess for its bonds, $x$. The exchange rate $e^c$ is largely capital account driven and would tend to appreciate more rapidly in response to this excess demand among private investors, so that

$$\dot{e}^c = e^c(\chi); f'(\chi) < 0$$

We could further expect a fall in $e^c$ to fuel excess demand among private investors.

$$\chi = \chi(e^c); \chi'(e^c) < 0$$

This positive feedback effect leads to the unstable dynamics of the exchange rate adjustment with:

$$\frac{\delta \dot{e}^c}{\delta e^c} > 0$$

For debtor countries in the periphery, as long as the central bank under attack (or facing continual deficits) has reserves (through export earnings) or creditworthiness to borrow it is able to compensate for the decreases in reserves. However, the process is not without a limit and the country would be forced into a deflationary stance, and would have to resort to raising interest rates and maintaining greater fiscal austerity. The US, on the other hand, is not constrained by a depleting stock of reserves and its role in financial intermediation eases the external constraint on its economy. International liquidity is generated through the mechanism of the US deficit.

## CONCLUSION

The growing global imbalance increases the financial fragility of the international system. The debtor countries of the periphery bear the brunt of deflationary pressures and face financial crises because of their asymmetric integration into global financial markets. This creates the conditions that make them vulnerable to financial crisis, and exacerbates the imbalances. In fact, holdings of foreign exchange reserves as a hedge against capital flight could worsen the underlying global imbalance, and perpetuate structural vulnerability.

Even the peripheral surplus countries (that are not competing with the dollar as international money) are closely tied in to the appetite for imports of the US economy because of their strategy of export-led growth.[12] A lot of the current debates are focused on this aspect. This paper focuses on how private capital flows in the emerging markets of the periphery play a crucial safety valve role in sustaining US deficits. This mechanism rests on the hegemony of the dollar as 'international money'.

In developing the argument, we have ignored the role of the euro, and the implications of the possibility that it might displace the dollar as the international money. However, this framework suggests that displacing the dollar would also involve dismantling the triangular pattern of settlements that underwrites the dollar's role in financial intermediation. For peripheral debtor countries, the analysis brings out the need for 'national level policy reforms' in cushioning them from the structural vulnerability to financial crisis that arises from the pattern of integration with the international monetary system under an International Dollar Standard. Capital controls, diversification of reserve portfolios, and rebalancing of demand and investment are all integral to addressing this vulnerability.

[12]Mckinnon (2005) talks about 'the conflicted virtue' of such a strategy, and has begun to stress the need for some capital controls in ensuring a 'credible commitment commitment' to the rules of the game of a dollar standard.

## REFERENCES


Blecker, R.A. (1996), 'The New Economic Integration: Structuralist Models of of North South Trade and Investment Liberalization', *Structural Change and Economic Dynamics*, Vol. 7.

Boratav, K. (2004), 'Some Recent Changes in the Relations between the Metropoles and the Periphery of the Imperialist System', Paper presented at the IDEAs conference on The Economics of New Imperative 22–4 January, Jawaharlal Nehru University New Delhi.

Bordo, M and B. Eichengreen (2002), 'Crises Now and Then: What Lessons from the Last Era of Financial Globalization', NBER Working Paper 8716.

D'arista, J. (2004), 'Dollars, Debt, and Dempendence: The Case for International Monetary Reform', *Journal of Post Keynesian Economics*, Vol. 26, No. 2, pp. 557–72.

Dooley, M., D. Folkerts-Landau, and P. Graber (2004), 'An Essay on the Revived Bretton Woods System', NBER Working Paper 9971, September.

Dutt, A.K.(1989), 'Uneven Development in Alternative Models of North South Trade', *Eastern Economic Journal*, Vol. 15, No. 2, pp. 91–106.

Eichengreen, B. (2004), 'Global Imbalances and the Lessons of the Bretton Woods', NBER Working paper 10497.

Erturk, K. (2006), 'Currency Crisis and the Instability of Capitalism', *International Papers in Political Economy* (forthcoming).

Foley, D. (2001), 'Financial Fragility in Developing Economies', in A.K. Dutt and J. Ros (eds), *Development Economic and Structuralist Macroeconomics: Essays in honour of Lance Taylor*, Edward Elgar, Cheltenham.

Foley, D. and M. Sidrauski (1971), *Monetary and Fiscal Policy in a Growing Economy*, Macmillan, New York.

Frenkel, R. (2002), 'Capital Market Liberalization and Economic Performance in Latin America', in J. Eatwell and L. Taylor (eds), *International Capital Markets: Systems in Transition*, OUP, New York.

Godley, W (1999), 'Open Economy Macroeconomics Using Models of Closed Systems', Levy Economics Institute Working Paper 281, Annandale, Hudson September.

Godley, W. and M. Lavoie (2003), 'Two Country Stock-Flow Consistent Model Macroeconomics Using a Closed Model within a Dollar Exchange regime', Working Paper 10, Cambridge Endowment for Research in Finance, Working Paper 10, University of Cambridge, Cambridge.

—— (2004), 'Simple Open Economy Macro with Comprehensive Accounting: A Radical Alternative to the Mundel Flemming Model', Cambridge Endowment for Research in Finance, University of Cambridge, Working Paper 15, April.

—— (2006), 'Comprehensive Accounting in Simple Open Economy Macroeconomics with Endogenous Sterilization or Flexible Exchange Rates', *Journal of Post-Keynesian Economics*, Vol. 28, No. 2, pp. 241–66.

Gray, H.P. and J.M Gray (1989), 'International Payments in a Flow of Funds Format', *Journal of Post-Keynesian Economics*, Winter, Vol. 11, No. 2, pp. 241–60.

Izurieta, A. (2003), 'Dollarization as a Tight Rein on Fiscal Stance', in L.P. Rochon and M. Seccareccia (eds) *Dollarization: Lessons for Europe and the Americas*, University of Cambridge, Cambridge.

—— (2005), 'Can the Growth Patterns of the US Economy be Sustained by the Rest of the World', Cambridge Endowment for Research in Finance Working Paper, Cambridge.

Kindleberger, C., W. Salant and E. Desprez (2000), 'The Dollar and World liquidity: A Minority View', in S. Walter (ed.), *Comparative Political Economy: A Retrospective*, MIT Press, Cambridge and London, pp. 207–18.

Kregel, J. (1999), 'Yes it Did Happen Again—A Minsky Crisis Happened in Asia', Working Paper 234, Levy Economics Institute of Bard College, Annandale, Hudson.

—— (2004a), 'Negative Resource Flows as a Minskian Hedge Profile and the Stability of the International Financial System', Paper available at the website of IDEAS, *http://www.networkideas.org/featart/nov2004/IFS.pdf.*

—— (2004b), 'Can We Create a Stable International Financial Environment that Ensures Net Resource Transfers to Developing Countries?', *Journal of Post Keynesian Economics,* Vol. 26, No. 4, M. E. Sharpe, Inc.

Mckinnon, R. I (2005), 'Trapped by the International Dollar Standard', *Journal of Policy Modeling,* Vol. 27.

Neftci, S. (1999), 'FX Short Positions, Balance Sheets and Financial Turbulence', in J. Eatwell and L. Taylor (eds) *International Capital Markets: Systems in Transition,* Oxford University Press, New York.

Patnaik, P. (1997), *Accumulation and Stability under Capitalism,* Clarendon Press, London.

—— (2002a), 'Money, Finance and the Contradictions of Capitalism', in C.P. Chandrasekhar and J. Ghosh (eds), *Work and Well being in the Age of Finance,* Tulika, India.

—— (2002b), 'The Theory of Money and World Capitalism', Paper presented at the IDEAS conference on International Money and Developing Countries, Muttukadu.

Taylor, L. (1981), 'South–North Trade and Southern Growth: Bleak Prospects from the Structuralist Point of View', *Journal of International Economics,* Vol. 11, pp. 589–602.

—— (1998), 'Lax Public Sector, Destabilizing Private Sector: Origins of Capital Market Crises', Working Paper, Centre for Policy Analysis, New School University.

—— (2004a), 'Exchange Rate Indeterminacy in Portfolio Balance, Mundell Flemming, and Uncovered Interest Parity Models', *Cambridge Journal of Economies,* Vol. 28, No. 2, pp. 205–27.

—— (2004b), *Reconstructing Macroeconomics: Structuralist Proposals and Critiques of the Mainstream,* Harvard University Press.

Vasudevan, R. (2006a), 'International Trade, Finance and Money: Essays in Uneven Development', unpublished dissertation, New School for Social Research.

—— (2006b), 'Financial Intermediation and Fragility: The Role of the Periphery', unpublished.

# 6

# Economic Openness, Financial Fragility, and Corporate Finance

## A Minskyan Perspective on Argentina's 2001 Crisis

MARTÍN P. ABELES*

## INTRODUCTION

Financial and capital account liberalization, applied in conjunction with fixed exchange rate regimes, tends to result in currency appreciation, as in Argentina between 1991 and 2001.[1] This seems to have been the case in most liberalization-cum-fixed exchange-rate regime experiments carried out in the last couple of decades across the developing world (Taylor 1998). As pointed out by Palma (2003), high liquidity in international financial markets (the 'push' factor behind surges of capital inflows to the developing world) played a key role financing mounting current account deficits during this period. Concurrent trade liberalization only contributed to further deterioration in current accounts. The resulting situation is, in principle, consistent with economic growth, so long as net capital inflows continue to finance current account deficits ('debt-led growth'). It is also consistent with increasing foreign reserves—another usual occurrence that has often predisposed institutional investors and financial authorities into a false sense of security. However, it is not sustainable.

In the upswing euphoric phase of the cycle (to use a Kindlebergian term), foreign borrowing normally finances consumption of durables (to an increasing extent imported, given the combined effect of trade liberalization and currency appreciation), real estate, and the expansion of relatively more profitable non-tradable sector firms.[2] Foreign finance is

*I am grateful to María Angélica Barrientos, Roberto de Miguel, and Cristina Pessagno at INDEC (Instituto Nacional de Estadísticas y Censos, Argentina) for their invaluable help and insightful methodological suggestions. I would also like to thank Philip Arestis for his comments on a previous version of this paper. The usual caveats apply. Finally, I gratefully acknowledge financial support by the Janey Program for Latin America Studies Summer Research Grant, which made the gathering of the data utilized in this paper possible.

[1]In the case of Argentina, the domestic currency was already overvalued before the parliamentary introduction of a fixed exchange rate regime (Convertibility Law) in March 1991. Still, as of that date, it tended to appreciate further, as inflation did not immediately go down to manageable levels in the context of a fixed nominal exchange rate.

[2]In spite of their lower profitability, some firms in the tradable sector may also find such a macroeconomic context propitious to invest, particularly in the acquisition of relatively inexpensive (due to currency

assured by the combination of a fixed exchange rate (or any similar monetary arrangement that makes the short-term behaviour of the exchange rate easy to forecast; see Neftci 2002) and significant interest rate spreads, which give way to momentous arbitrage gains (while reinforcing currency overvaluation).[3]

As pointed out by Taylor (1998), '[a]fter some months or years of this process, the balance sheet of the local financial system will be risky overall, short on foreign currency (FC) and long on local assets'. The servicing of escalating foreign liabilities depends on residents' earnings, mostly denominated in domestic currency. Such is the case of durables consumption and mortgage loans, whose payments largely depend on domestically generated earnings (wages), as well as of government liabilities, since tax revenues are of course collected in domestic currency.[4]

Kregel (1998) and Taylor (1998), among others, have expressly drawn attention to the serious risk of insolvency engendered by this type of currency mismatch in the financial sector. In a similar vein, in this paper I intend to focus on the financial position of the non-financial sector, paying special attention to non-tradable sector firms, whose ability to service foreign loans is also decidedly dependent on domestic currency revenues. Indeed, as non-tradable sector firms experience higher profitability and engage in 'speculative' finance (a la Minsky), they contribute to intensifying overall financial fragility, given that an increasing proportion of the country's foreign, non-financial sector debt is taken up precisely by one of the sectors that would most severely endure the deflationary impact of currency devaluation.

In order to empirically assess this phenomenon for Argentina prior to the 2001 crisis, I develop and seek to operationalize a set of financial indicators that draw on Minsky's distinction between hedge, speculative, and Ponzi financing positions. The paper is organized as follows. In the second section, I present an outline of Minsky's approach, concentrating on the relationship between finance, investment, and financial fragility. In the third section I describe the empirical evidence to be analysed and develop a criterion for the assessment of financial fragility at the level of the firm. In the fourth section, following the methodology developed in the previous section, I carry out a sectoral examination of Argentina's corporate balance sheets between 1998 and 2001. The last section concludes.

## MINSKY'S ANALYTICAL FRAMEWORK

Hyman Minsky was interested in the analysis of advanced capitalist economies, characterized by complex financial relationships. He underlined the fact that modern capitalist

appreciation) imported capital goods. However, this is not an option available across the board. It is typically restricted to firms large enough to have direct access to international capital markets, which belong to sectors that either enjoy some natural competitive advantage (for example, agribusiness in Argentina) and/or that benefit (or have benefited in the past) from some sort of government support or subsidy. Overall, despite certain successful examples, financial and capital account liberalization has resulted in severe de-industrialization, especially (but not necessarily) when applied in tandem with trade liberalization (Patnaik 2003).

[3]For an explanation of the persistence of interest rate spreads in the face of swelling capital inflows, see Frenkel (2004).

[4]The fact that banks may be allowed to make foreign currency domestic loans (as was the case in Argentina during the 1990s) does not rule out the emergence of currency mismatches between banks' assets and liabilities, since most foreign currency debtors' earnings (including the government's) are denominated in the domestic currency.

economies entail costly and long-lived capital assets which, in turn, require financing of some sort. According to Minsky, it is in the relationship between finance and investment that Keynes' notion of fundamental uncertainty develops, engendering the characteristic instability of capitalist economies (Minsky 1975a).

Counter to the Modigliani–Miller theorem—according to which there is no difference whether positions in capital assets are financed out of earnings, equity, or debt-Minsky's analysis paid special attention to the liability structure of firms.[5] The current purchase of capital assets is validated (or not) by future income flows, which implies that contractual financial commitments, when incurred in order to finance positions in capital assets, may not be met. If past financial commitments are not met, expectations about the future are likely to be affected (revised 'downwards')—almost certainly reducing current investment, and with it current income—making past financial commitments even more difficult to meet, and so forth.

Naturally, the higher the extent to which firms resort to external finance (debt), the larger the second-round effects to be expected from the interruption in any significant financial commitment. This is where financial institutions enter the scene. As the proportion of debt service payments increases relative to firms' cash flows, financial institutions become increasingly exposed to non-performing loans. If under such circumstances (that is, a widespread increase in leverage ratios) financial institutions increase their liquidity preference or become more risk averse, either due to a fall in their own cash flows or just out of sheer precaution, the availability of new loans (as well as the possibility of refinancing old ones) may be frustrated, precisely in the stage where demand for finance tends to become more inelastic to changes in interest rates.

The situation described here is likely to reduce investment, bringing profits down with it as Kalecki (who maintained that capitalists 'earn what they spend') would have predicted. Given existing financial commitments, falling profits tend to increase the demand for finance, exerting an upward pressure on interest rates, worsening the financial situation of firms even more. If at some point in this sequence firms resort to selling assets in order to meet debt payments ('sell position to make position', as Minsky would have put it) a Fisher-type debt deflation is likely to develop. Certainly, then, exactly 'how' a position is financed 'does' make a difference.

## Hedge, Speculative, and Ponzi Finance

As pointed out by Schroeder (2002), from Minsky's point of view the very act of borrowing to finance accumulation is the crucial determinant of financial instability. Further, Minsky argued that in a world of interlocked balance sheets, financial crises are endogenous—even if the eventual trigger of the crisis depends on specific institutional conditions and may be related to particular historical episodes, because the increase of financial fragility is itself endogenous.

A financially fragile firm is one that faces increasing payment commitments vis-à-vis its gross profits. Financial fragility may result from an increase in the firm's leverage ratio or from a modification (shortening) of the maturity structure of its outstanding liabilities. In any case, according to Minsky, fundamental to the distinction between robust and fragile

[5]Of course, he also paid attention to liability structures of households and financial institutions (see, for example, Minsky 1975b).

financial structures is the distinction among hedge, speculative, and Ponzi finance. In his own words:

A unit engages in hedge finance when the cash flow from the operations exceeds the cash payments due on contracts; a household mortgage is an example. A unit engages in speculative finance when the cash flow from operations falls short of the payment commitments on contracts, although cash flow from operations exceeds the interest charges. Speculative finance occurs when term to maturity of liabilities is short relative to asset life; banks normally engage in speculative finance, as do corporations that have a floating debt in the form of bank loans and commercial paper. A unit engages in 'Ponzi' finance when interest charges on outstanding debt exceed cash flow from operations. Units that are constructing facilities with long gestation periods or whose cash flow from operations or contracts falls short of anticipations are engaged in 'Ponzi' finance (Minsky 1975b, p. 7).

In other words, a hedged unit is one whose assets are expected to produce cash inflows from operating projects that exceed financing costs and operating expenses, including dividends to shareholders, 'by a sufficient "margin of safety" or cushion capable of absorbing any unforeseen changes in cash inflows and outflows' (Kregel 1998). To be precise, the 'margin of safety' comprises the difference between cash inflows and outflows from assets and liabilities, respectively; a 'cushion' that should be large enough so as to absorb any unexpected decrease in inflows (for example, a fall in gross profits) or any unexpected increase in outflows (for example, a rise in the interest rate on outstanding debt).

Likewise, a firm engages in speculative finance as its 'margin of safety' declines and the probability of it being unable to meet pending financial commitments increases, so that at some point over the life of the loan the firm may require an extension from its creditors or a reduction in the amount of dividends normally paid out to shareholders. This comprises a speculative position because both the lender and the borrower are speculating that by the end of the project, resources will suffice to repay interest and principal, despite occasional shortfalls.

Arestis and Glickman (2002) point out an aspect of speculative finance that is crucial when extending Minsky's framework to deal with an open economy:

Minsky characterizes the *speculative-financing* unit in two closely related but not entirely overlapping ways. On the one hand, he offers a definition in terms of such a unit's own cash prospects. Thus he writes that 'the balance sheet cash flows from a unit can be larger than the expected income receipts so that the only way they can be met is by rolling over ... debt; units that roll over debt are engaged in speculative finance' (Minsky 1986). At the same time, he also refers to the *speculative-financing* unit in terms of the impact on it of changes in financial market conditions (Arestis and Glickman 2002).

Indeed, there are two facets to speculative finance: the first is related to inflow prospects, for example, future sales; the second to outflow prospects, for example, future interest rates on outstanding debt. From the second perspective, that is considering the exposure of a firm to an unexpected rise in interest rates, any indebted unit, even one that enjoys a hedged position (according to the first criterion) may all of a sudden find itself bearing a speculative, or even a Ponzi position.

It is this second dimension of Minsky's definition of speculative finance that becomes crucial in an open economy framework, where firms are allowed to borrow foreign funds and are, therefore, exposed to unexpected changes in exchange rates. Indeed, in an open economy set-up, where firms assume foreign liabilities, currency depreciation gives rise to the same effect on cash flow commitments as rising interest rates in a closed economy set-up. For this reason '[c]ushions of safety would ... have to be larger for firms operating in countries with open capital markets' (Kregel 1998).

Finally, a unit is engaged in a Ponzi position when its 'margin of safety' is nil, that is, when shortfalls are likely to occur almost throughout the entire maturing phase of the project, so that the firm needs to borrow additional funds just to be able to meet interest payments; to 'increase debt to pay debt', as Minsky put it.

Summing up, for Minsky, '[t]he relative robustness/fragility of the financial structure is determined by the proportion of units engaged in hedge, speculative and 'Ponzi' finance; the greater the proportion engaged in hedge finance, the more robust the financial system' (Minsky 1975b). The attempt to extend and operationalize this proposition for an open economy comprises the thrust of this paper.

### Financial instability hypothesis

Minsky's financial instability hypothesis can be summarized as follows. Over prolonged financially tranquil periods the success of past investments, that is, the validation of capital assets purchased in the past, reduces firms' aversion to risk, inducing them to increase debt finance and to implicitly commit an increasing proportion of future cash flows to servicing the debt generated by new liabilities.[6]

Over the tranquil period, hedge finance tends to prevail. But '[i]n a world dominated by hedge finance and in which little value is placed on liquidity ... the interest rate structure yields profits opportunities in financing positions in capital assets' (Minsky 1986; quoted by Arestis and Glickman 2002). As units (firms, households, banks, etc.) engage in speculative finance and their demand for assets increases, asset prices tend to increase as well, giving rise to capital gains—reinforcing the disposition which motivated the speculative finance in the first place. In short, success induces agents to reduce their 'margins of safety':

> [I]n a world of uncertainty, given capital assets with a long gestation period, [...] the successful functioning of an economy within an initially robust financial structure will lead to a structure that becomes more fragile as time elapses. Endogenous forces make a situation dominated by hedge finance unstable... (Minsky 1986; quoted by Arestis and Gilckman 2002).

In other words, a prolonged period characterized by the predominance of hedge finance endogenously leads to speculative finance. But as speculative finance spreads, an increasing number of units are exposed to falling into Ponzi positions. Speculative units may be involuntarily pushed into Ponzi positions due to an increase in interest rates and/or due to a fall in gross profits. However, the likelihood of such an event increases due to the very increase in the proportion of debt service payments relative to firms' cash flows. While financial institutions may perceive their increased exposure and react by reducing the amount and increasing the cost of finance, firms may themselves (out of precaution) divest their funds towards more liquid assets (Keynes' 'precautionary' motive for demanding money), cutting down investment plans and reducing aggregate profits.

Interestingly, as pointed out by Papadimitriou and Wray (1999), while the

[6] '[S]uccess breeds the disregard of the possibility of failure: the absence of serious financial difficulties over a substantial period leads to the development of a euphoric economy in which increasing short-term financing of long positions becomes a normal way of life' (Minsky 1986, quoted by Arestis and Glickman 2002).

'shift toward speculative positions, or fragility, occurs intentionally (and more-or-less inevitably because of the way in which expectations are affected by success in a boom) [...] the shift from speculative toward Ponzi finance is mainly unintentional'.[7] Once Ponzi positions are significant enough, any 'spark' can trigger a debt-deflation.

### THE ROLE OF INSTITUTIONS

In a well-known collection of articles, Minsky (1982) sought to explain why 'it' (the Great Depression) did not happen again. Minsky laid emphasized the favourable impact of 'big government' and 'big bank'—the two chief institutional innovations with which capitalism emerged after the Second World War. A 'big government' not only contributes to setting a minimum level for aggregate demand (via the multiplier effect, as in the standard textbook approach), thus having a beneficial impact on cash flows; it also has a 'portfolio effect', as government deficits provide safe assets ('near monies') for private portfolios (Papadimitriou and Wray, 1999). Referring to the US economy, Minsky claimed that post-war recessions had been unusual and, most importantly, had not developed into severe depressions precisely because government deficits tended to place a floor on employment, personal income, and cash flows.

Minsky also thought that an active central bank ('big bank') willing to intervene in support of asset prices was also crucial in preventing financial crises. Indeed, Minsky believed that a 'big government' might not suffice in the event of a debt deflation. Given the interlocked nature of balance sheets, an asset price meltdown may still arise after, say, a large firm or bank defaults, forcing creditors to default as well, despite the presence of 'big government'. Hence, a lender of last resort—willing to lend or promise to lend to creditors in difficulty (provided they do not shut out debtors) or even to purchase assets of dubious value and issue risk-less liabilities—is crucial if financial instability is to be thwarted. For Minsky, this—and not the control of inflation—should be the primary purpose of a central bank.

Insofar as 'big government' and 'big bank' are successful in nurturing financial tranquility, detrimental side effects are liable to develop, as some risky economic operations tend to be rewarded (or not penalized as they might have otherwise been). Minsky was well acquainted with the dynamic implications of successful 'big government' and 'big bank' interventions. As pointed out above, in the absence of financial turmoil economic agents may tend to modify their expectations, engage in riskier positions (shifting from hedge to speculative positions), thus increasing overall financial fragility. Despite these 'side effects', Minsky conceived of institutions in an optimistic fashion, as contributing to stability,[8] in contrast

[7] In a very volatile context, the shift from hedged to speculative financing positions may be unintentional as well. In any case, it should be noted that as regards individual financial positions, the causal sequence might often go from the macroeconomic level (for example, changes in exchange rates, interest rates, etc.) to the microeconomic level. In other words, a given unit may not be able to effectively decide which financial position it would rather bear at a particular moment in time.

[8] '[I]nstitutions and interventions thwart the instability breeding dynamics that are natural to market economies by interrupting the endogenous process and "starting" the economy again with non-market determined values as "initial conditions"' (Minsky and Ferri 1991; quoted by Papadimitriou and Wray 1999).

to the orthodox 'moral hazard' gist, which tends to view institutions as barriers to achieving equilibrium.[9]

## The Minskyan open economy

Minsky's work predates the current era of financial liberalization. Partly for this reason it tended to consider a closed economy framework. It has, therefore, to be broadened in order to incorporate exchange rate and other risks associated with free international capital mobility. In recent years (particularly after the 1997 East Asian Crisis) several authors have innovatively tried to extend Minsky's approach to financial fragility to deal with the case of open economies.

According to Kregel (1998), an open economy is vulnerable to a financial crisis earlier in the business cycle than a closed economy because in the former, the 'margins of safety' need to be higher in order to handle the potential damage that exogenous changes in exchange rates and/or foreign interest rates may exert on cash flows. For Kregel, susceptibility to a financial crisis depends upon the economy surpassing a particular point in the business cycle; a point at which 'margins of safety' become too thin to cushion unforeseen changes in cash flows.[10]

According to Dymski (1999), an open economy is susceptible to generating major macroeconomic imbalances if capital inflows cannot be channeled into productive investment projects. For Dymski (1999), financial crises are more likely to emerge in developing economies, which lack the institutional capacity to cope with massive capital inflows. Indeed, the tendency of capital inflows to be channeled into speculative investments instead of productive investments in developing economies is what sets the ground for a Minsky crisis, as the reversal (or 'sudden stop') in capital flows punctures the resultant asset bubbles, triggering a debt-deflationary process.

According to Arestis and Glickman (2002), as argued by Kregel (1999), financial crises are likely to arise earlier in the business cycle in an open economy than in an closed economy due to the exposure to exchange rate variations. They believe that international capital mobility tends to internationalize the move towards higher levered positions (from hedge to speculative finance), as the initial validation of profits-cum-capital gains reduces domestic financial conservatism, driving the economy into a 'state of internationalized financial fragility':

> Openness vastly expands the drive toward financial innovation and extends the opportunities for 'making on the carry'. As a result, it decidedly broadens the routes by which units, including the state itself, can shift from hedged to speculative and Ponzi conditions. The economy is thus driven endogenously into a fragile condition in which it becomes increasingly exposed to disruptive events which, if domestic in origin, will amplify themselves via their external consequences and, if initially external, will bring adverse domestic repercussions in their train (Arestis and Glickman 2002, p. 244).

[9]Of course, 'side effects' have to be handled, just as with ordinary medicine. However, just as in the case of ordinary medicine, the existence of side effects need not invalidate the medicine's primary corrective effect. In fact, anticipating the effect of lender-of-last-resort-type of interventions on agents' perception of risk, Minsky supported balance sheet supervision and macro-prudential regulations as key complementary, regulatory devices.

[10]For a discussion about the timing followed by the Minskyan phases in an open economy, see Schroeder (2002).

According to Felix (1999), financial and capital account liberalization, by exposing the economy to exchange rate volatility tends to increase the 'hurdle rate', predisposing investible funds towards projects with faster expected pay-offs.[11] A bias towards shorter gestation projects may, therefore, be expected to emerge.[12] For Felix (1999), the Minskyan contention that financial market dynamics are inherently unstable and give rise to endogenous financial fragility comprises a fertile point of departure in understanding the problems experienced under the current international financial liberalization period. The extension of Minsky's policy advice to the open economy set-up is problematic, given the absence of an international lender of last resort:

> [Minsky] assumed a single central bank that could effectively intervene as lender of last resort (LOLR) and a large public sector with a progressive tax structure and expenditure commitments that would allow automatic fiscal stabilizers to set a high floor under aggregate demand... Adapting these *apercus* to a global setting of decontrolled financial markets with no global LOLR, and national economies with varying policy goals, is, however, a complex exercise in political economy (Felix 1999, p. 27).

[11]The hurdle rate is 'the minimum expected return that induces investment in projects involving front-end outlays—that is, fixed costs—and delayed revenue flow. Since information about the time-shape of future costs and revenues becomes more uncertain the longer the life of the project, delaying the project may reduce risk by allowing more information to be gathered. The hurdle rate of return adds a premium for 'waiting' to the cost of capital in investment calculations. The premium is the present value of the expected income stream from postponing the project divided by the expected present value of starting the project now. Greater expected volatility raises the hurdle rate...' (Felix 1999, p. 18).

[12]For example, this bias is evidenced in the current prevalence of mergers and acquisitions over greenfield investments in connection with FDI flows.

The ideas rendered above offer only a primer of a much more abundant and multi-faceted literature, which has sought to extend Minsky's ideas to an open economy framework. Still, they provide a propitious background for both the methodological development and the empirical investigation pursued further in the paper.

## THE ANALYSIS OF CORPORATE FINANCIAL FRAGILITY

In this section I develop a criterion for the assessment of financial fragility at the level of the firm in the context of an open economy. It may be useful, however, to describe the nature of the available empirical evidence before developing the set of financial indicators meant to distinguish among hedged, speculative, and Ponzi positions.

### The Panel

The empirical assessment of financial fragility requires detailed balance sheet information. In Argentina, the most comprehensive and reliable information available from this standpoint is provided by the ENGE (acronym for 'National Survey of Large Firms'), carried out by INDEC (acronym for 'National Bureau of Statistics and Censuses'). The panel includes the 500 largest non-financial corporations (listed and not-listed) operating in Argentina, both foreign and domestic, which represent approximately 15per cent of Argentina's GDP.

I shall refer to the firms in the panel as 'INDEC 500' hereafter. This is a recent survey, for which no information was available prior to 1995.[13] For the sake of subsequent analysis, the firms in the panel have been classified into foreign and domestic firms, on the one hand,

[13]Moreover, some of the information required for this paper is only available as of 1998.

and tradable and non-tradable sector firms, on the other, as shown in Table A6.1, which gives a broad picture of INDEC 500's composition.[14]

## CASH FLOWS AND FINANCIAL FRAGILITY[15]

As already argued, financial fragility ultimately arises from firms borrowing funds to finance production. According to Minsky, an economy is financially fragile if the bankruptcy of one firm can set off a chain reaction of bankruptcies of other firms, giving way to a recursive negative spiral. Hence, the likelihood of a systemic breakdown depends on the distribution of firms' financial positions along a line that goes from more robust (*hedged*) to more fragile positions (Ponzi). In other words, 'increased fragility of individual firms implies that the economy as a whole becomes financially unstable' (Schroeder 2002).

Minsky analyses financial fragility through firms' cash flow accounting categories, focusing on the extent to which income flows from the productive part of the firm may satisfy previously contracted financial obligations. The cash flow of a firm equates the source of funds from net operating revenues ($R$) and borrowing ($B$), to its uses for investment ($I$), servicing debt ($i^{\star}D$), and dividend payments ($Div$):

$$R + B \equiv I + i^{\star}D + Div \qquad (6.1)$$

or,

$$RE + B \equiv I + i^{\star}D \qquad (6.2)$$

where $i$ stands for the interest rate on outstanding debt $D$, $RE$ for retained earnings, and $RE = R - Div$. Net operating revenues or profits ($R$) are equal to gross profits minus tax payments. Note that (6.1) and (6.2) comprise accounting identities.

Both for both operational and analytical purposes it may be useful to make a distinction between financial investment ($I_{Fi}$) and productive investment ($I_{Pr}$). In addition, when considering an open economy, it may be worth classifying financial investment into domestic ($I^D_{Fi}$) and foreign ($I^F_{Fi}$). So, too, as regards firms' borrowing. Hence, Identity (6.1) may be re-expressed as:

$$R + B^D + (B^F \star e) \equiv I_{Pr} + I^D_{Fi} + (I^{F\star}_{Fi} e) + i^{\star}D^D + (i^{F\star}D^{F\star} e) + Div \qquad (6.3)$$

where $B^D$ and $B^F$ stand for domestic and foreign borrowing; $D^D$ and $D^F$ for domestic and foreign debt; $i^F$ for the foreign interest rate; and $e$ for the nominal exchange rate (domestic currency per unit of FC).

The distinction between the purchase of domestic and foreign financial assets may be important in assessing the nature and dynamics of a crisis. Note, for instance, that from a balance of payments perspective, the latter denotes capital outflows. An increase in the share of foreign financial assets in firms' portfolios may exert additional pressure on the balance of payments, which may be of particular importance in the case of countries experiencing foreign sector constraints. A sudden shift to foreign financial assets may, in turn, exert severe downward pressure on the value of domestic assets, including the domestic currency, triggering devaluation and/or debt-deflation.

Exposure to financial fragility in the case of an open economy depends crucially on the decomposition of debt between foreign and domestic.[16] In addition, when dealing with the

[14]Foreign firms have been identified according to the conventional 10per cent minimum equity share to foreign stockholders.

[15]This and the following subsection draw essentially on Foley (2003).

[16]Of course, the maturity structure of debt is also crucial, as became evident during the 1997 East Asian

corporate sector, the sectoral composition of foreign debt should also be taken into account. As suggested above, in the context of an open economy it is not the same whether foreign debt is mainly held by the tradable or the non-tradable sector (the latter also includes the government and the bulk of the population). Indeed, a non-tradable sector firm borrowing FC can instantly become insolvent due to currency devaluation.[17]

This seems to have been relevant in the case of Argentina. As shown in Table A6.2, foreign liabilities as a share of total liabilities had a tendency to increase between 1995 and 2001, together with the general increase in leverage ratios.[18] Notice the increasing exposure of non-tradable sector firms to currency risk throughout this period.[19] Even if non-tradable sector firms tended to exhibit a slightly lower proportion of foreign to total liabilities than tradable sector firms, it should be noted that their foreign liabilities were equal to 25 per cent of their total assets by 2001.[20]

A further decomposition of sources of funds may be useful for the assessment of corporate exposure to currency risk. Net operating revenues ($R$) may be classified into operational or 'productive' profits proper ($R_P$), on the one hand, and interest and dividend receipts ($R_F$) on the other. The latter may in turn be broken up into domestic ($R_F^d$) and foreign ($R_F^f$) currency financial proceeds, as shown in (6.4):[21]

$$R_{Pr} + R_{Fi}^{D} + (R_{Fi}^{F} \star e) + B^{D} + (B^{F} \star e) \equiv I_{Pr} + I_{Fi}^{D} + (I_{Fi}^{F} \star e) + i \star D^{D} + (i^{F} \star D^{F} \star e) + Div \quad (6.4)$$

## Operationalizing Hedge, Speculative, and Ponzi Positions

In order to analyse a firm's financial position we need to consider its net worth ($NW$), that is, the difference between the value of its assets ($A$) and its debts ($D$):

$$NW = A - D \quad (6.5)$$

As already discussed, Minsky defines three possible financial positions—hedged, speculative or Ponzi. Following Foley (2003), a *hedged* firm is one for which net operating revenues exceed its debt service obligations and investment plans, including dividends for shareholders, so that its net worth is increasing and its debt decreasing. According to the above representation of sources and uses of funds, as summarized in (6.4), this implies:

$$R_{Pr} + R_{Fi}^{D} + (R_{Fi}^{F} \star e) > I_{Pr} + I_{Fi}^{D} + (I_{Fi}^{F} \star e) + i \star D^{D} + (i^{F} \star D^{F} \star e) + Div \quad (6.6)$$

crisis. I have not developed this issue here for lack of relevant data.

[17]The tendency of private investment to shift in the direction of the non-tradable sector comprises one of the characteristic features of Palma's (2003) 'route 1' to financial crises.

[18]According to Bebczuk (2004), who develops a 'concentrated ownership model' in order to explain dividend policies in companies with highly concentrated ownership (as is often the case in developing countries), debt may act as an insurance device, which enables risk sharing with creditors. Interestingly, foreign subsidiaries of transnational corporations may be inclined to behave in a similar way, exhibiting high leverage and dividend repatriation ratios (Abeles 2004).

[19]Most notably, 61 per cent of foreign non-tradable sector firms' liabilities had been contracted abroad.

[20]Given this 0.25 ratio of foreign liabilities to total assets, a 50 per cent real devaluation would make the foreign liabilities to total assets ratio equal to 0.5, driving many of these non-tradable sector firms into insolvency. (Argentina's currency depreciated by more than 70 per cent between 2001 and 2002.)

[21]FC proceeds are important in this context since the impact of currency devaluation on firms' foreign debt and net worth could be compensated by foreign asset holdings (Abeles 2004).

so that:

$$B = B^D + (B^F \star e) \leq 0 \tag{6.7}$$

A speculative firm is one for which net operating revenues exceed its debt service obligations, including dividend payments, but do not completely suffice to afford investment plans. A speculative firm hence needs to borrow 'external' funds to finance expansion. Both its net worth and indebtedness are growing:

$$R_{Pr} + R_{Fi}^D + (R_{Fi}^F \star e) \geq i^\star D^D + (i^{F\star} D^F \star e) + Div \tag{6.8}$$

but:

$$R_{Pr} + R_{Fi}^D + (R_{Fi}^F \star e) \leq I_{Pr} + I_{Fi}^D + (I_{Fi}^F \star e) + i^\star D^D + (i^{F\star} D^F \star e) + Div \tag{6.9}$$

so that:

$$0 \leq B = B^D + (B^F \star e) \leq I = I_{Pr} + I_{Fi}^D + (I_{Fi}^F \star e) \tag{6.10}$$

Finally, a Ponzi firm is one for which net operating revenues fail to cover its debt service obligations (including dividend payments), so that it has to borrow to pay back previously contracted debt ('increase debt to pay debt'). A Ponzi firm increases its liabilities and decreases its net worth, which may eventually become negative:[22]

$$R_{Pr} + R_{Fi}^D + (R_{Fi}^F \star e) < i^\star D^D + (i^{F\star} D^F \star e) + Div \tag{6.11}$$

so that:

$$B = B^d + (B^f \star e) > I = I_{Pr} + I_{Fi}^D + (I_{Fi}^F \star e) \tag{6.12}$$

Financial distress at the level of the firm may arise due to different reasons. Given a firm's liabilities and dividend payments schedule, a reduction in net operating revenues may force a hedged unit into a speculative position, or a speculative unit into a Ponzi position. Alternatively, in order to preserve its financial position, a firm experiencing a fall in profitability may cut back on its dividend payments or reduce its investment plans. In the latter case, however, other firms' cash flows would eventually suffer as well.

An increase in domestic interest rates on outstanding debt may also drive a hedged unit into a speculative position, or a speculative unit into a Ponzi position. Note, however, that the impact of rising domestic interest payments may be offset by interest accrued on domestic financial assets. The overall impact of an increase in domestic interest rates, therefore, depends on the net (debtor or creditor) position of the firm. In case of a net debtor position, yet again, the firm may cut back on its dividend payments or investment plans in order to preserve its original financial position.

Currency devaluation (increase in $e$) could also put a firm, facing significant foreign liabilities, into severe financial trouble, turning a hedged into a speculative unit, and further into a Ponzi unit, or putting a Ponzi unit out of business altogether.[23] Again, the extent to

[22]As in Foley (2003), the same taxonomy can be expressed by means of intensive variables. Aggregating profits, borrowing, investment, and debt services back into single homogenous variables as in equation (6.1), it may be possible to distinguish Minsky's trinity in terms of a firm's growth rate $g$ (investment over assets), profit rate $r$ (profits over assets), and the interest rate paid $i$ (interest payment over stock of debt). In the case of a hedged unit the rate of profit exceeds both the growth rate of the firm's capital ($r > g$) and the rate of interest ($r > i$); in the case of a speculative unit, the rate of growth of assets exceeds its profit rate, which in turn exceeds the rate of interest ($g > r > i$); finally, in the case of a Ponzi unit, the interest rate exceeds the profit rate ($i > r$). Schroeder (2002) applies this taxonomy at the macroeconomic level to analyse the case of Thailand in the 1990s.

[23]Arestis and Glickman (2002) have dubbed firms that issue foreign liabilities in order to expand, exposing

which currency devaluation actually affects a firm's financial position depends on its net international (debtor or creditor) position. As pointed out above, a firm can hedge its foreign liabilities against the risk of domestic currency devaluation by increasing its holdings of foreign assets.[24]

Finally, note that financial distress could also arise, ceteris paribus, from a simple increase in dividend payments. This is not just a hypothetical situation. Dividend payments have become more burdensome with financial liberalization and the development of capital markets, as pointed out by Eatwell (1996):

As liquidity increases with the creation of ever more sophisticated financial products, the stock market begins to operate like a bond market. Institutional investors increasingly demand that dividend rates should be maintained, irrespective of corporate performance, thereby imposing a further deflationary burden on corporate cash flow.

In other words, a mere reduction in retention rates could weaken a firm's financial position. As shown in Table A6.3, the scale of dividend payments in Argentina can be deemed as anything but negligible.

## Indicators of Financial Position (IFP)

Minsky visualized firms in an economy as being virtually distributed along a line where more robust financial positions (hedged) lie on one end and more fragile ones (Ponzi) on the other. Given the necessary information, it may be possible to identify each firm's financial position according to Minsky's trinity and analyse the evolution of their distribution over time. With this in mind, I have employed two sets of indicators of financial position (IFP). The first set of indicators excludes dividend payments from the uses-of-funds side:

$$IFP^1_{b/Dividends} = \frac{R_P + R^D_{Fi} + R^F_{Fi} \cdot e}{I + DDS + FDS \cdot e} \quad (6.13)$$

$$IFP^2_{b/Dividends} = \frac{R_P + R^D_{Fi} + R^F_{Fi} \cdot e}{DDS + FDS \cdot e} \quad (6.14)$$

where $IFP_{b/Dividends}$ stands for 'Indicator of Financial Position *before* Dividend payments'; $I$ stands for investment, including both productive ($I_{Pr}$) and financial ($I_{Fi}$) investment flows; $DDS$ for domestic debt services, including both interest and principal payments; and $FDS$ for foreign debt services, also including both interest and principal payments. Note how the indicators depicted in (6.13) and (6.14) draw from (6.6), (6.8), and (6.11).

There is a slight difference between these two indicators, denoted by their superscripts '1' and '2'. While the first, $IFP^1_{b/Dividends}$, includes investment expenditures ($I$) in the denominator (as part of the uses of funds), the second, $IFP^2_{b/Dividends}$, excludes them. It is necessary to make this (apparently insignificant) distinction in order to identify each firm's financial position. While the first indicator, $IFP^1_{b/Dividends}$, may indisputably show whether a given firm bears a hedged position or not, it cannot show (in the case the firm is not hedged) whether the firm bears a speculative or a Ponzi position. Likewise, while the second indicator, $IFP^2_{b/Dividends}$, may indisputably show whether a firm bears a Ponzi position or not, it cannot show (in the case the firm is not in engaged in a Ponzi scheme) whether the firm bears a hedged or a speculative position. Still, resorting to both indicators in unison the following classification ensues:

themselves to foreign exchange-rate movements as 'super-speculative-financing units'.

[24] Of course, an increase in foreign interest rates $i^F$ would inflict a similar effect, as was the case prior to the 1980s Latin American debt crisis.

Table 6.1: Classification of IFP *before* Dividend payments

| Hedged | Speculative | Ponzi |
|---|---|---|
| | $IFP^1_{b/Dividends} < 1$ | |
| $IFP^1_{b/Dividends} > 1$ | and | $IFP^2_{b/Dividends} > 1$ |
| | $IFP^2_{b/Dividends} > 1$ | |

*Source*: Author.

In other words, if a firm exhibits $IFP^1_{b/Dividends} > 1$, it means its net operating revenues, indicated by the numerator in equation (6.13), more than suffice to pay back its debt and finance its investment plans, indicated by the denominator. This firm is engaged in hedge finance. However, if $IFP^1_{b/Dividends} < 1$, it is necessary to resort to the second indicator, $IFP^2_{b/Dividends}$, to distinguish whether the firm bears a speculative or a Ponzi position. If the firm exhibits $IFP^2_{b/Dividends} < 1$, it means its net operating revenues are not even sufficient to service its debt (let alone finance investment); this firm bears a Ponzi position. The intermediate case (a firm that exhibits $IFP^1_{b/Dividends} < 1$ and $IFP^2_{b/Dividends} > 1$) denotes speculative finance. Note that this classification leaves dividend payments to shareholders aside. That is not the case with the second set of indicators. In fact, the second set of indicators differs from the first only in that it includes dividend payments when accounting for uses of funds:

$$IFP^1_{a/Dividends} = \frac{R_P + R^D_{Fi} + R^F_{Fi} \cdot e}{I + DDS + FDS \cdot e + Div} \quad (6.15)$$

$$IFP^2_{a/Dividends} = \frac{R_P + R^D_{Fi} + R^F_{Fi} \cdot e}{DDS + FDS \cdot e + Div} \quad (6.16)$$

where $IFP_{a/Dividends}$ stands for 'Indicator of Financial Position after Dividend payments'. From (6.15) and (6.16) an analogous classification results:

Table 6.2: Classification of IFP *after* Dividend payments

| Hedged | Speculative | Ponzi |
|---|---|---|
| | $IFP^1_{a/Dividends} < 1$ | |
| $IFP^1_{/Dividends} > 1$ | and | $IFP^2_{a/Dividends} < 1$ |
| | $IFP^2_{a/Dividends} > 1$ | |

*Source*: Author.

The same reasoning described before applies here. Arguably, this second set of indicators entails a more realistic representation of firms' actual financial position, given that firms normally pay out dividends to shareholders. It is nevertheless interesting to analyse the different results obtained from sorting the panel among hedged, speculative, and Ponzi positions under each of these two sets of indicators, as this may indicate to what extent dividend policies may have contributed to firms' financial constraints.

## THE EMPIRICAL EVIDENCE

In this section I carry out a sectoral examination of Argentina's corporate balance sheets between 1998 and 2001, classifying them into hedged, speculative and Ponzi positions, according to the criteria described in the third section. Table A6.4, presents the evolution of the distribution of hedged, speculative, and Ponzi positions within INDEC 500, classified according to $IFP^1_{b/Dividends}$ and $IFP^2_{b/Dividends}$, as in Table 6.1 above; that is, under the assumption that firms paid no dividends to shareholders. As expected, hedged and speculative positions tended to give way to Ponzi positions as the 1998–2001 recession proceeded and the financial breakdown came closer.

In other words, even under the assumption that firms paid no dividends to shareholders at all, about half of the firms in the panel had to borrow funds in order to service their debt and stay in business during 2001. The situation was all the more severe given the record-low investment figures that year, as shown in Table A6.5.

As pointed out above, exposure to financial fragility in an open economy set-up depends very much on the composition of debt and its sectoral distribution—exposure to currency risk is significantly much higher in the case of non-tradable than in the case of tradable sector firms. As shown in Table A6.6, which breaks up the panel into tradable and non-tradable sector firms, the latter seem to have followed a fairly steeper path in the direction of financial fragility. Indeed, along with the increasing weight of non-tradable sector firms in the panel, the proportion of Ponzi firms within the non-tradable subset more than doubled, going from 22 per cent in 1998 to 46 per cent in 2001. Tradable sector firms reveal a similar proportion of Ponzi units in 2001 (47 per cent), but their increase vis-à-vis 1998 was less spectacular.[25]

It may also be important to distinguish behaviour of foreign firms as compared to domestic firms see Table A6.7. Interestingly, the table seems to show that foreign firms moved faster into financially fragile positions than domestic ones. The proportion of Ponzi units among foreign firms rose from 27 per cent to 48 per cent between 1998 and 2001.[26] Domestic firms revealed a higher proportion of Ponzi units in 1998 (31 per cent) and a lower proportion in 2001 (43 per cent), that is, their path towards financial fragility seems somewhat more moderate.

Recall that the various classifications presented in the paper are based on the first set of indicators, $IFP^1_{b/Dividends}$ and $IFP^2_{b/Dividends}$; that is, they have been obtained under the assumption that firms paid out no dividends to shareholders. On the one hand, this assumption exposes the true cash flows of firms ex ante, as determined by the totality of firms' gross profits; on the other hand, it tends to inflate firms' cash flows ex post, concealing their correct financial position.

Table A6.8 reveals the distribution of hedged, speculative, and Ponzi positions according to $IFP^1_{b/Dividends}$ and $IFP^2_{b/Dividends}$ (that is, according to the classification derived from Table 6.1), together with the corresponding distribution that results from employing $IFP^1_{a/Dividends}$ and $IFP^2_{a/Dividends}$ (that is, according to the classification derived from Table 6.2), which includes dividend payments to shareholders.

Note that financial positions deteriorate significantly once dividend payments are taken into account. In 1998, the first (and in terms of Argentina's macroeconomic performance, 'best') year in this short series, the proportion of Ponzi units increased from 28 per cent (*before* dividend payments) to 40 per cent (*after* dividend payments). This means that a significant number of firms were actually borrowing funds simply to meet their dividend payments. In 2001, once dividend payments were computed, 57 per cent of the firms in the sample held Ponzi positions, instead of 47 per cent, as accounted before dividend payments.

Table A6.9 breaks up the INDEC 500 panel into tradable and non-tradable sector firms, as in Table A6.6, but in this case taking dividend

[25] Recall that this paper's working hypothesis hinges on the idea that substantial inflows of capital to Argentina during the 1990s (which contributed to sustaining a perceptibly overvalued domestic currency) led to an unsustainable boom in the non-tradable sector, exacerbating the overall financial fragility.

[26] Note that foreign firms' significance within the panel also grew during the same period.

payments into account. The difference between the behaviour of tradable and non-tradable sector firms' here is not as noticeable as in Table A6.6. It should be noted, however, that the share of non-tradable firms in the panel increased significantly between 1998 and 2001, overshadowing the growth in the share of non-tradable sector firms bearing a Ponzi position. Indeed, in 1998, 26 per cent of the firms in a Ponzi situation belonged to the non-tradable sector; whereas in 2001, 34 per cent of the firms in that situation belonged to the non-tradable sector. Recall that, as indicated in Table A6.2, in 2001, 45 per cent of non-tradable sector firms' total debt was foreign debt.[27]

In turn, Table A6.10 differentiates between foreign and domestic firms' behaviour, as in Table A6.7, but this time taking dividend payments into consideration. Here, again, the deterioration seems much more pronounced in the case of foreign vis-à-vis domestic firms. Indeed, 60 per cent of foreign-owned firms found themselves in a Ponzi position after paying out dividends (compared to 48 per cent before paying out dividends, as shown in Table A6.7). Domestic firms bearing a Ponzi position also increased significantly, from 43 per cent before dividend payments (Table A6.7) to 52 per cent after dividend payments (Table A6.10).

As I have argued elsewhere, dividend repatriation may be expected to increase significantly during the downward phase of the business cycle (Abeles 2004). Quite remarkably, however, as observed in Table A6.11, in 2001, foreign firms repatriated two and a half times their profits (net of interest payments), implying that transnational subsidiaries' remittances greatly exceeded their profits, to include also past earnings, depreciation funds, and probably even borrowed funds. This explains why 60 per cent of foreign firms are found to be in Ponzi positions once dividend payments are taken into account.[28] In the case of domestic firms, their falling into Ponzi positions seems to have had less of a discretionary component, given their negative aggregate profitability (net of interest payments).

## CONCLUSIONS

In recent years, several authors have innovatively sought to extend Minsky's approach to financial fragility, originally developed in the context of closed economies, to deal with the case of open economies.[29] The overriding theme in this literature is the destabilizing nature of private finance, exacerbated by free international capital mobility. Inspired by these contributions, I have attempted to operationalize Minsky's taxonomy of hedge, speculative, and Ponzi finance at the level of the firm for the case of open economies and to provide new empirical evidence on non-financial corporate vulnerability for Argentina prior to the December 2001 crisis. The mere approach to private finance contrasts the one-sided orthodox insistence on fiscal vulner-

[27]The weight of FC liabilities was actually much higher than foreign liabilities proper (as accounted for in the balance of payments), since firms were allowed to borrow FC in the domestic banking system. FC liabilities to the domestic banking system were partially rescued ('pesified') by the Argentine government after the devaluation of 2002.

[28]Note that total dividend repatriation by foreign firms included in INDEC 500, which amounted to \$3.4 billion in 2001, represented more than $^1/_4$ of Argentina's total loss of foreign reserves (which fell by \$12 billion) during 2001.

[29]Including Arestis and Glickman (2002), Dymski (1999), Felix (1999), Foley (2003), Kregel (1998), Schroeder (2002), among others.

ability as the ultimate cause of Argentina's latest financial breakdown.[30]

While not meaning to relegate the influence of fiscal imbalances in the build-up of Argentina's 2001 crisis, the empirical evidence provided in this paper points in a somewhat different direction. Indeed, diminishing corporate cash flows may have themselves had an effect on fiscal revenues and not the other way round, as is claimed conventionally. In fact, private foreign over-indebtedness gave way to momentous defaults after the 2002 currency devaluation, in conjunction with the public sector's (more notorious) default.

According to a private survey carried out by a financial consulting firm (AGM),[31] out of a sample of 60 non-financial corporations whose liabilities exceeded US$100 million, adding up to a total US$ 27.4 billion debt,[32] 41 companies fell into arrears with their (mostly foreign) creditors, for a total of US$ 22.2 billion; that is, 81per cent of the sample's total indebtedness.[33] Of the aforesaid US$ 22.2 billion of irregular debt, 15 per cent corresponded to exporting companies, 37per cent to non-exporting companies, and 48per cent to public utility companies, according to AGM's own classification. That imples that, even if all the 'non-exporting' companies cannot be categorized as strictly belonging to the non-tradable sector, as expected, the bulk of arrears undoubtedly pertained to the non-tradable sector firms.[34]

Minsky's analytical framework comprises a particularly fruitful source for understanding current open economy issues, particularly in today's era of financial globalization. Even though I do not say that Argentina's 2001 crisis should be characterized as a 'Minsky crisis' proper, there are many elements, both at a conceptual and methodological/empirical level, which seem to make more sense when examined through a Minskyan lens.

## REFERENCES

Abeles, Martín (2004), 'Financially Destabilizing Aspects of Inward FDI: The Case of Argentina during the 1990s,' Paper presented at the International Seminar on 'Challenges to Development in the 21st Century', Institute of Economics, State University of Campinas, Sao Paulo, Brazil, 6–7 December 2004.

Arestis, Philip and Murray Glikman, (2002), 'Financial Crisis in Southeast Asia: Dispelling Illusion the Minskyan Way,' *Cambridge Journal of Economics*, Vol. 26, pp. 237–60.

Baker, Dean and Mark Weisbrot, (2002), 'The Role of Social Security Privatization in Argentina's Economic Crisis', Centre for Economic and Policy Research, Washington, DC.

Bellofiore, Riccardo and Piero Ferri (2001), 'Introduction: Things Fall Apart, the Centre Cannot Hold', in Riccardo Bellofiore and Piero Ferri (eds), *Financial Fragility and Investment in the Capitalist Economy: The Economic Legacy of Hyman Minsky*, Volume II, Edward Elgar, New York.

Damill, Mario, Roberto Frenkel, and Luciana Juvenal (2003), 'Las cuentas públicas y la crisis de la convertibilidad en Argentina' CEDES, Buenos Aires.

Dymski, Gary (1999), 'Asset Bubbles and Minsky Crises in East Asia: A Spatialized Minsky Approach,' Research Paper, University of California, Riverside.

[30]Noteworthy exceptions include Damill, Frenkel, and Juvenal (2003), Kregel (2002), Lozano and Schorr (2001), and O'Connell (2002).

[31]Aguirre-González-Marx Associates.

[32]Mostly, though not entirely foreign debt.

[33]According to official balance of payments data, total non-financial private sector foreign debt amounted to US$ 61 billion in December 2001.

[34]In fact, 74.5 per cent of the 60 companies' total US$ 27.4 debt corresponded to 'non-exporting' and public utility companies, whereas only the remaining 25.5 per cent corresponded to 'exporting' companies.

Eatwell, John (1996), 'International Capital Liberalisation: The Impact on World Development', New School University, Centre for Economic Policy Analysis, Working Paper No. 1.

Felix, David (1999), 'Open-Economy Minsky-Keynes and Global Financial Crises,' Paper presented at the 9th Annual Hyman P. Minsky Conference on Financial Structure, Jerome Levy Economics Institute, 21–23 April 1999.

Foley, Duncan (2003), 'Financial Fragility in Developing Economies,' in Amitava Dutt (ed.), *Festschrift for Lance Taylor*, Edward Elgar, New York.

Frenkel, Roberto (2004), 'Del auge de los flujos de capital a las trampas financieras,' in Jose Antonio Ocampo (ed.) *El desarrollo economico en los albores del siglo XXI*, Alfaomega, Bogota.

Kregel, Jan (1992), 'Minsky's "Two Price" of Financial Instability and Monetary Policy: Discounting versus Open Market Intervention', in Steven Fazzari and Dimitri Papadimitrou (eds), *Financial Conditions and Macroeconomic Performance. Essays in Honor of Hyman P. Minsky*, M.E. Sharpe, New York and London.

____ 1998. 'Yes, "It" Did Happen Again: A Minsky Crisis Happened in Asia', Levy Economics Institute, Working Paper No. 234.

____ 2002. 'Revised draft for DGDS Argentina Paper' mimeo.

Lozano, Claudio and Martin Schorr (2001), 'Estado Nacional, Gasto Publico y Deuda Externa' IDEP, Buenos Aires.

Minsky, Hyman (1975a), *John Maynard Keynes*, Columbia University Press, New York.

____ (1975b), 'Financial Resources in a Fragile Financial Environment', *Challenge*, July–August 1975, pp. 6–13.

____ (1982), *Can 'It' Happen Again?* M.E. Sharpe, New York.

____ (1985), 'The Legacy of Keynes', *The Journal of Economic Education*, Vol. 16, No. 1, pp. 5–15.

____ (1986), *Stabilizing an Unstable Economy*, Yale University Press, New Haven.

Neftci, Salih (2002), 'FX Short Positions, Balance Sheets, and Financial Turbulence', in John Eatwell and Lance Taylor (eds), *International Capital Markets: Systems in Transition*, Oxford University Press, Oxford and New York.

O'Connell, Arturo (2005), 'The Recent Crisis of the Argentine Economy: Some Elements and Background', in Gerald Epstein (ed.), *The Financialization and the World Economy*, Edward Elgar, New York.

Palma, Gabriel (2001), 'The "Three Routes" to Financial Crises: Chile, Mexico, Argentina [1]; Brazil [2]; and Korea, Malaysia and Thailand [3]', in Ha-Joon Chang (ed.), *Rethinking Development Economics*, Anthem Press, London.

Papadimitrou, Dimitri and L. Randall Wray (1999), 'Minsky's Analysis of Financial Capitalism', Levy Economics Institute, Working Paper No. 275.

Patnaik, Prabhat (2003), 'On the Economics of "Open Economy" De-industrialization', V.V. Giri Memorial Lecture, delivered at the Annual Conference of the Indian Society of Labour Economics, Kolkata, December 2003.

Schroeder, Susan (2002), 'A Minskyan Analysis of Financial Crisis in Developing Countries', New School University, Centre for Economic Policy Analysis, Working Paper 2002–09.

Taylor, Lance (1998), 'Capital Market Crises: Liberalization, Fixed Exchange Rates, and Market-Driven Destabilization', *Cambridge Journal of Economics*, Vol. 22, pp. 663–76.

# 7

# Trust, Freedom, and Wealth Creation
## A Political Economy of Dollarization in Lebanon

Armen V. Papazian*

The Asian financial crisis that spread across emerging markets during the 1990s, and the fact that most of the affected countries had some sort of a fixed or pegged exchange rate has spawned a new debate on the viability of alternative exchange rate regimes (Mendoza 2001). At the centre stage is the bipolar view (Fischer 2001) that perceives intermediate exchange rate regimes as unsustainable in the long run. The view proposes that the real choice for emerging markets and developing countries is between floating rates or hard pegs. Indeed, for some, the alternatives are floating arrangements or full dollarization (Yeyati and Sturzenegger 2003).

Full dollarization describes a situation where an FC is used as the sole legal tender instead of the domestic currency. It is considered an extreme case of a fixed exchange rate, whereby the exchange rate is actually eliminated along with the local currency. Dollarization is a general term, and does not imply that the FC is actually the US dollar (US$). As such, if US citizens opted for the Lebanese Pound (LBP) for their local transactions, the process or phenomenon would still be called dollarization. This has been referred to as full, official, or de jure dollarization. While very few cases of full dollarization exist today, the issue has become a debated alternative for many Latin American countries. Indeed, the full dollarization of Ecuador in 2000 and El Salvador in 2001 could explain the renewed interest in exploring the costs and benefits of such a drastic solution to macroeconomic imbalances.[1]

*This research paper was completed while the author held Assistant Professorships at the Lebanese American University in Beirut-Lebanon, and the American University in Dubai, UAE.

I am grateful to colleagues in the Department of Finance at the Lebanese American University Business School and the American University in Dubai for helpful discussions and suggestions. I also thank my graduate and undergraduate students in the Financial Management and Senior Study in Finance Courses at the Lebanese American University. I would like to acknowledge the able research assistantship of Humaya Harati, Mohamad Tarabay, Maya Youssef, and Nabil Husseini. Mistakes remain my own.

[1]The recent revival of the dollarization literature closely follows the currency substitution literature. See

While a major part of the debate focuses on the theoretical implications of full dollarization, partial or unofficial dollarization (de facto) has also attracted significant attention (Schuler 2000; Reinhart, Rogoff, and Savastano 2003; and Yeyati and Sturzenegger 2003). Partial or unofficial dollarization describes situations where an FC is used alongside the domestic currency. The initial stage of partial dollarization concerns the 'store of value' function of money and has been called 'Asset Substitution'. This is when residents start holding foreign bonds and deposits abroad in order to protect themselves against wealth losses due to inflation in the domestic currency. The second stage involves 'Currency Substitution', when FC deposits are held in the domestic banking system and later on foreign notes are used as a medium of exchange. In such scenarios, 'wages, taxes, and everyday expenses such as groceries and electric bills continue to be paid in domestic currency, but expensive items such as automobiles and houses are often paid (for) in FC' (Schuler 2000, p. 2).

Parallel to partial deposit dollarization, a recent wave of academic research has looked into liability dollarization (LD) as a crucial factor in macroeconomic stability and as a potential source for currency crises and bankruptcies in case of devaluation (Honig 2004). Indeed, deposit and liability dollarization are perceived to mirror each other (Yeyati and Sturzenegger 2003).

Whether full or partial, dollarization has been explained as a response to macroeconomic mismanagement, high inflation, and lack of public financial discipline. Indeed, it is perceived to be the least 'bad' alternative to local macroeconomic mismanagement and wealth destroying policies. The proposition, naturally, is addressed to emerging markets and developing countries where there is a proven historical record of bad policymaking, and where policymakers lack credibility. For advocates of dollarization, the benefits of the process include: reduced transaction costs, higher credibility, and lower country risk.

The costs and benefits of dollarization have been the subject of intense disagreement. Given the scarcity of material evidence on the performance of dollarized economies, and given their small number and size, it can be argued that most of the benefits are really speculative (Edwards 2001). Critics of dollarization identify heavy costs with the loss of the local currency as it implies loss of: (i) seignorage revenue, (ii) independent monetary policy, and (iii) the central bank's role as a lender of last resort. It also implies exposure to shocks experienced by the anchor currency (the FC), and no guarantee that it will actually work. Moreover, dollarization is being advised to emerging markets when no real evidence exists that it delivers its promises (Edwards 2001). Dollarization takes away the money printing powers of the state, but does not guarantee fiscal discipline.

Previous studies on currency substitution have suggested that countries, mainly in Latin America, have hysteresis in their dollarization ratios (Dornbush and Reynoso 1989; Clements and Schwartz 1992). Hysteresis describes the persistently high dollarization ratios despite declining inflation rates and increasing real rates of return on domestic currency assets. The tendency of dollarization ratios to stay high has been explained by the costs associated with the process. Indeed, costs of financial adaptation make de-dollarization hard to achieve (Dornbush, Sturzenegger, and Wolf

---

also Alesina and Barro (2001); Berg and Borensztein (2000), Calvo and Vegh (1992, 1993, 1996), Chang (1994); and Chang and Velasco (2001).

1990), even if stabilization and inflation targets have been met. Recent studies identify only four countries that have been able to de-dollarize, namely Mexico, Israel, Poland, and Pakistan (Reinhart et al. 2003).

For somewhat understandable reasons, the debate on dollarization has focused on Latin America. Subsequently, dollarization in Lebanon has attracted very little attention. Mueller (1994), whose study is one of the very few studies on dollarization in Lebanon, predicts that dollarization ratios would stay high, given the high costs and little incentive to switch back to the domestic currency. Indeed, Lebanon is a partially dollarized economy depicting significantly high ratios of deposit and liability dollarization (see also, Shahin and Freiha 2005).

Inflation and macroeconomic instability have characterized Lebanon during the 1980s and early 1990s (Saidi 1986; Dibeh 2002). High rates of inflation and a collapsing currency were the economic consequences of the fiscal and monetary policies adopted throughout the 1975–90 civil war. Since then, inflation has been tamed in peacetime, and was around 3 per cent in 2005. Interestingly, dollarization ratios have stayed high despite an initial decline in the early 1990s.

This study proposes that persistently high dollarization ratios in Lebanon can be explained from a political economy perspective. Indeed, the nature of the post-war state, the sectarian nature of institutional and government power, the interests of commercial banks, and the military presence of Syria are all factors that have postponed de-dollarization. This study suggests that Lebanon's de-dollarization process, while on its way until 1997, failed to achieve a solid ground of trust and credibility for the LBP.[2] Indeed, in early 2005, dollarization stood at its 1992 level. However, given the recent socio-political developments in the country, it is possible to argue that Lebanon has taken its first steps towards real political independence.[3] While sectarianism is still to be abolished, the recent elections (May–June 2005) and the popular demand for a technocratic, fair, and efficient government might be a singular opportunity for Lebanese monetary authorities to resuscitate the marginal and tarnished image of the LBP.

The contributions of this paper are four-fold.

1. I explore dollarization in Lebanon in a comparative context using Latin America. Given the earlier focus in the literature, bringing Lebanon into the picture makes it necessary to look at the institutional dimensions of dollarization.

2. I interpret persistently high rates of dollarization in Lebanon from a political economy perspective, and argue that it is lack of trust and freedom that undermine the wealth creating potential of the Lebanese state. As such, I view dollarization as the result of local institutional and leadership weakness.

3. Using an institutional perspective, I propose that de-dollarization is about reclaiming economic identity, and is a fundamental expression of societal trust. Thus it is far more elemental than exchange rate policy, and rests on the foundations of local wealth creation.

4. Finally, I propose de-dollarization as the right course of action for Lebanon, and suggest

[2]While all Lebanese banknotes since 1964 depict the name Lira, recently, financial authorities have opted for the name Pound. We follow their practice, even though we find it symptomatic and a fact that reflects the lack of trust in the currency.

[3]Following the assassination of former PM Rafiq El Hariri, and the ensuing political demonstrations and the departure of Syrian ground troops from Lebanon, the country went through parliamentary elections that defined its will to establish independence and a technocratic government (May–June 2005).

that, given necessary institutional reform, a new Lebanese Lira could provide the required incentives and inspire the much needed trust.

The paper is structured as follows. The next section explores dollarization in Lebanon using different measures and perspectives. The third section proposes a possible interpretation of the persistently high rates of dollarization in Lebanon, using a political economy framework. The fourth section three provides a discussion of de-dollarization, and the last section concludes.

## PARTIAL DOLLARIZATION IN LEBANON

The vast majority of the recent studies on dollarization deal with Latin American countries, and a smaller proportion look at Eastern Europe and the former Soviet Republics. Lebanon is hardly ever mentioned in theoretical or empirical studies investigating currency substitution in different parts of the world. However, currency substitution has been on the research agenda of Lebanese economists since the very beginning of the experienced crisis (Osseiran 1987; Saidi 1986).

One of the major difficulties faced with studies that look at partial dollarization is the issue of data availability. Indeed, much of the developing world and the so-called emerging markets have no accurate and detailed data regarding the use of FC. Lebanon has a significant amount of data available through its Central Bank the Banque du Liban (BDL) and other private banks. One could possibly ascribe this fact to the open and liberal economic culture of Lebanon, and the fact that very early on in its history (after World War II), Lebanon had free capital flows. Moreover, the advanced and developed status of the banking industry in Lebanon has helped in the creation of relevant databases, which would have otherwise been absent.

The data upon which this study is based have been retrieved from the Central Bank of Lebanon, the Ministry of Finance, the Association of Lebanese Banks, and the Bank Audit Research Department. Most of the sources are not always clear enough about the definitions they use, and on many instances one could observe significant differences in estimates. Nevertheless, the data are available and are clear enough to allow a fairly accurate analysis.

Like most other developing countries, Lebanon has no data on the FC in circulation. Indeed, it is very hard to find out exactly how much foreign currency paper money (or FC) is being used by citizens. However, Lebanon has enough data, covering at least the last decade, on FC deposits in the domestic banking system, liabilities, and external public debt.

The simplest starting point for an analysis of dollarization in Lebanon is the ratio of FC deposits to total deposits in the domestic banking system. This ratio reflects the nature of liquidity within the banking system. Figure 7.1 depicts the ratio of FC deposits by the non-financial sector in commercial banks to the total deposits of the non-financial sector.

Figure 7.1 shows that FC deposits have been significant in relative terms even before the war. Indeed, free capital flows and an open economy may be held responsible for this. We observe that the ratio of FC deposits to total deposits registered its most significant rise during the war (1983 onwards), reaching its peak of 93 per cent in November 1987. While the economic history that coincides with this chart is fascinating in its own right, the focus here is on the post-war period, namely between 1992 and 2005. We observe that in 1992 the deposit dollarization ratio reached a second peak of 87 per cent. The high inflation rates witnessed during that year (reaching 120 per cent) could explain the ratio's upward jump.

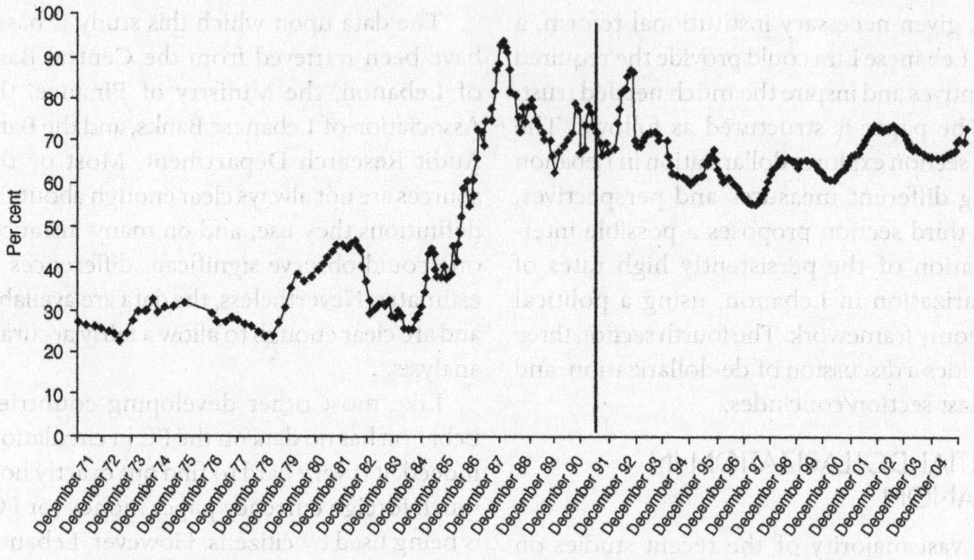


Figure 7.1: Deposit Dollarixation, FC Deposits / Total Deposits of the Non-financial Sector, 1971–2005

*Data Source:* Banque Du Liban

With the advent of the Rafiq Hariri government, the use of the US$ as an anchor currency for the LBP, and the Horizon 2000 project for reconstruction and development, the ratio declined consistently to reach 55 per cent in April 1997.

The ratio of deposit dollarization rose again after 1997 to reach a level of 70 per cent in January 2005. Interestingly, this was not far from the level it had reached in February 1992 (74 per cent). While the reversal in 1997 has been explained by the Asian financial crisis and the turmoil that followed in international financial markets, the full circle is indicative of the inability of the post-war governments to establish the necessary level of credibility. There are many possible reasons behind the inability of the LBP to regain its place in the economic and financial life of the country. Suffice it to say at this point that the LBP today seems as marginal as it was in 1992.

Before exploring other measures of dollarization, a possible issue of concern must be addressed regarding the source of the FC deposits. Indeed, given banking secrecy laws, remittances received from the Lebanese diaspora, and other regional investments, it is interesting to find out what proportion of these FC deposits belong to non-residents. Figure 7.2 depicts the proportion of FC deposits by non-residents.

We observe a clear pattern of decline during the civil war period (between the bars). Non-resident FC deposits declined from the 30 per cent level before the war to the 7 per cent level in 1991, rising thereafter. However, the rise in non-resident FC deposits did not reach pre-war levels, and currently stands at 21 per cent of total FC deposits by the non-financial sector. Note that total FC deposits have grown from US$ 11.4 billion in January 1997, to US$ 39.8 billion in January 2005. Thus, FC deposits by residents and by non-residents have both been rising in value terms.

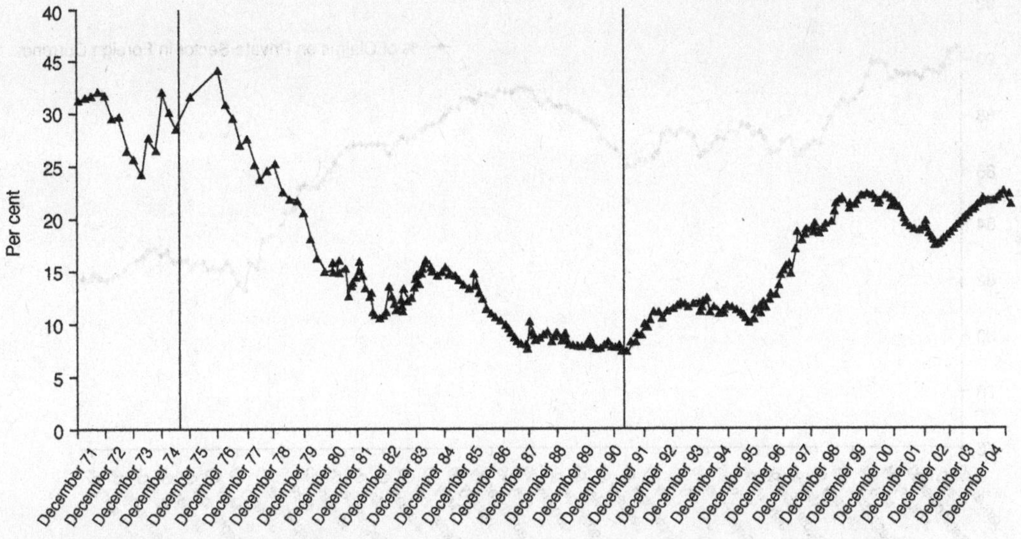


Figure 7.2: Proportion of Total FC Deposits by Non-Residents, 1971–2005

*Data Source:* Banque Du Liban

The second measure we use is LD. Liability or debt dollarization concerns both the private and public sectors. To assess private sector LD we explore FC claims on the private sector as a share of total claims on the private sector. Naturally, this is a domestic measure as it is based on commercial bank data extracted from the Central Bank archives. Figure 7.3 depicts the ratio over the last 12 years.

While it is widely understood that deposit and liability dollarization would mirror each other to some extent, Figure 7.3 reveals that the ratio for domestic private sector LD is much higher and in January 2005 stood at around 82 per cent. LD can indeed be a significant source of instability, and in case of possible devaluation, it could cause waves of bankruptcy. This is the case for businesses and individuals whose income is in local currency, but loan payments (interest and principal) are in FC. In other words, LD is a potential source of systemic crisis. In Lebanon, the ratio of domestic private sector LD has been above 80 per cent throughout the last 12 years, and above 86 per cent until 2001.

Public sector LD can be measured by the external public debt as a share of total net public debt. Indeed, this ratio reveals the extent to which the public sector will need FC in order to repay its financial obligations. Figure 7.4 depicts the ratio of external public debt to total net public debt. We observe that the ratio is high and has been rising throughout the last decade.

The external public debt ratio was 55 per cent in January 2005. The true meaning of this ratio can only be understood if one looks at the external public debt as a share of GDP. Figure 7.5 depicts external debt and total net public debt as a share of GDP. In 2004, external debt stood at 84 per cent of GDP, and total net public debt stood at 166 per cent of GDP. Note that both curves seem to be relatively stable in 2004.[4]

[4]This is explained by the liquidity provided by the Paris II Conference and the easing of debt issuing requirements (*BDL, Quarterly Bulletin, Q4*, 2003)

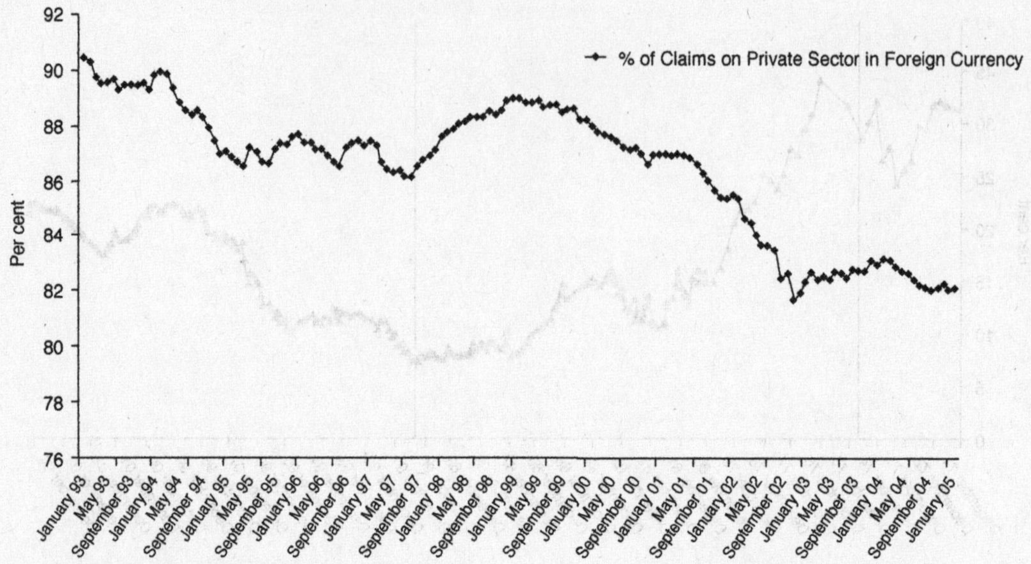


Figure 7.3: Percentage of Claims on Private Sector in FC, Commercial Banks, 1993–2005

*Data Source:* Banque Du Liban

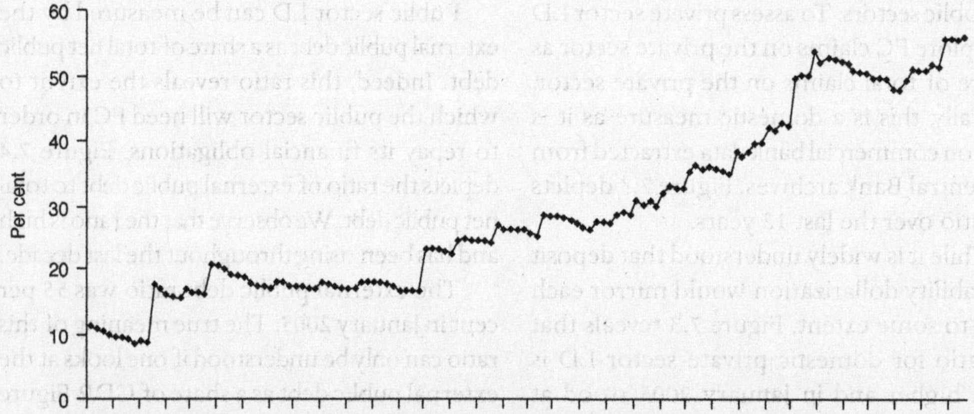


Figure 7.4: External Public Debt as a Share of Total Net Public Debt, 1993–2005

*Data Source:* Banque Du Liban

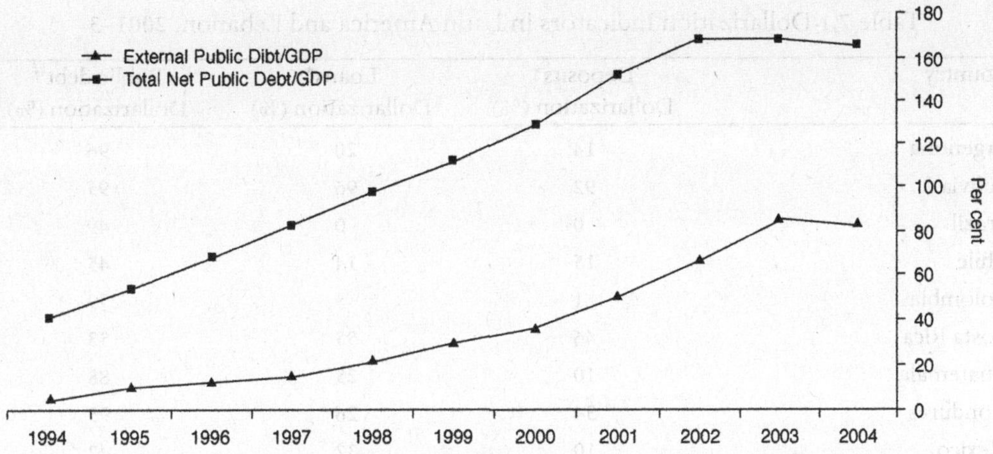


Figure 7.5: External Public Debt as a Share of GDP, Total Net Public Debt as a share of GDP, 1994–2004

*Source:* Banque Du Liban, Bank Audi Research Department.

To sum up the measures explored here, we observe that in January 2005 Lebanon had 70 per cent deposit dollarization, 82 per cent private LD, 55 per cent public LD, and an external debt that stood at 84 per cent of GDP (2004). Moreover, we also observed that, (i) current levels of deposit dollarization date back to the war years following the mid-1980s; (ii) even though the deposit dollarization ratio fell in the early 1990s, reaching 55 per cent in April 1997, there was a reversal and it increased 1992 levels in 2005; (iii) private LD, while declining, stayed high above the 80 per cent for much of the decade; (iv) public LD rose steadily in the post-war era, starting off around 10 per cent in the early 1990s, reaching 55 per cent in early 2005, and the same can be said of the external public debt as a share of GDP.

For a comparative perspective on these ratios, Table 7.1 compares the above discussed dollarization indicators for Latin America and Lebanon (adopted from Galindo and Leiderman 2005).

Highly geared and highly dollarized, the Lebanese economy seems to be a singular case of dollarization when compared to other countries in Latin America where the recent debate on full dollarization is centred. Indeed, Lebanon seems to be even a better candidate for full dollarization than most of the Latin American countries. We observe in Table 7.1 that in terms of deposit dollarization, Lebanon ranks 5th for the period mentioned. In terms of loan dollarization, Lebanon ranks 2nd alongside Nicaragua. In terms of public debt dollarization, Lebanon ranks last. However, it should be noted that the ratio increases drastically in the years following 2001 and 2002, reaching 55 per cent in early 2005.

This section explored dollarization in Lebanon using a number of different measures, and found Lebanon to be amongst the most

Table 7.1 Dollarization Indicators in Latin America and Lebanon, 2001–3

| Country | Deposits* Dollarization (%) | Loans* Dollarization (%) | Public debt# Dollarization (%) |
|---|---|---|---|
| Argentina | 14 | 20 | 96 |
| Bolivia | 92 | 96 | 95 |
| Brazil | 0 | 0 | 49 |
| Chile | 15 | 14 | 45 |
| Colombia | 1 | 5 | 59 |
| Costa Rica | 46 | 55 | 53 |
| Guatemala | 10 | 25 | 88 |
| Honduras | 34 | 26 | 95 |
| Mexico | 10 | 32 | 42 |
| Nicaragua | 71 | 84 | 98 |
| Paraguay | 64 | 57 | NA |
| Peru | 74 | 79 | 92 |
| Uruguay | 85 | 61 | 96 |
| Venezuela | 0 | 1 | 67 |
| Average LAC | 37 | 40 | 75 |
| Average other emerging mkts@ | 22 | 19 | 39 |
| Lebanon | 70 | 84 | 31** |

*Notes*: *USD deposits/Total deposits and USD loans/total loans in the domestic financial system. Data for 1999, 2001, 2002, 2003; Source: Arteta (2003), Honohan (2003), and Bank Superintendencies. #USD debt/total public sector debt. Data for 2001 and 2002; Source: Calvo, Izquiedero, and Mejia (2003) and Central Banks and Finance Ministries. @Includes: Bulgaria, Czech Republic, Hungary, Israel, Korea, Malaysia, Morocco, Nigeria, Philippines, Poland, Rusiia, Slovak Republic, Thailand, and Turkey.
*Author's Note*: Data for Lebanon is the average for years 2001, 2002, and 2003 for deposit and loan indicators, and 2001 and 2002 for Public Debt indicator. **Note that public debt dollarization had reached 55 per cent by 2005.
*Source*: Galindo and Leiderman (2005).

highly dollarized countries in the developing world. The following section explores a possible explanation to the persistently high rates of dollarization in peacetime, and after inflation rates had been tamed.

## PERSISTENT DOLLARIZATION: AN INTERPRETATION

While relative macrostability and low/declining inflation rates were achieved in the early 1990s, dollarization has proven to be hard to reverse. Figure 7.6 depicts the inflation rate (right axis) and the exchange rate (left axis) between 1991 and 2004. We notice that inflation was in the single digit range since 1994, and steadily declining after 1995, reaching –0.4 in 2000 and 2001. The exchange rate reached a more stable level by 1993, declining and stabilizing from 1994 onwards. Indeed, pegging the LBP to the US Dollar was one of the crucial macro-stabilization policies adopted by the central bank since the early-1990s. The system

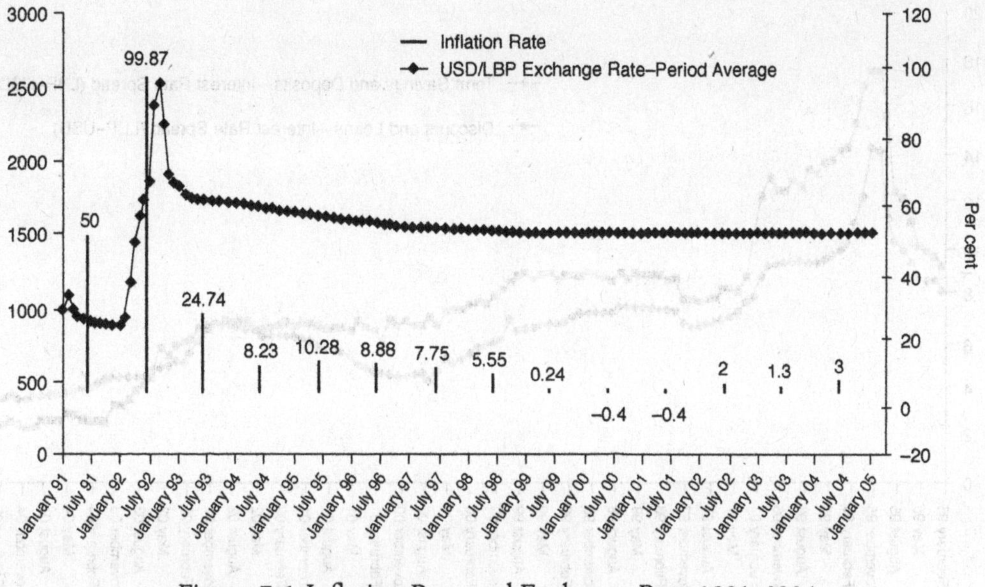


Figure 7.6: Inflation Rate and Exchange Rate 1991–2004

*Notes*: Inflation rate is yearly and in percent; Exchangerate is LBP/US$ (monthly) and value is given.
*Data Source*: Rate is LBP/US$ (monthly) and value is given
*Source:* Banque Du Liban.

looks like a hard peg at 1507 LBP for 1US$ after 1997.

Figure 7.7 depicts the interest rate spread between LBP and US$ interest rates on term deposits/savings, and loans in commercial banks. Adjusting for inflation, LBP savings and term deposit accounts earn higher returns than US$ accounts. Given a fixed exchange rate, this spread should, in principle, encourage LBP savings. However, this is not what happens for the simple fact that US$ lending rates are actually much lower than LBP lending rates (the spread is also positive). Under a fixed exchange rate regime, an LBP account holder and a US$ account holder will both opt for US$ denominated loans, as they are cheaper than LBP loans.

It is argued here that this difference is a major factor in the high LD rates observed in the second section. It makes no sense to borrow in LBP, even if you are earning in LBP, when you can get the same loan and pay less in US dollars, given fixed exchange rates. Naturally, this situation implies high bankruptcy risk for the borrowers with LBP income, as a possible devaluation will curtail, and might destroy, their ability to repay the US$ loan. Moreover, such a situation exposes bank balance sheets to higher risks, given the exposure to borrowers with income/liability currency mismatches. As long as LBP interest rates are higher than US$ interest rates, LD is here to stay. In fact, continued dollarization is partly due to the combined effect of inflation targeting, exchange rate stability maintained by a peg, and high real domestic interest rates relative to the anchor currency. Simply put, it is impossible to expect higher LBP loans, and

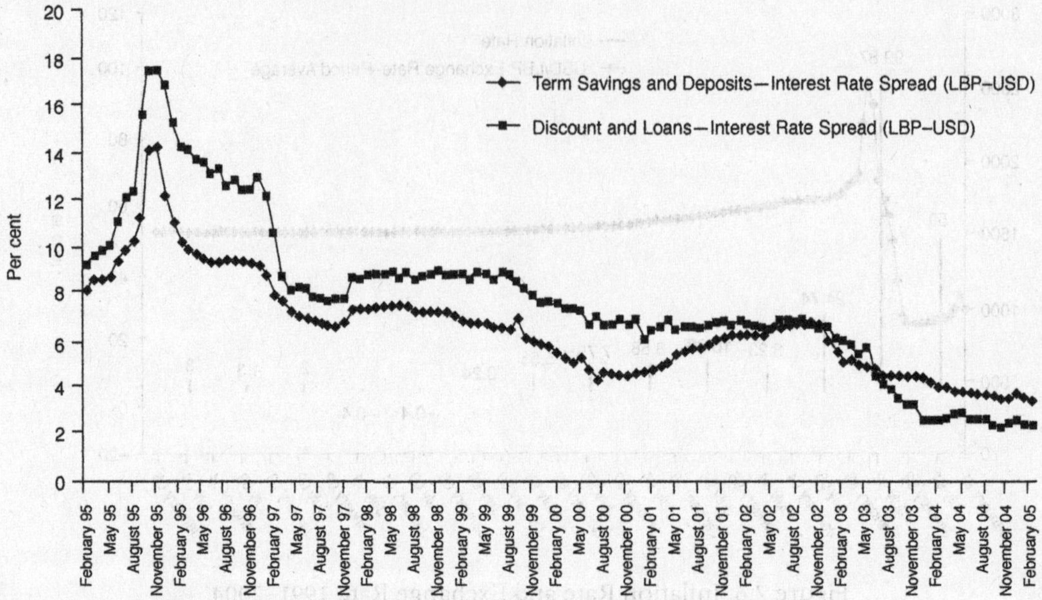


Figure 7.7: Term Savings and Deposits, and Discount and Loans—Interest Rate Spreads, 1995–2005

*Data Source*: Banque Du Liban.

thus new LBP deposits, and then new loans and new deposits, if it is more expensive to borrow in the local currency.

While this argument is valid, the discussion above does not exhaust the reasons behind the persistently high rates of deposit and liability dollarization. Using a political economy framework of analysis, we propose that the persistent dollarization in Lebanon is a market response that aims at protecting private wealth from the potentially damaging actions of an unfree and co-opted State.[5] Indeed, the underlying credibility issue, which led to the starting of the process, is far from solved.

Looking back, the evolution of Lebanese monetary structures reveals a very close historical connection with Syrian monetary structures. Indeed, it was only in 1964 (Code of Money and Credit) that Lebanon witnessed the establishment of an independent Central Bank (Oughourlian 1982). Prior to 1964, Lebanon had two major phases of monetary history (post-WWI). The first period extending from 1919 to 1924, coincided with the French mandate. During this time, Lebanon's monetary unit was the Syrian Pound issued by the The Banque De Syrie, a French company affiliate of the Ottoman Bank.[6]

The second stage spanned the period 1924–64. In 1924, the Lebanese and Syrian states negotiated with the Banque du Syrie, which

[5]Melvin (1998) considers dollarization in Latin America as a market imposed monetary reform.

[6]Of the 510,000 shares of BDS, about 22 per cent were owned by the Ottoman Bank, and 78 per cent by French shareholders.

later on became Banque du Syrie and du Liban (BSL), and granted BSL the sole right to issue the French Franc based Lebanese Syrian currency in Lebanon and Syria. By 1937, BSL had the right to issue a Lebanese currency in Lebanon. Between 1937 and 1964 there were two series of notes, one with the name 'Liban' (Lebanon) and the other 'Syrie' (Syria). However, Lebanon moved towards monetary independence after gaining independence in 1943. By 1949, the Lebanese currency was freed from the French Franc, and by 1964, Lebanon had established its independent central bank, the BDL.[7]

Not long after the establishment of monetary independence in 1964, Lebanon was plunged into a civil war (1975), which led to the eventual collapse of the currency in the mid-1980s. Emerging from almost two decades of destruction, in 1989, different Lebanese factions agreed to the Taef Agreement that established new principles for a new Lebanon. With the end of hostilities in 1990–1, Lebanon took its first steps towards real peace. However, the continued Syrian military presence since 1976, and the ensuing intervention in the affairs of government resulted in a State apparatus that was run according to Syrian priorities. At the same time, the fragmented and sectarian nature of government institutions (and power) further eroded the possibility of a unified, free, and efficient public sector. Sectarian interests and elites have also played a crucial role in perpetuating vertical patron-client relationships.[8] A weak institutional framework, vested interests, and sectarian rent-seeking have made the post-war state not only unfree, but also a co-opted state that served private and fractional interests rather than the welfare of all its citizens.

The collapse of the currency during the war (1980s), which was a result of excessive monetization of public debt, led to the high dollarization rates in deposits (reaching 90 per cent in 1987; see discussion in the second section). With an entrenched liberal economic culture, high levels of openness to the world economy, and free capital flows after World War II, Lebanon's private sector has reacted to the lack of discipline and rigour in macroeconomic management through dollarization. Moreover, dollarization was a response to the collapse of state structures into the hands and pockets of sectarian interest groups, which led to further erosion of government credibility and public trust in monetary and other policies of the State.[9]

Indeed, the end of the civil war did not imply true and complete autonomy due to the continuing Syrian influence and intervention in the domestic affairs of the State. Thus, the post-war Lebanese state was still an unfree state, and very much at the mercy of private and sectarian interest groups. Therefore, there has not been any true incentive or attempt to de-dollarize, independent of the fixed and other costs of financial adaptation.

However, recent socio-political developments, which were triggered by the assassination of the former Prime Minister Rafiq Al Hariri on 14th of February 2005, ushered in a new era for Lebanon. The massive demonstrations against the Syrian presence, and the eventual departure of Syrian military troops and intelligence services, prepared the ground

[7]This was done through the Code of Money and Credit enacted by decree No. 13513 dated 1 August 1963. The BDL started effective operation on 1 April 1964.

[8]Acosta (2001) raises the issue of self-seeking and incompetent elites as a possible explanation to the adoption of full dollarization in Latin America.

[9]Melvin (1998) also looks at dollarization as a market imposed condition.

for the recently completed parliamentary elections. Symbolizing national unity, although not necessarily complete and flawless, the 2005 elections are beyond any doubt the beginning of the future. Indeed, Lebanon could be facing a singular opportunity to set things right and introduce the appropriate institutional reforms in order to embark on a sustainable process of development. While the legitimacy aspect of the Lebanese State has been more or less restored after the departure of Syrian troops, the fact remains that sectarian rent seeking, vertical patron–client relationships, and weak institutions undermine the development of cohesive developmental policies. Thus, a local consensus based on the eventual abolishment of sectarian government could signal the second stage of Lebanon's fight for freedom, whereby the state and its citizens enter a new type of a relationship by dismissing the middlemen—the sectarian elites.[10]

If the appropriate reforms and policies are implemented, Lebanon could well see a reversal in the conditions that triggered dollarization. This paper suggests that the choice is a Lebanese one, and requires a new partnership between the private and public sectors. The latter should be able to exercise its power with discipline and efficiency, and the former should choose to trust and compete in an open and fair environment.

## WHY DE-DOLLARIZATION?

The debate on the costs and benefits of dollarization has revealed intense disagreements. Advocates of dollarization perceive it to be a better alternative to macroeconomic mismanagement and wealth-destroying policies by central banks. Critics of dollarization identify heavy costs with the loss of the local currency (discussed in the first section).

Advocates of dollarization suggest that countries with weak currencies are better off with dollarization, which is perceived as the least 'bad' alternative for countries whose attempts at macrostability and growth have yielded no tangible results. Dollarization is said to reduce transaction costs in international trade. Indeed, based on the Optimal Currency Area Theory developed by Mendell and McKinnon, dollarization could increase international trade flows by reducing the costs of transacting (Rose 2000).

The basic unit of analysis for advocates of dollarization is the individual. Proponents discuss the 'One Nation / One Money myth' (Cohen 1998; Schuler 2000), and propose a different perspective on money. Indeed, Schuler (2000) proposes the idea of free banking versus central banking, and argues that individual consumers should have the freedom to choose amongst alternative currencies. This freedom becomes particularly relevant when a weak local currency threatens the wealth and future of citizens.[11]

For the opponents of dollarization, the unit of analysis is the nation-state. A major part of the argument alongside the economic costs of

[10]The July 2006 war between Israel and Hisbollah (Sectarian militant political faction) in the south of Lebanon has provided ample proof of the unfree and co-opted nature of the Lebanese State. Indeed, this state had no real authority over its land, and sectarian political factions have shown greater military strength than the state army.

[11]The recently observed de-territorialization of money, that is the breaking down of the state monopoly on money through the growth of pseudo-currencies and money substitutes seems to indicate that new ways of thinking on money and monetary policy will emerge in the near future. However, it is far too early to advise emerging markets to give up their local currencies for a future that is yet to be created. Moreover, for a free banking system to emerge in the future there are many political barriers that need to be broken.

dollarization, which will be discussed further, is the historical evolutionary analysis of the currently strong currencies such as the US Dollar and the British Sterling. If one looks back at 19th century America, one observes how multiple bank notes and a chaotic banking system were organized and developed through the imposition of the US dollar as the only legal tender. Similar experiences have been observed in England. The development of formal and informal institutions, and the protection of property rights by the State have been crucial determinants of economic development in the United Kingdom and elsewhere (Schuler 2000).

Dollarization, as argued by critics, has significant costs as well. The first being the loss of seignorage revenue. Net seignorage is the difference between the cost of putting money in circulation or printing, and the value of the goods that the money can buy. Seignorage applies to all notes and coins and to bank reserves—that is, to the whole monetary base. Thus, by giving up the local currency, monetary structures are deprived of a significant segment of revenues, which now accrue to the foreign central bank (Fischer 1982; Berg and Borensztein 2000).

Another important argument against dollarization is based on a critique of fixed exchange rates. Flexible exchange rates are perceived to act as a buffer zone, isolating the local economy from potentially destabilizing shocks. Dollarization, however, leads to an unnecessary exposure to the adopted FC and potential shocks to the foreign economy. The loss of monetary independence has other implications for the monetary authorities. Under full dollarization, there is no room for counter-cyclical monetary policy (Sachs and Larrain 1999).

One of the most important and convincing arguments made by opponents of dollarization concerns the fact that dollarization is being advised to emerging markets when no real evidence exists that it fulfills its promises (Edwards 2001). Moreover, dollarization removes the money printing powers of the state, but does not guarantee fiscal discipline. Indeed, the initial institutional factors that lead to dollarization must still be addressed. Edwards suggests that not much is known about the performance record of dollarized countries, and dollarization cannot be prescribed blindly (Edwards 2001).

While the debate on the costs and benefits of dollarization is a subject of research in its own right; this paper suggests that the eventual conclusion regarding dollarization is based on domestic variables, local institutional development, and monetary and fiscal reform. More specifically, this study proposes yet another reason or rationale for de-dollarization. This argument is borne out of the insights brought forth by institutional economics.

Any community with a certain level of organized life could become an economy of its own, if it created structures that could print money. Indeed, the recent creation of the Euro zone is an example of how a new money printing structure can be created. I acknowledge, of course, that the Euro zone is itself a new experiment in the history of money printing structures. The factors that make the creation of such a powerful capacity possible are credibility, co-operation, and trust.

The planetary entities that print money, that is, states, manage the economic game of the local populace.[12] They manage the local economic game because they also print certificates of land ownership.[13] Indeed, real

[12]This is currently true despite the growing deterritorialization of money and the birth of private monies and money substitutes.

[13]Naturally, the printing of certificates of land ownership and currency is done through different state structures.

estate transactions imply the exchange of papers printed by the State. In truth, without the papers provided by the State, none of us would have anything to exchange. Leaving aside the metaphysical and philosophical ramifications of this thought, the economic implications are fascinating. Indeed, if trading is about exchanging rights, that is, pieces of paper, and those rights are defined and ascribed by the State, then the most important agents in today's globalized economy are the printing states. The successful printing states are those which take their responsibility seriously and develop the knowledge to print and spend with finesse and strategy.[14]

John Maynard Keynes once wrote that 'the political problem of mankind is to combine individual liberties, social justice, and economic prosperity'.[15] The printing state has a difficult task ahead. It must not only provide the papers to exchange, it must also set the rules, and tone of the game. A fair, free, and prosperous game is what all economies seek.

Shubik (2000, p. 1) describes fiat money as follows: 'Fiat money is a creation of both the state and society. Its value is supported by expectations which are conditioned by the dynamics of trust in government, the socio-economic structure and by outside events such as wars, plagues or political unrest'.

Thus, money in its basic abstract sense is the very symbol of societal trust. If a society/state is unable to have a currency of its own, or is unable to value its paper, the question could be one of macroeconomic policy regarding the exchange rate regime, but also a fundamental problem of economic identity and integrity. Indeed, dollarization is an example of the process through which a money structure absorbs the space and people of another money structure. Without trust, freedom, co-operation and credibility, no money printing structure can have an optimal performance. Only a successful state can create a successful market.

It is suggested here that de-dollarization is about reclaiming Lebanon's economic identity. Indeed, it is not about the exchange rate regime, no matter how important exchange rate policy is, but about the very existence and raison d'être of the Lebanese State/market as an economic entity or space.

There are three main reasons why de-dollarization is possible in Lebanon. The first is related to the causes that led to the high inflation rates and the resultant collapse of the currency in the mid-1980s. The high inflation rates which led to deposit dollarization were due to macroeconomic mismanagement in war times, not in peace times. This implies that under normalized conditions of life, people would have no reason to mistrust the intentions or goodwill of the policymakers. In other words, if trust in intentions is regained through the professional development of the public bureaucracy and policymakers, trust in competence would follow suit.

The second reason concerns human capital and technocratic know-how. Lebanon has the human resources that would make the thinking and implementation of sophisticated monetary and fiscal policies possible. While these human resources exist and are available to the state, they are hardly ever utilized in an organized manner. In other words, Lebanon has the human capital that could lead its economy into a better and more prosperous future. However

[14]It should be noted that other forms of money are being ignored here for convenience and clarity. Indeed, electronic forms of money can also be, at some level, be reduced to paper money. Moreover, all assets whether stocks, bonds, or any other, are expressed in the form of contractual agreements that are also written down on paper.

[15]John Maynard Keynes, *Essays of Persuasion*, 1932.

this is subject to bureaucratic reform, and the creation of professional performance standards within the public sector. In other words, the lack of trust of the Lebanese in the competence of their policymakers can be easily remedied.

The third reason why Lebanon should follow active de-dollarization policies is its very attachment to open markets and free trade. Simply put, a super fixed exchanged rate sounds contradictory to a Lebanese market-oriented economic philosophy. Indeed, a freely floating rate fits Lebanon's free market economics more naturally, than the fixed exchange rate which seems to be more the result of a 'fear of floating' (Reinhart et al. 2003).

However, true political and institutional reform must precede the de-dollarization policies, simply because dollarization is exactly a vote of no-confidence in the institutions and policies of the state. Subsequent to institutional reform, the elimination of rent seeking, corruption, and sectarianism, Lebanon has the human capital to manage its economic game with world standards of openness and freedom.

Once convinced of the necessity of de-dollarization, the question that arises next is: how to de-dollarize? I have suggested elsewhere (Papazian 2005) that a new Lebanese Lira can be the answer. It can provide the necessary incentives to elites and people, and it can inspire trust and confidence. However, the possible routes to de-dollarization are a subject of research in their own right and outside the scope of this paper.

## CONCLUSION

This study explored dollarization in Lebanon and revealed that Lebanon is amongst the most highly dollarized countries in the world. In January 2005, Lebanon had 70 per cent deposit dollarization, 82 per cent private LD, 55 per cent public LD, and an external debt that stood at 84 per cent of GDP (2004). Moreover, we also observed that (i) current levels of deposit dollarization date back to the war years following the mid-1980s; (ii) even though deposit dollarization fell in the early 1990s, reaching 55 per cent in April 1997, it reached 1992 levels in 2005; (iii) private LD, while declining, stayed high above 80 per cent for much of the decade; (iv) public LD rose steadily in the post-war era, starting off around 10 per cent in the early 1990s, reaching 55 per cent in early 2005, and the same can be said of the external public debt as a share of GDP.

Looking into a possible explanation of the persistently high rates of dollarization after inflation has been tamed, this study proposes that it is the unfree and co-opted nature of the post-war state that has led to the postponement of de-dollarization. The fact that the end of the civil war did not imply true and complete independence has been the crucial reason behind the continuous alienation people from the state. Moreover, the failure to abolish sectarian government and institutional power has led to the perpetuation of rent-seeking activities by certain interest groups. Thus, the sectarian elites have sought maximization of power rather than the welfare of citizens.

Following the recent socio-politican Transformations in Lebanon, the study identifies a unique opportunity for reform in Lebanon. The recent elections and the envisaged changes in local governance provide a special context to initiate de-dollarization policies. Moreover, the recent July 2006 war between Israel and Hizbollah has once again revealed the necessity of a legitimate, free, and non-sectarian state. Lebanon is a perfect candidate for de-dollarization for three main reasons: (i) the availability of highly skilled human capital; (ii) the fact that wartime macroeconomic mismanagement was the cause of dollarization and *not* chronic peacetime macroeconomic mismanagement, and finally (iii) Lebanon's free and open economic culture is best served by a floating exchange rate, rather than a hard peg.

While choosing between de-dollarization or the current status quo, the Lebanese have to keep in mind that the 'best' they could ever be to the US economy is a non-voting province, whereas the LBP can open the gates of locally created and managed prosperity. The recent elections and the hope to establish a technocratic, efficient, and representative government indicate that Lebanon might be faced with a once in a lifetime opportunity to set things right.

While outside the scope of this paper, I have suggested here that the issuing of a new Lebanese Lira might be the answer. Indeed, a new Lira can be a powerful incentive to the elites, the people, the government, and all stakeholders to engage and re-engage in the building of a non-sectarian state. Moreover, it could act as a catalyst for trust and confidence, and offer an opportunity for a new beginning. Yet again, without institutional reform, a new Lira would be a simple paper change with no significant impact.

One of the most important economic functions of the nation state is the provision of a currency invested with everybody's trust. This tool of economic exchange and interaction is the key variable in the economic game of nation states. Indeed, money-printing structures can create prosperity if the currency they supply is trusted and respected by the people. However, states and governments can also distribute poverty. Also, they cannot manage the economic game of a nation/people, if citizens choose not to play. Thus, while governments must assume responsibility, the people must choose to trust.

Dollarization might be perceived to be the least bad alternative to macroeconomic mismanagement in the short term, but it is beyond any doubt the worst alternative to learning the tools of wealth creation in the long term. Moreover, the short-term freedom of consumers to choose from alternative currencies is soon replaced with a long-term frustration, as the adopted FC State does not consider them a relevant constituency.[16] Indeed, one day, the world may see fewer currencies as new regions and blocs are formed, following the example of Europe. However, dollarization without such economic and institutional arrangements to share power, benefits, responsibilities, and decision making can in no way lead to societal welfare.

## REFERENCES

Acosta, Alberto (2001), 'The False Dilemma of Dollarization,' Global Policy Forum, New York.

Alami, Tarik (2000), 'An Econometric Investigation of Dollarization in Egypt', *Journal of Development and Economic Policies*, Vol. 2, No. 2, June, pp. 7–24.

—— (2001), 'Currency Substitution Versus Dollarization: A Portfolio Balance Model', *Journal of Policy Modeling*, Vol. 23, No. 4, May, pp. 473–79.

Alesina, Alberto and Robert J. Barro (2001), 'Dollarization', *American Economic Review*, Vol. 91, No. 2, May, pp. 381–5.

Barajas, A. and A. Morales (2003), 'Dollarization of Liabilities: Beyond the Usual Suspects', IMF Working Paper No. 03/11.

BDL (2003), *Banque Du Liban*, Quaterly Bulletin, Q4.

Beckerman, P.L. (2001), 'Dollarization and Semi-

[16]Indeed, recent attempts at passing a Bill on Dollarization have failed in the US, and the US position on other countries adopting the US dollar as their legal tender is still in debate (Fidler 2000). The Bill spells out a formula for share Seignorage.

Dollarization in Ecuador', World Bank Working Paper, 2643, July.

Berg, A. and E. Borensztein (2000), 'The Dollarization Debate', *Finance and Development*, Vol. 37, No. 1, March, pp. 38–41.

Bogetic, Z. (1999–2000b), 'Seigniorage Sharing Under Dollarization', *Central Banking*, Vol. XI, No. 4, pp. 77–87.

____ (2000a), 'Full Dollarization: Fad or Future?', *Challenge*, Vol. 43, No. 2, March-April, pp. 17–48.

Calvo, Cuilleumo (1996), *Many Exchange Rates and Output*, MIT Press, Cambridge, Massachusets.

Calvo, G. A. and Carlos A. Vegh (1992), 'Currency Substitution in Developing Countries: An Introduction', International Monetary Fund Working Paper 92/40, May.

____ (1993), 'Currency Substitution in High Inflation Countries', *Finance and Development*, Vol. 30, No. 1, March, pp. 34–7.

____ (1996), 'From Currency Substitution to Dollarization and Beyond: Analytical and Policy Issues', in Calvo (1996), pp. 153–75.

Chang, Roberto (1994), 'Endogenous Currency Substitution, Inflationary Finance, and Welfare', *Journal of Money, Credit and Banking*, Vol. 26, No. 4, November, pp. 903–16.

Chang, R. and A. Velasco (2001), 'Monetary Policy in a Dollarized Economy Where Balance Sheets Matter', *Journal of Development Economics*, Vol. 66, No. 2, December, pp. 445–64.

Clements, B. and G. Schwartz (1992), 'Currency Substitution: The recent experience of Bolivia', IMF Working Paper WP/92/65.

Cohen, B.J. (1998), *Geography of Money*, Cornell University Press, Ithaca and London.

De Nicolo, Fianni, P. Honohan, and A. Ize (2003), 'Dollarization of the Banking System: Good or Bad?', World Bank Policy Research Working Paper 3116.

Dibeh, Ghassan (2002), 'The Political Economy of Inflation and Currency Depreciation in Lebanon 1984–92', Middle Eastern Studies, Vol. 38, No.1, January, pp. 33–52.

Dornbusch, R. and A. Reynoso (1989), 'Financial Factors in Economic Development', AEA Papers and Proceeding, Perspectives on Economic Development, May.

Dornbusch, R., F. Sturzenegger, and H. Wolf (1990), 'Extreme Inflation: Dynamics and Stabilization', *Brooking Papers on Economic Activity*, Vol. 2, pp. 1–84.

Edwards, Sebastian (2001), 'Dollarization: Myths and Realities', *Journal of Policy Modeling*, Vol. 23, No. 3, April, pp. 249–65.

Eichengreen, Barry (2001), 'What Problems Can Dollarization Solve?', *Journal of Policy Modeling*, Vol. 23, No. 3, April, pp. 267–77.

Fidler, Stephen (2000), 'US Treasury Opposes Bill on Dollarization', *Financial Times*, 25 July.

Fischer, Stanley (1982), 'Seigniorage and the Case for a National Money', *Journal of Political Economy*, Vol. 90, No. 2.

____ (2001), 'Exchange Rate Regimes: Is the Bipolar View Correct?', *Journal of Economic Perspectives*, Vol. 15, No. 2, pp. 3–24.

Fontaine, Juan Andres (2000), 'Official Versus Spontaneous Dollarization', *Cato Journal*, Vol. 20, No. 1, Spring–Summer, pp. 35–42.

Galindo, Arturo and Leonardo Leiderman (2005), 'Living with Dollarization and the Route to Dedollarization', Research Department Inter American Development Bank and Tel Aviv University, Working Paper.

Giovannini, Alberto and Bart Turtelboom (1992), 'Currency Substitution', NBER Working Paper 4232, December.

Guidotti, Pablo E. (1993), 'Currency Substitution and Financial Innovation', *Journal of Money, Credit and Banking*, Vol. 25, No. 1, February, pp. 109–24.

Hale, David D. (1999), 'Should Argentina Dollarize? Part 2: No Way', *International Economy*, Vol. 13, No. 3, May-June, pp. 58–89.

Hetata, Sherif (1998) 'Dollarization, Fragmentation, and God', in Fredric Jameson and Masao Miyoshi (eds), *The Cultures of Globalization. Post-Contemporary Interventions Series*, Duke University Press, Durham and London, pp. 273–90.

Honig, Adam (2004), 'A Model of Liability Dollarization and Myopic Governments', Working Paper, Department of Economics, Amherst College.

Keynes, J.M. (1932), *Essays in Persuasion*, Harcourt Brace, New York.

LeBaron, Blake and Rachel McCulloch (2000), 'Floating, Fixed, or Super-Fixed? Dollarization Joins the Menu of Exchange-Rate Options', *American Economic Review*, Vol. 90, No. 2, May, pp. 32–37.

Levy-Yeyati, Eduardo and Federico Sturzenegger (2000), 'Is EMU a Blueprint for Mercosur?', *Cuadernos de Economia*, Vol. 37, No. 110, April, pp. 63–99.

Maynard, Geoffrey (1970), 'The Economic Irrelevance of Monetary Independence: The Case of Liberia', *Journal of Development Studies*, Vol. 6, No. 2, January, pp. 111–132 (Liberia)

Mendoza, Enrique G. (2001), 'The Benefits of Dollarization When Stabilization Policy Lacks Credibility and Financial Markets are Imperfect', *Journal of Money, Credit and Banking*, Vol. 33, No. 2, Part 2, May, pp. 440–74.

Melvin, Michael (1998), 'The Dollarization of Latin America as a Market-Enforced Monetary Reform: Evidence and Implications', *Economic Development and Cultural Change*, Vol. 36, No. 3, April, 543–8 (Latin America).

Melvin, Michael and Jerry Ladman (1991), 'Coca Dollars and the Dollarization of South America', *Journal of Money, Credit and Banking*, Vol. 23, No. 4, November, 752–63 (South America).

Melvin, Michael and Bettina Peiers (1996), 'Dollarization in Developing Countries: Rational Remedy or Domestic Dilemma?', *Contemporary Economic Policy*, Vol. 14, No. 3, July, pp. 30–40.

Mueller, Johannes (1994), 'Dollarization in Lebanon', International Monetary Fund Working Paper 94/129, October (Lebanon).

Ortiz, Guillermo (1983), 'Currency Substitution in Mexico: The Dollarization Problem', *Journal of Money, Credit and Banking*, Vol. 15, No. 2, May, 174–85, Mexico.

Osseiran, F. (1987), 'Currency Substitution in Lebanon 1977–1986', *Banque Du Liban Quarterly Bulletin*, No. 35.

Oughourlian, J. (1982), 'One Money, One state: A History of the Lebanese Currency', Eres.

Papazian, Armen V. (2005), 'Why Lebanon Needs a New Lebanese Lira', *The Certified Accountant*, LACPA, Beirut, Lebanon.

Portes, Richard and Helene Rey (1998), 'The Emergence of the Euro as an International Currency', National Bureau of Economic Research, Working Paper 6424, February.

Reinhart, Carmen, Kenneth Rogoff, and Miguel Savastano (2003), 'Addicted to Dollars', NBER Working Paper 10015.

Rose, Andrew (2000), 'One Money, One Market: Estimating the Efect of common currencies on Trade', Paper, Haas School of Business.

Sachs, Jeffrey and Felipe Larrain (1999), 'Why Dollarization is More Straitjacket than Salvation', Foreign Policy, Fall, pp. 80–92.

Saidi, N. (1986), 'Economic Consequences of the War in Lebanon', *Banque Du Liban, Quarterly Bulletin*, Nos. 28–30, pp. 5–17.

Shahin, N. Wassim and Fadi G. Freiha (2005), 'Hysterisis in Currency Substitution: The Middle East and North Africa', in Simon Neaime and Nora Colton (eds), *Renewal in Middle East Economics, Vol. 6, Money and Finance in the Middle East: Missed Opportunities or Future Prospects?* Elsevier, pp. 165–81.

Salvatore, Dominick (2001), 'Dollarization for the Americas? Editor's Introduction', *Journal of Policy Modeling*, Vol. 23, No. 3, April, 237–9.

Schuler, Kurt (1999), 'Encouraging Official Dollarization in Emerging Markets', Staff report, Office of the Chairman, Joint Economic Committee, U.S. Congress, April.

—— (2000), 'Basics of Dollarization', Staff Report Joint Economic Committee, US Congress, January.

Shubik, Martin (2000), 'The Theory of Money',

Cowles Foundation Discussion Papers 1253, Yale University.
Studart, Rogerio (2001), 'Dollarization: An Intellectual Fad or a Deep Insight?', Journal of Post-Keynesian Economics, Vol. 23, No. 4, Summer, pp. 681–61.
Uribe, Martin (1995), 'Hysteresis in a Simple Model of Currency Substitution', Board of Governors of the Federal Reserve System, International Finance Discussion Papers 509, May. (Published in *Journal of Monetary Economics*, Vol. 40, No. 1, September 1997, pp. 185–202.)
White, Lawrence H. (2000), 'Review of: The Geography of Money', *Journal of Economic Literature*, Vol. 38, No. 4, December, pp. 951–53.
Willett, Thomas D. (2001), 'Truth in Advertising and the Great Dollarization Scam', *Journal of Policy Modeling*, Vol. 23, No. 3, April, pp. 279–89.

# 8

# 'Good Governance' in Monetary Policy and the Negative Real Effects of Inflation Targeting in Developing Economies

GILBERTO A. LIBANIO*

## INTRODUCTION

The idea of governance has been applied in different contexts to explain economic events and to provide guidance to economic policy. 'Good governance'—either in terms of the behaviour of firms or in terms of government policies—is now recognized in academic circles and among international organizations as an important component of 'sound economic fundamentals'. As is well-known, the central principles of 'good governance' are the notions of transparency and accountability. When the concept is applied to the case of monetary policy, it usually supports the so-called 'new consensus'[1] and in particular the adoption of inflation targeting regimes.

There is no complete agreement on the definition of inflation targeting as a framework for monetary policy in the literature. However, in a general description, it involves the public announcement of a quantitative inflation target, an institutional commitment to price stability as the primary objective of monetary policy, a high degree of transparency in the decisions of policymakers, and the imposition of accountability on the central bank. This framework has received widespread attention from academic economists and policymakers since it was first adopted by countries such as New Zealand, Chile, and Canada in the early 1990s, and it has been used as a guideline to policy by a significant number of developed and developing countries in the last ten years.

Controversies and debates around monetary policy regimes are recurring themes in the history of economics. Just like other frameworks, inflation targeting has its supporters and its critics. The main advantages listed by the former group relate to the fact that inflation targeting provides a 'nominal anchor' to guide the actions of policymakers and the expectations of the public and, at the same time, allows for some discretion to adjust monetary policy in face of new information and unexpected events. The critics, in turn,

*The author would like to thank Jaime Ros, Amitava Dutt, and Jose Ricardo Costa e Silva for useful comments on an earlier draft. The usual disclaimer applies. Financial support from CNPq/Brazil and from the Kellogg Institute for International Studies is gratefully acknowledged.

[1]See Taylor (2000). For a criticism, see Lavoie (2002).

claim that inflation targeting may, in some circumstances place unnecessary constraints on the action of the central bank, and that the regime focuses excessively on inflation and does not pay sufficient attention to real outcomes. The empirical evidence available thus far does not help resolve the dispute. The performance of inflation targeters seems to be for the most part favourable, but it is also subject to controversy (as I discuss later in the chapter). Indeed, the dispute around the empirical evidence is not surprising, given the limited span of time in which the framework has been implemented.

The use of inflation targeting regimes by emerging market economies is a more recent phenomenon, which has its origins in the late 1990s. A growing literature has discussed the specific issues surrounding the adoption of the framework in these economies.[2] Some of the main challenges for the conduct of monetary policy in general—and the adoption of inflation targeting in particular—in developing countries are the magnitude of external shocks (such as 'sudden-stops' in capital inflows), large exchange rate volatility, and weaknesses in domestic financial sectors.

Despite the large theoretical and empirical literature on inflation targeting in both developed and developing countries, it is clear that very little attention has been given to the influence of monetary policy on output growth rates. Although short-run effects on the output gap are discussed, medium-term and especially long-term considerations are virtually absent. This is hardly surprising, given that the inflation targeting framework is usually associated with the idea of money neutrality in the long run. As Bernanke et al. (1999) put it in their widely quoted book on inflation targeting: 'In the long run the only macroeconomic variable that the central bank can affect systematically is the inflation rate. It is unlikely that monetary policy can be used to reduce the unemployment rate *on average* over any substantial period of time' (Bernanke et al. 1999, p. 14).

In other words, inflation targeting can be seen as the latest representative of a tradition that excludes real variables from the set of possible influences of monetary policy. This tradition is ultimately based on the belief that there exists some sort of long-run equilibrium (natural) rate of output or employment that is independent of monetary variables. In this case, even if monetary policy is not neutral with respect to real variables in the short run, any attempt to systematically explore the short-run trade-off between inflation and output will lead to higher inflation rates and no permanent gains in terms of output.

The purpose of this chapter is to consider the prospects for the adoption of inflation targeting regimes in emerging market economies. In particular, it will focus on the case of three Latin American economies where inflation targeting regimes have been implemented, namely Brazil, Chile, and Mexico.[3] In Brazil, an inflation targeting mechanism has been in operation since mid-1999, after the abandonment of the quasi-fixed exchange rate regime that was the basis of the real stabilization plan (1994–9). Chile was one of the pioneers in the adoption of inflation targeting (1990), but

[2]Chile is an early inflation targeter among developing countries (starting in 1990), but the Chilean monetary policy framework cannot be described as a pure case of inflation targeting during the whole decade. I will address this point later. On the Chilean experience, see Blejer et al. (2000, ch. 8) and Schmidt-Hebbel and Werner (2002).

[3]In Latin America, besides Brazil, Chile, and Mexico, inflation targeting has also been adopted by Colombia and Peru. However, these cases will not be discussed here.

this was also accompanied by an exchange rate target until 1999. In Mexico, the adoption of inflation targeting was gradual, and the first steps in this direction were taken in the aftermath of the Tequila Crisis (1994–5). Since 1999, the inflation target has been the major guide to monetary policy in Mexico.

One of the main issues to be addressed in this study is the pro-cyclical character of monetary policy under inflation targeting, especially in developing countries with liberalized capital accounts and flexible exchange rates. In addition, the paper will discuss whether (and how) pro-cyclical monetary policies may bring about negative effects on output and employment in the long run. It will be argued that not only is monetary policy pro-cyclical under inflation targeting, but also that it is likely to react in an asymmetric way to fluctuations in economic activity and exchange rates (too 'tight' during recessions, not so 'loose' during expansions). Such a pattern may generate a downward bias in aggregate demand, with negative long-run real effects on output growth.

Two qualifications to this argument are necessary. First, pro-cyclical monetary policy in developing countries does not occur only under inflation targeting regimes. It is also a feature of countries with fixed exchange rates and open capital accounts, and in which monetary policy is mainly conditioned by international capital flows. Second, this paper does not argue that inflation targeting should not have been adopted by any developing country, or that any specific country would be better-off by not adopting the regime. It just explores some important (although often neglected) features of the regime in a few countries where inflation targeting was actually implemented.

The remainder of this chapter is organized as follows. The next section will review the main features of the inflation targeting framework and the rationale behind its adoption. In the following sections, I will focus on the case of emerging market economies, and discuss the additional problems and challenges faced by these economies with respect to macroeconomic policies. Further the pro-cyclical and asymmetrical nature of monetary policy will be analysed, and the possible long-run effects on output and employment will be considered. Finally, a specification for testing whether monetary policy has been pro-cyclical and asymmetrical in Brazil, Chile, and Mexico under inflation targeting will be outlined, and some results will be presented.

## THE INFLATION TARGETING FRAMEWORK

Inflation targeting as a framework for monetary policy in a general sense, involves the public announcement of a quantitative inflation target, an institutional commitment to price stability as the primary objective of monetary policy, a high degree of transparency in the decisions of policymakers, and the imposition of accountability on the central bank.

A slightly different definition is provided by Mishkin and Schmidt-Hebbel (2001, p. 3):

> Full-fledged inflation targeting is based on five pillars: absence of other nominal anchors, an institutional commitment to price stability, absence of fiscal dominance, policy instrument independence, and policy transparency and accountability.

In practice, it is fair to say that the design and implementation details of inflation targeting regimes vary widely across countries. Central banks have adopted different target price indexes, target horizons, escape clauses, and mechanisms of communication, evaluation, and accountability. Besides, inflation targeting regimes are accompanied by different arrangements for fiscal and exchange rate policies.[4]

The theoretical rationale behind the adoption of inflation targeting in many countries rests on three elements (Bernanke et al. 1999). First, as mentioned before, the idea of money neutrality in the long run. In this case, even if monetary policy is not neutral with respect to real variables in the short-run, any attempt to systematically explore the short-run trade-off between inflation and output will lead to higher inflation rates and no permanent gains in terms of output.

The second element in support of inflation targeting is the idea that the maintenance of low and stable rates of inflation is an important precondition for achieving other macroeconomic objectives, such as high rates of growth in the long run. In this case, the main arguments are: (i) inflation is harmful to economic efficiency because it can distort the production, investment, and consumption decisions of economic agents as they are unable to distinguish between changes in the general price level and those in relative prices; (ii) the effort to insulate agents from the effects of inflation has its own costs, 'including costs of attention and calculation as well as the cost of resources devoted to (for example) the development of alternative financial instruments' (Bernanke et al. 1999, p. 17). It is worth noting that this element is more controversial than the previous one (long-run money neutrality). In fact, there is empirical evidence suggesting that the negative effects are only important at very high levels of inflation, and are negligible at annual rates below 8 per cent or so (Sarel 1996).[5]

The third argument, and perhaps the most important one according to Bernanke et al. (1999), is that inflation targeting provides a nominal anchor to monetary policy. As a target rate of inflation communicates to the public the price level the central bank is aiming to achieve in the future, it provides a guide for expectations of financial markets and the general public, and a reference point to evaluate a posteriori whether the central bank has been able to accomplish the goals of monetary policy. This argument is thus related to two of the main aspects of inflation targeting regimes, namely transparency and accountability.

For one reason or another, inflation targeting frameworks in different forms have been adopted by several countries in the past years, and more countries are likely to move in the same direction. Truman (2003) lists the following countries as inflation targeters: Australia, Brazil, Canada, Chile, Colombia, Czech Republic, Finland, Hungary, Iceland, Israel, Korea, Mexico, New Zealand, Norway, Peru, Philippines, Poland, South Africa, Spain, Sweden, Thailand, and UK.[6]

After more than a decade of inflation targeting in the world, there is now an extensive empirical literature that evaluates how

[4] It is true, however, that the first condition outlined above by Mishkin and Schmidt-Hebbel (2001), rules out fixed exchange rate regimes, currency boards, or other arrangements in which the exchange rate is seen as the main anchor to expectations and inflation.

[5] See also Stanners (1993) for empirical evidence that suggests no correlation between inflation and growth rates.

[6] Some authors (for example, Ball and Sheridan 2003) also include Switzerland in the group of inflation targeters. Note also that Finland and Spain joined the Euro in the late 1990s and, therefore, have their monetary policy subordinated to the European Central Bank (that does not formally adopt the framework).

successful it has been. This question is not straightforward since (as is recognized by many authors in this literature), there are a few methodological points that require attention and which suggest that we should consider any inferences with caution. Some of the issues are the controversy surrounding the definition of inflation targeting and the choice of the sample, potential selection bias, possible equivalence of some aspects of inflation targeting and other monetary regimes, and simultaneous causation of inflation-targeting adoption and the performance of the economy.[7]

## INFLATION TARGETING IN DEVELOPING COUNTRIES

A growing number of developing countries have adopted the inflation targeting framework, particularly since the late 1990s—Brazil, Chile, Colombia, Czech Republic, Hungary, Israel, Mexico, Peru, Philippines, Poland, South Africa, South Korea, and Thailand. The specific details and the circumstances that led to the adoption of the framework vary from country to country. In some cases, the inflation targeting regime was implemented gradually, with the sequential introduction of the mechanisms that formally characterize the framework. In others, it was introduced rapidly, as a response to financial or currency crises that caused the abandonment of previous monetary arrangements and led to the search for new 'nominal anchors' for monetary policy.[8]

The empirical evidence concerning the performance of countries under inflation targeting is limited, given the fact that most of them have adopted the framework very recently. However, there is at this point a relatively large literature that discusses specific problems and challenges related to the design and implementation of inflation targeting mechanisms in emerging market economies. Mishkin (2004) provides a useful summary of the main institutional aspects of developing countries that should be considered in the formulation and execution of inflation targeting policies. These are: (i) weak fiscal and financial institutions; (ii) low credibility of monetary institutions; (iii) currency substitution and LD; and (iv) greater vulnerability to external shocks (particularly, 'sudden stops' of capital inflows).[9]

To a greater or lesser extent, such characteristics can explain some stylized facts about the behaviour of some macroeconomic indicators in emerging market economies after the adoption of inflation targeting. Fraga, Goldfajn, and Minella (2003) compare developed and developing inflation targeters with respect to the volatility of inflation, exchange rates, GDP growth and interest rates, as well as average rates of inflation and GDP growth. Their findings suggest that emerging market economies show higher volatility in all the variables considered, and these results are explained by a combination of fragile institutions and higher vulnerability to external shocks. It is interesting to note that the variability of

[7] A comprehensive review of the empirical literature on the performance of inflation targeters in the developed world is beyond the scope of this paper. See, for instance, Bernanke et al. (1999), Mishkin and Schmidt-Hebbel (2001), Neumann and Von Hagen (2002), Ball and Sheridan (2003).

[8] Among the three countries that will be discussed in this study, Chile and Mexico appear to belong to the first group, whereas Brazil fits better in the second group. I will return to this point later.

[9] On the effects of volatile capital flows in developing countries, see Ffrench-Davis (2003) and Ocampo (2003a, 2003b). On inflation targeting in emerging market economies, see also Blejer et al. (2000), Caballero and Krishnamurthy (2003), and Truman (2003).

interest rates is the variable that presents the greatest difference between developed and developing countries (the average of standard deviation is more than four times higher in the second group of countries). As I will argue in the next section, this result is related to the pro-cyclical character of monetary policy under inflation targeting in emerging market economies.

## INFLATION TARGETING AND PRO-CYCLICAL MONETARY POLICY

It is widely recognized that macroeconomic policies in developing countries tend to operate in a pro-cyclical way, and are strongly influenced by international capital flows (Ffrench-Davis 2003; Ocampo 2003a). The recent experience of emerging market economies and the financial and currency crises in the 1990s suggest that capital account cycles decisively affect domestic policies and are subject to high levels of volatility and contagion. Moreover, the rapid process of financial liberalization during the last decade seems to have increased the vulnerability of these economies to swings in the international capital markets.[10]

Concerning monetary policy, it can be shown that a pro-cyclical pattern may emerge in developing countries with liberalized capital accounts under different exchange rate arrangements. In case of fixed exchange rates, the explanation is straightforward, since monetary policy is passive to capital flows (according to basic open economy macroeconomic theory). Net inflows lead to expansionary monetary policy while net outflows lead to monetary contractions.[11]

The case of flexible exchange rates is more interesting for the purpose of this study, since it has been adopted by many developing countries in Latin America and elsewhere and is more commonly associated with the inflation targeting framework. In this paper, I will make a case that inflation targeting contributes to the pro-cyclical character of monetary policy in emerging market economies with liberalized capital accounts and flexible exchange rates. Most importantly, I want to argue that pro-cyclical monetary policies are not only caused by large external shocks or crises, but they are a feature of the regime even under 'normal' times and do not depend on the occurrence of significant capital inflows or outflows.[12]

So, the question to be addressed is: if monetary policy is pro-cyclical under inflation targeting, what mechanisms can explain such behaviour? First of all, country risk perception tends to increase when economic activity slows down. For instance, consider an emerging market economy in which fiscal revenues depend highly on value added taxes or other forms of taxation that are sensitive to economic activity. When the economy faces a recession or simply slows down, fiscal revenues tend to decline and it is likely that government expenses do not fall in the same proportion or

[10]Caballero and Krishnamurthy (2003) acknowledge the effects of 'sudden stops' in capital flows in emerging economies. In order to minimize the pro-cyclical character of monetary policy, they propose two alternatives, namely, a state-contingent inflation targeting regime and a target that overweighs non-tradable inflation.

[11]The case of 'fear of floating' (Calvo and Reinhart 2002), in which countries that are considered to have a flexible exchange rate regime do not allow their currencies to fluctuate freely, can also explain pro-cyclical monetary policies.

[12]But see also Calderon and Schmidt-Hebbel (2003), who argue that the ability to pursue countercyclical policies depends on the country-risk premium, that is, countries with low risk-premium would be able to do it, while the ones with high risk-premium would not.

with the same speed (for example, due to 'rigidities' in certain types of expenses or due to political constraints). Therefore, it is clear that the fiscal surplus tends to be reduced (or fiscal deficit tends to be amplified) and this may lead to an increase in country risk premium, given the lower capacity of the country to repay external debt. As the recent experience of emerging markets with flexible exchange rates has shown, an increase in country risk premium may lead to a change in the portfolio of private investors and, consequently, to the depreciation of the domestic currency. Depreciation, in turn, impacts the expectations of inflation in the next periods, due to increase in the price of tradable goods.[13] Under inflation targeting, the central bank would react to the rise in inflation expectations by tightening the monetary policy (that is, increasing interest rates), which would amplify the decline in economic activity by reducing private spending and also affecting public spending (since higher interest rates imply higher interest payments on existing public debt and the necessity to generate a higher primary surplus).[14]

In principle, the same mechanism would operate in periods of economic expansion: higher fiscal revenues would lead to a decrease in country risk premium and a consequent appreciation of the domestic currency. I would argue, however, that monetary policy does not operate in a symmetrical way under these circumstances. In other words, the central bank under inflation targeting would, in general, react more strongly to exchange rate depreciations than to exchange rate appreciations. The reason for this behaviour is the weight of inflation stabilization in the central bank's reaction function: when the domestic currency is depreciating, prompt reaction is needed if the inflationary effects of depreciation are to be offset; when the currency is appreciating, the deflationary effects are not counterbalanced with the same intensity, since they may help the central bank to achieve the target for inflation, especially in periods of disinflation or after the economy has suffered negative supply shocks. In sum, this asymmetric reaction is likely to occur in developing countries under inflation targeting and flexible exchange rates, and may generate a downward bias to aggregate demand which bring about negative long-run effects on output and employment.

It is interesting to note that inflation targeting per se, that is, the formal mechanism of announcing a target for inflation to guide expectations, the search for increasing transparency by the publication of inflation reports, and so on, is not the main problem. In principle, such a framework is also consistent with directing monetary policy towards real objectives such as output and employment. As many supporters (for example, Bernanke et al. 1999) have emphasized, inflation targeting does not imply a rigid monetary policy rule, and provides enough flexibility for the central bank to respond in various directions to changes in the environment. However, the problem is that, in practice, central banks under inflation

[13]For many countries, this impact occurs especially through the increase in prices of capital goods and intermediate goods (such as oil), since it affects the production costs of many sectors of the economy.

[14]There is a limiting case in which the reaction of the central bank can lead the system to divergent behaviour. This happens when the effect of the rise in interest rates on government debt leads to the perception that the debt trajectory is unsustainable and that the government will not be able to honour its payments. In this case, we would observe capital flight, further currency depreciation, leading to further increases in interest rates and so on. This is the classic example of 'fiscal dominance', and will not be explored here (see Blanchard 2004, for an analysis of fiscal dominance in the Brazilian economy).

targeting tend to place an increased focus on inflation and be less concerned with output fluctuations. As Benjamin Friedman (2002, p. 7) puts it:

> Notwithstanding the compatibility in principle of inflation targeting as a conceptual framework for implementing a monetary policy in which real outcomes matter as well as inflation, an observer who has paid attention to the last quarter century of debate about monetary policy is entitled to suspect that a powerful motivation for adopting this framework, at least in some quarters, is the hope that if explicit discussion of central bank's policy is carried out entirely in terms of an optimal inflation trajectory, concerns for real outcomes may somehow atrophy or even disappear from consideration altogether.

In fact, most of the discussion about monetary policy under inflation targeting is devoid of any explicit reference to real outcomes, except for the recognition that an increase in interest rates may cause a decline in aggregate demand in the short run, and this is one of the channels through which monetary policy may affect inflation. Mishkin (2002) provides a theoretical rationale for central bank behaviour under inflation targeting and argues that 'too much focus' on output fluctuations in discussion of monetary policy is likely to produce worse outcomes for output and inflation. This argument is based on two elements: (i) monetary policy that responds actively to output fluctuations tends to be sub-optimal, since it is hard to measure the output gap, and its theoretical concept is controversial; (ii) 'language which stresses output goals can make a central bank's communication strategy less effective and can thereby weaken monetary policy credibility' (Mishkin 2002, p. 1).

There is also empirical evidence which shows that central banks have become more focused on inflation after the adoption of inflation targeting. Cecchetti and Ehrmann (1999) compare central bank behaviour in 23 developed and developing countries, and find that inflation targeters exhibit an increasing aversion to inflation variability and decreasing aversion to output variability. Moreover, they show that inflation targeting countries were able to reduce inflation volatility at the expense of an increase in output variability. Minella et al. (2003) estimate a reaction function for the central bank of Brazil, and show that the monetary authority has reacted strongly to inflation expectations. At the same time, it is interesting to note that the coefficient on output gap is not statistically significant in most of the specifications.

In summary, it is clear that inflation targeting regimes imply a strong emphasis on inflation stabilization, with low concerns for real effects on output and employment. As discussed earlier, such central bank behaviour may generate a pro-cyclical and asymmetrical pattern on monetary policy and deepen economic contractions, especially in emerging market economies with liberalized capital accounts. This problem is minimized in a framework that assumes away the long-term real effects of monetary policy and, more generally, of aggregate demand fluctuations. However, as I argue in the next section, there are theoretical as well as empirical reasons to question this assumption.

## MONETARY POLICY, AGGREGATE DEMAND, AND LONG-TERM REAL EFFECTS

As mentioned before, the inflation targeting framework rests on a number of theoretical and empirical foundations. In particular, it depends on the assumption that long-term equilibrium of real variables is independent of nominal magnitudes, and that there is a given equilibrium trajectory to which the economy returns in the long run. In this case, the NAIRU 'is unaffected by the time path of the economy and (...) the rate of growth of the economy is in effect predetermined (or at least set on the supply side of the economy without influence from the demand side)' (Arestis and Sawyer 2002, p. 2) Moreover, it is implied that no long-run trade-off between inflation and unemployment exists, which leads to the well-known argument that there is nothing central banks can do about real variables in the long run.

This section questions the assumption of a unique and stable natural rate of unemployment and briefly presents theoretical and empirical evidence that aggregate demand, in general, and monetary policy, in particular, may have long-term effects on economic activity. In other words, I argue that the quasi-consensus among academic economists and central bankers about the ineffectiveness of monetary policy in the long run does not entirely reflect the theoretical knowledge and the empirical evidence on the issue. Therefore, this study espouses the concern expressed by Friedman (2002, p. 4): 'the evidence for the natural rate model has never been as strong as the prevailing consensus within the economics profession (not to mention the case for inflation targeting) has let on'.

We start by pointing out the concept of hysteresis.[15] In general, hysteresis in labour markets relates to the idea that the long-term equilibrium unemployment rate depends on the history of the actual unemployment rate. There are several reasons why this may happen, including the effects of unemployment on workers' skills and overall productivity, and the distinction between insiders and outsiders in the process of wage setting (Blanchard and Summers 1986). Hysteresis brings in path-dependence and, therefore, opens room for aggregate demand fluctuations to affect the long-term path of the economy.

Another possible way to explore aggregate demand effects on growth is to consider the existence of increasing returns to scale. In particular, Kaldorian models of growth assume increasing returns in manufacture and explain economic growth by a mechanism of mutual and cumulative causation between output growth and labour productivity (as described by the so-called Verdoorn's Law). Besides, the idea of increasing returns in macroeconomics is usually associated with the existence of multiple equilibria. In this case, as shown by Hahn and Solow (1995), macroeconomic policy can have permanent effects by affecting the equilibrium toward which the economy will eventually converge.

Dutt and Ros (2003) present a broad review of models in which aggregate demand contractions have long-term effects on output. Firstly, they analyse models in which the trend-reverting tendencies of the economy are weakened by some sort of path dependence, which change the long-run position of the economy itself. This includes the effects of hysteresis in labour markets, the existence of multiple equilibria associated with increasing returns to scale, and the effects of currency overvaluation in open economies with balance of payment constraints.

The second group of models presented by Dutt and Ros (2003) explore situations in which automatic adjustment tendencies are absent or offset, even if 'frictions' or 'rigidities' are removed from the economy. The reasons for non-convergence relate to: (i) regressive income redistribution due to changes in money

[15] The literature of hysteresis in economics is large and will not be reviewed here. References can be found in Blanchard and Summers (1986) and Cross (1995).

and prices, and consequent effects on the propensity to consume; (ii) negative effects of deflation on investment, due to increase in the real value of firms' debts; (iii) changes in expectations due to falling prices and wages, which can paralyze consumption or investment decisions in case of pervasive uncertainty; (iv) liquidity trap, which prevents further reduction in the interest rate and, therefore, prevents recovery of investments; and (v) endogeneity of money.

Lavoie (2002) focuses more directly on monetary policy, and uses a simple monetary model (that he calls 'new consensus model') in which the central bank sets the interest rate according to a Taylor rule. Lavoie (2002) changes one of the equations of the model by introducing path-dependence and allowing aggregate demand to have an impact on the actual growth rates in the long run. His justification for this procedure is very much in line with the arguments presented in this section.

> Fast growth rates of demand imply fast growth rates of output; the latter encourages learning by doing but also a fast pace of capital accumulation, which on its own drives up the rate of technical progress; faster growth rates also encourage potential workers to enter the workforce, and they also encourage foreign workers to immigrate to the area where growth proceeds at a faster pace. The two main components of the natural rate of growth, the growth rate of the labor force and the rate of technical progress, are thus positively linked to the rate of growth of demand (Lavoie 2002, pp. 13–4).

Using this amended model, Lavoie (2002) analyses central banking behaviour under inflation targeting. He shows that a temporary increase in interest rates (in response to deviations of inflation from the target) induces a permanent decline in the natural rate of growth and, therefore, that restrictive monetary policies have negative long-run effects on economic performance.

The critique to the assumption of a unique and stable natural rate of unemployment (and the associated idea of money neutrality) also finds support in empirical evidence.[16] Ball (1997) analyses the behaviour of unemployment in Europe during the 1980s, and argues that the non-accelaratin-inflatin rate of unemployment (NAIRU) has increased in most of the region during that decade. Moreover, he finds that countries which had longer disinflation periods and larger drops in inflation rates presented higher increases in structural unemployment. Ball (1997) concludes that the increase in the NAIRU is associated with tight monetary policies adopted to reduce inflation rates.

Leon-Ledesma and Thirlwall (2002) pursue a similar investigation by focusing on the endogeneity of the natural rate of growth. They estimate the sensitivity of the *natural* rate of growth to the *actual* rate of growth for 15 OECD countries over the period 1961–95. Their findings support the idea that the natural rate is endogenous to the actual rate of growth and, therefore, that aggregate demand may influence the performance of the economy in the long run. Ahmed and Rogers (2000) examine the effects of inflation on output, consumption, and investment using long-term US data (1889–1995). Their results suggest that a permanent unanticipated rise in inflation has a positive long-run effect on the three variables and is associated with an increase in the share of investment in GDP.

[16] Akerlof (2002) reviews empirical evidence on the natural rate of unemployment. He rejects the vertical long-run Phillips curve and asserts: 'Econometric evidence further suggests that the natural rate theory rests on shifty sand rather than bedrock' (Akerlof 2002, p. 420).

Ball and Croushore (2003) focus on the effects of monetary policy, and analyse the effects of changes in the US federal funds rate on output and inflation during the period 1968–95. They find that monetary policy has strong effects on real output, but that these effects are not so strong on expected output. They explain this result with a simple macroeconomic model with sticky prices, and show that monetary policy has real effects if agents systematically underestimate the effects of policy on aggregate demand.

## INFLATION TARGETING AND PRO-CYCLICAL MONETARY POLICY: AN EMPIRICAL ESTIMATION

This paper intends to test whether monetary policy has presented a pro-cyclical and asymmetrical behaviour in emerging economies that adopted the inflation targeting framework. In particular, it focuses on three of the Latin American economies where the framework was adopted: Brazil, Chile, and Mexico.

There is a growing literature (although not yet very extensive) that analyses the experience of inflation targeting in Latin America. The focus is usually on the behaviour of inflation, the influence on expectations, and the possible credibility gains associated with the strategy.

To the best of my knowledge, only a few studies provide empirical estimates on the pro-cyclical character of monetary policy in Latin America. Calderon and Schmidt-Hebbel (2003) analyse a panel of eleven emerging market economies over the period 1996–2002 (annual data). Their findings suggest that the cyclical character of monetary policy depends on country risk premium: policy is pro-cyclical when country risk is high and countercyclical when it is low.

Costa e Silva (2004) provides a test for pro-cyclical monetary and fiscal policy in Argentina, Brazil, Chile, and Mexico using annual data for the period 1970–2000. The focus of his study is the influence of capital flows on macroeconomic policy and the feedback effect of policy on capital flows, while no particular attention is given to inflation targeting. Costa e Silva (2004) finds that monetary policy has been pro-cyclical in three of the four countries analysed, and that it has been correlated to the fluctuations of international capital flows.

In this study, I analyse the pro-cyclical and asymmetrical character of monetary policy under inflation targeting by estimating the relationship between economic activity and interest rates. In other words, I want to evaluate how monetary policy has responded to fluctuations in output, especially during the downturn of the cycle. Since it is also expected that interest rates affect economic activity, this study will use a Vector Autoregression (VAR) model, in order to allow for these feedback effects. In the structural form, the model can be written as:

$$i_t = A_1 + \sum_{j=0}^{n} \alpha_{1j} \Delta y_{t-j} + \sum_{j=1}^{n} \alpha_{2j} \cdot i_{t-j} + B_1 X_t + \varepsilon_{1t} \quad (8.1)$$

$$\Delta y_t = A_2 + \sum_{j=1}^{n} \beta_{1j} \Delta y_{t-j} + \sum_{j=1}^{n} \beta_{2j} \cdot i_{t-j} + B_2 X_t + \varepsilon_{2t} \quad (8.2)$$

where $i$ represents short-term real interest rates (deflated by consumer price indexes), $y$ corresponds to the level of output, and X are the control variables, namely, changes in oil prices (to capture supply shocks) and in US interest rates (to capture changes in international liquidity).[17] In this case, a negative sign

[17] I have estimated the model with both control variables, with only one of them, and with none. In general, I used lagged values of the variables to allow for

for the parameters $\alpha_{1j}$ would suggest that monetary policy follows a pro-cyclical pattern, that is, the central bank tightens monetary policy in periods of declining economic activity.

On the other hand, by separating periods of expansion and contraction, I intend to assess the asymmetrical character of monetary policy, and verify whether the monetary authorities in Brazil, Chile, and Mexico have responded in different ways during various phases of the business cycle. This task will be accomplished by creating two dummy variables: (i) GOOD, which takes the value 1 in periods when GDP is above a linear trend, and 0 otherwise, and (ii) BAD, which is symmetrical to GOOD. By multiplying the dummy variables with the rates of growth in the three economies, I create two separate series describing 'good times' and 'bad times', and then proceed to estimate whether or not monetary policy has responded differently to booms and recessions. In this case, the resulting equations are as follows:

$$i_t = A_1 + \sum_{j=0}^{n} \alpha_{1j} \Delta yGOOD_{t-j} + \sum_{j=0}^{n} \alpha_{2j} \cdot \Delta yBAD_{t-j} + \sum_{j=1}^{n} \alpha_{3j} \cdot i_{t-j} + B_1 X_t + \varepsilon_{1t} \quad (8.3)$$

$$\Delta yGOOD_t = A_2 + \sum_{j=0}^{n} \beta_{1j} \Delta yGOOD_{t-j} + \sum_{j=0}^{n} \beta_{2j} \cdot \Delta yBAD_{t-j} + \sum_{j=1}^{n} \beta_{3j} \cdot i_{t-j} + B_2 X_t + \varepsilon_{2t} \quad (8.4)$$

$$\Delta yBAD_t = A_3 + \sum_{j=0}^{n} \delta_{1j} \Delta yGOOD_{t-j} + \sum_{j=0}^{n} \delta_{2j} \cdot \Delta yBAD_{t-j} + \sum_{j=1}^{n} \delta_{3j} \cdot i_{t-j} + B_3 X_t + \varepsilon_{3t} \quad (8.5)$$

a delayed response of monetary authorities to external shocks. Due to space constraints, not all the results are provided here, but can be made available upon request.

Since the implementation of full-fledged inflation targeting regimes in Brazil, Chile, and Mexico is fairly recent, I have used monthly data in order to have as many observations as possible. I have estimated the outlined model for the period when inflation targeting had been fully implemented in these economies (1999–2005). The proxies used for GDP are: (i) for Brazil: Industrial Production Index, from IBGE; (ii) for Chile: Monthly Economic Activity Index, from the Chilean Central Bank; (iii) for Mexico: Global Economic Activity Index, from INEGI. In the three cases, the series with seasonal adjustment were used. The data on the rates of interest are derived from the Central Banks of the three countries.

Before proceeding to the estimation, I checked for stationarity of the series using the Augmented Dickey–Fuller (ADF) test, and the null of unit roots was rejected at 10 per cent for all series. In addition, the choice of lags for the endogenous variables in the VAR was based on the Schwarz Information Criterion, which tends to be 'conservative' in terms of lag lengths. The same was also used for the choice of lags of control variables.

For the most part, the estimation provides support to the arguments presented in this chapter. In the case of Brazil, the negative coefficients on GDP growth in equation (8.1) suggest that monetary policy has been pro-cyclical under inflation targeting. The results regarding the asymmetric behaviour of monetary policy are also in line with what was expected. Policy has been pro-cyclical in good and bad times, but the central bank reaction tends to be stronger in bad times: 'too tight during contractions, not so loose during expansions' (see Tables A8.1.1 and A8.1.2).[18]

[18]Impulse response functions are provided in Appendix A8.2.

The results for Chile also conform to expectations: monetary policy had a pro-cyclical character in the period 1999–2005, and also reacted in an asymmetric way to the business cycle. Estimations suggest that it has been countercyclical in good times and pro-cyclical in bad times. As argued before, such behaviour would bring about a negative bias in aggregate demand. These results are robust to all the different specifications analysed here (see Tables A8.1.3 and A8.1.4).

The Mexican case confirms only in part the results found for Brazil and Chile. The estimated coefficients in equation (8.1) suggest that monetary policy has been countercyclical to changes in GDP. When periods of expansions and contractions are discriminated, we found results which are similar to ones in the case of Chile: positive coefficients on the variable $\Delta y.GOOD$, which indicates that policy has been countercyclical in 'good times', and negative coefficients on the variable $\Delta y \cdot BAD$, suggesting a pro-cyclical behavior in 'bad times'. However, the reaction of the central bank appears to be stronger (in absolute value) in periods of prosperity than it is in periods of recessions, and this may explain the overall countercyclical character of monetary policy. In other words, the behaviour in good times seem to 'dominate' that in bad times (see Tables A8.1.5 and A8.1.6 and the impulse response functions in Appendix A8.2).

Overall, the results suggest that inflation targeting regimes in Brazil, Chile, and Mexico may bring about a negative bias in aggregate demand, given the asymmetrical reaction of central banks to the business cycle. However, as I will argue in the conclusion, further research on the relation between interest rates, exchange rates, and GDP growth is needed in order to better elucidate this question. The work of Galindo and Ros (2005) presents a promising avenue for research by estimating the asymmetric response of monetary policy to exchange rate movements in Mexico. The authors show that the inflation targeting framework has contributed to the appreciation of the real exchange rate, and this has had contractionary effects on output in the long run.[19]

## CONCLUSIONS

This paper has discussed the potential long-term growth effects of inflation targeting regimes, an aspect usually neglected in the literature. The main question under consideration is whether or not monetary policy reacts in a pro-cyclical and asymmetrical way to economic activity in developing countries. The paper suggests that such behaviour is likely to produce a downward bias in aggregate demand, and bring about negative effects on growth rates in the long run.

An empirical model has been estimated to evaluate monetary policy in Brazil, Chile, and Mexico during the period 1999–2005. The results suggest: (i) that monetary policy has been pro-cyclical in Brazil and Chile, and countercyclical in Mexico; and (ii) that it has reacted asymmetrically to GDP growth rates in Brazil, Chile, and Mexico, in different ways: while the first case is better described by the expression 'too tight during contractions, not so loose during expansions', the other ones can be described as 'countercyclical in booms, procyclical in recessions'. In all cases, it can be argued that monetary policy under inflation targeting has been detrimental to aggregate demand.

[19] See also Ball and Reyes (2004), for an empirical estimation of the relations between exchange rates, interest rates, international reserves, and inflation for Mexico.

The results described here partly confirm the findings of Costa e Silva (2004) who used annual data during the period 1970–2000 to find a pro-cyclical monetary policy in Brazil and countercyclical policy in Mexico. Also, they do not contradict the results of Calderon and Schmidt-Hebbel (2003), who found a correlation between country risk premium and the response of monetary policy to GDP growth.

I conclude with a few comments on further avenues for empirical research that would help to clarify some of the issues not resolved here. First, the sample can be expanded to include other developing countries in Latin America and elsewhere which adopted the inflation targeting framework. Second, the procedure suggested by Galindo and Ros (2005), who found that inflation targeting contributes to the appreciation of the real exchange rate in Mexico, can be applied to the other countries studied here.

Another comment relates to the theme of aggregate demand and growth. It seems that the empirical analysis in this paper does not provide a response to whether long-run output growth is demand-driven or not. The idea that aggregate demand can influence growth in the long run is assumed a priori, and the paper explores the consequence of this assumption when monetary policy is guided by inflation targeting procedures. In this case, the main contribution of this study is to point out the potential negative real effects of inflation targeting that are usually neglected in the literature, simply because of the assumption that aggregate demand fluctuations are irrelevant to long-term outcomes.

Finally, if it is true that monetary policy is pro-cyclical and asymmetric under inflation targeting, and that demand changes can have long-lasting effects, the main economic policy implication of this study is that central banks should consider the real effects of monetary policy more seriously. In particular, the analysis would imply that the trade-off central bankers face is not only between inflation and short-run output losses, but also between inflation and long-lasting effects on output and employment.

## REFERENCES


Ahmed, Shaghil and John Rogers (2000), 'Inflation and the Great Ratios: Long Term Evidence from the US', *Journal of Monetary Economics*, Vol. 45, No. 1, February, pp. 3–35.

Akerlof, George (2002), 'Behavioral Macroeconomics and Macroeconomic Behavior', *American Economic Review*, Vol. 92, No. 3, June, pp. 411–33.

Arestis, Philip and Malcolm Sawyer (2002), 'Can Monetary Policy Affect the Real Economy?', The Levy Economics Institute Working Paper 355, October.

Ball, Christopher and Javier Reyes (2004), 'Inflation Targeting or Fear of Floating in Disguise: The Case of Mexico', *International Journal of Finance and Economics*, Vol. 9, pp. 49–69.

Ball, Laurence (1997), 'Disinflation and the NAIRU', in Christina Romer and David Romer (eds), *Reducing Inflation: Motivation and Strategy*, University of Chicago Press, Chicago.

Ball, Laurence and Dean Croushore (2003), 'Expectations and the Effects of Monetary Policy', *Journal of Money, Credit and Banking*, Vol. 35, No. 4, August, pp. 473–84.

Ball, Laurence and Niamh Sheridan (2003), 'Does Inflation Targeting Matter?', *IMF* Working Paper 03/129, June.

Bernanke, Ben, Thomas Laubach, Frederic Mishkin, and Adam Posen (1999), *Inflation Targeting: Lessons from the International Experience*, Princeton University Press, Princeton, NJ.

Blanchard, Olivier (2004), 'Fiscal Dominance and Inflation Targeting: Lessons from Brazil', NBER Working Paper 10389, March.

Blanchard, Olivier and Lawrence Summers (1986),

'Hysteresis and European Unemployment Problem', *NBER Macroeconomics Annual*, Vol. 1, September, pp. 15–77.

Blejer, Mario, Alain Ize, Alfredo Leone and Sergio Werlang (eds) (2000), *Inflation Targeting in Practice: Strategic and Operational Issues and Application to Emerging Market Economies*, International Monetary Fund, Washington, DC.

Caballero, Ricardo (2002), 'Using Counter-Cyclical Monetary Policy Against Financial Crises', http://www.nzz.ch/english/background/2002/05/03_latin_america_economies.html.

Caballero, Ricardo and Arvind Krishnamurthy (2003), 'Inflation Targeting and Sudden Stops', NBER Working Paper 9599, April.

Calderon, Cesar and Klaus Schmidt-Hebbel (2003), 'Macroeconomic Policies and Performance in Latin America', *Journal of International Money and Finance*, Vol. 22, No. 7, December, pp. 895–923.

Calvo, Guillermo A. and Carmen M. Reinhart (2002), 'Fear of Floating', *Quarterly Journal of Economics*, Vol. 117, No, 2, May, pp. 379–408.

Cecchetti, Stephen and Michael Ehrmann (1999), 'Does Inflation Targeting Increase Output Volatility? An International Comparison of Policymakers' Preferences and Outcomes', NBER Working Paper 7426, December.

Costa e Silva, Jose Ricardo (2004), 'Essays on Finance and Business Cycles', unpublished PhD Dissertation, Washington University, St. Louis.

Cross, Rod (ed.) (1995), *The Natural Rate of Unemployment: Reflections on 25 Years of the Hypothesis*, Cambridge University Press, Cambridge.

Dutt, Amitava and Jaime Ros (2003), 'Contractionary Effects of Stabilization and Long Run Growth', University of Notre Dame, unpublished manuscript.

Ffrench-Davis, Ricardo (2003), 'Financial Crises and National Policy Issues: An Overview', in Ffrench-Davis, Ricardo and Stephany Griffith-Jones (eds), *From Capital Surges to Drought: Seeking Stability from Emerging Economies*, Palgrave Macmillan, Basingstoke.

Fraga, Arminio, Ilan Goldfajn, and Andre Minella (2003), 'Inflation Targeting in Emerging Market Economies', NBER Working Paper 10019, October.

Friedman, Benjamin (2002), 'The Use and Meaning of Words in Central Banking: Inflation Targeting, Credibility, and Transparency', NBER Working Paper 8972, June.

Galindo, Luis Miguel and Jaime Ros (2005), 'Inflation Targeting in Mexico: An Empirical Appraisal', Paper presented at the Amherst/CEDES Conference on Inflation Targeting, Buenos Aires, May.

Hahn, Frank and Robert Solow (1995), *A Critical Essay on Modern Macroeconomic Theory*, MIT Press, Cambridge, Mass.

Lavoie, Marc (2002), 'A Post-Keynesian Alternative to the New Consensus on Monetary Policy', Paper presented at the ADEK Conference, Dijon, France, November.

Leon-Ledesma, Miguel and Anthony Thirlwall (2002), 'The Endogeneity of the Natural Rate of Growth', *Cambridge Journal of Economics*, Vol. 26, No. 4, July, pp. 441–59.

Minella, Andre, Paulo Springer de Freitas, Ilan Goldfajn, and Marcelo Kfoury Muinhos (2003), 'Inflation Targeting in Brazil: Constructing Credibility under Exchange Rate Volatility', *Journal of International Money and Finance*, Vol. 22, No. 7, December, pp. 1015–40.

Mishkin, Frederic (2002), 'The Role of Output Stabilization in the Conduct of Monetary Policy', NBER Working Paper 9291, October.

—— (2004), 'Can Inflation Targeting Work in Emerging Market Countries?', NBER Working Paper 10646, July.

Mishkin, Frederic and Klaus Schmidt-Hebbel (2001), 'One Decade of Inflation Targeting in the World: What Do We Know and What Do We Need to Know?', NBER Working Paper 8397.

Neumann, Manfred and Jurgen von Hagen (2002), 'Does Inflation Targeting Matter?', *The Federal Reserve Bank of St. Louis Review*, Vol. 84, No. 4, July–August, pp. 127–46.

Ocampo, Jose Antonio (2003a), 'Developing Countries' Anti-cyclical Policies in a Globalized World', in Amitava Dutt and Jaime Ros (eds), *Development Economics and Structuralist Macroeconomics*, Edward Elgar, Northampton, MA.

——— (2003b), 'Capital-Account and Counter Cyclical Prudential Regulation in Developing Countries', in R. Ffrench-Davis and S. Griffith-Jones (eds), *From Capital Surges to Drought: Seeking Stability from Emerging Economics*, Palgrave Macmillan, Basingstoke.

Sarel, Michael (1996), 'Nonlinear Effects of Inflation on Economic Growth', IMF Staff Papers, Vol. 43, No. 1, March, pp. 199–215.

Schmidt-Hebbel, Klaus and Alejandro Werner (2002), 'Inflation Targeting in Brazil, Chile and Mexico: Performance, Credibility and the Exchange Rate', *Economia*, Vol. 2, No. 2, pp. 31–89.

Stanners, Walter (1993), 'Is Low Inflation an Important Condition for High Growth?', *Cambridge Journal of Economics*, Vol. 17, No. 1, March, pp. 79–107.

Taylor, John (2000), 'Teaching Modern Macroeconomics at the Principles Level', *American Economic Review*, Vol. 90, No. 2, May, pp. 90–4.

Truman, Edwin (2003), *Inflation Targeting in the World Economy*, IIE, Washington, DC.

# Part III

# Labour and Employment

# 9

# The Dynamics of Manufacturing Employment in South Africa

Fiona Tregenna*

## INTRODUCTION

The objective of this study is to understand the components, as well as the possible causal determinants, of the changes in manufacturing employment in South Africa. Over the past two decades, the level of employment has hovered within a fairly narrow range of approximately 8, 150, 000 to 8, 550, 000, with the 2004 figure near the mid-point of this range at 8, 388, 697.[1] This stagnant level of employment together with rapidly growing labour supply has brought the levels of unemployment to crisis proportions. The 'broad' unemployment currently stands at 40.5 per cent, while the 'narrow' rate (excluding discouraged job seekers) is at 26.5 per cent (Statistics South Africa 2005). While total employment has been stagnant, manufacturing employment has declined significantly. The latter is currently at levels last seen in the early 1970s, although there does appear to be some stabilization since the year 2000.

This paper focuses on the relationships between capital stock, capacity utilization, relative factor utilization, and employment. Basic decomposition techniques are used to investigate the extent to which changes in employment between 1970 and 2004 can be accounted for by these factors. Although this analysis does not explain underlying causal relationships, it may be helpful in understanding the various changes that have taken place as well as shedding light on priorities for further research. From a policy perspective, identifying the critical blockages to employment growth may be helpful in designing focused key interventions currently prevailing to reduce the devastating levels of unemployment.

The next section of the paper reviews relevant empirical trends in South African manufacturing, notably those pertaining to changes in output, capital stock, capacity utilization, relative factor utilization, and

*Financial support for this research from the Human Sciences Research Council is gratefully acknowledged.

[1]All data used throughout this paper are sourced from the South African Standardized Industry Database (SASID) unless otherwise indicated.

employment. The third section begins by briefly discussing some relevant conceptual issues, particularly concerning the relationship between changes in capital stock and employment. Decomposition techniques are then used to disaggregate changes in employment into a capital stock effect, capacity utilization effect, and relative factor utilization effect. The results are presented for manufacturing as a whole, as well as by sector. The fourth section discusses the results and possible policy implications.

## EMPIRICAL TRENDS

This section provides an overview and analysis of trends in capital accumulation, capacity utilization, factor utilization, and employment in South African manufacturing over the period 1970–2004. The reason for the focus on these particular variables is that they are the components of the identity relationship, posited in the next section, that forms the basis of the decomposition analysis.

### CAPITAL ACCUMULATION, CAPACITY UTILIZATION, FACTOR UTILIZATION, AND EMPLOYMENT

Figure 9.1 shows the trends in real fixed capital stock, capacity utilization, labour intensity (measured as the ratio of employment to effective capital), and employment for the manufacturing sector. Capital stock rose by about 3.8 per cent per annum from 1971 to 2003. Capacity utilization fluctuated in an apparently cyclical fashion, varying between about 77 per cent and 86 per cent over the three decades, with an overall slight downward trend. Of course, given the construction and nature of the capacity utilization measure, one would not expect as much variation in this measure as with the other series shown. Labour intensity fell dramatically and almost continuously, with the exception of a short period in the mid-

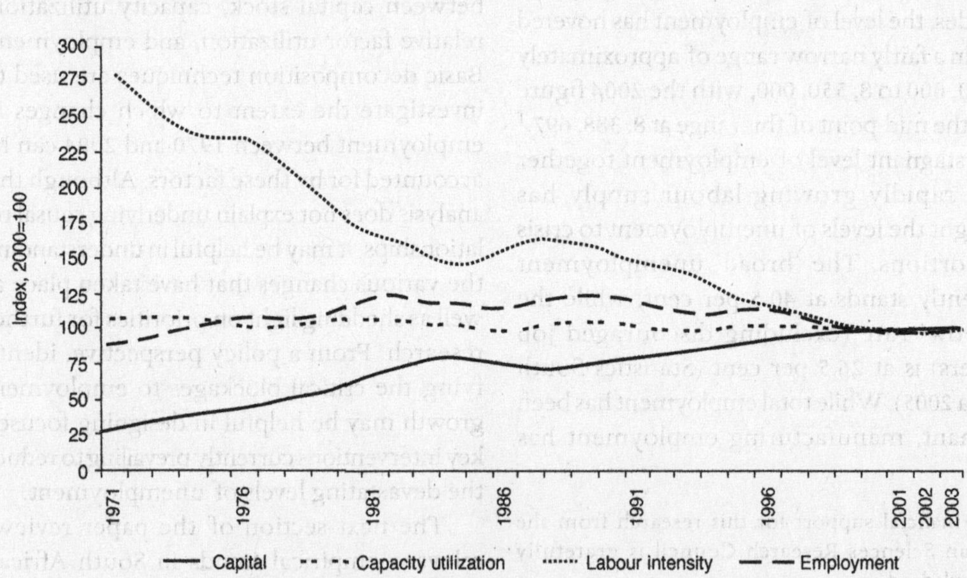


Figure 9.1: Trends in Fixed Capital Stock, Capacity Utilization, Labour Intensity, and Employment: Manufacturing Sector, 1972–2003

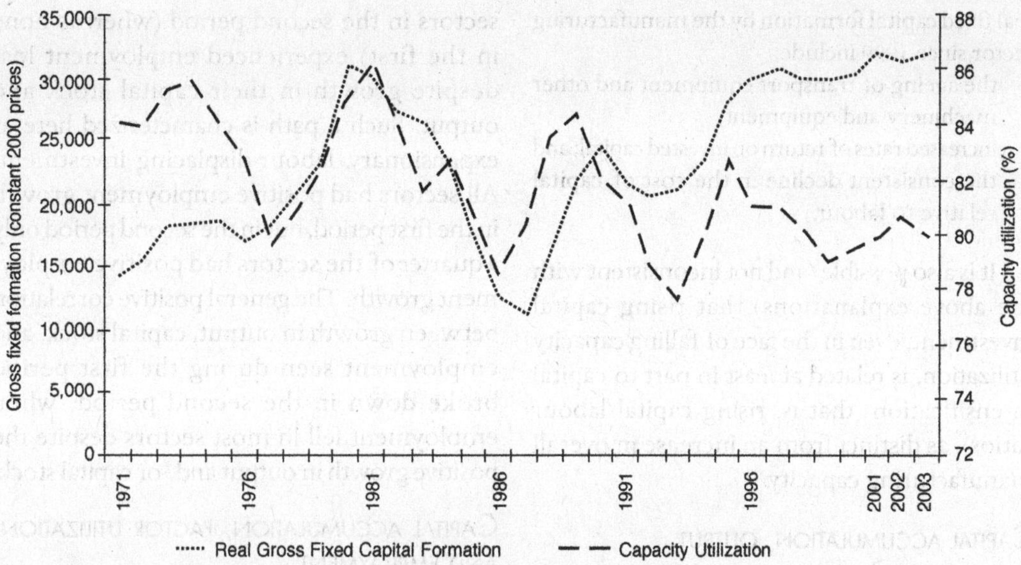


Figure 9.2: Real Gross Fixed Capital Formation and Capacity Utilization in the Manufacturing Sector, 1971–2003

late 1980s. After hitting highs at the beginning and at the end of the 1980s, employment in manufacturing has now fallen back to levels experienced in the early 1970s.[2] Total employment has also fallen from its 1989–90 peak, though not as dramatically as the fall in manufacturing employment. Given the dramatic rise in labour supply, unemployment rates have risen significantly.

Figure 9.2 shows the changing relationship between gross fixed capital formation and capacity utilization in manufacturing. It is interesting to note what appears to be an increasing divergence between the two series since about 1990, and in particular since about 1995 when real gross fixed capital formation continued to increase despite the low and declining rates of utilization of existing manufacturing capacity.

Smith (2003, p. 82) reports the comments of the Reserve Bank:

> Prior to about 1995, rising rates of capacity utilization in the manufacturing sector usually coincided with heightened investment activity and, conversely, declining capacity utilization rates with a slowdown in investment activity. This fairly well established relationship broke down in the second half of the 1990s when low and falling rates of capacity utilization in the manufacturing sector were accompanied by a fairly vigorous pick-up in investment spending. The reasons for this deviation from the established pattern are not entirely clear, but it is thought that the expenditure on new technology expanded the absolute capacity of the manufacturing sector by more than what was anticipated, resulting in an increased under-utilization of capacity at the prevailing levels of output. Other factors contributing to the rise in

[2]Part of the reported decline might be attributed to outsourcing of manufacturing jobs to service providers classified in the services sector.

real fixed capital formation by the manufacturing sector since 1999 include:

- the ageing of transport equipment and other machinery and equipment;
- increased rates of return on invested capital; and
- the consistent decline in the cost of capital relative to labour.

It is also possible (and not inconsistent with the above explanations) that rising capital investment, even in the face of falling capacity utilization, is related at least in part to capital intensification (that is, rising capital labour ratios), as distinct from an increase in overall manufacturing capacity.

## Capital Accumulation, Output, and Employment

Table 9.1 presents a typology of possible combinations of changes in output, capital stock, and employment, as well as an analysis of the number of sectors that fell into each category over the periods 1970–90 and 1991–2004 (without taking into account at this point of the relative size of different sectors). Sectors that experienced an increase in output are characterized as 'expansionary' while those whose output fell are characterized as 'contractionary'; these are further categorized according to whether (net) investment or disinvestment occurred (on the basis of the change in capital stock); as well as whether employment increased or decreased. Productivity changes are imputed from the changes in output and in capital and labour, respectively.

It is striking that 26 out of the 28 manufacturing sectors in the first period—but only six in the second period—saw increases in output, capital stock, and employment.[3] Thirteen sectors in the second period (whereas none in the first) experienced employment loss despite growth in their capital stock and output. Such a path is characterized here as expansionary, labour-displacing investment. All sectors had positive employment growth in the first period, but in the second period only a quarter of the sectors had positive employment growth. The general positive correlation between growth in output, capital stock, and employment seen during the first period broke down in the second period, when employment fell in most sectors despite the positive growth in output and/or capital stock.

## Capital Accumulation, Factor Utilization, and Employment

Figure 9.3 analyses changes in capital stock and relative factor utilization for the 28 manufacturing sectors. Three points are plotted for each sectoral cluster: 1970, 1990, and 2004. Each of these points is a combination of the level of real capital stock and relative factor utilization (measured as the labour–capital ratio) for that sectoral cluster for the relevant year. The key information conveyed in Figure 9.3 is, however, the overall trend rather than specific sectoral information.

A movement of a sector in a north–easterly direction would indicate both an increase in real capital stock and an increase in the labour capital ratio, that is, both capital investment and labour-intensification, with an unambiguously positive effect on employment. Conversely, a movement south–west would represent falling capital stock and falling relative factor utilization, in other words disinvestment together with capital-intensification, as well as an unambiguously negative change in employment. Third, movement north-west would mean that a sector had falling real capital stock with increasing relative factor utilization,

[3] Of course, the changes in capital stock and employment would generally not be proportional, an aspect which is explored further in this paper.

Table 9.1: Typology and Empirical Occurrence of Sectoral Accumulation Path

| Change in Output | Change in Capital Stock | Change in Employment | Description | Productivity Changes | No. of Sectors 1970–90 | No. of Sectors 1991–2004 |
|---|---|---|---|---|---|---|
| + | + | + | Expansion, labour-absorbing investment | Changes in capital and labour productivity depend on relative changes in output, capital, and employment | 26 | 6 |
| + | + | – | Expansion, labour-displacing investment | Change in capital productivity depends on relative changes in output and employment; Rising labour productivity | – | 13 |
| – | + | – | Contraction, labour-displacing investment | Falling capital productivity; Change in labour productivity depends on relative changes in output and labour | – | – |
| – | + | + | Contraction, labour-absorbing investment | Falling capital and labour productivity | 1 | – |
| – | – | – | Contraction, disinvestment, employment loss | Changes in capital and labour productivity depend on relative changes in output, capital, and employment | – | 2 |
| – | – | + | Contraction, disinvestment, employment creation | Change in capital productivity depends on relative changes in output and capital; Falling labour productivity | – | – |
| + | – | – | Expansion, disinvestment, employment loss | Rising capital and labour productivity | – | 6 |
| + | – | + | Expansion, disinvestment, employment | Rising capital productivity; Change in labour productivity depends on relative changes in output and employment | 1 | 1 |

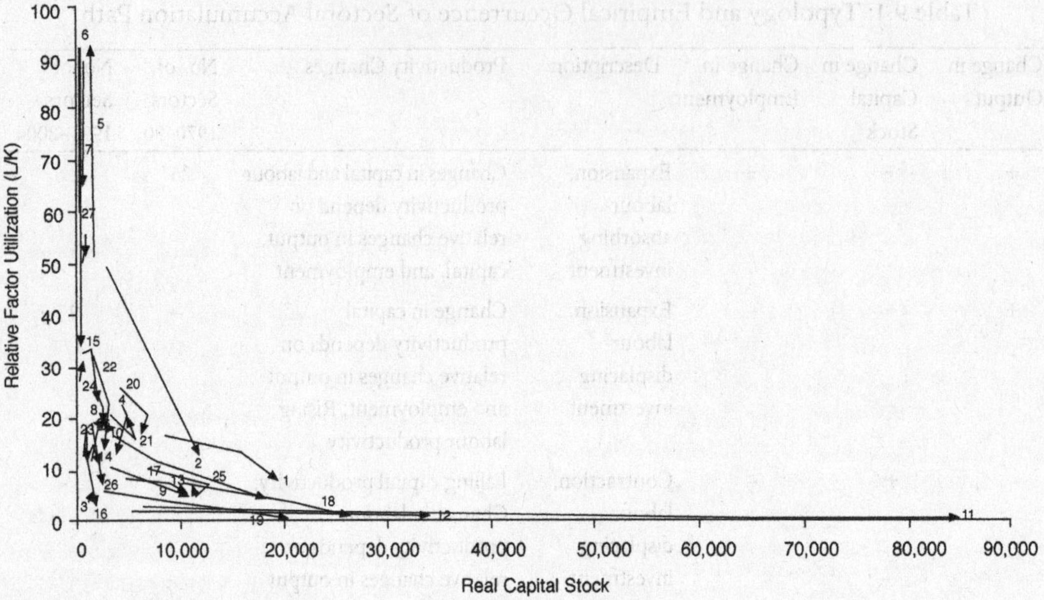


Figure 9.3: Sectoral Trends in Capital Stock and Relative Factor Utilization, 1970–1990–2004

Key:

| Sector name | SIC | Key | Sector name | SIC | Key | Sector name | SIC | Key |
|---|---|---|---|---|---|---|---|---|
| Food | 301–304 | 1 | Coke & refined petrol | 331–333 | 12 | Machinery & equipment | 356–359 | 22 |
| Beverages | 305 | 2 | Basic chemicals | 334 | 13 | Electrical machinery & apparatus | 361–366 | 23 |
| Tobacco | 306 | 3 | Other chemicals & man-made fibers | 335–336 | 14 | TV, radio, & comm. equipment | 371–373 | 24 |
| Textiles | 311–312 | 4 | Rubber products | 337 | 15 | Professional, & scientific equipment | 374–376 | 25 |
| Wearing apparel | 313–315 | 5 | Plastic products | 338 | 16 | Motor vehicles, parts, &accessories | 381–383 | 26 |
| Leather & leather products | 316 | 6 | Glass & glass products | 341 | 17 | Other transport equipment | 384–387 | 27 |
| Footwear | 317 | 7 | Non-metallic minerals | 342 | 18 | Other manufacturing | 392–393 | 28 |
| Wood & wood products | 321–322 | 8 | Basic iron & steel | 351 | 19 | | | |
| Paper & paper products | 323 | 9 | Basic non-ferrous metals | 352 | 20 | | | |
| Printing, publishing, & recorded media | 324–326 | 10 | Metal products excl. machinery | 353–355 | 21 | | | |
| Furniture | 391 | 11 | | | | | | |

meaning that there had been capital disinvestment and labour intensification, with an ambiguous net effect on employment. Finally, a movement south-east would be indicative of increasing capital stock with falling relative factor utilization, that is, capital investment with capital intensification, again with an ambiguous net effect on employment.

A general movement of sectors in the south-east direction is evident, that is, most sectors become less labour intensive while increasing their real capital stock. A second noteworthy feature of this chart is the 'axis-hugging' movement of sectors. This indicates that sectors that started out as highly intensive tended to see significant falls in their labour intensity, without growing dramatically in terms of capital stock. On the other hand, sectors that started out with high levels of capital stock and low levels of capital intensity tended to have significant further rises in capital stock, with relatively stable but slightly declining levels of labour intensity. Overall, sectors that were previously highly labour-intensive have tended to become less so, while highly capital-intensive sectors have generally increased their capital stock without becoming more labour-intensive.

To conclude this section on background empirical analysis, the following key empirical trends can be highlighted.

- Manufacturing employment was at its highest levels at the beginning and end of the 1980s, but has since fallen and is currently at levels not seen since the early 1970s. Total employment in the economy has also fallen from the peak levels of 1989–90.
- Capital stock rose by about 3.8 per cent per annum between 1971 and 2003.
- Capacity utilization has varied between about 71 per cent and 86 per cent, with an overall slightly downward trend.
- Since about 1995, investment has increased despite declining capacity utilization.
- Manufacturing has become increasingly capital intensive, almost continuously since 1971.
- Since 1991, only a quarter of the total manufacturing sectors had positive employment growth, and the previous correlation at the sector-level between positive output and investment and employment growth broke down.
- Most manufacturing sectors have become increasingly capital-intensive. Further, sectors that were initially highly labour-intensive have tended to become less labour-intensive, while initially highly capital-intensive sectors have generally increased their capital stock without becoming more labour-intensive.

## ANALYSIS

### Introduction: The Relationship Between Investment and Employment

Any given level of capital stock or of investment could be associated with different accumulation paths, each with particular distributional and employment implications, as well as differing degrees of long-term sustainability.

Accumulation may be capital widening or capital deepening. With satisfactory rates of profitability, firms may invest in a capital-widening manner, expanding capacity without any significant changes in the composition of capital or capital–labour ratios. Under these conditions, we would expect to see increases in output, capital stock, and employment, without a dramatic change in the labour–capital ratio.

However, as employment rises, the bargaining power of workers as well as wage rates rise, thus squeezing profitability. A squeeze on profitability would tend to push firms into capital deepening investment. Firms are driven to acquire more 'efficient' capital in order to remain competitive against domestic and foreign competitors. Investment under these conditions would tend to be investment in cost-cutting capital goods. This would manifest in rising capital intensity.

South Africa has a huge reserve army of labour, given that the 'broad' unemployment rate exceeds 40 per cent. It may thus seem counterintuitive that the type of mechanism described here—where high and rising employment increases workers' bargaining power and squeezes profitability—would be especially powerful. However, the political and institutional dynamics in South Africa give rise to similar effects, notwithstanding the high levels of unemployment. For example, factors such as the high levels of unionization and working class mobilization, political alliance between the trade union federation COSATU and the governing ANC, the relatively favourable labour market legislative regime, and the institutionalized access of organized workers to policy through fora such as Nedlac,[4] contribute to similar effects even in the face of high rates of unemployment.

As discussed further elsewhere in this paper, non-cost factors also appear to be particularly relevant to relative factor utilization decisions. Anecdotal evidence suggests that firms may choose to engage in labour-displacing capital investment even where this is not strictly cost-efficient. Such dynamics need to be located within a broader socio-political context, including considerations of race and power.

Further, different types of competitive regimes may foster different investment patterns with associated differences in factor intensity and employment. Faced with intense competitive pressure—which could arise domestically or from (actual or potential) import penetration—firms may respond by investing all available resources, those deriving from profits as well as those that can be borrowed through financial markets. Under such 'coerced investment', firms must accumulate in order to survive, under the threat that failure to invest adequately may result in their being driven out of the marketplace. Such investment will tend to be capital-deepening and labour-displacing.

[4]The National Economic Development and Labour Council, the statutory bargaining institution on economic and social policy.

The relationship between changes in fixed capital stock and employment is thus complex and conjuncturally specific. Even in the short- to medium-term, and even abstracting from the broader factors raised above, investment could have various (potentially opposing) effects on employment, with an ambiguous overall effect. These effects may be conceptualized as follows.

Changes in capital stock (that is, net investment) are of course related to changes in relative factor utilization. The effect of new investment in fixed capital stock on measured relative factor utilization is contingent on the magnitude of any associated increase in employment. Investment that actually displaces labour, or that is associated with a less than proportionate increase in employment, would (ceteris paribus) lower the labour intensity of production. Investment associated with a proportionate increase in employment would of course (ceteris paribus) have no effect on relative factor utilization, while labour-absorbing investment associated with a more than proportionate increase in employment would (ceteris paribus) increase the labour intensity of production.

## Decomposition Analysis of Changes in Employment

A basic model is conceptualized in which employment is a function of productive capacity, the degree of utilization of this capacity, and relative factor utilization. First, the overall level of 'capacity' in the economy is an indicator of the potential output of the economy if all the capital were to be fully utilized, and is proxied by the entire fixed

Table 9.2: Possible Effects of Changes in Capital Stock (Net Capital Investment) on Employment

| Effect | Rationale | Expected sign |
|---|---|---|
| Output effect (extensive investment) | Investment may be undertaken in order to increase production using existing technologies and production methods (labour-absorption) | Positive |
| Substitution effect (intensive investment) | Capital-deepening investment may displace labour at any given level of production | Negative |
| Productivity effects from investment | Efficiency effect—if output does not increase or does not increase proportionately, fewer workers are required than previously | Negative |
| | Output effect—higher productivity may lower costs which, if there is a simultaneous increase in demand, may lead to an increase output and hence employment; this may mitigate the negative 'efficiency effect' of the productivity increase. | Positive |

capital stock. Second, capacity utilization measures the extent to which the overall capacity in the economy is actually being used. Together, the levels of capital stock and of capacity utilization indicate the level of 'utilized capital' or 'effective capital'. Third, this 'effective capital' can be utilized with a range of combinations of factors of production, or different ratios of labour to 'effective capital'.

Each of these three levels—capacity, capacity utilization, and labour intensity can be understood as having a variety of (direct and indirect) determinants, with substantial overlap. Further, the identification of these factors and their relative prioritization would be affected by the ideological and theoretical stance taken, as well as by empirical methodologies and results. This conceptualization thus allows for different views and interpretations of factors that would influence each of the three levels, making it a conducive framework for analysing the determinants of employment.

One way of explaining the overall level of employment is thus through the underlying causal determinants of each of these three components and the interrelationships between them. Understanding the relative importance and the nature of the determinants would be important to getting to grips with the basic factors affecting the level of employment, and hence potentially shedding light on areas for policy intervention in order to increase the same.

First, determinants of capital stock could potentially include factors such as rates of profit and expectations of future profits, the level and composition of public investment, political and social conditions, access to and cost of borrowed capital, enterprise balance sheets and cash flows, savings rates, net capital flows, risk and uncertainty, relative investment conditions and international rates of return, the tax structure and industrial incentives, the structure and conduct of financial institutions, and the rates of utilization of existing capacity.

It should also be noted that capital stock is not homogenous and the relationship between capital stock and potential output is neither linear nor even monotonic. Various characteristics of the capital stock such as its sectoral distribution and its state of technology would be relevant to its potential productivity.

The second component, the rate of capacity utilization, would tend to be influenced primarily by the level and composition of effective demand, which in turn could be influenced by factors such as income distribution, gross wages, employment, net import penetration, and the level and composition of government expenditure.[5]

Third, relative factor utilization (labour intensity) could be influenced by factors such as relative factor productivity as well as relative factor costs, factor substitutability, political, social, and distributional issues, the labour market regime, work organization, fiscal policy, skills, exogenous technologies, and class and bargaining power.

[5]In addition, careful interpretation is called for, particularly capacity utilization, especially given that it is measured as a percentage and hence cannot rise beyond a ceiling, unlike the other variables. Even if capacity utilization and aggregate demand are in fact causally significant, one would not expect to see a prolonged high capacity utilization effect. If rising aggregate demand pushes up the level of capacity utilization, this may prompt new investment such that the capital stock is expanded. This may result in little apparent change in the measured level of capacity utilization, or even a short-term decline. In other words, some of the effects of high or rising demand (whether at the aggregate, sectoral, or firm level) may be manifested in high levels of capacity utilization, and to some extent in increasing capital stock. Even if aggregate demand is highly causally significant, this would not necessarily reflect in an ongoing rise in capacity utilization, as rising capacity utilization (probably over a certain threshold) would trigger higher investment.

Formalizing the conceptual approach outlined here, the relationship between capital stock, capacity utilization, relative factor utilization, and employment, can be expressed as follows.

$$L_t = \alpha_t \bullet \lambda_t \bullet K_t$$

where:

$L_t$ = employment at time t
$\alpha_t$ = relative factor intensity at time t
$\lambda_t$ = capacity utilization at time t
$K_t$ = capital stock at time t

or as an identity, and omitting the time subscripts:

$$L \equiv \frac{L}{\lambda K} \bullet \lambda \bullet K$$

where $\frac{L}{\lambda K} = \alpha$ is the ratio of labour to utilized capital.[6]

This allows for a three-stage decomposition for the manufacturing sector, for which capacity utilization is available.[7] The decomposition analysis is based on the following:

$$\Delta L = \alpha_1 \lambda_1 K_1 - \alpha_0 \lambda_0 K_0$$

$$= \underbrace{(\alpha_1 - \alpha_0)\left(\frac{\lambda_0 K_0 + \lambda_1 K_1}{2}\right)}_{\textit{factor utilization effect}}$$

$$+ \underbrace{(\lambda_1 - \lambda_0)\left(\frac{K_0 + K_1}{2}\right)\left(\frac{\alpha_0 + \alpha_1}{2}\right)}_{\textit{capacity utilization effect}}$$

$$+ \underbrace{(K_1 - K_0)\left(\frac{\lambda_0 + \lambda_1}{2}\right)\left(\frac{\alpha_0 + \alpha_1}{2}\right)}_{\textit{capital stock effect}}$$

[6]Or in growth rates, $\ln L = \ln \frac{L}{\lambda K} + \ln \lambda + \ln K$.

[7]Note that the period is truncated by a year on either side for this analysis given the availability of capacity utilization data.

The results of this decomposition of manufacturing sector employment into the capital effect, the capacity utilization effect, and the factor utilization effect are shown in Table 9.3 and Figure 9.4. The table summarizes the changes over two broad periods, 1971–90 and 1991–2003, while the figure shows the decomposition of the changes on a year-on-year basis.

Comparing the two broad periods (see Table 9.3), it is notable that the capital effect was positive in both periods, while the capacity utilization and factor utilization effects were both negative. However, there was a major shift in relative magnitudes of the different effects in the two periods, associated with the fact that there was positive employment growth in the first period but employment losses in the second. While the capital effect was significantly greater than the factor utilization effect between 1971 and 1990, during the period 1991–2003 the factor utilization effect far exceeded the capital effect.

Figure 9.4 shows that, on an annual basis the capital effect was positive with the exception of a period in the late 1980s, although it did seem to show a declining trend overall. There appears to be a broad positive relationship between the capital and capacity utilization effects, particularly in the earlier years. The factor utilization effect was fairly volatile, but was negative for 27 of the 32 years.

Table 9.3: Decomposition of Changes in Manufacturing Employment: Summary of Results

| | 1971–90 | 1991–2003 |
|---|---|---|
| Capital effect | 1,265,302 | 335,606 |
| Capacity utilization effect | –40,927 | –23,510 |
| Factor utilization effect | –812,620 | –575,411 |
| Total employment change | 411,755 | –263,315 |

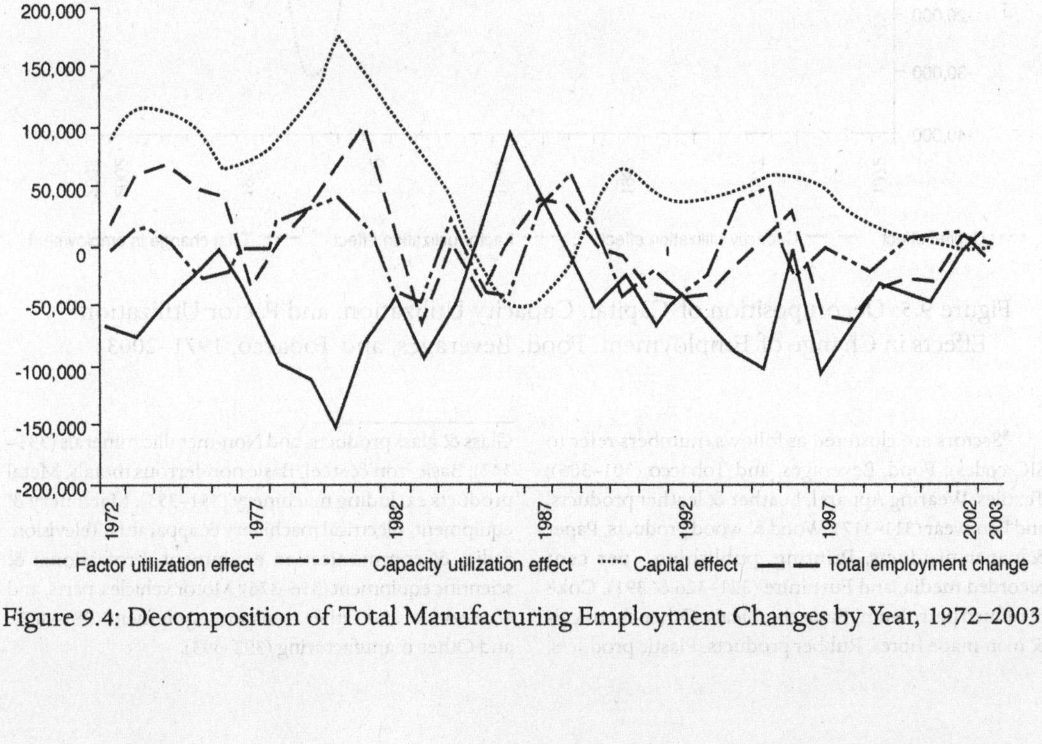


Figure 9.4: Decomposition of Total Manufacturing Employment Changes by Year, 1972–2003

Although these results do not elucidate the underlying causal relationships, they do suggest the importance of the factor utilization effect in accounting for the poor employment performance of the manufacturing sector, particularly since about 1989. These results are discussed fully in the fourth section.

## Sectoral Analysis

The following series of figures presents the results of the decomposition analysis for all the manufacturing sectors. The sectors are clustered into 19 groups of related sub-sectors for brevity of exposition.[8]

Figure 9.5 decomposes the capital, capacity utilization, and factor utilization effects for the food, beverages, and tobacco sub-sectors. The capital effect is generally positive, although it is noteworthy that it is negative from 1999 onwards. Visual inspection suggests a positive association between the capital and capacity utilization effects for much of the period. The factor utilization effect is mostly negative, but is volatile.

One of the striking features of the trends in the textiles, wearing apparel, leather and leather products, and footwear sectors (Figure 9.6) is that the capital effect does not appear

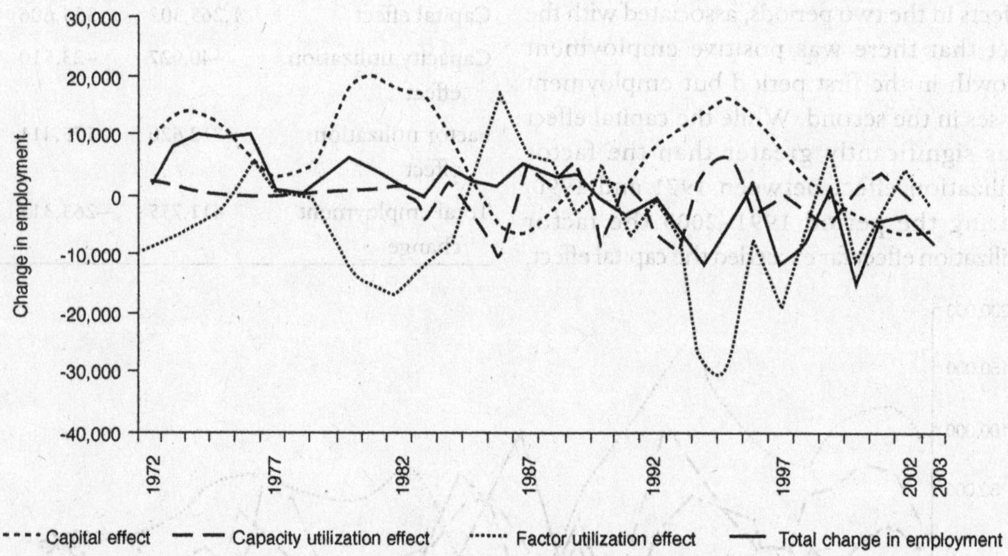


Figure 9.5: Decomposition of Capital, Capacity Utilization, and Factor Utilization Effects in Change of Employment: Food, Beverages, and Tobacco, 1971–2003

[8]Sectors are clustered as follows (numbers refer to SIC codes): Food, Beverages, and Tobacco (301–306); Textiles, Wearing Apparel, Leather & leather products, and Footwear (311–317); Wood & wood products, Paper & paper products, Printing, publishing, per cent recorded media, and Furniture (321–326 & 391); Coke & refined petroleum, Basic chemicals, Other chemicals & man-made fibres, Rubber products, Plastic products, Glass & glass products, and Non-metallic minerals (331–342); Basic iron & steel, Basic non-ferrous metals, Metal products excluding machinery (351–355); Machinery & equipment, Electrical machinery & apparatus, Television, radio, & communication equipment, Professional & scientific equipment (356–376); Motor vehicles, parts, and accessories, and Other transport equipment (381–387); and Other manufacturing (392–393).

to be particularly significant (in magnitude) for this sector, unlike that in many other sectors. In certain periods in particular—such as most of the 1980s and the period from the mid-1990s onwards—the overall change in employment appears to be particularly strongly associated with the factor utilization effect. Interestingly, this is not only during periods of job loss, but also during periods of job growth.

Two periods of job growth, with apparently distinctive dynamics, can be commented on in this regard. First, in the mid- to late-1980s, there was employment growth, together with labour-intensification of production, and a fall in the real capital stock. This might suggest a time of little investment (or even capital stripping) and a more labour-intensive use of existing capital stock, as well as rising capacity utilization of that capital stock. This can be distinguished from the apparent dynamics of the brief period of job creation in the mid-1990s, when labour intensification went along with a positive capital effect and a negative capacity utilization effect. A possible story compatible with these results would be moderate but positive levels of investment, but which was labour-absorbing in nature.

Next, we look at a cluster of sub-sectors including wood and wood products, paper and paper products, printing, publishing, and recorded media, and furniture (see Figure 9.7). A striking result in this case is the apparent inverse association between the capital and factor utilization effects, which appear to be of opposite sign and moving in opposite directions for virtually the entire period. This might be taken as suggesting that capital and labour could be substitutes in the production process in these sub-sectors, to a greater extent than in other sectors.

Figure 9.8 shows the results for the chemical and related sectors. The picture varies considerably for different periods of time. One

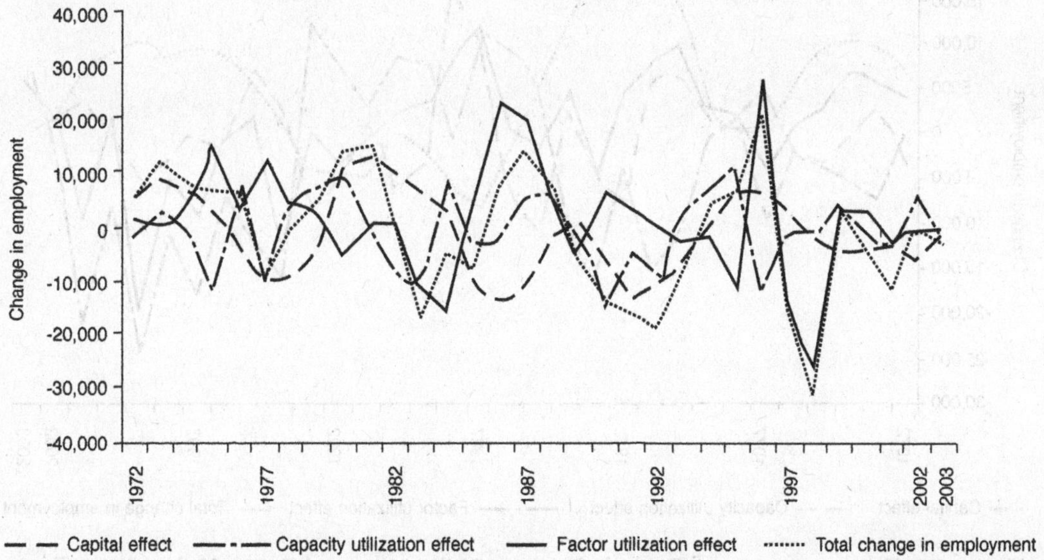


Figure 9.6: Decomposition of Capital, Capacity Utilization, and Factor Utilization Effects in Change of Employment: Textiles, Wearing Apparel, Leather & Leather Products, Footwear, 1971–2003

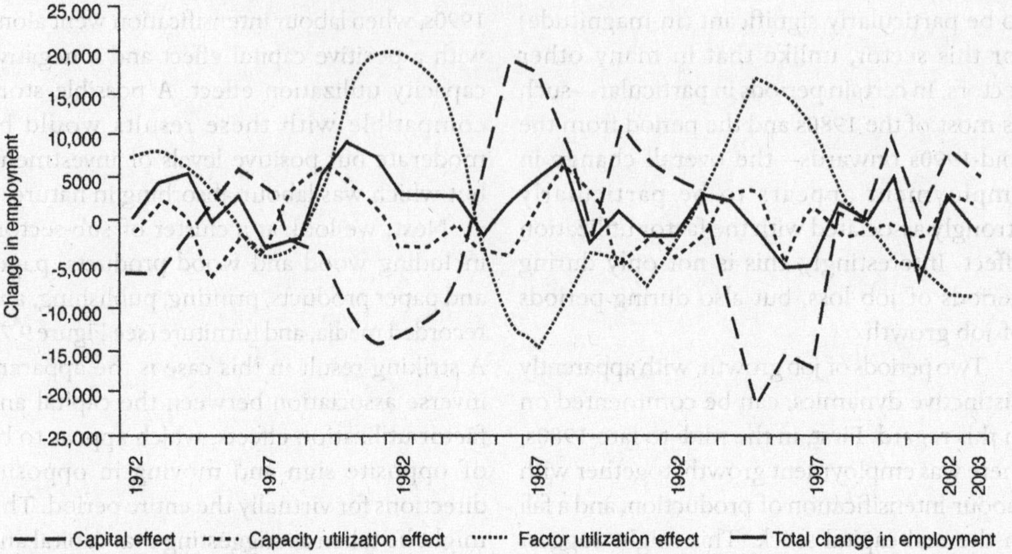


Figure 9.7: Decomposition of Capital, Capacity Utilization, and Factor Utilization Effects in Change of Employment: Wood & Wood Products, Paper & Paper Products, Printing Publishing & Recorded Media, & Furniture, 1971–2003

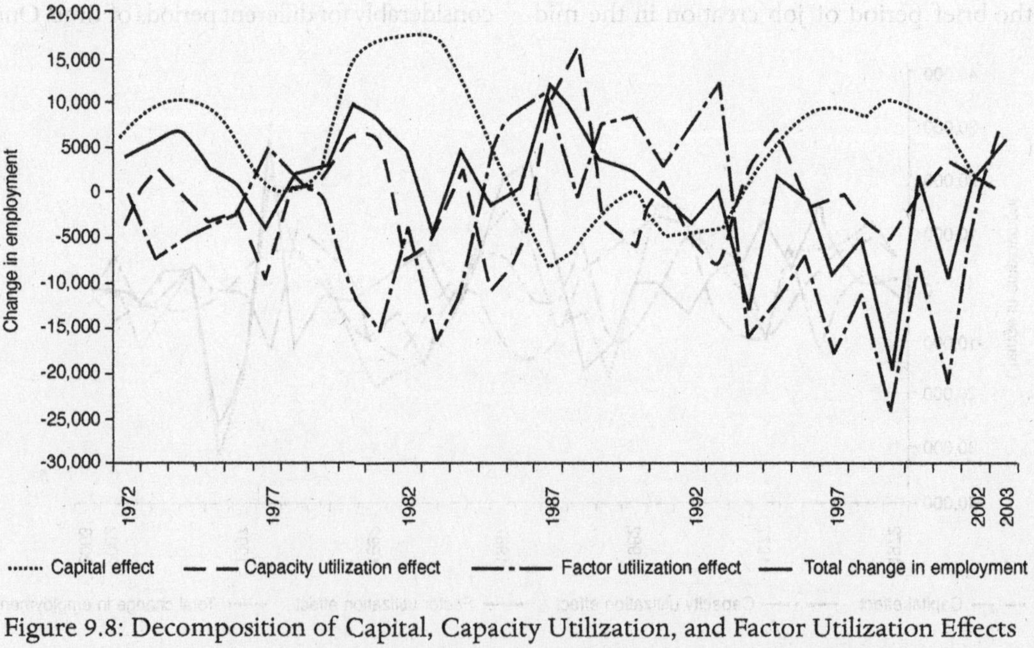


Figure 9.8: Decomposition of Capital, Capacity Utilization, and Factor Utilization Effects in Change of Employment: Coke & Refined Petroleum, Chemicals, Rubber, Plastic, Glass & Glass Products, and Non-metallic Minerals, 1971–2003

noticeable difference from most other sectors is the significant relative contribution of the capacity utilization effect, which in this case shows substantial variation and is also large in size. In the 1990s, the capital effect is positive, but this is more than outweighed by the increasing capital intensity of production in the sub-sectors.

Next, the trends are analysed for the basic iron and steel, basic non-ferrous metals, and metal products (excluding machinery) sub-sectors (see Figure 9.8). It is difficult to ascertain clear trends from which conclusions can be drawn in this case. The capital effect is mostly positive, although it has been negative since 1998. The capacity utilization effect varies in a possibly cyclical manner. The factor utilization effect also varies considerably, although it is more negative than positive.

Figure 9.10 presents the results of the decomposition analysis for the following sectors: machinery and equipment, electrical machinery and apparatus, television, radio, and communications equipment, and professional and scientific equipment. The overall change in employment seems to be closely associated with the capital and capacity utilization effects until about the mid-1980s, after which there appears to be a continued close association between the overall employment change and the capacity utilization effect. Since about 1996, the overall employment change appears to be most closely associated with the factor utilization effect. There is considerable volatility in all three effects over the entire period.

Figure 9.11 shows the trends for the motor vehicles, parts, and accessories, and other transport equipment sub-sectors. In this case, the capital effect is positive for almost the entire period, and it has been positive with an increasing trend since 1989. Spikes in employment growth appear to be associated

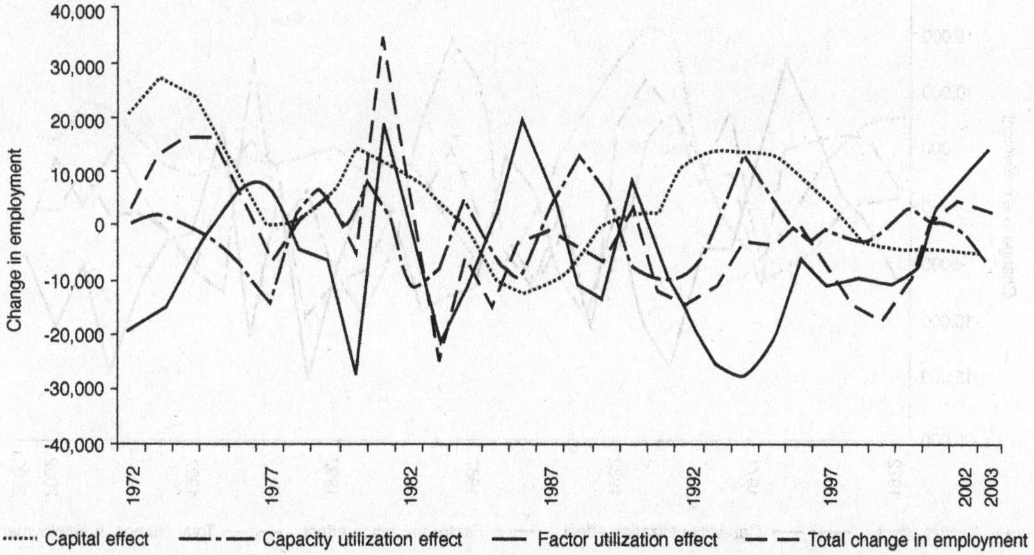


Figure 9.9: Decomposition of Capital, Capacity Utilization, and Factor Utilization Effects in Change of Employment: Basic Iron & Steel, Basic Non-ferrous Metals, Metal Products excl. Machinery, 1971–2003

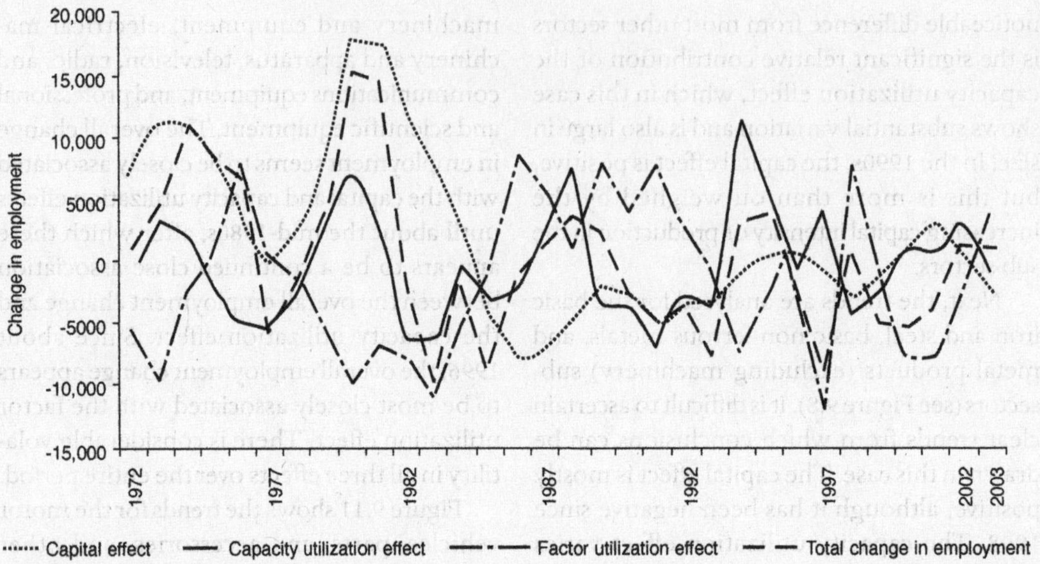


Figure 9.10: Decomposition of Capital, Capacity Utilization, and Factor Utilization Effects in Change of Employment: Machinery & Equipment, Electrical Machinery & Apparatus, TV, Radio & Communications Equipment, Professional & Scientific Equipment, 1971–2003

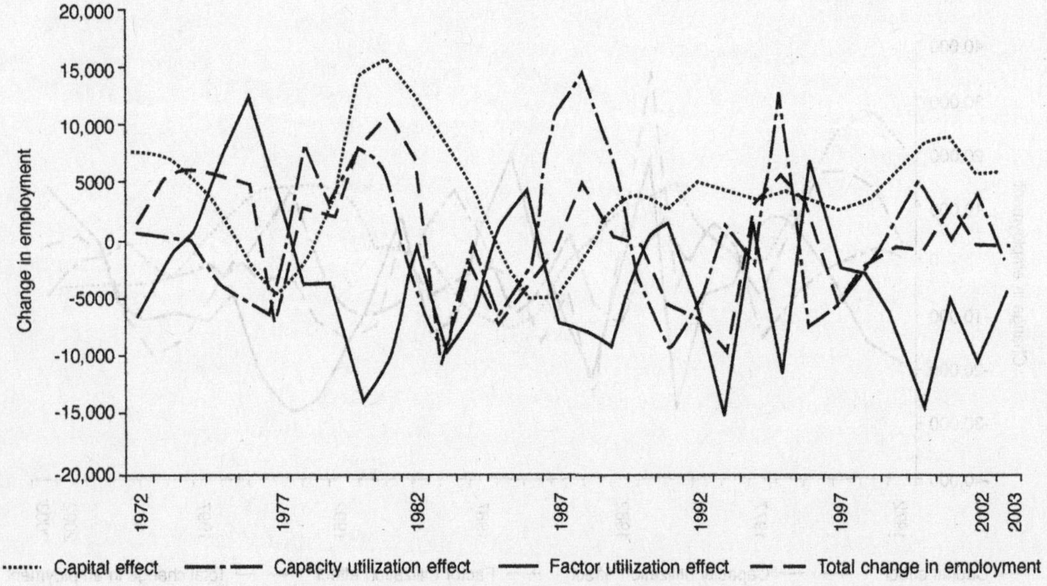


Figure 9.11: Decomposition of Capital, Capacity Utilization, and Factor Utilization Effects in Change of Employment: Motor Vehicles, Parts & Accessories, and Other Transport Equipment, 1971–2003

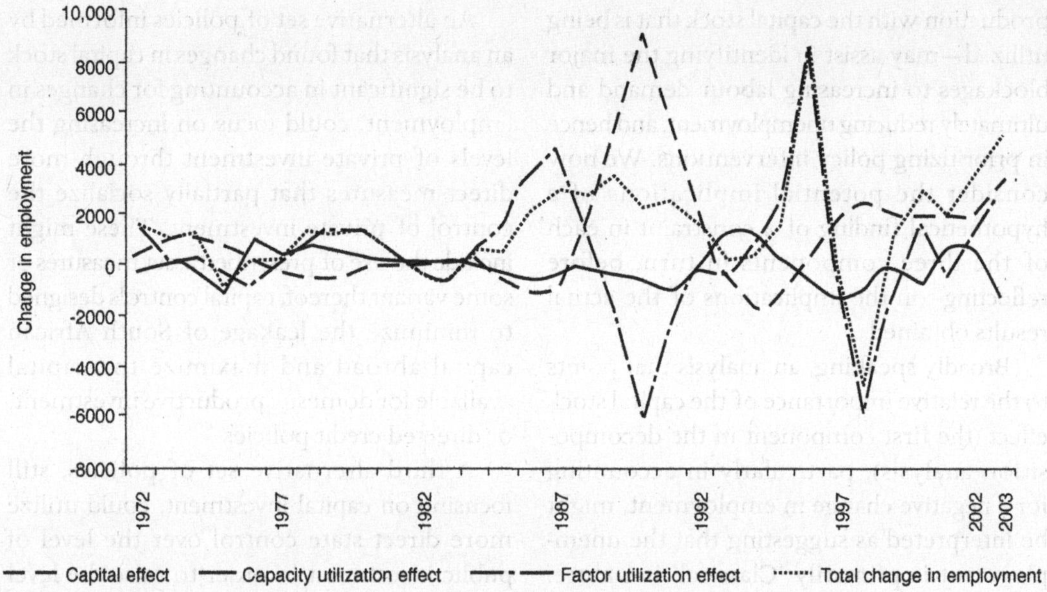


Figure 9.12: Decomposition of Capital, Capacity Utilization, and Factor Utilization Effects in Change of Employment: Other Manufacturing, 1971–2003

with periods in which the capacity utilization effect was positive and large. The factor utilization effect varies but is mostly negative, and has been negative since 1997.

Finally, the effects for the 'other' manufacturing subsectors are decomposed and shown in Figure 9.12. Not much change is evident until the mid-1980s, and there is considerable volatility thereafter. The capital effect is mostly positive, the capacity utilization effect varies around 0, and the factor utilization effect is mostly positive. There appears to be a very strong positive association between the factor utilization effect and overall employment change since the early 1990s.

## DISCUSSION

The objective of the decomposition exercises and other empirical analysis undertaken in this paper is to get some sense of the relative importance of changes in capital stock, capacity utilization, and relative factor utilization, respectively, in accounting for changes in employment in South Africa. Decomposition analysis, albeit a rather mechanical accounting exercise, can at least point towards possible explanations and directions for further research. In this section we discuss how to interpret the decomposition analysis and possible implications of different possible outcomes, before commenting on the particular results obtained in this paper.

The simple model used as the basis for the decomposition exercise in this paper is intended as an initial analytical tool for the analysis of employment in particular periods, rather than being theoretically pre-emptive. Understanding where the major constraints to labour demand lie in a particular conjuncture—whether with: (i) insufficient capital stock, (ii) low levels of utilization of existing capital stock, or (iii) highly capital-intensive production with the capital stock that is being utilized—may assist in identifying the major blockages to increasing labour demand and ultimately reducing unemployment, and hence in prioritizing policy interventions. We now consider the potential implications of a hypothetical finding of a constraint in each of the three components in turn, before reflecting on the implications of the actual results obtained.

Broadly speaking, an analysis that points to the relative importance of the capital stock effect (the first component in the decomposition analysis), particularly in accounting for a negative change in employment, might be interpreted as suggesting that the unemployment is primarily 'Classical' in nature. Such an analysis might suggest the need for increasing the overall level of capacity in the economy by increasing the overall level of capital stock. There could be various policy interventions consistent with such an analysis, with varying political and economic implications, particularly in terms of distribution. Three such approaches to increasing capital stock are briefly reviewed here.

In one approach policy informed by such a result could focus on increasing the future profit expectations of private investors, as well as bolstering the certainty with which these expectations are held. Interventions in this vein could include fiscal policies that increase enterprise profitability or dividend payouts, measures to reduce the share of output going to workers and increase the share going to capitalists measures to increase worker productivity, infrastructure that increases the returns on private investment, and policies that increase investors' perception of the overall certainty of the political and economic environment.

An alternative set of policies informed by an analysis that found changes in capital stock to be significant in accounting for changes in employment, could focus on increasing the levels of private investment through more direct measures that partially socialize the control of private investment. These might include the use of prescribed asset measures or some variant thereof, capital controls designed to minimize the leakage of South African capital abroad and maximize the capital available for domestic productive investment, or directed credit policies.

A third alternative set of policies, still focusing on capital investment, could utilize more direct state control over the level of public investment in order to raise the level of aggregate investment. This could involve significantly boosting public spending on physical capital. Such interventions would prima facie increase the public component of aggregate capital stock, as well as affecting the level of private investment.

The possible sets of policy interventions discussed above—focusing on capital stock—are not necessarily mutually exclusive, although they would tend to be consistent with different views of the primary constraints on increasing investment in the South African economy, and on the appropriate political and economic roles of the state and private capitalist sector, respectively. This, however, is not the focus of this particular paper.

Second, an analysis that pointed to the relative importance of the capacity utilization effect in accounting for changes in the level of employment might point to problems of realization, where firms are unable to sell all output at full value, and hence lower their levels of production. Domestically, problems of realization are indicative of an imbalance between the structure of production and the distribution of demand, which is a function of the distribution of income which is, in turn, determined by factors such as technology and class struggle.

A finding of the relative significance of the capacity utilization effect might suggest that unemployment is more 'Keynesian' in nature, with sellers being on the long end of both the labour and goods markets. Such a finding could point to policies geared towards increasing levels of capacity utilization, primarily through increasing the level of aggregate demand in the economy. In most Keynesian models of investment, capacity utilization is the key determinant of investment (via effective demand).

Policies designed with the above in mind would be consistent with some of the possible measures already mentioned with respect to increasing capital stock. However, tensions are likely to arise between measures to increase capacity utilization and other potential policies increasing capital stock, notably with the first set of policies mentioned here. For example, 'profit-led' interventions intended to induce higher levels of private sector investment by reducing the share of output going to workers would be likely to depress the level of aggregate demand in the economy and actually deepen the capacity utilization constraint.

Policies to increase the level of aggregate demand in the economy, and hence the level of capacity utilization, might thus include increasing the share of output going to workers, increasing redistributive public spending to the poor, increasing public expenditure, export promotion, and protection of domestic industry through trade and industrial measures. Of course, as with the policy options to increase investment discussed above, various measures could be proposed to increase aggregate demand, with different implications distributionally and in other ways.

Third, should the evidence suggest that changes in relative factor utilization (labour intensity) are significant in accounting for changes in employment, it would imply that merely increasing the levels of capital stock or of capacity utilization would be unlikely to decisively address the high levels of unemployment in South Africa. Various policy interventions could then be conceptualized towards changing the relative factor utilization. Appropriate measures in this regard would depend on the root causes of the level and changes in relative factor utilization.

If the level of, or change in, relative factor utilization is primarily driven by relative factor prices, this could point to policies intended to affect the relative prices or productivity of capital and / or labour. We also hypothesize that relative factor utilization is influenced by broader political economy issues, such as patterns of distribution, class and bargaining power, and work organization. Addressing these would involve broader transformation.

Policies addressed to each of the three dimensions of the analytical framework employed in this paper—capital stock, capacity utilization, and relative factor utilization—could have distinct distributional implications. Changes in either the levels of capital stock, of capacity utilization, or of relative factor utilization, each at an order of magnitude associated with the same increase in employment, would bring differential returns to capital and labour. Changing relative factor utilization in a labour-intensive direction would possibly be more beneficial to labour relative to capital, from a distributional perspective. Of course, any assessment of the distributional implications of changes in capital stock, capacity utilization, and relative factor utilization would be contingent on the manner in which such changes are brought about. For example, with respect to capital stock, three different policy paradigms have been discussed, each of which would have very different distributional implications.

Following on from the above general interpretation of the decomposition analysis and possible policy implications, we now turn to commenting on the conclusions that can be drawn from the results of the actual analysis in this paper.

The capital effect accounts for a positive contribution to labour demand throughout, with the exception of a period in the late 1980s. The changes in labour demand accounted for by changes in capacity utilization vary over different years, but with an overall negative contribution. The most striking result is in terms of relative factor utilization (labour intensity), with a dramatic and almost continuous fall in the ratio of labour employed to utilized capital. The drop in the labour intensity of production accounts for an overwhelmingly negative change in labour demand in manufacturing. During the period 1991–2003, when a net loss in employment was observed, the negative factor utilization effect significantly exceeded the positive capital effect.

Although this paper is restricted to the manufacturing sector, due to space constraints, the rest of the South African economy was also analysed in the framework and using the methods discussed here. As capacity utilization data are not available for the non-manufacturing sectors, a two-stage decomposition analysis was carried out—decomposing changes in employment into a capital effect and a labour intensity. A similar picture obtains as with manufacturing. The capital effect was positive and the factor utilization effect negative in both periods 1970–90 and 1991–2004. However, there were important shifts in their relative magnitudes. In the first period, with positive employment growth, the capital effect was more than double the labour intensity. By contrast, in the second period, with an overall employment loss, the factor utilization effect somewhat exceeded the capital effect.

The finding of the overwhelmingly negative contribution (in a simple decomposition sense) of the labour intensity effect to changes in manufacturing employment, is consistent with other results in the literature (derived using different methodologies). It is noteworthy that South Africa's economy has become increasingly capital intensive, despite the rising unemployment and the fact that levels of unemployment are much higher than those of South Africa's trading partners and other countries at similar levels of development.

One difficulty in interpreting the results obtained from this research arises from the fact that one would expect capital stock to rise over time with the growth of the economy, and in addition that the labour intensity of production would typically fall over time with an economy's development and with technological advances. In this light, the finding that the capital stock effect 'accounts' for a positive growth in employment, and the factor utilization effect 'accounts' for a loss in employment, is hardly surprising. It is important to evaluate to what extent the trends in South Africa are 'normal' and consistent with the country's level and pace of economic development, and to what extent they are anomalous or excessive. South Africa's rate of capital intensification does appear to be high relative to that in comparable countries. Further, South Africa's current level of capital intensity does appear to be significantly higher than would be predicted on the basis of relative factor costs and labour abundance.

Further research, not fully discussed here owing to constraints of space analyses changes in relative factor utilization in the South African economy in greater detail. Inter alia, decomposition techniques were used in an attempt to separate out the extent to which changes in economy-wide relative factor utilization can be accounted for by intersectoral changes (shifts in the sectoral composition of the economy) as opposed to intrasectoral changes.[9] From 1970–90, both the composition and sectoral effects were negative, and were of a roughly similar order of magnitude. During 1991–2004, by contrast, the composition effect was marginally positive, and the sectoral effect negative. This would suggest that in the second period, it was intra-sectoral changes in the labour–capital ratio (that is, falling labour-intensity with sectors), rather than changes in the sectoral composition of the economy (towards less labour-intensive sectors), that accounted for the overall decline in the labour-capital ratio.

## CONCLUDING REMARKS

The results of this research suggest that capital investment alone is insufficient for employment creation. In fact, certain types of capital investment may actually reduce employment. Under certain political and institutional conditions, investment could substitute employment by 'artificially' increasing the capital-intensity of production. There thus need to be a positive relationship between investment and employment. It appears that much of the investment that has occurred in South African manufacturing has been labour-displacing rather than labour-absorbing. Of course, in a complete aggregate and dynamic analysis, the latter types of labour-displacing investment may create employment elsewhere in the economy, through enhanced efficiency and multiplier effects of increased output. Nevertheless, the overall relationship between capital investment and employment remains ambiguous and contingent on the nature of the investment.

The aggregate capital-labour ratio is likely to be higher than the socially optimal level, given that decisions of private firm with respect to investment and production method do not factor in the social benefits of higher employment that are not captured by the individual private firm, and similarly the social costs of labour-displacing private investment that are not borne by the individual firm.

If the capital intensification of the economy continues, increasing net investment would be required simply to maintain the current, inadequate levels of employment; even higher rates of increase in net investment would be required to absorb net new labour entrants

[9]The labour–capital ratio was decomposed into the composition and sectoral effects as follows:

$$\Delta\gamma = \underbrace{\sum_{i=1}^{n}(k_t^i - k_{t-1}^i)\left(\frac{\gamma_{t-1}^i + \gamma_t^i}{2}\right)}_{\textit{composition effect}} + \underbrace{\sum_{i=1}^{n}(\gamma_t^i - \gamma_{t-1}^i)\left(\frac{k_{t-1}^i + k_t^i}{2}\right)}_{\textit{sectoral effect}}$$

where $\gamma$ is the overall labour / capital ratio and $\gamma_t^i$ is the ratio in sector i at time t, and $k_t^i$ is sector i's share of total fixed capital stock at time t. A similar method was used to decompose changes in the labour–output ratio.

and maintain the current levels of unemployed people; and still higher rates of increase in net investment would be required to begin to reduce the number of unemployed people. Shifting towards more labour-intensive production—either through sectoral shifts, and/or through changes in technology—would mean that lower levels of net new investment would be required than would otherwise be the case in order to achieve a reduction in unemployment; or to put it differently, greater reductions in unemployment can be achieved at the same levels of net new investment.

This serves to emphasize that it is not merely the overall quantity of capital stock (or the level of investment) that is important, but also the 'quality' of this capital. 'Quality' could have various dimensions, one of particular relevance to this paper being the degree to which it is labour-absorbing in a sustainable manner (also that it is not labour displacing as an objective in itself). This would be influenced by various factors, including the sector, type of product within the sector, technology choices, and so on. All of these could be subject to policy interventions intended to make investment more labour-absorbing rather than labour-displacing. With a shift towards more labour-absorbing investment, a higher labour demand growth path may actually require lower absolute levels of capital investment than otherwise would be the case.

An analysis that points to the importance of capital intensification in accounting for employment losses (and the absence of employment creation) does not, in itself, automatically point to the reversing of capital intensification as the obvious and central policy intervention for employment creation. More important is the overall employment-intensity of a sector, including both direct employment and indirect employment multipliers.

Further, this analysis should not be interpreted as ignoring or downplaying the need for new investment. As discussed in the initial conceptualization, labour demand can be increased through an increase in capacity, in capacity utilization, or in the labour intensity with which capacity is utilized. Further, there are obviously limits to the extent to which employment can be generated through increasing the labour intensity of production. Particularly in an open economy, competitiveness could be undermined when the individual firm costs of more labour intensive production become individually 'inefficient'.

This serves to emphasize the need for an integrated approach including supportive macroeconomic, industrial, and trade policies. One of the central apparent paradoxes of the South African economy is the combination of extremely high rates of unemployment and a process of capital-intensification. That this is occurring with rather low rates of overall capital investment that makes the displacement of labour by capital even more noteworthy. Further, wages are not especially high relative to countries which are in a similar level of development. It appears that there is a degree of 'excess' capital intensification that needs to be understood in terms of South Africa's political and institutional context.

## REFERENCES

Bhorat, Haroon (1999), 'Decomposing Shifts in Labour Demand in South Africa'. *Southern African Journal of Economics*, Vol. 67, No. 3, p. 348.

—— 'The Impact of Trade and Structural Changes on Sectoral Employment in South Africa', *Development Southern Africa*, Vol. 17, No. 3, pp. 437–66.

Bhorat, Haroon and Morné Oosthuizen (2005), 'The Post-Apartheid South African Labour Market', Development Policy Research Unit Working Paper 05/93, April.

Bhorat, Haroon, Sten Dielten, and James Hodge, 'The Impact of Structural and Production Method Changes on Employment Growth of Occupational Groups in South Africa', HSRC, Pretoria, unpublished paper.

Crotty, James (1993), 'Rethinking Marxian Investment Theory: Keynes-Minsky Instability, Competitive Regime Shifts, and Coerced Investment', *Review of Radical Political Economics*, March 1992, Vol. 25, No. 1, pp. 1–26.

—— (1993), 'Neoclassical and Keynesian Approaches to the Theory of Investment', *Journal of Post Keynesian Economics*, Vol. 14, No. 4, Summer 1992, pp. 483–96.

Edwards, L. (1999), 'Trade Liberalisation, Structural Change and Occupational Employment in South Africa', Paper presented at TIPS 1999 Annual Forum, Muldersdrift.

—— (2001), 'Trade and the Structure of South African Production, 1984–97', *Development Southern Africa*, Vol. 18, No. 4, October, pp. 471–91.

Fedderke, Johannes, Simon Henderson, Mautine Mariotti, and Prabhat Vaze (2000), 'Changing Factor Market Conditions in South Africa: The Labour Market—a Sectoral Description of the Period 1972–1997', Econometric Research Southern Africa, Policy Paper No. 5.

Heintz, J. (2001), 'Investment, Labour Demand and Political Conflict in South Africa', PhD Dissertation, University of Massachusetts Amherst, May.

Levy, Brian (1992), 'How Can South African Manufacturing Efficiently Create Employment? An Analysis of the Impact of Trade and Industrial Policy', Informal Discussion Paper on Aspects of the Economy of South Africa No.1, Southern Africa Department, World Bank, Washington.

Malinvaud, E. (1977), *The Theory of Unemployment Reconsidered*, Basil Blackwell, Oxford.

Nattrass, N. (2000), 'Is South Africa's High-productivity Growth Strategy Appropriate in a Labour-surplus Economy?', Paper presented at TIPS Annual Forum 2000.

Poswell, Laura (2002), 'The Post-Apartheid South African Labour Market: A Status Report', Development Policy Research Unit, Rondebosch.

Smith, H. (2003), 'Note on the Changing Structure of the Manufacturing Sector', *South African Reserve Bank Quarterly Bulletin*, March, pp. 79–87.

Statistics South Africa (2005), *Labour Force Survey March 2005*, Statistics South Africa, Pretoria.

Tregenna, Fiona (2003), 'Background Paper on Determinants of Labour Demand in South Africa' Report prepared for Employment and Economic Policy Research, HSRC, Pretoria.

Wakeford, Jeremy (2004), 'The Productivity-Wage Relationship in South Africa: An Empirical Investigation', *Development Southern Africa*, Vol. 21, No. 1, March, pp. 109–132.

# 10

# The Evolution of Wage Differentials under the Export-led Regime in Turkish Manufacturing Industry

## A Cluster Analysis

EMEL MEMIS*

## INTRODUCTION

One of the highly controversial debates in the literature has been the persistent inter- and intra-industry wage differentials. Conventional theory, until recently, offered arguments that went against the evidence for wage differentials, with the underlying assumptions of competitive labour and capital markets. In a perfectly competitive world, returns to factors of production are determined by behavioural choices (Hicks 1963). Hence inequalities, as such, are affirmed to be either temporary anomalies or consequences of rational behaviour (Becker 1964). Later in the literature, departures from perfect competitive market assumptions generated new theoretical explanations. Efficiency wage theory, internal labour markets, and rent sharing models based on the extent of managerial altruism are some of the examples (Krueger and Summers 1987; Dickens and Katz 1987; Doeringer and Piore 1971; Akerlof and Yellen 1986).

Heterodox economists have repeatedly criticized conventional theorists for failing to discern the evidence. They argue that institutional factors, that is, industrial concentration, unionization, policy changes, laws, norms, and many other regularities in the economy usually induce permanent structural artifacts such as persistent wage differentials. The monopoly pricing of firms and segmented labour market theory are the most well-known explanations (Edwards 1979; Reich 1984; Gordon et al. 1982). As opposed to conventional arguments, heterodox theories have considered wage inequalities as an inherent matter of fact. That is, they believe that the existing nature of the economic system per se sustains and transforms certain systematic patterns of inter- and intra industry wage differentials (Botwinick 1993).

*Erol Taymaz and Yumiko Yamamato deserve my warmest thanks for providing access to data used in this research. I also would like to thank Al Campbell, Korkut Erturk, Erdogan Bakir, Kagan Parmaksiz, Manuel Montes, Benan Eres, Fuat Ercan, Peter Jacobs, and participants of the ACDC in 2005 for their very useful questions and comments on a previous draft of this paper. Any remaining errors are mine.

Over the last thirty years, the integration of the world economy shifted the earlier debates towards changes in the world division of labour and its impacts on income distribution, in general, and on the wage structure, in particular. Persistent inequalities within countries could no longer be analysed in isolation from differential levels of economic development between nations. Alternatively, the main question explored became the impact of increased trade/openness on the wage structure in advanced/developing economies[1] and the issue has become much more complicated.

Conventional trade theory suggests that increased trade reduces wage inequalities in developing countries. In its simplest form, the Heckscher–Ohlin theory argues that countries export those commodities, which use abundant factors intensively, thus increasing the demand for the abundant factor. Since the abundant factor in developing countries is 'unskilled' labour, higher exports from sectors employing 'unskilled' labour create higher demand for this type of labour reducing the wage disparities between 'skilled' and 'unskilled' labour. Simultaneously, the theory predicts the opposite for advanced countries. While the studies for advanced countries continued to explore the question: 'Are your wages set in Beijing?' (Freeman 1995), studies in developing countries have confirmed that wage dispersion has increased in contrast to the standard prediction, even though empirical evidence in developing countries is still rare compared to that in advanced countries.

Given this background, the main purpose of this study is to measure the extent of inter-industry wage differentials in Turkish manufacturing industry from 1980 to 2000, displaying further evidence on wage differentials in developing countries. The Turkish economy is a case in point. To the extent that wage dispersion is a major component of income inequality, this study also provides some insights into the pattern of distribution of income, primarily on the pattern of intra-class distribution of income over time. In these respects, analysis of the extent of wage dispersion in general is a crucial issue for equality and development purposes. On the other hand, given the period of examination of this study, which starts with the shift of Turkish economy to the export-led regime in 1980, our empirical analysis can account for the impact of such a policy shift. These policies were intended to generate 'economic growth' and were specifically targeted towards the manufacturing industry, playing major roles on industrial development (or lack thereof).

Another contribution of this study lies in the method deployed for the empirical analysis. One interesting remark by Berner and Galbraith (2001) is that at the theoretical level, most of the literature focuses on the determination of wage rates to explain the sources behind the evidence of wage differentials. Yet, the empirical evidence is derived from industrial data sets that are constructed by standard classifications based on product characteristics. And accordingly, these data sets split the pattern of wages into discrete

[1]While some studies presented evidence for long-run stability in wage differentials, according to which, any type of structural changes led by policy shifts would not affect the pervasive wage structure through time and even among different countries; other studies have show that since the mid-1980s, increased openness has widening impacts on wage differentials (see Katz and Summers 1989; Krueger and Summers 1987; Arbache, Dickerson, and Green 2001; Wood 1995, 1997 for more details).

components as 'industries' that is, groups of firms classified by similarities in other aspects rather than the wage pattern per se. However, it is clear by now that common wage structure does not necessarily reflect similarity of product market characteristics, but may reflect other similarities, for example, common institutional sources. Based on this theoretical justification, following Berner and Galbraith (2001), empirical analysis in this chapter implements a cluster analysis, necently introduced method in the field of economics. Using the clustering method we regroup industries[2] primarily using the historical pattern of the main variable of analysis, which is the wage differential in our case.

The evidence obtained demonstrates that the extent of the wage-differentials in the Turkish manufacturing industry has widened over the period of analysis, suggesting a counterargument against conventional theoretical explanations. And the results do mark the importance of reclassifying industrial data based on the variable to be analysed. The paper is organized as follows: the next section presents a brief summary of the overall developments in the Turkish economy together with earlier findings on the industry wage structure. In the third section we describe the data empirical methodology, as well as findings. In the fourth section we review several policies and regulations implemented through the restructuring of the economy under an export-led regime. Using relevant analytical tools we also derive possible explanations for the evidence from the overview of policies and practices. Finally, in the last section, we summarize the main findings and present the concluding remarks.

[2]Data used are at the three-digit aggregation level, which is the most disaggregated level provided by the OECD STAN dataset.

## THE TURKISH ECONOMY AND EARLIER EVIDENCE ON INDUSTRY WAGE STRUCTURE

From the post-world war II period until the 1970s, as in many other developing countries, industrialization was considered the most significant objective for development in Turkey. Turkey became a significant producer of manufactured goods, shifting away from a peripheral agrarian economy. This was mainly the outcome of ISI policies applied just after the war. The main objective of these policies was first to create an industrial base in order to achieve sustainable economic growth as elsewhere. Yet, by the late 1970s, the Turkish economy, similar to Latin American countries, was faced with severe balance of payments difficulties, high unemployment, and high inflation. The major underlying problem was the economy's inability to generate sufficient foreign exchange.[3] The 1980s started with a radical restructuring, moving away from ISI and leaning towards an export-oriented plan with the 24 January 1980 Reform Package. This shift, as has been the case in elsewhere, did not happen as a simple smooth economic change for the economy and the society as a whole. The restructuring through neo-liberal policies came through fundamental changes in the political and social structure in Turkey. The standard elements of these policies were the liberalization of the trade regime, the introduction of new measures to promote exports, financial deregulation and deregulation of prices, deregulation of the labour market

[3]Various sub-sectors of manufacturing industry were heavily dependent on imported intermediate goods. Though imports for the production of consumer durables declined with the shift to intermediate commodities, the demand for oil and new technology created a foreign exchange bottleneck at the end of the 1970s.

and privatization to reduce the size of the public sector, under an overall framework of liberalization both internally and externally. These came along as part of the programme implemented by a short-lived military regime that came to power in a right-wing coup following a period of economic crisis and social turmoil. Just before the end of the decade, the last stage of the liberalization process was completed with full financial liberalization in 1989.[4] Despite the standard expectations such as the creation of an efficient financial market through which savings would be turned into investment at a lower cost and would finance high budget deficits, such a financing scheme became a vicious cycle for public debt, given the fact that with financial liberalization interest rates were tied to the foreign exchange regime and to the need to attract (and retain) foreign capital.[5] Hence, the Turkish economy followed a speculation-led development path, which warped the economic system into a deeply fragile state, both in terms of the domestic structure and in its vulnerability to short-term speculative capital attacks (Yeldan 2001). Three major crises over the recent decade, in 1994, 2000, and 2001 reveal the fragility of the financial structure.

One stylized fact that characterizes the new restructuring period in Turkey has been the increasingly unequal income distribution. The sources and mechanisms behind income inequality depend on many different historical and social factors. Yet, economic policies have always been very significant in reshaping the structure of income distribution. There are many studies on income distribution and profitability on Turkish manufacturing sector that provide insights into wage inequalities in this sector.[6] However, there are only a few studies that specifically discuss the pattern of wage differentials over time. Erdil (1993) analyses inter-industry wage differentials in Turkish Manufacturing Industry over the period 1964 to 1989 and shows the persistence of inter-industry wage differentials in Turkish manufacturing industry. Bagdadioglu and Ercan (2001) provide estimates that wage inequality is higher in the private than public sector.[7] Yet, these studies take the standard classification of industries as given, unlike the analysis in this study. The usefulness of our method becomes clearer, particularly in a time-series analysis. The common statistical technique used traditionally is to calculate the standard deviation of differences of wage levels of each industry from the average wage level. However, standard deviation does not provide the information to identify those industries that follow a similar path. In other words, which industry stands where over a period of time is not obtained from calculations of standard deviation. This is how the cluster analysis we use in this study is different from the traditional method. Moreover, earlier

[4]In addition the export-led growth strategy that was dependent on wage suppression, depreciation of currency, and export incentive systems reached its limits by 1988. Hence, in a sense, this setting-up of the system exhausted itself. Thus, financial liberalization was seen as an exit away from this boundary.

[5]As a result, interest payments absorbed almost all of the public sector disposable income (Yeldan 2001, p. 1). Inflation rates increased to as high as 90 per cent and nominal interest rates sky-rocketed to three digit levels in the second half of the 1990s.

[6]See Çagatay (1986), Ozmucur (1992, 1996), Metin-Özcan, et al. (2002), and Onaran and Yentürk (2003) for more details.

[7]There are two more studies to the best of my knowledge that focus on the role of ownership on wage structure. Ozmucur (1997) presents the differences in wages and analyses disparities between public and private sector wage structures. Similarly, Bayazıto_lu and Ercan (2001) state that ownership plays a significant role in wage dispersion.

studies focus mainly on determining factors of wage rates, without discussing changes in policies, or transformations of institutional factors or even changes in the trade structure of these industries. Thus, we aim to partly fill these lacunae in the literature.

## EMPIRICAL ANALYSIS

In this study we use two different data sources: the Annual Manufacturing Industry Statistics[8] (AMIS) database and the OECD STAN dataset. The period of analysis covers the years 1980 to 2000. AMIS, which is based on the international standard industrial classification of all economic activities, revision number two (ISIC-Rev.2), is compiled from information collected from employers.[9] It includes all public and private establishments with more than ten employees. We used AMIS for the following variables: wage payments, value-added, and working hours. For trade indicators, the STAN dataset was used. The first estimates of exports and imports at current prices were derived from detailed information from OECD's International Trade in Commodities Statistics (ITCS) database. This dataset is based on ISIC-Rev.3. For consistency, a standard conversion from the ISIC-Rev.3 to ISIC Rev. 2 was used[10] via an industry equivalence table from STAN.

Instead of taking the international standard classifications as given, we make use of a different industry grouping that is based upon the specific variable to be analysed. The theoretical justification of such a method goes back to the 'wage contours' approach suggested by Dunlop (1979). He defined wage contours as congruities of wage-setting behaviour, which do not necessarily reflect a common process, location, or product characteristic that may have given rise to those harmonized behaviours (Galbraith and Calmon 1996, p. 433). Thus, common wage characteristics, he argues, are linked not only to the similarity of product markets but also to similar sources of the labour force or common labour market institutions (Dunlop 1979). Many earlier studies either use more detailed levels of aggregation level in order to not lose information but nevertheless result in dividing what should be a homogeneous group and/or obtaining spurious results. Or they use a descriptional unit of analysis, such as sales as the basis for clustering, which fixes the reference point on the movements of a different variable. However, for the reasons given above, both are problematical (Galbraith and Calmon 1996, p. 435). Berner and Galbraith (2001, p. 18) said that considering each industrial category as a discrete unit of observation is a mistake. And the effort to obtain information on the variations of the different wage structure becomes more complicated when that information is concealed under the classification of industrial data sets. In order to reduce complications to detect the patterns of structures, for example wage patterns, Berner and Galbraith (2001) introduce a statistical tool, cluster analysis, which permits one to come up with a fundamental structure in time series data based on patterns of behaviour over time. Its usefulness in this study comes from its ability to be

[8] *http://www.die.gov.tr/konularr/iy_sanayi.htm* The wage cost is the gross wage payments by the employer which include all fringe benefits, overtime payments, and income tax but excludes the social security payments and retirement benefits paid by the employer. Working hours and wage payments correspond to production workers only.

[9] The most reliable data resource on employment in Turkey is the household survey which has individual information and is issued twice a year by the Institute of Statistics (SIS). However, the absence of wage information in this survey leaves us with the second best choice.

[10] Please go to website: *http://unstats.un.org/unsd/cr/registry/regcst.asp?Cl=2* for more details.

applied to the rates of dispersion of the wage data over a period of time.

For our purposes, first, we chose the best possible indicator for wage differentials, which is *the deviation of hourly wage cost within each industry from the weighted average of manufacturing as a whole.*[11] Our intent here is to explain intuitively the logic behind this method. Next, using Ward's method, we applied the clustering procedure.[12] It is observed that clustering effectively isolates low wage paying sub-industries from others, even though they might belong to same product group (See Table A10.2.1). For example, the manufacture of scientific and optical instruments (385) is assigned to the low wage cluster (cluster 2), which also includes the machinery and equipment industry. This indicates that the scientific and optical instruments sector is a low wage industry, even though it uses a high level of technology. Similarly, the textiles and textile products sector and food, beverage and tobacco industries are segregated into two clusters as lowest wage and low wage groups (clusters 1 and 2). Other examples are separation of manufacturing of plastic products and manufacturing of fabricated metal products except machinery and optical goods, in the low tech-low wage cluster (cluster 2) from high and medium tech–high wage group (cluster 4). The manufacturing of non-metallic mineral products are separated into three clusters: manufacturing of glass and glass products is included in the high wage cluster (cluster 4), manufacturing of pottery and earthenware is low wage paying (cluster 2), whereas the other non-metallic mineral manufacturing is among the average wage paying industries (cluster 3). This is evidence that within standard

[11]The percentage difference is used in order to convert the series into a unit free one. The average hourly wage ($w_{it}$) is calculated by dividing the yearly total payments ($W_{it}$) to workers by the total hours of working ($L_{it}$) for each industry. The calculations can be formalized as follows: hourly wage for industry $i$ at time $t$: $w_{it} = W_{it}/L_{it}$ Then, mean deviation of wage ($dev_{it}$) for industry $i$ at time $t$ is the percentage difference from whole manufacturing wage at time $t$ ($\overline{w}_t$) and is calculated as: $dev_{it} = ((w_{it} - \overline{w}_t)/\overline{w}_t)*100\%$

The weighted average wage for the whole manufacturing industry is calculated as: $\overline{w}_t = \sum_t (L_{it}/L_t)w_{it}$ where the share of number of hours worked for each industry in total manufacturing are used as the weights.

The data consists of 21 (from 1980 to 2000) annual measures of 29 three-digit ISIC sectors in manufacturing industry hourly wage percentage differences from the average hourly wage.

[12]Ward's method performs clustering by seeking at each step the minimum ratio within clusters to the total variance in whole differences set and existing cluster means. Ward's method is a hierarchical type of agglomerative nesting method. It follows iterative steps. In the first step it treats all industries as separate clusters. Then checking the dissimilarity among the industries according to an index formed based on their distance from the centroid of the cluster, either the latter is merged or not. This iterative step goes on until all the industries are members of clusters. At each step, cluster numbers are reduced from N to 1 in a way to minimize the specified objective function. The objective function Ward used is the increase in total sum of squares or the geometric distance from each data point to the centre of its cluster. Here, the error sum of squares (ESS) for cluster $c$ is: $ESS_c = R_c - 1/m_c \sum_t D_{ct}^2$ where $D_{ct} = \sum_t dev_{itc}$ and $R_c = \sum_t \sum_i dev_{itc}^2$

$R_c$ is the sum of squared mean deviation in all years for all industries in the $c$th cluster;

$D_{ct}$ is the sum of mean deviation of wages at time $t$ for industries in the $c$th cluster;

$m_c$ is the number of industries in cluster $c$; and

$dev_{itc}$ is the mean deviation of wage at time $t$ for the $i$th industry among $m_c$ industries in the $c$th cluster.

Following these, in order to test whether Ward's clustering method gives appropriate results, the average linkage method is used as well. Since both methods give the same results it can be concluded that the results passed the assessment tests. For more details see Galbraith and Lu (1999) as well as Kaufman and Rousseeuw (1990) (Detailed printed results can be provided on request).

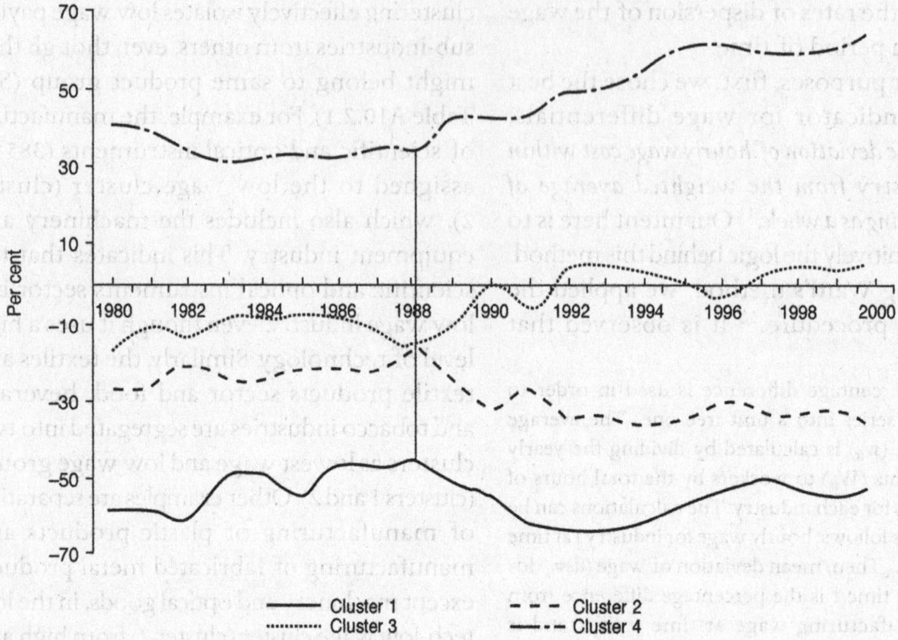


Figure 10.1: Percentage Deviation of Hourly Wages from the Average

product type groups there are different wage patterns.

The wage differentials obtained as percentage differences of each cluster's weighted[13] average compared to the overall average can be seen in Figure 10.1. The figure shows the time path of the differentials by clusters over the period. We observe two interesting facts here: first, the wage across clusters is hierarchical; and, second, it seems clear that wage patterns experienced substantial changes after the year 1988. Note particularly, the rising trend in the high wage cluster and the falling trend in the lowest and low wage clusters. During 1982–8, all paths follow a comparatively a stable course. However, after 1988, they diverge drastically from the average (except cluster 3). The most extreme divergence is observed between the low average wage clusters (cluster 2 and 3) that is 40 per cent points, which denotes 2000 per cent rise in the degree of deviance from 1988 to 2000.[14]

In the literature, productivity differentials are known to offer the most significant source for wage differentials. Figure 10.2 shows the trend in labour productivity differentials[15]

[13]For each cluster, a single weighted average hourly wage is calculated considering only the industries included in that cluster where the number of hours worked is used as weights.

[14]The divergence between low wage (cluster 2) and high wage (cluster 4) clusters increased by 106 per cent. The lowest wage (cluster 1) and low wage (cluster 2) clusters diverged from each other by 86 per cent. Last, the lowest change is seen between lowest wage (cluster 1) and high wage (cluster 4) clusters 50 per cent.

[15]Labour productivity is calculated as value added (deflated by GNP deflator 1980=100) per labour hour. Cluster deviance from the whole industry average

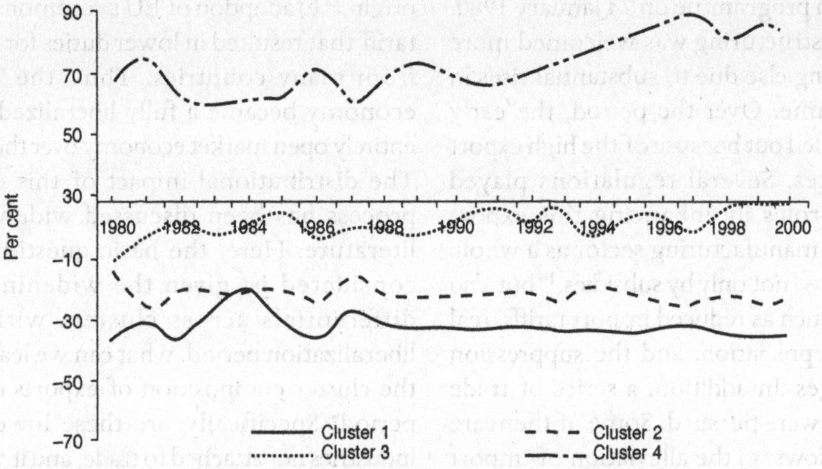


Figure 10.2: Labour Productivity Differentials

across clusters over the period. This figure somewhat confirms the results of traditional literature; nonetheless, it is clear that changes in the structure of productivity deviations are not as severe as wage deviations.[16] The disparity between low wage and average wage clusters (clusters 2 and 3) rises by only 30 per cent[17] in the 1990s as compared to the 1980s. And this is the highest figure of divergence obtained across clusters. For instance, between the high wage (cluster 4) and the lowest wage (cluster 1) as well as with the low wage (cluster 2) cluster the degree of divergence is 20 and 21 per cent, respectively in the 1990s compared to the 1980s. The results suggest that though productivity differentials reflect on the wage structure in Turkish industry, they do not fully describe changes in its trend.

It is also possible to look at simple correlations between productivity and wage deviations to see the exent to which the two trends reflect each other. The results show that the correlations decline in 1990s compared to the 1980s particularly in two clusters that is, lowest wage and average wage clusters (clusters 1 and 3) (see table A10.2.5). This reflects the fact that the explanatory power of productivity variation declines in the 1990s. One interesting result is that correlations are negative for cluster 2 and, even more interesting, that the figure doubles in 1990s compared to the 1980s. As the productivity disparity falls, the wage disparity rises, which is counter to common expectations.

## DOES LIBERALIZATION REDUCE WAGE DISPARITY IN TURKISH MANUFACTURING INDUSTRY?

Turkey, as mentioned earlier in this paper, increased its openness by the enactment of a

---

labour productivity is calculated as taking the industry average as 100, the productivity index for each cluster is calculated. Then, the average is normalized at zero in order to reach percentage deviations.

[16]The evolution of labour productivity index across clusters confirms this fact more clearly. Due to space limitations we could not include the picture of labour productivity indexes here.

[17]The figures correspond to geometric averages of annual differentials over the period mentioned.

stabilization programme on 24 January 1980. The new restructuring was welcomed more than anything else due to substantial rises in export volume. Over the period, the early 1980s is singled out because of the high export growth rates. Several regulations played important roles in enhancing this export boom. The manufacturing sector as a whole was supported not only by subsidies,[18] but also by policies such as reduced import tariffs, real currency depreciation, and the suppression of real wages. In addition, a series of trade regulations were pursued. Some of them are listed as follows: a) the alleviation of import restrictions in 1983,[19] b) reductions in import protection tariff,[20] starting in 1992, c) GATTI-UR Agreement is signed in 1993 after a seven year period of continuing discussions,[21] d) enforcement of EU Customs Union agreement in 1996, which established zero duty rates and no quotas for non-agricultural items of EU and European Free Trade Association (EFTA) origin,[22] e) adoption of EU's common external tariff that resulted in lower duties for imports from many countries. Thus, the Turkish economy became a fully liberalized and an entirely open market economy over the period. The distributional impact of this opening process has been discussed widely in the literature. Here, the basic question being considered is: given the widening wage differentials across clusters within the liberalization period, what can we learn from the cluster composition of exports over the period? Specifically, are these lower wage industries not attached to trade, and if yes, does not liberalization not reduce wage disparity?

We checked the trend in manufacturing exports by clusters (see Figure 10.3). The shares of the lowest wage and low wage clusters (clusters 1 and 2) are combined together due to a data issue.[23] In line with the conventional trade theory, it is observed that commodities produced by using low technology are exported, in other words, the export structure of Turkish manufacturing sector confirms the argument that export goods are labour intensive ones from economies where labour is the abundant factor. The shares of the lowest and low wage clusters (clusters 1 and 2) sum up to more than half of the total manufacturing exports.[24] Note particularly, following the

[18]The amount of export subsidies was roughly 30 per cent of the value of exports in the early 1980s (Taymaz 1998).

[19]The positive import lists were changed to negative lists. The import lists were classified under three groups: the prohibited list (commodities that are not allowed to be imported), the approval list (commodities that require official permission to import) and the fund list (luxury goods that can be imported freely, on condition of paying a levy). After 1983, the positive lists under these classifications were changed to negative lists, allowing all other goods free importation unless listed. This process involved almost all consumer goods imports; as such 60 per cent of 1983 imports were liberalized.

[20]Though tariff rates remained constant in the early 1980s; they increased in late 1980s and then declined post-1992.

[21]This agreement resulted in greater liberalization for the developing world whereas it formed the basis for monopolizing for the advanced world via intellectual property rights.

[22]An importer only needs a tax number not a licence or document to import all but restricted items.

[23]Given two different data sets it is not possible to separate these clusters from each other due to difficulties in converting ISIC Rev.3 to ISIC Rev.2.

[24]Except the four years from 1984–8 the cluster's path lies above 50 per cent. Moreover, not only within manufacturing but in total exports (in all industries) as well, the combined cluster of lowest and low wage (clusters 1 and 2) has the highest share over the period. Their share lies above 40 per cent in the 1990s (essentially after 1988) and reaches 50 per cent of the total exports in 2000.

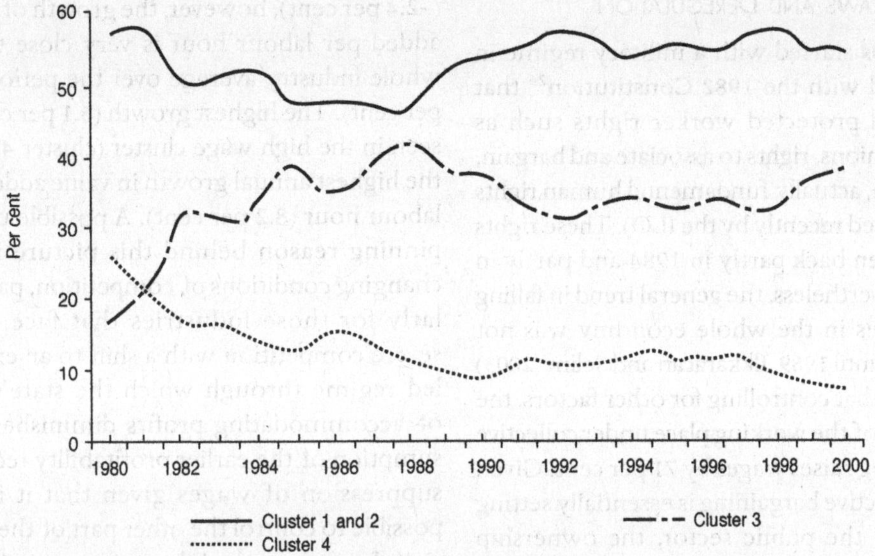


Figure 10.3: Cluster Shares in Manufacturing Exports

falling portion over the period 1980–8 that exports of these two clusters climb almost to 60 per cent, rising to half of the 1988 figure. However, employees in these industries kept earning lower wages counter to conventional expectations. Despite the openness of the economy and the implementation of export-led strategies, the fact that the majority of export goods are produced by low paying manufacturing industries has not changed.

Given the evidence here for the Turkish manufacturing industry, one can safely argue that Turkey's experience builds a picture that goes against traditional arguments—supporting critical views. The automatic mechanism in the Heckscher–Ohlin theory cannot be confirmed in the Turkish case. Then, the challenge is to explain other possible sources of the persistent inter-industry wage differentials which are likely to be found as the outcomes of structural features inherent within the economic system or of post-liberalization policies and practices, or both.[25] Post-1980 restructuring policies may, in fact, reveal more about wage disparities. Next follows an overview of other policies as well as their impact on the wage structure and income distribution. Beyond the trade agreements and regulations referred to briefly, there are several other policies implemented along with the whole package of the stabilization and structural adjustment programmes.

[25]The theoretical justification of this argument is based on an alternative framework which posits the very existence of capitalist competition as an explanation for wage differentials. The ongoing competition among capital, per se, sustains and transforms certain systematic patterns of inter- and intra industry wage differentials. Most of the persistent pattern of wage differentials, as already mentioned, is the result of different dynamics intertwined all together: the ongoing competition and profitability differentials, continuing generation of a reserve army of unemployed, and the uneven efforts of organized workers to raise their wages within the strict limits defined by competition (Botwinick 1993).

## Labour Laws and Deregulation

The 1980s started with a military regime in place and with the 1982 Constitution[26] that outlawed protected worker rights such as joining unions, rights to associate and bargain, which are, actually, fundamental human rights (recognized recently by the ILO). These rights were given back partly in 1984 and partly in 1987. Nevertheless, the general trend in falling real wages in the whole economy was not reversed until 1989. Ilkkaracan and Selim (2003) estimate that controlling for other factors, the coverage of the working place under collective bargaining raises wages by 71 per cent. Given that collective bargaining is essentially setting wages in the public sector, the ownership distinction across clusters might be a significant factor that explains the pattern of wage differentials (see Tables A10.2.6 and A10.2.7 for public sector shares across clusters over time).

Moreover, in order to see the possible impacts of these labour laws on labourers' bargaining power across clusters, we decomposed the average annual growth in real wages into average annual growth rate in wage share and the real value added per labour hour, considering the growth rate in the wage shares as a proxy for labour's bargaining power. (see Table 10.1). The figures verify significant differences across clusters. The lowest growth (3.9 per cent) is obtained in the low wage cluster (cluster 2); with the highest stagnation in wage share (–2.4 per cent), however, the growth of value added per labour hour is very close to the whole industry average over the period (6.3 per cent). The highest growth (6.1 per cent) is seen in the high wage cluster (cluster 4) with the highest annual growth in value added per labour hour (8.2 per cent). A possible underpinning reason behind this picture is the changing conditions of competition, particularly for those industries that face more severe competition with a shift to an export-led regime through which the state's role of accommodating profits diminishes. Resumption of the earlier profitability requires suppression of wages given that it is not possible to control the other part of the costs as it depends on mainly on imports. As it is clear from Table 10.1, over the whole period, all the clusters show a negative annual average growth rate in wage share.[27] This offers evidence for a steady change in income distribution favouring profits vis-à-vis wages during the period. Note particularly the figures in 1980s, when none of the clusters show positive growth but instead present drastically large negative growth rates. This finding is supported by earlier studies as well. Eres (2005) states that the whole manufacturing industry profit rate shows explosive growth (546 per cent) from 1968 to 1988, for which the distributional arrangements played a significant role. After 1988, except for a four-year

[26]With the 1982 Constitution and 1983 Labour Code, a suppressive labour regime is deployed. The Supreme Board of Arbitration was established by this code. The determination of the real wage began to be closely monitored and substantially repressed by continual state intervention (Eres 2005). Then, by the end of 1980s a very brief populist period followed, starting in 1989 and lasting till 1991. Yet, the detrimental effects on not only wage incomes but also on bargaining power of labour could not recover even until the end of the 1990s.

[27]Moreover, the following quote may offer an intuition on the direction of wage movements after the year 2000. In 2001, after the 2001 financial crisis and the new Minister of Treasury, Kemal Dervis, mentioned during his presentation in July 2003 as a part of the World Bank's Practitioners in Development Series that though it was very hard to do, he had to decrease the real wages by 20 per cent since 2001. Dervis took office shortly after the collapse of the Turkish lira (halved its value) and overnight the interest rates increased to more than 5000 per cent.

Table 10.1: Annual Growth of Real Wage, Wage Share, and Value Added per Hour (per cent)

| Cluster | 1980–2000 | | | 1980s | | | 1990s | | |
|---|---|---|---|---|---|---|---|---|---|
| | Real wage | Wage share | Value added per hour | Real wage | Wage share | Value added per hour | Real wage | Wage share | Value added per hour |
| 1 | 4.8 | −1.3 | 6.1 | 2.1 | −5.4 | 7.5 | 3.4 | 1.6 | 1.9 |
| 2 | 3.9 | −2.4 | 6.3 | −0.2 | −5.9 | 5.7 | 0.6 | −1.6 | 2.2 |
| 3 | 6.0 | −1.4 | 7.5 | 0.0 | −8.0 | 7.4 | 1.6 | −1.5 | 3.1 |
| 4 | 6.1 | −2.1 | 8.2 | −0.9 | −8.2 | 7.3 | 2.6 | −1.8 | 4.4 |
| All Industries | 5.0 | −1.7 | 6.6 | −0.8 | −7.1 | 6.3 | 1.2 | −1.4 | 2.6 |

*Note*: Calculations[28] are done by estimating the regression coefficients of Equation 10.1

recovery period, the profit rate growth started falling with a volatile trend that had further adverse effects on the wages.

There is one other policy that had adverse implications on the industry wage structure. The domestic terms of trade between agriculture and manufacturing deteriorated against agriculture through state price regulations that kept agricultural support prices lower than the inflation rate over the period. This deterioration shifted the agricultural population to other sectors usually filling jobs in the low-paid, low-technology industries and increasing the reserve army of labour. This definitely had both direct and contagion effects on the wage structure. Yeldan (2001) estimates the share of marginal and informal labour in total manufacturing industry employment as 41 per cent in 1980. This number increased to 49 per cent in 1994.[29] Hence, the marginalization phenomenon turned out to be a structural feature of the labour market over the period. The creation of free trade zones and EPZs[30] also created an impetus for

[28]The compounded annual percentage growth rates:

Equation 10.1: ln(var) = $a + bt$ where t states for time variable, b*100 per cent provides annual average growth rate in percentage. Decomposition of average real wages is performed by converting the following equation into the growth rates equation.

Equation 10.2: $RW_c = (W/VA)_c$ / $*(RVA/L)_c$ where RW stands for hourly real wage for cluster c, W, VA, RVA, and L represent nominal value of wage payments, nominal value of value added, real value added, and total number of hours worked, respectively. RVA/L, value added per labour hour is used as a proxy for labour productivity. By equation 10.2, the growth rate of real wages in each cluster on the left-hand side is equal to the sum of the growth rates of the terms on the right-hand side as shown by equation 10.3:

Equation 10.3: $gRW_c = g(W/VA)_c + g(RVA/L)_c$

[29]Besides, the acceleration of capital movements leading to volatility in the real sector, it inflicts bankruptcies, particularly of small and medium sized establishments where majority of workers are informal, marginal and coming from vulnerable segments of the society. Even among formal employment, women workers particularly, are in the majority within small and medium sized establishments. Ozler (2000) shows evidence for increase in female share of employment in a plant when its exports to output ratio increases using Turkish manufacturing industry plant level data for 1983–5.

[30]There are many different types of EPZs focusing mainly on textiles and garments, electronics, and leather industry production. Investing countries are France, USA, Netherlands, Germany, Switzerland, UK, Italy, and Japan. In Turkey there is the single industry zone—the leather industry zone. In 2003, the export share of EPZs

marginalization, which became the social basis of exporting industries.[31] With the enactment of the Free Trade Zones Law in 1985, all the duties, taxes, and charges are treated differently by legislation. Income and revenue generated in free trade zones are exempted from income or revenue taxes, along with several incentives.

## Privatization

Privatization policies were the other significant set of policies that induced informalization in the labour market. Deregulation of price controls on commodities produced by SOEs, imposing user charges for public goods and services,[32] contracting-out, and selling shares of assets were implemented as a solution to budget deficits.[33] Several statutory monopolies such as Tea and Tobacco Monopoly and Electricity Power Monopoly were devastated using the same justification.[34] All these apparently had huge impacts not only on the wage structure but also on the employment structure of industries. Privatization led to significant employment losses and earning losses in re-employments (Tansel 2001). Comparing the pre- and post-dismissal job earnings of re-employed workers she concludes that they can only earn 33 per cent of their SOE earnings.[35] The study also reveals that the post-dismissal jobs were not only worse in terms

in total exports was 45 per cent (for EPZ resources see *http://www.ilo.org/public/english/dialogue/sector/themes/epz.htm)*

[31]Moreover, in 1986, a supplementary decree titled Foreign Capital Framework Decree was enacted, widening the content of the Law Concerning the Encouragement of Foreign Capital issued in 1954. Some of the exemptions provided to foreign capital were as follows: 100 per cent customs duties exemptions for all machinery and equipment required for investment, between 30 per cent and 100 per cent exemption on corporate tax paid for fixed capital investment, exemption of charges, taxes and duties on credits if 20 per cent of the production is committed for exportation; and rewards though several premiums such as investment premiums or resource allocation support premium. As a result, through the figures are low compared to other developing countries, with these generous incentives, FDI increased significantly. At the end of 1999, the share of manufacturing sector in total FDI was 46.1 per cent and its share increased in the sectoral distribution of number of permissions allowed since 1997 (SPO, 8th Five Year development plan, FDI Commission Report 2000). The share of foreign firms in the private sector of manufacturing industry increased from 1 per cent in 1983 to 2 per cent in 1999 and further to 3.5 per cent in 2000. And the share of these firms in manufacturing employment increased gradually from 6 per cent in 1983 particularly after the year 1988 to 11 per cent in 2000 (Taymaz and Lenger 2004). Taymaz and Lenger (2004) further state that the full liberalization of the financial system in 1989 provided an additional driving force for foreign investment.

[32]Besides other public goods such as tolls, fees in public hospitals, or tuitions in higher education at public universities were implemented by the law passed in 1984, which also allowed for establishment of private schools that are exempt from personal or corporate taxes.

[33]These policies were put forward as action commitments, in order to achieve economic growth, in the 5th five year development plan (1985-90) and the 6th five year development plan (1990-4). In the former plan it was announced that public investment would focus only on infrastructure. In the latter several other policies were announced for public enterprises.

[34]In 1986, the law concerning the de-nationalization of SOEs was passed, appointing the Prime Ministry as the agency to carry out the process. Privatization of SOEs, which was expected to be a solution for public budget deficits, became an arena for wild competition and corruption and led to employment losses on the one hand and increases in imports of intermediate goods that were provided by SOEs earliers, on the other. The efforts to promote private entrepreneurship ended up in some cases as additional burdens for the state and, therefore, for the people.

[35]This is also supported by the ILO report 'Labour market policy for restructuring in Turkey: The need for more active policies'. Downloadable at *www.ilo.org/public/english/ employment/strat/download/ep51.pdf.*

of pecuniary earnings but worse in terms of quality, that is, lower labour standards, and provided no premiums or fringe benefits.

In order to see the cluster differences in the context of public/private ownership, the immediate indicators to look at are public sector shares in value added and employment across clusters (see Tables A10.2.6 and A10.2.7). It is observed that in the low wage (cluster 2) and lowest wage (cluster 1) clusters, public shares are negligible compared to higher wage clusters (clusters 3 and 4) essentially after 1995. Given the fact that public sector hourly wages are higher than those in the private sector in all clusters (see Table 10.2.4) a part of the wage differentials also reflects the disparity between public and private sector wage trends, thus confirming earlier findings mentioned above.

## RESULTS AND CONCLUDING REMARKS

In this paper we present empirical measurements of hourly wage differentials in the Turkish manufacturing industry over the period of the export-led regime, using a cluster analysis. The results demonstrate the importance of reclassifying industrial data based on the variable to be analysed. The clustering method effectively isolates different wage patterns among the industries even though they might belong to same product group. This shows evidence that within standard product type groups there are different wage patterns.

The results of our empirical analysis indicate that wage differentials between sub-industries represent a substantial change in the wage patterns in the late 1980s, when the economy moved to full-liberalization. This is one of the findings that suggests that inter-industry wage differentials in the Turkish case do not support conventional arguments. Further, we also present evidence against the claims that wage structure is stable over time, the argument that implicitly presumes that wage structure is neutral to policy changes. On the contrary, wage patterns exhibit drastic divergence as the trend of the high wage industries rises whereas the low wage clusters show falling trends. Standard interpretation of such changes in wage structure would be the similar changes in productivity differentials. Yet, evidence here suggests that productivity differentials do not fully describe changes in wage differentials.

Analysis of the industries based on their trade structure shows that more than half of the total manufacturing exports are pursued by low paying clusters, which are highly labour intensive and use less advanced technology. One interesting finding is related to the evolution of this trade structure. Despite the policies for openness and the export-led strategies, the majority of exports are still carried on by the low-paying manufacturing industries. Even though we may not be able to conclude that if those policy steps were not taken, the low wage-paying industries would no more be among the low-paying groups; yet we can safely argue that the Turkish experience builds a picture that goes against the conventional arguments. The automatic equalizing mechanism mentioned in conventional trade theories cannot be confirmed in this case.

In order to explore the factors behind the persistence and, more than that, widening patterns of wage dispersion, unlike many other studies, we review the restructuring policies and practices with a view that they may clarify the issue better. We point to the fact that with the evidence presented, underpinning factors behind the patterns of wage differentials in Turkish manufacturing industry can be partly found in the distributional changes that accompanied the regime shift in the Turkish economy. This shift changed the conditions of external competition drastically. And along with that the state's role of accommodating these industries diminished, resulting in suppression of wages—the extent of which depended on specific conditions. However, further research is still needed to support these arguments using different analytical tools. And it might be interesting to see the implications of the evidence found here, that is, implications of the widening wage inequality on economic performance, both at the sectoral and macroeconomic levels in order to come up with alternative policies and practices.

## REFERENCES

Akerlof, G.A. and J. Yellen (1986), *Efficiency Wage Models of the Labor Market*, Cambridge University Press, Cambridge.

Arbache, J.S., A. Dickerson, and F. Green (2001), 'Assessing the Stability of the Inter-industry Wage Structure in the Face of Radical Economic Reforms', *Studies in Economics from Department of Economics*, University of Kent.

Bagdadıoglu, E. and H. Ercan (2001), 'Union-Nonunion Average Wage Series in Turkish Manufacturing', in T. Bulutay (ed.), *Wages, Income and Wage Distributions*, State Institute of Statistics, Printing Division, Ankara, pp. 163–206.

Bayazıtoglu, B. and H. Ercan (2001), 'Turkish Manufacturing Wages: Inter-Industry Earnings Inequality', in T. Bulutay (ed.), *Wages, Income and Wage Distributions*, State Institute of Statistics, Printing Division, Ankara, pp. 207–42.

Becker, G. (1964), *Human Capital*, Columbia University Press, New York.

Berner, M. and J.K. Galbraith, (ed.) (2001), *Inequality and Industrial Change A Global View*, Cambridge University Press, New York.

Boratav, K. (1990), 'Inter-Class and Intra-Class Relations of Distribution under SA: Turkey During the 1980s', in T. Aricanli, and D. Rodrik (eds), *The Political Economy of Turkey: Debt, Adjustment and Sustainability*, June, St. Martin's Press, New York.

Botwinick, H. (1993), *Persistent Inequalities: Wage Disparity under Capitalist Competition*, Princeton University Press, Princeton.

Cagatay, N. (1986), *The Interindustry Structure of Wages and Markups in Turkish Manufacturing*, Unpublished PhD. Thesis, Standford University.

Dickens, W. T. and L.F. Katz (1987), 'Inter-industry Wage Differences and Industry Characteristics', in Lang and Leonard (eds), *Unemployment and the Structure of Labor Market*, Basic Blackwell, London.

Doeringer, P. B. and M. J. Piore (1971), *Internal Labor Markets and Manpower Analysis*, Heath, Lexington.

Dunlop, J.T. (1979), 'Wage Contours', in M. J. Piore (ed.) *Unemployment and Inflation: Institutionalist and Structuralist Views*, ME Sharpe, Armonk.

Edwards, R. (1979), *Contested Terrain: The Transformation of the Workplace in the Twentieth Century*, Basic Books, New York.

Erdil, E. (1993), 'Inter-Industry Wage Differentials in Turkish Manufacturing Industry, 1964–1989', Unpublished MS Thesis, Department of Economics, Middle East Technical University.

Eres, B. (2005), 'The Profit Rate in the Turkish Economy: 1968–2000', Unpublished PhD Dissertation, Department of Economics, University of Utah.

Freeman, R. (1995), 'Are Your Wages Set in Beijing?', *Journal of Economic Perspectives*, Summer, pp. 15–32.

Galbraith, J.K. and D. P. Calmon (1996), 'Wage Change and Trade Performance in US Manufacturing Industries', *Cambridge Journal of Economics*, Vol. 20, pp. 433–50.

Gallbraith, James K. and J. Lu (1999), 'Cluster and Discriminant Analysis on Time-Series as a Research Tool', UTIP Working Paper, No. 6.

Gordon, D., R. Edwards, and M. Reich (1982), *Segmented Work, Divided Workers: The Historical Transformation of Labor in the US*, Cambridge University Press, New York.

Hicks, J. R. (1963), *The Theory of Wages*, 2nd edition, St. Martin's Press, New York.

Ilkkaracan, I. and R. Selim (2003), 'The Role of Unemployment in Wage Determination: Further Evidence on the Wage Curve from Turkey', *Applied Economics*, Vol. 35, No. 14, pp. 1589–98.

Katz, L. and L. Summers (1989), 'Industry Rents: Evidence and Implications,' *BPEA Microeconomics Annual*, pp. 209–75.

Kaufman, L. and P. J. Rousseeuw (1990), *Finding Groups in Data: An Introduction to Cluster Analysis*, Wiley, New York, chapter 4.

Krueger, A. and L. Summers (1987), 'Reflections on the Interindustry Wage Structure' in K. Lang and J. Leonard (eds), *Unemployment and the Structure of Labor Markets*, Basic Blackwell, London, pp. 17–48.

Metin-Ozcan, K., Voyvoda, E., and E. Yeldan (2002), 'The Impact of the Liberalization Program on the Price-Cost Margin and Investment of Turkey's Manufacturing Sector after 1980', *Emerging Markets Finance and Trade*, Vol. 38, No. 5, pp. 72–103.

Onanan, O. and N. Yenturk (2003), 'The Mark-Up Rates in Turkish Private Manufacturing Industry during Trade Liberalization', *Journal of Income Distribution*, Vol. 11, No. 3–4, pp. 21–41.

Ozmucur, S. (1996), 'Yeni milli gelir serisi ve gelirin fonksiyonel dagilimi, 1968–1994' (The New GDP Series and the Functional Distribution of Income in Turkey, 1968–1994', with English summary), *Middle East Technical University Studies in Development*, Vol. 23, No. 1, pp. 85–127.

—— (1997) 'Productivity and Profitability in the 500 Largest Firms of Turkey, 1980–1995', ERF Working Paper, No. 9713

Ozler, S. (2000), 'Export Orientation and Female Share of Employment: Evidence from Turkey', *World Development*, Vol. 28, No. 7, pp. 1239–48.

Reich, M. (1984), 'Segmented Labor: Time Series Hypotheses and Evidence', *Cambridge Journal of Economics*, Vol. 8, pp. 63–81.

Tansel, A. (2001), 'Effects of Privatization on Labor in Turkey', Economic Research Center (ERC), Research Papers, 2001/03, Middle East Technical University.

Taymaz, E. (1998), 'Trade Liberalization and Employment Generation: The Experience of Turkey in the 1980s', in A. Revenga (ed.), *Turkey: Economic Reforms, Living Standards, and Social Welfare Study*, Vol. 2, World Bank, Washington, DC.

Taymaz, E. and A. Lenger (2004), 'Multinational Corporations as a Vehicle for Productivity Spillovers in Turkey', DRUID Working Papers 04–09, DRUID,

Wood, A. (1995), 'How Trade Hurt Unskilled Workers', *Journal of Economic Perspectives*, American Economic Association, Vol. 9, No. 3, pp. 57–80, Summer.

—— (1997), 'Openness and Wage Inequality in Developing Countries: The Latin American Challenge to East Asian Conventional Wisdom', *World Bank Economic Review*, Oxford University Press, Vol. 11, No. 1, pp. 33–57, January.

Yeldan, E. (2001), *Kuresellesme Surecinde Turkiye Ekonomisi: Bolusum, Birikim, Buyume* (Turkish Economy throughout the Globalisation Process: Distribution, Accumulation, Growth), 2001, Iletisim Yay, Istanbul.

# 11

# Labour Market Participation Decisions of Married Women

## Evidence from Turkey

A. Burça Kizilirmak*

## INTRODUCTION

This chapter examines the determinants of married women's labour force participation in Turkey. In particular the effect of husband's labour market status on the wife's labour market behaviour is investigated.

High female participation in the labour market implies both an advance in the relative socioeconomic position of women and also an increased utilization of human potential for economic development. Thus, it is necessary to identify the determinants of employment decisions of women in order to implement policies that tackle gender gaps and encourage female participation in the labour market.

The special features of employment decisions of the married women require a separate analysis. In general, labour force participation rates of married women are lower than those of single women. Moreover, the effect of the husband's employment situation on the wife's participation is a good indicator of women's status in the labour market, specifically of their 'secondary worker' status. There are two hypotheses regarding the effect of the husband's employment situation on the wife's participation decisions. The first one is the 'added worker effect' hypothesis. According to this one, the wife who is inactive in the labour market decides to work temporarily in order to compensate the income loss due to the unemployment of her husband. The second hypothesis is the 'discouraged worker effect' whereby the wife's search for work decreases due to unfavourable labour market conditions facing the whole family. In this case, as the husband is unemployed due to an economic downturn, the wife is pessimistic about her employment prospects as well and is less likely to search for work.

Empirical evidence on the effect of the husband's employment situation on the wife's participation decisions is mixed. While some

*A preliminary version of this paper was presented at the ACDC in India and at the ESPRU/CHILD Workshop on Discrete Choice Labour Supply Models held in Ireland. I am grateful to the conference and workshop participants for helpful comments and suggestions. I would also like to thank Hasan Sahin for his valuable comments in the preparation of this work.

early studies in the UK and US during the 1970s and early 1980s found small but significant added worker effect (Heckman and MaCurdy 1980; Lundberg 1985), others found no evidence of the same (Layard et al. 1980; Maloney 1987 and 1991). More recent work, including that in European countries, found evidence of either the discouraged worker effect or no impact of the husband's unemployment on his wife's labour force status (Davies et al. 1992; Giannelli and Micklewright 1995; and Prietro-Rodriguez and Rodriguez-Gutierrez 2003). On the other hand, in their study on Italy in 1995, Del Boca et al. (2000) concluded that the effect of the unemployment status of the husband is negligible. However, they also found that this effect is mediated by other variables that reflect the family's attitudes towards work. Bingley and Walker (2001) used the UK data from 1978 to 1992 and found that husband's unemployment does not affect the wife's labour supply if the husband's unemployment is a short-term one. However, longer durations of unemployment of the husband lead to the discouraged worker effect.

Contrary to the trends in many countries in the world, female labour market participation has been decreasing in Turkey in the last decades. According to the State Institute of Statistics (SIS), the female labour force participation rate in Turkey dropped from 45.8 per cent to 25.4 per cent between 1980 and 2004. In general, studies show that traditions and responsibilities at home still seem to be important factors that keep female labour force participation low in Turkey (Özar and Günlük-Senesen 1998; KSSGM 2000).

Several empirical studies have examined the participation decisions of females in Turkey. However, to the best of my knowledge, effects of the labour market status of the husbands were studied only by Baslevent and Onaran (2003). The authors estimated a bivariate probit model for the years 1988 and 1994. They found that the labour market participation of the wives and employment status of their husbands are negatively correlated. The current paper is based on this finding of the added worker effect. The main question asked here is, whether the entry of women into the work force due to an economic crisis, results in a permanent integration of women into the formal labour market. If the women, who start working as a response to the unemployment of their husbands, get permanent jobs rather than temporary ones, a permanent advance in their economic and social conditions is more likely. Thus, this study aims to identify the effect of the labour market status of husbands on both the participation decision and the employment outcomes for their wives.

Data from the 2003 Household Budget Survey conducted by SIS are used in this paper. The year 2003 in Turkey is particularly useful in analysing the labour market in an economic recession. Turkey faced a severe economic crisis in 2001 which gradually deepened in the following years and led to a deep recession in production and employment. The unemployment rate continued to increase from 6.5 per cent to 10.5 per cent between 2000 and 2003. Thus, the problem of unemployment was still persistent during the year under study in this paper.

By assuming that individuals who decide to participate in the labour market also choose the kind of employment, both a multinominal and a conditional logit model are used in the estimations.[1] Four states of the labour market are considered: non-participation, self-

[1]This approach has been used by Hill (1983), Tiefenthaler (1994), Soopramanien and Johnes (2001), and Falzone (2000) among others.

employment, temporary wage employment, and permanent wage employment.

The paper is organized as follows. The next section describes the methodology. The third section gives an overview of the Turkish labour market. The fourth section reports the data, variables, and the empirical results. The fifth section contains the concluding remarks.

## METHODOLOGY

It is assumed that an individual may choose from m mutually exclusive alternatives. The maximum utility attainable for individual i from choosing alternative j is:

$$V_{ij} = \beta'_j x_{ij} + \alpha'_j y_i + \varepsilon_{ij}, \quad j = 1,\ldots, m \quad (11.1)$$

where $x_{ij}$ and $y_j$ are two vectors of independent variables, $\beta'_j$ and $\alpha'_j$ are parameter vectors, and $\varepsilon_{ij}$ is an unobservable error term. The vector $x_{ij}$ consists of attributes of the choices and $y_i$ consists of characteristics of the individual. Alternative j is chosen when the maximum utility obtained by choosing alternative j is higher than that obtained by choosing other alternatives: $V_{ji} > V_{ki}$ (for $j$ $k$ and $j = 1,\ldots, m$).

Assuming that the disturbances $\varepsilon_{ji}$ have independent and identical Weibull distributions, this specification leads to the conditional logit model. The probability that individual i chooses alternative j is given by:[2]

$$P_{ij} = \frac{\exp(\beta'_j x_{ij} + \alpha'_j y_i)}{\sum_{k=1}^{m} \exp(\beta'_k x_{ik} + \alpha'_k y_i)} \quad (11.2)$$

and is estimated by the maximum likelihood method.

Explanatory variables in $x_{ij}$ are earnings in different participation states. As the earnings information of the non-working women is not available, earnings in each state must be predicted for all women using the information available for working women. However, due to the sample selection bias, it is necessary to correct the earnings equations for sample selection. This is done by Lee's (1983) method that requires the estimation of probabilities of selection into each participation state. Thus the estimations in this study are carried out in the following three stages.

In the first stage, the probability of selection into each participation state is estimated by fitting a reduced form participation equation. The reduced form equation is the following multinominal logit model:

$$P_{ij} = \frac{\exp(\alpha'_j y_i)}{\sum_{k=1}^{m} \exp(\alpha'_k y_i)} \quad (11.3)$$

Using the predicted probabilities obtained from this model, the following selectivity term (the inverse of Mills ratio) is calculated:

$$\lambda_{ij} = \phi(H_{ij}) / \Phi(H_{ij})$$

where $\phi(.)$ is the standard normal density function, $\Phi(.)$ the normal distribution function, and $H_{ij} = \Phi^{-1}(P_{ij})$.

In the second stage, the selectivity term that is computed from these probabilities is used as an additional regressor in the earnings equations in order to control for the selectivity bias. Finally, in the third stage, predicted wages are used as explanatory variables in the participation equation (11.2) and the model is estimated by the maximum likelihood method.

## BACKGROUND

One notable feature of the Turkish labour market is the high growth rate of the working age population, averaging 1.3 per cent annually

[2]See Maddala (1983), ch. 2.

during the 2000–5 period.[3] However, employment opportunities either declined or rose slowly in the same period, with an average growth rate of only 0.4 per cent per year. As a result, the unemployment rate increased from 6.5 per cent to 10.3 per cent between 2000 and 2005.

The increase in the unemployment rate is partly due to the economic recessions of the last years, and partly due to economic programmes that aim to stabilize the economy. After experiencing a series of severe economic crises and fluctuating growth throughout the 1990s, Turkey went through another series of crises in November 2000 and in February 2001. According to SIS statistics, the decline in real GNP was 9.5 per cent in 2001. The deep recession in production and employment gradually deepened in the following years and the unemployment rate continued to increase. In 2003, the unemployment rate was 10.5 per cent. Thus, the problem of unemployment was still persistent during the year under study in this paper.

Another striking feature of the labour market in Turkey is the declining labour force participation rate of women. According to the general population censuses of SIS, the female participation rate was 45.8 per cent in 1980. In 2005, according to the SIS Household Labour Force Survey, it fell to 24.8 per cent. Both the participation rate and the decline in it, point to a more severe condition for women than for men in Turkey. The male participation rates were 79.8 per cent and 72.2 per cent in 1980 and 2005, respectively.

Several explanations have been put forward for the decrease in female participation rate in Turkey (Tansel 2001; Başlevent and Onaran 2003; Dayıoğlu and Kasnakoğlu 1997; and Dayıoğlu 1999). First, there has been a decline in the participation of younger population due to increased enrolment rates. Second, decrease in the share of agriculture in the economy and migration from rural to urban areas led to the withdrawal of some women from the labour force. The women previously working in agriculture may have to stop working after migration to the city. The main reasons are cultural values that determine the attitudes towards women's work, migrant women's lack of qualifications for work, and unfavourable demand conditions in the city.

Several empirical studies have examined the participation decisions of females in Turkey.[4] These studies highlight education, economic growth, and employment share of agriculture as factors that increase participation of women in the labour market. Presence of especially young children and being married, on the other hand, have negative effects. In general, traditions and responsibilities at home seem to be still important factors that keep female labour force participation low in Turkey (Özar and Günlük-Şenesen 1998; KSSGM 2000).

Another feature of the Turkish labour market is the large informal sector. Share of the informal sector in employment is estimated to be between 21 per cent and 53 per cent depending on the measure used.[5] One widely used measure is the share of workers who are not registered with the social security institutions in total employment. This rate is 52 per cent on average in the 2000–5 period. There is also a big gender difference: 44 per

[3] All data in this section are from the SIS Household Labour Force Survey, unless otherwise indicated.

[4] Dayıoğlu and Kasnakoğlu (1997), Dayıoğlu (1999), Tansel (2001), Tunalı (1997), Tunalı and Başlevent (2004), and Yanik and Assaad (2004).

[5] See for example Özar (1996, 2000), Ansal et al. (2000); and Kasnakoğlu and Yayla (2000).

cent of men and 68 per cent of women are working without social security in Turkey.

## THE DATA AND EMPIRICAL RESULTS

It is assumed here that an individual may choose from four mutually exclusive alternatives: non-participation (not working in the formal sector), working as self-employed, working as a temporary employee, and working as a permanent employee (indexed as *n*, *s*, *t*, and *p*, respectively). Family workers and unemployed are included in the 'not working in the formal sector' group.[6] 'Self-employed' includes self-employed and employers. 'Temporary employees' are irregular employees without a contract and employees with a fixed term contract. 'Permanent employees' have continuous jobs in the firms where they are working.

The 2003 Household Budget Survey is used in the estimations.[7] The data set contains data on 107,614 individuals and 25,764 households. The sample used here includes 13,896 married couples living in urban areas, with wives in the 15–55 age group. Of the wives in the sample, 89 per cent are non-participants, 1.3 per cent work as self-employed, 2.6 per cent work in temporary wage employment, and 7.1 per cent work in permanent wage employment.[8]

The explanatory variables considered here are potential work experience of the wife (*exper*), dummies representing education level (*nodiploma*, *element*, *high*, and *univ* which take value 1 if the wife has no diploma, elementary school diploma, high school diploma, and university diploma, respectively), non-wife income (*nwinc*), children in the 0–5 and 6–18 age groups (*kidun6* and *kidov6*, respectively), a dummy which equals 1 if the husband is unemployed (*unemp*), number of months the husband did not work in the last year (*duration*), predicted earnings in the three employment states ($pearn_s$, $pearn_t$, $pearn_p$) and regional dummies.[9] The experience variable is also included quadratically ($exper^2$).

Table A11.1.1 presents the descriptive statistics of the independent variables. Elementary

[6]Ideally, the unemployed should be considered as a distinct category. However, the methodology used here requires the estimation of an earnings equation for each alternative and the unemployed have practically zero earnings. Turkey introduced unemployment insurance only in 2000 and the first benefit was paid in 2002. Nevertheless, the number of people eligible for the unemployment insurance has been very limited especially in the first years (around 60,000 people in 2003 according to the Turkish Employment Organization) and the benefits have been very small (equal to the monthly minimum wage at maximum) with little variance across the recipients. For these reasons and also because the data set used in this study does not have information on insurance benefits, estimation of an earnings equation for the unemployed would not be possible.

[7]The cross section data set is used since a panel data set for this kind of study is absent for Turkey.

[8]Labour force participation rate of the women in the sample (11 per cent) is lower than that given by the SIS general population census (25.4 per cent in 2004). The reason is that the sample here consists of only married women who generally have lower participation rates than single women. Including the single women (over age 15) in the sample, increases the female participation rate to 27 per cent which is closer to the rate in the population census.

[9]Potential experience is calculated as the difference between age and the total of number of years of education, and non-wife income is the natural logarithm of monthly income (billion TL) of the family except the wife's. Earnings of self-employed ($earn_s$) are calculated as the natural logarithm of monthly entrepreneurial income divided by monthly hours of work. Earnings of temporary and permanent employees ($earn_t$, and $earn_p$, respectively) are calculated as the natural logarithm of monthly salaries divided by monthly hours of work (all earnings are in million TL). Regional dummies are created for Istanbul, Marmara, Agean, Central Anatolia, Mediterranean, Black Sea, Eastern Anatolia, and Southeast Anatolia (*r_ist*, *r_mar*, *r_age*, *r_cnt*, *r_mdt*, *r_blc*, *r_est*, and *r_ste*, respectively).

school graduates constitute the biggest group in the overall sample except for permanent employees, for which university graduates have the highest share (at 45 per cent. The share of women with unemployed husbands is 3.4 per cent on average, lowest at 1.1 per cent for self-employed, and highest at 7.6 per cent for temporary employees. Average duration of unemployment of the husband is again the highest for temporary employees at 3.2 months, but lowest for permanent employees at 1.7 months. For all the women in the sample, predicted self-employment hourly earnings are the highest among earning types, averaging 3 million Turkish Lira (TL). These are followed by permanent employment and temporary employment earnings with means of 1.8 million TL and 1.2 million TL, respectively.

Estimation results of the reduced form participation equation are presented in Table A11.1.2. Potential experience has the expected sign in all participation states although it is statistically insignificant for the self-employed. Results imply that experience has a positive but decreasing effect on the probability that the wife gets wage employment. Women with any diploma, compared to women with no diploma have significantly higher participation probabilities in general. However, effects of different levels of education have different effects across employment types. The probability to be self-employed is higher for high school and university graduates and the probability to be a temporary worker is lower for middle and high school graduates. On the other hand, all levels of education increase the probability to become a permanent employee.

Co-efficient of non-wife income is also found to be statistically significant and has the expected negative sign for all employment types. The number of kids under 6 years of age significantly decreases the participation of women in wage employment and has no effect on the probability to be self-employed. On the other hand, number of children between ages 6 and 18 significantly increases the self-employment probability and decreases the permanent employment probability. The positive effect of older children on the probability to be self-employed may be due the fact that children may be able to help their self-employed mothers in their work.

The explanatory variables of central interest here are the ones related to the husband's economic status. After controlling for other relevant factors, wives with unemployed husbands have significantly higher permanent wage employment probabilities. However, these probabilities decrease as the duration of husband's unemployment increase. Effects of probabilities to be in other states of labour market participation are found to be statistically insignificant at the 5 per cent level. These findings point to the presence of the 'added worker effect' in the sense that the unemployment of husbands encourages their wives to work. The fact that these wives mostly find permanent wage employment is an indication of a permanent improvement of their socio-economic conditions as a result of an economic crisis. The 'duration' variable represents the severity of the crises facing the family. Its negative sign implies that the 'discouraged worker effect' dominates the 'added worker effect' as the extent of the crises increases.

Estimation results of the reduced form participation equation are used to correct sample selection bias in the earnings equation estimates. Table A11.1.3 presents the results from estimating the earnings equations for the three employment types. The experience variable is significant only for the permanent employee earnings with expected signs. Coefficients of education dummies are positive in all the earnings equations although they are not significant at all levels in self-employment and temporary employment equations. Number of kids under age 6 is found to depress all wages significantly, and the number of children between ages 6 and 18 significantly depresses permanent employee wages. Marginal effects of the regional dummies imply that earnings are lower in most of the regions compared to those in Istanbul.

Table A11.1.4 contains the estimation results of the participation model, including the predicted earnings. Productivity variables (experience and education) are not included in this model since the predicted earnings capture the effects of these variables. Coefficients and marginal effects are similar to the results in Table A11.1.2. The only exception is the effect of the number of children between ages 6 and 18 on the probability to be a temporary employee, which is found to be positive and significant.

## CONCLUSIONS

This paper has been concerned with analysing the labour supply of married women in urban Turkey, in order to determine the effect of the husband's economic status on the wife's labour market participation. Evidence of the 'added worker effect' is found in the sense that wives decide to participate in order to compensate for the loss of income due to husbands' unemployment. It is also found that wives with unemployed husbands tend to get permanent wage employment rather than temporary wage employment or self-employment. However, this 'added worker effect' vanishes and the 'discouraged worker effect' begins to dominate as the extent of the crisis increases. These findings indicate that although married women in Turkey still have the 'secondary worker' status in the labour market, increased participation during an economic crisis might lead to a permanent improvement of their socio-economic conditions, on the condition that the crisis does not persist.

Additional findings of the study are as follows. Non-wife income depresses participation of women in the formal labour market which is another indication of the 'secondary worker' status of women. Fertility depresses the participation of women in wage employment in the early years of maternity. Women with children between ages 6 and 18, on the other hand, tend to be engaged in self-employment and temporary wage employment rather than in permanent employment. And, finally, high school and university education of women increases their participation probabilities in the labour market, especially in permanent wage employment and self-employment. This last finding implies that education of women is crucial for attaining a permanent improvement in their socio-economic conditions.

## REFERENCES

Ansal, H., S. Küçükçifçi, Ö, Onaran-Benan and Z. Onbay (2000), *Türekiye Emek Piyasasının Yapısı ve Işsizlik*, Türekiye Ekonomik ve Toplumsal Tarih Vakfi, İstanbul.

Başlevent, C. and O. Onaran (2003), 'Are Married Women in Turkey More Likely to Become Added or Discouraged Workers?', *Labour*, Vol. 17, No. 3, pp. 439–58.

Bingley, Paul and Ian Walker (2001), 'Household Unemployment and the Labour Supply of Married Women', *Economica*, Vol. 68, No. 270, pp. 157–85.

Davies, Richard B., Peter Elias, and Roger Penn (1992), 'The Relationship between a Husband's

Unemployment and His Wife's Participation in the Labour Force', *Oxford Bulletin of Economics and Statistics*, Vol. 54, No. 2, pp. 145–71.

Dayıoğlu, M. (1999), 'Labour Market Participation of Women in Turkey', in F. Acar and A. Güneş-Ayata (eds), *Gender and Identity Construction: Women of Central Asia, Caucasus and Turkey*, E.S. Brill, Leiden.

Dayıoğlu, M. and Z. Kasnakoğlu (1997), 'Kentsel Kesimde Kadın ve Erkeklerin İşgücüne Katılımları ve Kazanç Farklılıkları', *METU Studies in Development*, Vol. 24, No. 3, pp. 329–61.

Del Boca, Daniela, Marilena Locatelli, and Silvia Pasqua (2000), 'Employment Decisions of Married Women: Evidence and Explanations', *Labour*, Vol. 14, No. 1, pp. 35–52.

Falzone, J. S. (2000), 'Labour Market Decisions of Married Women: With Emphasis on Part-time Employment', *International Advances in Economic Research*, Vol. 6, No. 4, pp. 662–71.

Giannelli, Gianna and John Micklewright (1995), 'Why Do Women Married to Unemployed Men Have Low Participation Rates?', *Oxford Bulletin of Economics and Statistics*, Vol. 57, No. 4, pp. 471–86.

Heckman, James J. and Thomas E. Macurdy (1980), 'A Life Cycle Model of Female Labour Supply', *Review of Economic Studies*, Vol. 47, No. 1, pp. 47–74.

Hill M.A. (1983), 'Female Labour Force Participation in Developing and Developed Countries-Consideration of the Informal Sector', *Review of Economics and Statistics*, Vol. 65, No. 3, pp. 459–68.

Kasnakoğlu, Z. and M. Yayla (2000), 'Türkiye'de Kayıtdı_ı Ekonominin Boyutları', in T. Bulutay (ed.), *Enformel Kesim (I)*, DİE, Ankara. pp. 50–84.

KSSGM (2000), *Kentlerde Kadınların İş Yaşamına Katılım Sorunlarının Sosyo-Ekonomik ve Kültürel Boyutları*, KSSGM (T.C. Başbakanlık Kadının Statüsü ve Sorunları Genel Müdürlüğü), Ankara.

Layard, R., M. Barton, and A. Zabalza (1980), 'Married Women's Participation and Hours', *Economica*, Vol. 47, No. 185, pp. 51–72.

Lee, L. (1983), 'Generalized Econometric Models with Selectivity', *Econometrica*, Vol. 51, No. 2, pp. 507–12.

Lundberg, Shelly (1985), 'The Added Worker Effect', *Journal of Labour Economics*, Vol. 3, No. 1, pp. 11–37.

Maddala, G. S. (1983), *Limited Dependent and Qualitative Variables in Econometrics*, Cambridge University Press, Cambridge.

Maloney, Tim (1991), 'Unobserved Variables and the Elusive Added Worker Effect', *Economica*, Vol. 58, No. 230, pp. 173–87.

Maloney, Timothy J. (1987), 'Employment Constraints and the Labour Supply of Married Women: A Reexamination of the Added Worker Effect', *Journal of Human Resources*, Vol. 22, No. 1, pp. 51–61.

Özar, S. (1996), 'Kentsel Kayıtdışı Kesimde İstihdam Sorununa Yaklaşımlar ve Bir Ön Saha Çalısması', *METU Studies in Development*, Vol. 23, No. 4, pp. 509–34.

____ (2000), 'Enformel Kesimin İstihdam Açısından Değerlendirilmesi', in T. Bulutay (ed.), *Enformel Kesim (II)*, DİE, Ankara. pp. 185–210.

Özar, S. and G. Günlük-Şenesen (1998), 'Determinants of Female (non)Participation in the Urban Labour Force in Turkey', *METU Studies in Development*, Vol. 25, No. 2, pp. 311–28.

Prietro-Rodriguez, Juan and Cesar Rodriguez-Gutierrez (2003), 'Participation of Married Women in the European Labour Markets and the "Added Worker Effect"', *Journal of Socio-Economics*, Vol. 32, No. 4, pp. 361–469.

Soopramanien, D. and G. Johnes (2001), 'A New Look at Gender Effects in Participation and Occupation Choice', *Labour*, Vol. 15, No. 3.

Tansel, A. (2001), 'Economic Development and Female Labour Force Participation in Turkey: Time-Series Evidence and Cross-Province Estimates', Department of Economics, Middle East Technical University, Ankara.

Tiefenthaler, J. (1994), 'A Multisector Model of Female Labour Force Participation: Empirical Evidence from Cebu Island, Philippines', *Economic Development and Cultural Change*, Vol. 42, No. 4, pp. 719–42.

Tunalı, I. (1997), 'To Work or Not to Work: An Examination of Female Labour Force Participation Rates in Urban Turkey', The Proceedings of the Economic Research Forum's Fourth Annual Conference on Regional Trade, Finance and Labour Markets, Beirut, 7–9 September 1997, pp.163–178.

Tunalı, I. and C. Başlevent (2004), 'Married Women's Participation Choices and Productivity Differentials: Evidence from Urban Turkey', Paper presented at Workshop On Gender, Work, And Family In The Middle East And North Africa, 7–11 June 2004, Mahdia, Tunisia.

Yanik and Assaad (2004), 'Women's Participation in Paid Work in Urban Turkey: Do Local Demand Factors Matter?', Paper presented at the ERF 11th Annual Conference, 14–16 December 2004, Beirut, Lebanon.

# Part IV

# Issues in Cross-national Growth Comparisons

# 12

# Fractionalization Indexes and Economic Growth
## Longitudinal Evidence from South Africa

J.W. Fedderke, J.M.Luiz, and R.H.J. de Kadt

## INTRODUCTION

The re-emergence of interest in the determinants of growth has focused attention on the puzzle of the apparent non-convergence of per capita income between low and high income countries. One response to this dilemma is what has come to be known as the 'endogenous growth' theory—which in various forms drops the assumptions of the exogeneity of technological change, and the homogeneity of investment opportunities across countries (see Romer 1986, 1990; and Lucas 1988 as seminal examples). The convergence prediction in Solow–Swan type growth models is, of course, conditional on the homogeneity of the savings rate, the labour force growth rate, and the technology of production. Once the possibility of heterogeneity of countries in the relatively limited dimensions provided by Solow–Swan type growth models is recognized, the possibility that heterogeneity in other dimensions may be of significance to growth follows readily. Thus, to name a few, differences in the level of human capital (Barro 1991; Mankiw, Romer, and Weil 1992), the depth of financial development (King and Levine 1993), the nature and quality of government intervention in economic processes (Barro 1990; Fischer 1991, King and Levine 1993), have all been controlled for in growth equations. Yet, even after correcting for a wide variety of additional explanatory variables, many growth equations struggle to account for cross-country variation in growth, particularly in Africa and Latin America (see for example Barro 1991; and Easterly and Levine 1997).

Easterly and Levine (1997, p. 1205), in an influential article, drew attention to the potentially important role of ethnic diversity in influencing economic growth: 'cross-country differences in ethnic diversity explain a substantial part of the cross-country differences in public policies, political instability, and other factors associated with long-run growth'. They find that ethnic diversity is an important predictor of economic performance, and of the African growth experience. Central to Easterly and Levine's perspective is the question of whether the level of ethnic fractionalization bears on the potential for distributional conflict. Specifically, they hypothesize that in the light of a significant body of recent literature, polarized societies will be prone to competitive rent-seeking that impedes agreement about the provision of public goods[1] and that creates positive incentives for growth-reducing policies. This is attributed either to the pursuit of redistributive policies defined along ethnic lines,[2] or to the fact that ethnically diverse societies are more prone to war and unrest which, in turn, are bad for economic growth.[3]

One limitation of all these studies on fractionalization is that whilst they emphasize cross-country evidence, they do not provide a basis for exploring the dynamics of the process; that is, they do not provide a basis on which to establish how growth interacts with ethnolinguistic diversity. There are at least two dimensions to this question. The first is that in evidence such as that presented by Easterly and Levine (1997), what is not explicit is that African economic growth fell dramatically from the 1960s to 1970s, and has remained dismal subsequently—at least for most of the continent. This leaves one with the puzzle of how it is that a variable, which remains a constant for all countries (the ethnolinguistic measure employed in many studies is for the single year 1960), can account for a series of growth rates that follow the shape of a step function, with the step occurring some considerable time after the point of measurement of the ethnolinguistic measure generally employed in these studies.

The second dimension to the question addresses the issue of whether or not it is legitimate to view ethnolinguistic fractionalization as a constant over time. Is it instead not at least feasible that ethnolinguistic

[1]This does, of course, beg the question, why rent-seeking mobilization should be along ethnic lines, rather than other forms of social distinction. In the current context, we note only the obvious point that rent seeking does not exclusively take ethnic form, and also that there exists an extensive literature exploring why ethnic mobilization is easier than some others. Argument goes towards lower information and transaction costs, lower monitoring costs, and lower enforcement costs in ethnic groupings. See for instance Collier's (2001) discussion of Posner (1980). Also see Alesina et al. (2002), Collier (2001), Knack and Keefer (1997), and Posner (2004). On a broader conception of institutions and their impact see Assane and Grammy (2003), Bhattacharyya (2004), and Hall and Jones (1999).

[2]Easterly and Levine (1997) and Easterly (2001) cite a vein of literature in support of this view. Thus Mauro (1995) and La Porta et al. (1999) find that ethnic diversity predicts poor quality of government services. Rodrik (1999) notes that ethnically divided nations react more adversely to external terms of trade shocks. Svensson (2000) reports that more foreign aid proceeds are diverted into corruption in more ethnically diverse contexts. Knack and Keefer (1997) find that ethnic homogeneity raises social capital which is associated with higher growth and productivity. Annet (2001) claims that linguistic or religious diversity leads to greater political instability which in turn leads to higher government consumption. Last, Collier (2001, p. 141) mentions the Kenyan case where during the time of President Kenyatta, a Kikuyu, the main Kikuyu city grew very rapidly at the expense of other non-Kikuyu cities. When President Moi a Kalenjin, took over, he responded by building a new international airport in the heartland of his own minor tribe, and filled certain parts of the civil service with Kalenjin. Evidence for rent seeking along ethnic lines in South Africa is legion. For evidence demonstrating that the historic pattern is replicating itself, see Luiz (2003).

[3]There appear to be two alternative explanations regarding the ethnic roots of instability. The first is primordial, arguing that different group identities influence the way in which people relate and interact with each other, leaving mute the question of whether its root cause could be biological, psychological, historical, mythical, or constructed. The alternate view suggests that ethnicity is not the real issue: conflict may come to be ethnically *patterned*, but not ethnically *caused*. Rather, ethnicity comes to be exploited, often for reasons of political expediency, rendering it a vehicle rather than a cause of conflict (see the discussion in Collier 2001, p. 151).

diversity changes with growth? If so, in what direction? And why might such a change occur? To answer these kinds of questions, a time series based study is required.

South Africa constitutes an interesting case in which to explore the claim of negative impact of ethnolinguistic fractionalization on growth. In terms of the Ethnolinguistic Fractionalization Index (ETHNIC) cited by Easterly and Levine (1997), South Africa (in 1960) ranked 6th out of 66 countries covered by this index with a value on the measure of 88 (that is a probability of 88 per cent that two randomly chosen individuals are of different ethno-linguistic origin). The most highly fractionalized country was Tanzania (score of 93) and the least fractionalized were Haiti, Japan, and Portugal (score of 1). South African census data collected since 1910 provide historical evidence of this fractionalization. Also important in the South African case is the fact that from 1948 up to the demise of Apartheid, a major attempt was made to socially and politically 'engineer' South Africa along the lines of supposedly 'essentialist' ethnic identities. At least with regard to the 'African' community these ethnic divisions were meant to coincide with linguistic identities. That South Africa continues to be linguistically highly fractionalized is registered, at least in part, by the fact that the present (post-1994) Constitution acknowledges linguistic diversity through the legal recognition of eleven official languages. If fractionalization is an important explanatory variable in the long-run growth process of a country, South Africa is ideal for testing this hypothesis. That data are also available for this case study renders it doubly interesting, since it can be subjected to rigorous analysis. This is reinforced by the fact that a number of studies have already demonstrated that the social, political, and institutional variables (SPIVs) available for South Africa prove to be important in driving the long-run economic performance of the economy.[4]

This chapter introduces, describes, and analyses three new sets of societal indicators and one set of political indicators for South Africa for the period 1910–97. The societal indicators are, respectively, linguistic, religious, and racial fractionalization.[5] The political indicator measures political fractionalization as measured by the distribution of members of the legislature across political parties (developed in Fedderke et al. 2001a). The choice of these indicators was occasioned by the desire to establish whether, and if so in what degree, social and political diversity might help to explain the long-run growth performance of the South African economy.[6] What is unique to the study is the use of time series data over an extended timeframe in a wide range of institutional dimensions.

The second section of the paper discusses a range of measurement issues relevant to the institutional variables employed in the study. The third section examines the significance of dynamics in the measures of fractionalization.

[4]On the impact of political instability on investment, see Fielding (2000) and Fedderke (2004). On the impact of political instability, and changes in political rights on short and long term capital flows as well as capital flight, see Fedderke and Liu (2002). On the impact of political instability on human capital production in black schooling in South Africa, see Fedderke and Luiz (2002). On the interaction of political instability, political rights, and economic growth in South Africa see Fedderke et al. (2001b).

[5]A fractionalization index measures the probability that any two randomly selected members of a statistical population will possess different properties in the dimension that is being measured.

[6]This study is part of a larger project that is concerned with addressing the institutional dimensions of long-term economic growth in South Africa. See Fedderke et al. (1999, 2000, 2001a, 2001 b, 2002, 2003).

The fourth section explores the question of whether the level of aggregation in fractionalization carries any analytical significance. The fifth section further examines the magnitude of impact of measurement error. The sixth section concludes.

## FRACTIONALIZATION: REFLECTING ON THE SIGNIFICANCE OF MEASUREMENT PROBLEMS

Measures of ethnolingusitic fractionalization have come to be widely used in growth studies. In addition, the literature has seen the introduction of at least two measures of such fractionalization.[7] Since the present study introduces a range of new measures of fractionalization, in a number of dimensions, we reflect briefly on some issues surrounding both the measurement and interpretation of linguistic and ethnic fractionalization.

The fractionalization indexes employed for the present study were constructed by consulting official South African government statistical sources which are based on census data. For the period 1910–60, our principal source has been the Union Statistics for 50 Years and various other official statistical yearbooks. Subsequently, the Central Statistical Services Reports were our primary sources; we also used various statistical reports of the apartheid-created 'independent homelands'.

We begin our discussion of fractionalization with a general methodological warning that applies repeatedly in what follows. Obtaining consistent and reliable data series on linguistic usage and other forms of fractionalization in South Africa was non-trivial. The scope and accuracy of coverage of different population groups has not been consistent over time. Particularly with respect to Africans, early years showed incomplete data collection, rendering the data unreliable. Moreover, under Apartheid and the repeated creation, redefinition, and disappearance of the supposedly ethnically defined 'homelands',[8] significant portions of the African population disappeared, moved classification, and reappeared in statistical sources. Finding, re-classifying, and reinserting such populations was not a trivial task. The implication is that the fractionalization data suffer substantially from data collection problems. After 1970, the active creation of homelands for Africans under Apartheid policies shifted responsibility for census data collection away from Pretoria. For example, data collection on first language orientation by homelands was negligible. The consequence is an error of measurement in any use of official data series, with a downward bias in the resulting linguistic fractionalization. Reported fractionalization indices in the present studies are corrected for any homeland exclusion.

The general point here is that given the demands of this undertaking even for a country such as South Africa, which relative to many other developing countries has fairly extensive and sound data collection procedures, this raises significant questions concerning the quality of data for developing countries in general—where data collection is frequently even more problematic than that in South

[7]The first, and most widely used measure in growth studies is the Atlas Narodov Mira (1964) measure, developed by Russian ethnological scholars. The second and more recent measure that we are aware of, is the Alesina et al. (2002) measure. Further, Posner (2004) has developed a new fractionalization index but only for Africa.

[8]Under Apartheid attempts were made to create 'independent' political entities defined ethnically—officially referred to as 'homelands'. Only a small number of the projected homelands pursued the goal of independence to any extent.

Africa, in the presence of high levels of fractionalization which require high levels of accuracy.

For example, the highest levels of linguistic fractionalization reported in Alesina et al. (2002) are for the Cameroon, Chad, the CAR, the DRC, Ethiopia, the Gambia, Guinea-Bisau, Kenya, Liberia, Mali, Mozambique, Nigeria, Philippines, South Africa, Tanzania, Uganda, and Zambia—all of which report a probability value of above 0.8. The countries with the highest levels of fractionalization are those most likely to have the most contentious data being employed in cross-sectional growth studies. Furthermore, the data employed by Alesina et al. for a wide range of countries rely on the *Encyclopedia Britannica*, the *CIA World Factbook*, Scarrit and Mozaffar (1999), Levinson (1998), and the *World Directory of Minorities* of the Minority Rights Group International (1997). The South African data come from the Levinson work and differ from that calculated in this paper from primary data. A cursory glance through these sources reveals some of the problems. For example, the *CIA Factbook* lists South African ethnic groups on the basis of the four racial population groups. While racial fractionalization in South Africa is undoubtedly important (and we deal with it in a separate section here), ethnic divisions cleave racial groupings also. This is well illustrated by the high degree of fractionalization within the African population group in South Africa, where linguistic grouping does correlate to some extent with ethnic identity. The *CIA Factbook* also lists the religious groups as follows: Christian, Muslim, Hindu, and Indigenous with no further differentiation, whereas for South Africa more detailed data are available. Note further that for other countries in the Alesina et al. data set, these categories are further disaggregated. An immediate question must, therefore, be whether 'like' is being compared with 'like' in international cross-country estimations.

In a similar vein, Posner (2004) criticizes the ethnolinguistic fractionalization index used in growth studies based on the *Atlas Naradov Mira* measures. He highlights the 'grouping problem' in which umbrella categories sometimes subsume groups that are clearly distinct and often highly antagonistic. He cites the Tanzanian example in which the Nyamwezi and Sukumo are collapsed into a single category despite the fact that these groups are very distinct (culturally, linguistically, and geographically) and are keen political competitors. In fact, both the Rwanda and the Burundi measures collapse the Hutus and Tutsis into a monolithic category, ignoring a fundamental cleavage which played a role in the devastation faced by both countries towards the end of the twentieth century. On other occasions, Posner points to the 'problem of inclusion' where distinct linguistic groups are produced in the Atlas study but which are irrelevant as political actors. Posner does not deny the importance of ethnic groups in the Atlas but claims that they are unimportant for the political measure that ethnolinguistic fractionalization is trying to test, namely the competition for power and resources.

Posner (2004) also takes issue with the use of Herfindahl indexes more generally and questions whether they are the best means of capturing a country's diversity because these are often insensitive to a great deal of variation in the ethnic landscapes being compared. Two countries can both have a Herfindahl measure of 0.5 but have vastly different ethnic landscapes. One can have two groups of equal size while the second contains three groups containing two-thirds, one-sixth, and one-sixth of the population, respectively. The dynamics of inter-group competition would be very different in the two countries but the same would not be captured by the formula. A further problem that he highlights is that the index contains no information about the depth of the divisions between different groups. It also provides no information about the relative political weights to be assigned to various ethnic groups. So for example, the white proportion in South Africa does not capture the impact of this group on the country's political landscape. The final problem presented by Posner is that these single measures contain multiple ethnic and political cleavages which change over time. He cites the Indian example of a population which is divided along ethnic, religious, linguistic, and caste lines and questions which group division is more relevant.

While issues of measurement are undoubtedly crucial, these extend beyond simple questions of accuracy of measurement. In the sections that follow, we consider a range of additional questions that arise in the context of appropriate construction, and interpretation of measures of fractionalization. The intention of the discussion is to move beyond the consideration of static measures with wide geographic sweep. Instead, the object of the discussion is to consider questions that arise from the introduction of time, and questions of aggregation that arise from in-depth evidence to emerge from a specific case study.

## DYNAMICS: DO CHANGES OVER TIME EXIST IN MEASURES OF FRACTIONALIZATION, AND DO THEY CARRY ANALYTICAL SIGNIFICANCE?

Data questions surrounding fractionalization extend beyond problems of measurement. An equally important set of considerations, to be explored over the course of the following sections, concerns appropriate interpretation of the evidence that emerges from the data.

The first question arises due to the fact that studies employing measures of fractionalization, frequently do so on the basis of data that have observations at a single time point (*Atlas Naradov Mira* 1964; Alesina et al. 2002). These observations bear a considerable analytical burden—as explanatory variables of dynamic processes in economic development, generally per capita GDP. Data sets have observations for distinct years across countries (the measure is not for the same year across countries). Implicit in the use of either set of fractionalization measures, is the presumption that measures of fractionalization are essentially static, and exogenous to processes of economic development. Only on this presumption would the time point of measurement and/or the time-invariant nature of the fractionalization measure be irrelevant to the estimation of the fractionalization impact. The immediate question then is whether the presumption of an unchanging magnitude of the fractionalization measures employed in studies is justified.

Evidence from South Africa on first blush suggests that it may be. Table 12.1 reports measures on linguistic and religious fractionalization for the aggregate South African population, for available census years in South Africa.[9] The presumption that measures of

[9] We follow the standard measure given by $F = 1 - \sum_{i=1}^{n} \left(\frac{n_i}{N}\right)\left(\frac{n_i - 1}{N - 1}\right)$, where $n_i$ denotes the number of members of households that cite the ith language as the principal medium of communication within the household, $N$ denotes the number of members in the population. $F$ thus computes the probability that two randomly chosen individuals speak different first languages. Symmetrically for religious fractionalization. Note that for linguistic fractionalization we suppressed

Table 12.1: Fractionalization Measures for Available South African Census Years

| | Fractionalization Measure | | |
|---|---|---|---|
| Census Year | Linguistic | Religious | Racial |
| 1911 | | | 0.49 |
| 1921 | | | 0.49 |
| 1936 | | 0.82 | 0.48 |
| 1945 | 0.86 | 0.84 | 0.48 |
| 1951 | 0.87 | 0.86 | 0.49 |
| 1960 | 0.87 | 0.88 | 0.49 |
| 1970 | 0.86 | 0.89 | 0.46 |
| 1980 | 0.86 | 0.88 | 0.44 |
| 1991 | 0.86 | 0.87 | 0.39 |
| 1996 | | | 0.38 |
| 2001 | | | 0.36 |

fractionalization appear to be relatively invariant over time, appears to be vindicated, with both linguistic and religious fractionalization changing by relatively little in aggregate for South Africa over a period of more than half a century.

However, the same cannot be said of the measure of racial fractionalization also reported in Table 12.1. While the measure remained fairly constant over the 1911–60 period (at a probability of approximately 0.49), during 1960–2001 fractionalization declined substantially, in relative terms, to end with a probability of 0.36 in 2001.

The distinction between the three measures of fractionalization is particularly important when placed in the context of the level of distributional conflict in South Africa. A number of studies have examined the impact of distributional conflict on growth in South Africa, including its impact on investment in physical capital stock. Results are unanimous in confirming a negative impact of a measure of political instability on output directly, or on investment rates.[10] Yet, the measure is not readily tied to our measures of fractionalization in any manner that conforms to the priors that arise from the literature on fractionalization. Figure 12.1 depicts the measure of political instability (as a proxy for distributional conflict),[11] as well as the measures of fractionalization.

The measure of distributional conflict in South Africa identifies a number of periods of intense conflict—during the 1960s, the 1970s, and particularly the 1980s. This much is conventional wisdom about South Africa. But note that the aggregate linguistic fractionalization measure for South Africa remains virtually unchanged, both over periods of stability (1946–64; the 1990s) as well as periods of relative instability. Similarly, the measure of

the 1936 observation, and for religious fractionalization the 1921 observation. While available, data collection problems resulted in clear outlier observations relative to the rest of the series.

[10]See Fielding (2000), Fedderke (2004), Mariotti (2002), Kularatne (2002), and Fedderke and Luiz (2005a).

[11]The measure of political instability is obtained from Fedderke et al. (2001a). One objection might query whether the measure of political instability is indeed a measure of distributional conflict. Instead political conflict in South Africa may be conceived of as a conflict not over access to resources but over political rights. However, Fedderke and Luiz (2005a) demonstrate that the primitive here is property rights, which influence both growth and political conflict, while political rights are an outcome variable from the interaction of economic and property rights developments. Effectively, the exclusion of most racial groupings in South Africa from access to resources by denying them relevant property rights renders questionable the suggestion that conflict was, at least exclusively, concerned with political rights, and not with rights over resources.

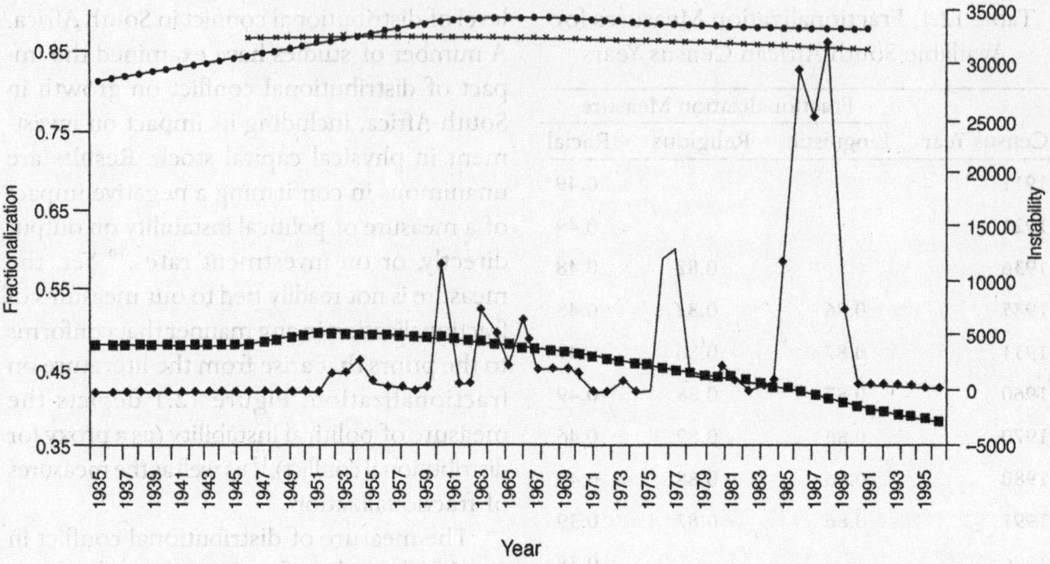


Figure 12.1: Fractionalization Measures and Distributional Conflict

religious fractionalization shows its period of increase before the periods of intense conflict, and remains virtually static over the period of intense conflict.[12]

Instead, the most likely source of distributional conflict, if such a source is to be found in a fractionalization measure, comes from the measure of *racial* fractionalization. This is the only fractionalization measure that demonstrates significant change from the period preceding significant distributional conflict, to the period in which distributional conflict rose dramatically.

That distributional conflict in South Africa might most plausibly be linked to racial divisions in the society does not seem to be a dramatic finding. After all, what could possibly constitute a more clichéd view of the South African political landscape? Indeed, it is precisely

[12]We recognize that this might lead to the conjecture that rising religious fractionalization might have led to distributional conflict, though with a lag. Two reasons suggest that this is unlikely. Barro and McCleary (2003) find that religious beliefs do influence economic performance and certainly this association goes back to the seminal work of Max Weber. The decision to measure religious diversity was in part occasioned by the fact that South Africa has historically been characterized by a considerable diversity of religions. It should be noted that, notwithstanding this diversity of religions, the country does not have a history of significant conflict between religious communities. Instead religious communities and institutions have been mobilized around political issues, notably with respect either to supporting or criticizing Apartheid. In this regard, many religious organizations came into conflict with the government. Some supported the Apartheid project and some were internally divided over the issue. The important point, however, is that these divisions were not primarily divisions between religious movements on specifically religious matters. They were divisions on the matter of the morality of Apartheid. See for instance the discussions in Research Institute for Theology and Religion (2000). We reflect further on questions of causality below.

the racial fractionalization measure that Alesina et al. (2002) employ for South Africa.

However, there are at least four considerations in relation to the empirical evidence that nuance the findings from cliché to insight. First, in contrast to the measure employed by Alesina et al. for fractionalization in South Africa, the measure of fractionalization most plausibly related to distributional conflict is not static, but strongly changes over the sample timeframe. Indeed, it is this very change in the fractionalization measure that usefully might be said to distinguish between periods of relative stability and instability in South Africa.

Second, the direction of change in the racial fractionalization variable is opposite to that predicted by the literature. It is not rising, but falling racial fractionalization that appears to be associated with rising political instability, though by the 1990s, political instability quietens again despite a continued decline in racial fractionalization which continues to this day. One response to this finding is to conjecture that the association between fractionalization and distributional conflict is more non-linear than generally hypothesized in the literature. Very high fractionalization measures may reflect iso-sized groups, in stable equilibrium rather than in distributional struggle. The relative strength of each grouping may be such as to render the cost of conflict prohibitive to each. Instead, it is precisely the disturbance of such an equilibrium through increased pressure toward homogenization, brought about by a relative gain in one or another of society's constituent groups, that may trigger distributional conflict, either through aggression (such as increased repression of a growing disadvantaged group), or as a defensive measure (for example, rising political resistance in the face of legislative measures designed to disempower). Eventually, the relative preponderance of one group may become sufficiently large to once again render the cost of conflict prohibitive for other groups, such that sufficiently high homogeneity in turn leads once again to political accommodation and relative stability.[13]

A third consideration might concern the direction of causality between instability and the fractionalization measure. Racial fractionalization might well have fallen at least in part due to white emigration, in the face of rising opposition to the maintenance of white privilege. Under this interpretation of the evidence, causality would run from instability to racial fractionalization, rather than vice versa. A further consideration here might be to question again the interpretation of the interaction between religious fractionalization and political instability, of whether rising religious fractionalization might have led to distributional conflict, though with a lag.

To investigate these questions we examine the interaction between the three measures of fractionalization and political instability, employing the bounds analysis of Pesaran, Shin, and Smith (2001).[14] We report the resultant F-tests in Table 12.2.

[13]In South Africa, this resulted in the Tricameral parliament of 1983 (which co-opted Coloureds and Asians into the formal legislative structures in the hopes of building new alliances and building critical mass) and then in 1989, in the unbanning of the African resistance movements (including the African National Congress and the Pan African Congress). The unbanning of these anti-apartheid movements in turn paved the way for the constitutional negotiations which led to democratic elections in 1994.

[14]See also the discussion in Pesaran (1997), Pesaran and Shin (1995a, 1995b), and Pesaran, Shin, and Smith (2001). Suppose that the question is whether there exists a long-run relationship between the set of variables $y_t$, $x_{1,t}, \ldots x_{n,t}$. Univariate time series characteristics of the data are not known for certain. The PSS approach to testing

Table 12.2: PSS F-tests for Direction of Association

| | Religious Fractionalization | Linguistic Fractionalization | Political Instability | Racial Fractionalization |
|---|---|---|---|---|
| Religious Fractionalization | – | 18.58* | 3.95 | 5.73** |
| Linguistic Fractionalization | 4.97 | – | 5.53** | 8.54* |
| Political Instability | 3.36 | 13.62* | – | 0.59 |
| Racial Fractionalization | 3.57 | 210.97* | 7.39* | – |

*Notes*: Row headings denote forcing variables; Column headings outcome variables; * denotes unambiguous significance of the test statistic, allowing the rejection of the null of no association; ** denotes an indeterminate test statistic.

The evidence is instructive. The causality tests unambiguously favour the direction of association to be *from* racial fractionalization *to* political instability, with no evidence in favour of the reverse direction of association.[15] Second, there is no evidence of religious fractionalization impacting on political instability, nor of religious fractionalization being influenced either by any other measure of social cleavage or by the political instability measure. Third, it is noteworthy that the different measures of fractionalization appear to hang together—with linguistic fractionalization particularly appearing as an outcome variable flowing from other forms of social cleavage.

The fourth and final implication that follows from the evidence is that the trigger for distributional conflict in a society is at least not universally associated with a single measure of social cleavage. In South Africa, linguistic fractionalization, at least at the aggregate level is difficult to associate with variations in political instability, while racial fractionalization is more readily so associated.

The general point thus is that while there may well be links between distributional conflict and measures of fractionalization, such links may prove to be contingent on history and social context. Appropriate measures of fractionalization associated with distributional conflict may thus be heterogeneous across societies.[16]

for the presence of a long run relationship proceeds by estimating the error correction specification given by:

$$\Delta y_t = \alpha_0 + \sum_{i=1}^{p} \beta_i \Delta y_{t-1} + \sum_{j=1}^{n}\sum_{i=1}^{p} \gamma_{j,i} \Delta x_{j,t-i} + \left( \delta_1 y_{t-1} + \sum_{k=2}^{n+1} \delta_k x_{k,t-1} \right) + \varepsilon_t$$

The test proceeds by computing the standard F-statistic for the joint significance of $\delta_1 = \delta_2 = \ldots = \delta_{n+1} = 0$, under all feasible alternative LHS variables. While the distribution of the test statistic is non-standard, with $x_{i,t}$~$I(0)$ $\forall i$ providing a lower bound value, $x_{i,t}$~$I(1)$ $\forall i$ an upper bound value to the test statistic. The test is analogous to a Granger causality test, but in the presence of non-stationary data. This renders the PSS F-test suitable in the current context.

[15]This direction of association is further favoured by the fact that emigration from South Africa accelerated during the 1980s and 1990s, considerably after the process of racial homogenization of the population began.

[16]A cursory examination of the international political landscape readily demonstrates that it is unlikely that ethnolinguistic fractionalization is necessarily the defining social fault line. While ethnolinguistic fractionalization may be the social cleavage which resulted in conflict in Rwanda and Burundi, it is not clear that this is the case in other conflicts. The long lasting conflict in Northern Ireland was ostensibly waged

## DOES DISTRIBUTIONAL CONFLICT EMERGE AT THE AGGREGATE LEVEL?

Thus far we have considered data only at the aggregate level for South Africa. Both the linguistic and the religious fractionalization measures ignored any information at more disaggregated levels, for instance, for racial groups.

Yet, given the evidence on the impact of racial fractionalization on political instability, it is not clear that aggregate measures of fractionalization are appropriate for capturing distributional conflict, at least in South Africa. Instead, distributional conflict may be the expression of developments that are placed at greater levels of disaggregation than can be captured by the simple summary measures reported thus far.

In order to examine the plausibility of this hypothesis we measure linguistic fractionalization, disaggregated so as to capture not only the overall level of fractionalization, but also the levels of fractionalization within the racial groups as they were officially designated in the period of segregation prior to 1948, and which became statutorily encoded after 1948 under Apartheid.[17] In this way we are better able to capture dynamic processes and potentially interesting patterns of change that might not be observed if one were to focus only on the aggregate data.

We have already noted that the aggregate measures of both linguistic and religious fractionalization in South Africa remain constant over protracted periods of time. In contrast, the disaggregated fractionalization indexes in both dimensions, when decomposed by race, show substantial variation over time. In effect, the aggregate evidence on linguistic and religious fractionalization in South Africa is

Table 12.3: Fractionalization Measures for Available South African Census Years—the Racial Breakdown

| Census | Linguistic | | Fractionalization | | | Religious Fractionalization | | | | |
|---|---|---|---|---|---|---|---|---|---|---|
| Year | White | Coloured | Asian | African | Total | White | Coloured | Asian | African | Total |
| 1945 | 0.52 | 0.19 | 0.80 | 0.81 | 0.86 | 0.75 | 0.83 | 0.48 | 0.74 | 0.84 |
| 1951 | 0.52 | 0.20 | 0.80 | 0.81 | 0.87 | 0.78 | 0.85 | 0.47 | 0.78 | 0.86 |
| 1960 | 0.52 | 0.20 | 0.80 | 0.82 | 0.87 | 0.77 | 0.84 | 0.47 | 0.83 | 0.88 |
| 1970 | 0.54 | 0.21 | 0.78 | 0.80 | 0.86 | 0.79 | 0.84 | 0.47 | 0.85 | 0.89 |
| 1980 | 0.58 | 0.29 | 0.46 | 0.83 | 0.86 | 0.79 | 0.85 | 0.51 | 0.82 | 0.88 |
| 1991 | 0.52 | 0.29 | 0.10 | 0.83 | 0.86 | 0.79 | 0.85 | 0.61 | 0.82 | 0.87 |

between Protestants and Catholics and was thus driven by a religious cleavage. The balkanization of Yugoslavia and the Soviet Union had many dimensions including ethnolinguistic and religious cleavages. The Huntington (1997) hypothesis of the clash of civilizations supports a number of fundamental cleavages in world politics and these could easily be translated intra-country, although this was not his intention. The current conflict in the Sudan, likewise, reveals a complex network of cleavages including religious and racial. It is, therefore simplistic to assume that the default cleavage for distributional conflict will necessarily be ethnolinguistic rather than other forms of social and political cleavages, including the most obvious ones of race and religion.

[17]The study employs the Apartheid racial classificatory system of African, Asian, Coloured, and White, given the prevalence of data collection under these categories.

misleading in the sense that it fails to reflect the substantial extent of social change that occurs within the society.

A number of features stand out from the evidence.

• Only two out of the eight racially decomposed measures of linguistic and religious fractionalization show stability of the same order as the aggregate measures—African linguistic fractionalization and Coloured religious fractionalization. All other racially disaggregated measures in either dimension report relatively strong change over time.

• Of the four racial groupings in South Africa, the two smallest groupings, those of Coloureds and Asians, show the most dramatic change over time. Most spectacular of all, Asian linguistic fractionalization falls from a probability measure of 0.78 in 1970, to 0.10 in 1991, reflecting a switch from a range of Indian first languages to English over the twenty year period. While linguistic fractionalization amongst Coloureds has risen rather than fallen strongly from 0.21 to 0.29 over the same period, it also has done so by virtue of a linguistic switch to English as first language, from Afrikaans in this instance. Over the period in which Asian linguistic fractionalization is falling dramatically, Asian religious fractionalization is increasing strongly, from 0.47 to 0.61.

• One of the two 'dominant' racial groups of South Africa also shows instances in which a stable pattern of fractionalization is disturbed. However, the disturbance is relatively temporary, with a reversion to the former stable fractionalization pattern over time. Thus, white linguistic fractionalization rises from 1970–80, with the entry of significant Portuguese immigration from the two former Portuguese colonies of Mozambique and Angola. However, the increase in fractionalization rapidly reverts to the former level of fractionalization by 1991, as the Portuguese immigrants are assimilated into the Anglophone white linguistic grouping.

Two general implications are suggested by this evidence. The first is that aggregate measures of fractionalization may prove to be substantively misleading as indicators of underlying potential for distributional conflict. In South Africa, the aggregate measure of linguistic fractionalization simply hides substantial movement in the extent of cleavage that emerges at more disaggregated levels, and which might conceivably have triggered distributional conflict. Linguistic fractionalization at the micro level appears considerably less stable, with dramatic and sustained change appearing over a relatively short time period. The corollary is that testing for the impact of fractionalization on instability or growth cannot necessarily simply have recourse to aggregate measures in any dimension, since the real change of relevance that triggers the conflict might not be observable at the aggregate level.

The second implication is potentially both more interesting, but also of greater significance for estimation purposes. We have already noted that larger marginalized minorities in South Africa show a relatively rapid degree of acceptance of the language of trade and industry: English. The preceding evidence reports that the Coloured, Portuguese, and particularly the Asian communities of South Africa show substantive tendencies to adopt English as their main language. Such changes may reflect decisions to improve employment and economic prospects by acquiring the linguistic currency of economic activity. In effect, this encompasses a choice to invest in more appropriate forms of both human and social capital in order to increase the prospects for both individual occupational mobility and the reduction of the transactions costs entailed in participation in the economy.[18] The suggestion is that at least larger, more significant minorities face considerable incentives to assimilate into dominant linguistic patterns.[19] By contrast, small minorities (such as the German and/or French speakers in the White population) may be able to retain linguistic identity longer since they are insignificant enough to be left alone and develop their own cultural enclaves within the broader society.

The net consequence of this may be that linguistic fractionalization at the micro level manifests the lack of stability discussed already. Importantly, we note that the implication is that linguistic fractionalization is no longer an exogenous (constant), but becomes endogenous to the potential of distributional conflict.[20] Those population groups most at risk from conflict (large minorities) have an incentive to assimilate, while larger groupings and/or small minorities have the means to maintain their identity over time.

This, in turn, carries a potential challenge for the notion that fractionalization necessarily leads to distributional conflict between linguistic groups. At the very least, one would have to recognize that in the South African context, minority groups had an incentive to integrate into the prevailing language of commerce and industry, and did so with alacrity. Perhaps this is true only of minorities, and in the presence of roughly equally sized groups (for example, in Belgium) the story might be different. Indeed the lengthy stand-off between White and African population groups in South Africa would suggest that where 'opponent' groups are of sufficient size or influence, distributional conflict may indeed be protracted and intense. Nevertheless, the evidence points to the importance and significance of nuance and clinical study as a valuable extension of aggregate or summary cross-sectional evidence.

## ACCURACY AND PRECISION: JUST HOW KEY ARE THESE WATCHWORDS?

A substantial sub-theme in the debate surrounding the impact of ethno-linguisitic fractionalization on economic and social development has come to focus on questions of accuracy in the measurement of fraction-

[18]In the case of Asians, additional factors would have included the policy decision in 1948 to terminate immigration from India, and to decrease, to the point of elimination, funding for private Indian schools (see Fedderke et al. 2000). Both measures prevented Indian linguistic usage from being sustained through investment in the stock of primary language users.

[19]Economic incentives towards linguistic assimilation need not be restricted to minorities. Sufficient economic pay-offs may induce even majorities to change. A tempting means of independent verification lurks here. Currently, the African population of South Africa has unprecedented access to schooling resources. A predicted change which follows from the interpretation of the data series presented above is that the African population too should come to manifest reduced levels of linguistic fractionalization, since the prevailing language of education, industry and commerce, and government in South Africa is English. This latent change in linguistic fractionalization would be hidden in current and past census data, since the primary language use of households is collected for heads of households. Only once the current population of school children and university students forms its own households would this change become evident.

[20]Questions surrounding the direction of association between variables in growth contexts are both pervasive and crucial. For discussions on methodological and estimation issues in these contexts see Awokuse (2005), Chang and Caudill (2005), Shan (2005), and Wahab (2004).

alization. Indeed, the second section of this paper added some additional reflections in this regard. Such deliberations are valuable. But they do beg the question of how practical significant errors of measurement might be in empirical work investigating say, the impact of fractionalization on economic growth. This question becomes all the more pressing if it is indeed true that fractionalization matters (for example, in distributional conflict), and if the measurement problems the literature refers to are as widespread as this and other studies suggest.

We provide two initial sets of consideration from the South African case study that shed some light on the practical question posed. From 1970, South Africa engaged in the creation of nominally independent 'homelands' that were subsequently excluded from official population census data for South Africa. Since the population of these homelands was essentially defined on linguistic grounds,[21] the linguistic groups in the official South African censuses were correspondingly under-enumerated. Table 12.4 reports the contrast between the uncorrected and the corrected census computations of Black and total South African linguistic fractionalization indexes for the 1980 and 1991 census observations (the only ones affected).[22] In addition, the official census populations, the populations of the up to four homelands, and the proportion of the relevant linguistic grouping excluded by virtue of the non-enumeration of the homelands are also reported.

Note that the exclusion of the homeland populations from the official South African census resulted in a substantial under-enumeration. Up to 50 per cent of a set of linguistic groups that together constituted approximately 40 per cent of South Africa's black population were thereby excluded from official census data (that is, approximately 20 per cent of the total population).

Unsurprisingly, therefore, a divergence emerges between uncorrected and corrected fractionalization indexes for the black population. But given the size of the underlying measurement error (20 per cent of the total population excluded), the divergence is surprisingly small—0.78 on the uncorrected fractionalization index versus 0.83 on the corrected index constitutes the maximal divergence, for the black population in South Africa. Moreover, for the aggregate total population fractionalization index, the divergence between the corrected and the uncorrected index is negligible—0.86 versus 0.85.

An immediate implication that follows is that while measurement error in the computation of fractionalization indexes is undoubtedly a serious concern and should be minimized, the fractionalization indexes used in the literature might be argued to be in fact fairly robust to measurement error. Of course, bias emerges in the fractionalization indexes—but it appears that the error of measurement would have to be fairly substantial before a significant divergence between the true and the biased fractionalization measure emerges.

There is a second sense in which the role of precision of measurement in fractionalization indexes can be investigated for the South African data. Table 12.5 reports a measure of

[21] Transkei and Ciskei were essentially Xhosa-, Bophutatswana Tswana-, and Venda Venda-speaking.

[22] The Homelands were created after 1970, and were reincorporated into official censuses after 1994. Thus only the 1980 and 1991 census years reported in this study were affected. Note that the remainder of the study reports only fractionalization indexes corrected for the under-enumeration.

## Table 12.4: Assessing Fractionalization Index Sensitivity to Error of Measurement

| Year | South African Official Census | | | Homeland Census | | | Homeland Census | | | South African Total Population | | | Fractionalization Index | | | |
|---|---|---|---|---|---|---|---|---|---|---|---|---|---|---|---|---|
| | Count | | | Count | | | Proportion of Total SA Population | | | Proportion of Linguistic Group in Total SA Population | | | Black | | Total | |
| | Xhosa | Tswana | Venda | Xhosa | Tswana | Venda | Xhosa | Tswana | Venda | Xhosa | Tswana | Venda | Uncorrected | Corrected | Uncorrected | Corrected |
| 1970 | 3,912,680 | 1,679,920 | 359,480 | – | – | – | – | – | – | 0.28 | 0.12 | 0.03 | 0.80 | | 0.86 | |
| 1980 | 2,791,981 | 1,346,383 | 160,135 | 2,323,650 | 1,323,315 | 315,545 | 0.45 | 0.50 | 0.66 | 0.23 | 0.12 | 0.02 | 0.79 | 0.83 | 0.86 | 0.86 |
| 1991 | 2,503,967 | 1,431,573 | 114,742 | 4,279,500 | 2,403,000 | 556,100 | 0.63 | 0.63 | 0.83 | 0.22 | 0.12 | 0.02 | 0.78 | 0.83 | 0.86 | 0.86 |

political fractionalization.[23] The index is computed on parliamentary representation, and only for the White House of Assembly, and reports the probability that two randomly chosen members of parliament would represent different political parties.[24] By its very construction, therefore, the measure cannot be said to capture the 'true' political fractionalization that prevailed in South Africa. But equally, the fractionalization measure nevertheless cannot be said to be devoid of any informational content.

Table 12.5: Measure of Political Fractionalization

| Year | Index | Year | Index |
|---|---|---|---|
| 1910 | 0.59 | 1958 | 0.50 |
| 1915 | 0.69 | 1961 | 0.48 |
| 1920 | 0.74 | 1966 | 0.40 |
| 1921 | 0.54 | 1970 | 0.43 |
| 1924 | 0.61 | 1974 | 0.43 |
| 1929 | 0.58 | 1977 | 0.33 |
| 1933 | 0.59 | 1981 | 0.33 |
| 1938 | 0.44 | 1987 | 0.47 |
| 1943 | 0.58 | 1989 | 0.57 |
| 1948 | 0.61 | 1994 | 0.55 |
| 1953 | 0.52 | 1999 | 0.46 |

The correlation between our measure of political fractionalization and a range of measures of political rights, civil liberties, political instability, and property rights is reported in Table 12.6. While for some measures of rights (Freedom House Political Rights) and political instability, there is little correlation with the political fractionalization measure, for others the correlation proves more substantial (the Fedderke et al. 2001a political freedoms and property rights measures, and the Freedom House Civil Liberties measure).

How might we interpret these correlations? We have just noted that these measure are imprecise—suffering from (potentially unknown) measurement error. For normally distributed data, the observed correlation between two variables is equal to the 'true' correlation between such variables if perfectly

Table 12.6: Political Fractionalization Correlations

| | Political Freedom (Fedderke et al. 2001a) | Political Rights (Freedom House) | Civil Liberties (Freedom House) | Political Instability (Fedderke et al. 2001a) | Property Rights (Fedderke et al. 2001a) |
|---|---|---|---|---|---|
| Political Fractionalization | 0.77 | –0.02 | 0.69 | –0.03 | 0.48 |
| True Correlation | 0.86 | –0.02 | 0.77 | –0.03 | 0.54 |

[23]The measure was first introduced in Fedderke et al. (2001a).

[24]From 1910–83 South Africa had only the House of Assembly as its formal legislative chamber. It essentially represented Whites, though even prior to 1983, representation of Africans, Coloureds, and Asians existed under the Representation of Natives Act (1936), and the Separate Representation of Voters Act (1955). Such representation was more notional than real. In 1983, South Africa introduced a three chamber parliament, with a White House of Assembly, the Asian House of Delegates, and the Coloured House of Representatives. Africans had no representation (outside of the notionally independent ethnically defined homelands), until 1994 and the introduction of the first democratic South African Parliament.

measured times the square root of the product of the reliability coefficients for each variable.[25] For many social datasets, reliability is not above 0.8 to 0.9. Thus, observed correlation coefficients of 0.6 to 0.8 are high, given the unreliability of measurement. To illustrate, suppose that the rights variables of Table 12.6 are each measured with a reliability of 0.8, while the parliamentary fractionalization measure is measured with no error at all (we can observe parliamentary composition without error). The implied 'true' correlations are reported in the final row of Table 12.6. What emerges is that the parliamentary fractionalization measure, despite its clearly partial and unsatisfactory provenance, nevertheless holds substantial information concerning a range of other institutional dimensions. Putting it another way: we would be hard-pressed to say that these correlated variables are measuring very different things.

We draw two final implications from these explorations. First, partial measures and even poorly measured variables still hold information. Second, the existence of dense webs of association between variables noted elsewhere,[26] suggests that a wide range of social indicators, even if at first sight relatively partial and incomplete, nevertheless may carry useful modeling opportunity, if employed with appropriate discretion.

We hasten to add that we do not mean to say that measurement error is a trivial concern. Much of the discussion in the preceding sections of this paper has pointed to the importance of measuring the right dimensions, at the right levels of aggregation, and accurately. But equally, measurement error is also just measurement error—it need not be the end of the analytical world.

## CONCLUSION: IMPLICATIONS FOR GROWTH STUDIES

The discussion in this chapter has mainly focused on the development of general methodological lessons associated with a specific time series case study. The following general conclusions emerge from the preceding discussion.

First, we note immediately that while many of the aggregate fractionalization indexes show considerable stationarity over time, this is not universally true (racial fractionalization), and even where it does hold, the aggregate stability hides substantial movement at the micro level. The implication is that indicators of social cleavage may themselves be subject to substantial change over time, rendering the question of what drives such changes (particularly whether economic development indicators do so) germane.[27]

Second, the evidence presented here is suggestive of a more substantive hypothesis. We have observed that linguistic fractionalization in South Africa is subject to a (though admittedly slight) downward trend, while religious fractionalization has been increasing. (The contrast is suitably dramatic for Asians.) One possible interpretation of the evidence is that the movement in the two indexes is due not so much to changes in underlying cleavages in South African society, but to changes in the nature of identity formation. In particular, the evidence is consistent with a shift of identity formation from one that is based on 'essentialist' linguistic (ethnic) roots, to one which is choice-based. Increased

[25] A reliability coefficient of 1.0 would indicate perfect agreement and no measurement error, 0 would indicate pure measurement error and no agreement.

[26] See the extensive investigation in Fedderke and Klitgaard (1998).

[27] This is a question we explore in greater detail in a separate paper (Fedderke et al. 2005b).

religious fractionalization might reflect the abandonment of religions of birth, in favour of religions of choice.

Third, we note the significant difficulties associated with collecting data on social cleavage. We note further that in cross-sectional contexts this issue is further complicated. Consistency, as well as reliability of data compilation must play a role across wide geographical reaches, and periods of time. Countries with the highest levels of fractionalization are those that are most likely to have the most contentious data being employed in cross-sectional studies.

We also note that measurement difficulties surrounding fractionalization indexes are not necessarily terminal. For the South African time series data we show that even relatively egregious problems of measurement do not necessarily bias fractionalization measures as much as one might have anticipated. Certainly the means of exploring the relationship between different measures of social and institutional context remain alive, even in the presence of measurement error.

Finally, the evidence on various fractionalization indexes reported here suggests that various social cleavages (for instance, religious and linguistic fractionalization) show a strong correspondence. Where the society is fractionalized in one dimension, it is tempting to conclude that it will be fractionalized in other dimensions also. Racial fractionalization may be mirrored in linguistic as well as religious diversity.

A further question that arises in this regard relates to the importance of the intentional mobilization of social cleavage which may itself be inherently latent, often through political agency.[28] How and when such mobilization may be successful will depend substantially on the institutional context. For instance, South Africa's historical institutional emphasis on racial cleavage as a means of economic and political exclusion had the effect of exacerbating distributional conflict, confirmed here by bounds analysis, thus harming growth. By contrast, religious fractionalization may have had very little or no impact at all on economic activity.

Anoher question is which particular line of social cleavage deserves close attention. With the suggestion that any one particular form of social cleavage may not be significant, what matters is the existence of cleavage, and the institutional means of exploiting such cleavage. Given the conclusions that have been reached in terms of the potential impact of fractionalization on long-run growth, it is essential to ensure that we use the right measures. This paper does not purport to have developed the 'right' measures but it has raised important caveats about the way in which cross-sectional growth studies employ the currently available fractionalization indexes.[29] It also suggests that the use of time series data for individual country case studies may be a fruitful new route for social scientists who are interested in the development prospects of developing countries.

[28]See, for instance, the discussion in Hamilton and Wright (1993) for the South African context.

[29]A caveat that Alesina et al. (2002, p. 18) are conscious of.

## REFERENCES

Alesina, A., A. Devleeschauwer, W. Easterly, S. Kurlat, and R. Wacziarg (2002), 'Fractionalization', NBER Working Paper 9411, Cambridge.

Annett, A. (2001), 'Social Fractionalization, Political Instability, and the Size of Government', IMF Staff Papers, Vol. 48, No. 3, pp. 561–92.

Assane, D. and A. Grammy (2003), 'Institutional Framework and Economic Development:

International Evidence', *Applied Economics*, Vol. 35, pp. 1811–7.

*Atlas Narodov Mira* (1964), Miklukho-Maklai Ethnological Institute at the Departmet of Geodesy and Cartography of the State Geological Committee of the Soviet Union, Moscow.

Awokuse, T.O. (2005), 'Exports, Economic Growth and Causality in Korea', *Applied Economics Letters*, Vol. 12, No. 11, pp. 693–6.

Barro, R.J. (1990), 'Government Spending in a Simple Model of Endogenous Growth', *Journal of Political Economy*, Vol. 98, No. 5, pp. S102–S125.

____ (1991), 'Economic Growth in a Cross Section of Countries', *Quarterly Journal of Economics*, Vol. 106, pp. 407–43.

Barro, R.J. and R.M. McCleary (2003), 'Religion and Economic Growth', NBER Working Paper 9682, Cambridge.

Bhattacharyya, S. (2004), 'Deep Determinants of Economic Growth', *Applied Economics Letters*, Vol. 11, No. 9, pp. 587–90.

Chang, T., and S.B. Caudill (2005), 'Financial Development and Economic Growth: The Case of Taiwan', *Applied Economics*, Vol. 37, No. 12, pp. 1329–35.

Collier, P. (2001), 'Ethnic Diversity: An Economic Analysis', *Economic Policy*, April, pp. 127–166.

Easterly, W. (2001), 'The Middle Class Consensus and Economic Development', Mimeo, World Bank, Washington DC.

Easterly, W. and R. Levine (1997), 'Africa's Growth Tragedy: Policies and Ethnic Divisions', *Quarterly Journal of Economics*, Vol. 112, No. 4, pp. 1203–50.

Fedderke, J.W. (2004), 'Investment in Fixed Capital Stock: Testing for the Impact of Sectoral and Systemic Uncertainty', *Oxford Bulletin of Economics and Statistics*, Vol. 66, No. 2, pp. 165–87.

Fedderke, J.W., R. De Kadt, and J.M. Luiz (1999), 'Growth and Social Capital: A Critical Reflection', *Theory and Society*, Vol. 28, pp. 709–45.

____ (2000), 'Uneducating South Africa: Government Policy and the Failure to Address Human Capital a 1910–1993 Legacy', *International Review of Education*, Vol. 46, Nos 3 and 4, pp. 257–81.

____ (2001a), 'Indicators of Political Liberty, Property Rights and Political Instability in South Africa: 1935–97', *International Review of Law and Economics*, Vol. 21, pp. 103–134.

____ (2001b), 'Growth and Institutions: A Study of the Link between Political Institutions and Economic Growth in South Africa—A Time Series Study: 1935–97', *Journal for the Study of Economics and Econometrics*, Vol. 25, No. 1, pp. 1–26.

____ (2003), 'Capstone or Deadweight? Inefficiency, Duplication and Inequity in South Africa's Tertiary Education System, 1910–93', *Cambridge Journal of Economics*, Vol. 27, pp. 377–400.

Fedderke, J.W. and R.E. Klitgaard (1998), 'Growth and Social Indicators: An Exploratory Analysis', *Economic Development and Cultural Change*, Vol. 46, No. 3, pp. 455–90.

Fedderke, J.W. and W. Liu (2002), 'Modelling the Determinants of Capital Flows and Capital Flight: With an Application to South African Data from 1960–95', *Economic Modelling*, Vol. 19, pp. 419–44.

Fedderke, J.W. and J.M. Luiz (2002), 'Production of Educational Output: Time-Series Evidence from Socio-economically Heterogeneous Populations—the Case of South Africa, 1927–1993', *Economic Development and Cultural Change*, Vol. 51, No. 1, pp. 161–188.

____ (2005a), 'The Political Economy of Institutions, Stability and Investment: A Simultaneous Equation Approach in an Emerging Economy—The Case of South Africa, 1927–1993, *Economic Development and Cultural Change*, Vol. 51, No. 1, pp. 161–88.

____ (2005b), 'Does Human Generate Social and Institutional Capital? Exploring Evidence from Time Series Data in a Middle Income Country', Unpublished mimeo.

Fielding, D. (2000), 'Manufacturing Investment in South Africa: A Time Series Model', *Journal of Development Economics*, Vol. 58, pp. 405–27.

Fischer, S. (1991), 'Growth, Macroeconomics, and

Development', *NBER Macroeconomics Annual*, pp. 329–64.
Hall, R.E. and C.I. Jones (1999), 'Why Do Some Countries Produce So Much More Output Per Worker Than Others?', *Quarterly Journal of Economics*, Vol. 114, No. 1, pp. 83–116.
Hamilton, C. and J.B. Wright (1993), 'The Beginnings of Zulu Identity: The Image of Shaka', *Indicator*, Vol. 10, No. 3.
Huntington, S.P. (1997), *The Clash of Civilizations and the Remaking of World Order*, Free Press, London.
King, R.G. and R. Levine (1993), 'Finance and Growth: Schumpeter Might be Right', *Quarterly Journal of Economics*, Vol. 108, pp. 717–37.
Knack, S. and P. Keefer (1997), 'Does Social Capital Have an Economic Payoff? A Cross-country Investigation', *Quarterly Journal of Economics*, Vol. CXII, No. 4, pp. 1251–88.
Kularatne, C. (2002), 'An Examination of the Impact of Financial Deepening on Long-run Economic Growth: An Application of VECM Structure to a Middle-income Country Context', *South African Journal of Economics*, Vol. 70, No. 4, pp. 647–87.
La Porta R., F. Lopez de Silanes, A. Shleifer, and R. Vishny (1999), 'The Quality of Government', *Journal of Law, Economics and Organization*, Vol. 15, No. 1, pp. 222–79.
Levinson, D. (1998), *Ethnic Groups Worldwide, A Ready Reference Handbook*, Oryx Press, Phoenix.
Lucas, R.E. (1988), 'On The Mechanics of Economic Development', *Journal of Monetary Economics*, Vol. 22, pp. 3–42.
Luiz, J.M. (2003), 'The Relevance, Practicality and Viability of Spatial Development Initiatives: A South African Case Study', *Public Administration and Development*, Vol. 23, No. 5, pp. 433–43.
Mankiw, N.G., D. Romer, and D.N. Weil (1992), 'A Contribution to the Empirics of Economic Growth', *Quarterly Journal of Economics*, Vol. 107, pp. 407–37.
Mariotti, M. (2002), 'An examination of the Impact of Economic Policy on Long Run Economic Growth: An Application of a VECM Structure to a Middle-income Context', *South African Journal of Economics*, Vol. 70 No. 4, pp. 688–724.
Mauro, P. (1995), 'Corruption and Growth', *Quarterly Journal of Economics*, Vol. 110, No. 3, pp. 681–712.
Minority Rights Group International (1997), *World Directory of Minorities*, Minority Rights Group International, London.
Pesaran, M.H. (1997), 'The Role of Economic Theory in Modelling the Long Run', *Economic Journal*, Vol. 107, pp. 178–91.
Pesaran, M.H. and Y. Shin (1995a), 'Long Run Structural Modelling', Unpublished manuscript, University of Cambridge.
—— (1995b), 'An Autoregressive Distributed Lag Modelling Approach to Cointegration Analysis', DAE Working Paper no 9514, Department of Applied Economics, University of Cambridge.
Pesaran, M.H., Y. Shin, and R. Smith (2001), 'Bounds Testing Approaches to the Analysis to the Testing of Level Relationships', *Journal of Applied Econometrics*, Vol. 16, pp. 289–326.
Posner, D.A., (2004), 'Measuring Ethnic Fractionalization in Africa', *American Journal of Political Science*, Vol. 48, No. 4, pp. 849–63.
Posner, R.A. (1980), 'A Theory of Primitive Society with Special Reference to Law', *Journal of Law and Economics*, Vol. 23, No. 1, pp. 1–54.
Research Institute for Theology and Religion (2000), *Violence, Truth and Prophetic Silence: Religion and the Quest for a South African Common Good*, UNISA, Pretoria.
Rodrik, D. (1999), 'Where Did All the Growth Go? External Shocks, Social Conflict and Growth Collapses', *Journal of Economic Growth*, Vol. 4, No. 4, pp. 385–412.
Romer, P.M. (1986), 'Increasing Returns and Long Run Growth', *Journal of Political Economy*, Vol. 94 (October), pp. 1002–37.
Romer, P. (1990), 'Endogenous Technological Change', *Journal of Political Economy*, Vol. 98, No. 5, pp. S71–S102.
Scarrit, J. and S. Mozaffar (1999), 'The Specification of Ethnic Cleavages and Ethnopolitical Groups

for the Analysis of Democratic Competition in Contemporary Africa', *Nationalism and Ethnic Politics*, Vol. 5, No. 1, pp. 82–117.

Shan, J. (2005), 'Does Financial Development "lead" Economic Growth? A Vector Autoregression Appraisal', *Applied Economics*, Vol. 37, No. 12, pp. 1353–67.

Svensson, J. (2000), 'Foreign Aid and Rent-Seeking', *Journal of International Economics*, Vol. 51, No. 2, pp. 437–61.

Wahab, M. (2004), 'Economic Growth and Government Expenditure: Evidence from a New Test Specification', *Applied Economics*, Vol. 36, pp. 2125–35.

# Part V
# Lessons from China

# 13

# Targeted FDI Promotion Strategy
## Attracting The 'Right' FDI for Development

Jinkang Zhang*

### INTRODUCTION

In 1989, John Williamson concluded that there was a 'Washington Consensus' about the desirability of openness to the world economy, liberalization of domestic markets, and macroeconomic stability (Gore 2000, Williamson 2000). In a lecture in the series 'Practitioners of Development' delivered at the World Bank on 13 January 2004, Williamson argued that:

> 'The Washington Consensus as I originally formulated it was not written as a policy prescription for development: it was a list of policies that I claimed were widely held in Washington to be widely desirable in Latin America as of the date the list was compiled' (Williamson 2004, p.1).

Williamson argued about ten liberalizing economic reforms: the seventh was the liberalization of flows of FDI. He stressed that 'barriers impeding the entry of foreign direct investment should be abolished' (Williamson 2004, p.8), and also explained that in 1989 there was still widespread reluctance to accept foreign investment, including FDI. The more important problem now is to restrain countries from competing for FDI by offering investment incentives, thereby handing an undue proportion of the benefits of FDI back to the companies that make the investments. One of the advantages of FDI that has been strongly emphasized, at least since the Asian crisis, is that the flow of FDI is much more stable than that of portfolio capital and certainly that of bank loans.

Williamson (1990, 2004) stressed that the original version of the Washington Consensus spoke quite specifically of liberalizing the inflow of FDI, and not of general liberalization of capital inflows. The regions that moved furthest in the direction of stabilization, liberalization, and integraton with the world economy were Latin America and the economies in transition. East Asia moved much less and, in his view, some of the movement, that is, rapid capital account liberation, was a mistake. China and South Asia both moved rather gradually, but the direction of movement

*This paper was presented at the *First ACDC* held in Neernrana, India, 2–4 December 2005. I wish to express my gratitude to Sanjaya Lall for suggestions, and to Aradhana Aggarwal, M. Albaladejo, and Philippa Biggs for comments.

was unambiguous. Sub-Saharan Africa moved spottily and grudgingly under foreign pressure. Williamson argued that the new consensus (Post-Washington Consensus) should not only be focused on economic growth but on achieving a broader range of goals: equitable development, sustainable development, and democratic development.

In 2004, Joshua Cooper Ramo from the European Think Tank (The Foreign Policy Centre in London) published a report titled 'The Beijing Consensus: Notes on the New Physics of Chinese Power'. Ramo was the former Foreign Editor of Time magazine and is currently a professor at Tsinghua University in Beijing. Ramo argues that there is a new 'Beijing Consensus emerging with distinct attitudes to politics, development and the global balance of power'. He argues that China offers hope to developing countries after the collapse of the Washington consensus.[1] In the report, he wrote 'What is happening in China at the moment is not only a model for China, but has begun to remake the whole landscape of international development, economics, society, by extension, politics.' (Ramo, 2004, p. 3). 'It does not believe in uniform solutions for every situation. It is defined by a ruthless willingness to innovate and experiment.' (Ramo 2004, p. 4).

Many scholars realize that China has its own path for development, which is admired by many other developing countries. However, the change is 'too fast to track back'—for scholars both from home and abroad, who can not explain these changes very clearly. All these issues are worth studying. But, a significant fact is that China is the second largest FDI recipient in the world followed by the US, and the largest in the developing world. The stock of FDI inflows in China to 2004 is over US$ 560 billion. There is a huge literature on China's FDI inflow and economic growth, FDI inflow and exports, as well as FDI policies. In terms of FDI policies, there is considerable literature dealing with the impact of tax concessions on inward FDI. The literature dealing with targeted FDI promotion strategy is relatively more modest, although it is widely used in some countries, and Singapore as a good example.

The objective of this paper is to present the role of the targeted FDI promotion strategy, which could be an effective tool for developing countries to attract 'the right' FDI in order to achieve their goal of development. In this paper, FDI promotion[2] is defined to include only certain marketing activities through which governments try to attract FDI. Promotion excludes the granting of incentives to foreign investors, the screening of foreign investment, and negotiation with foreign investors, even though many of the organizations responsible for conducting investment promotion activities may also conduct these other activities.

Moreover, this paper intends to discuss the characteristics of China's FDI policy and to argue that there is no 'best' FDI policy for every country at any time, just as there is no 'one for all' or 'one for always' solution for development. The term—foreign direct investment policy—in this paper means all the policy tools the host country uses to maximize the net benefits by using FDI. Considering host countries' practices, FDI policy can be divided into two basic categories: incentives and restrictions (regulatory policy). FDI incentives

[1]See the website of the Foreign Policy Centre: *http://fpc.org.uk/publications/123*

[2]From other literature, FDI promotion is defined as all the incentives, which includes fiscal incentives, financial incentives, investment guarantees, EPZs, offering information, and etc.

include: (i) providing information and technology assistance; (ii) facilitating financing; (iii) tax incentives; (iv) investment guarantee programme; (v) EPZs. This paper will focus only on the analysis of tax incentives and FDI promotion strategy.

The second section discusses the role of FDI on development, liberalization of FDI policy, and determinants of FDI inflows. The third section analyses the effects of tax incentives on inward FDI using the chinese experience. The fourth section provides the best practice of targeted FDI promotion strategy with an investigation of China's FDI promotion activities and institutions. The fifth section lists out recommendations for developing countries. The sixth section discusses are as for further studies in this field.

## FDI POLICY

### THE ROLE OF FDI IN DEVELOPMENT

In the 1960s and 1970s, there were many critiques of FDI and the activities of multinational corporations (MNCs) in developing countries. First, critics argued that MNCs transferred obsolete and 'inappropriate' technology to developing countries, often at inflated prices. Second, MNCs exercised enormous monopoly power over political and economic conditions within host economies. Third, MNCs evaded taxes by engaging in the practice of 'transfer pricing' between their subsidiaries. Fourth, MNCs discouraged domestic investment because local firms could not compete with foreign firms (Chang and Grabel 2004, p.138).

Recently, many developing countries have begun to treat FDI as the necessary resource for development in order to narrow the capital gap. In addition, FDI seems more stable than other types of foreign investment, say portfolio investment or foreign bank lending.

Standard propositions of the neoclassical theories suggest that FDI is likely to be an engine of host economic growth, because of the following reasons: (i) inward FDI may enhance capital formation and employment augmentation; (ii) FDI may promote industrial restructuring through competitive pressures or bring new activities or industries to host countries and then increase manufacturing export competitiveness; (iii) by its very nature, FDI may bring into host economies special resources such as management know-how, the access of skilled labour to international production networks, and established brand names; and (iv) FDI may result in technology transfers and spill-over effects (Hamdani 2001; Markusen and Venables 2000; UNCTAD 1992).

Moreover, FDI inflow has a crucial economic development role in host countries. There are some inherent advantages for development: risk sharing, market discipline, export orientation, and the transfer of technology and managerial expertise. Recent trends show that FDI can be an important and stable source of private capital for developing economies, particularly countries that are able to create a hospitable environment for new foreign investment (Singh and Kwang 1995).

Although FDI has positive effects on the host country, it does not guarantee that all of these positive results will occur in all countries. The possible benefits may be subject to varying human resource, financial system, and institutional constraints. Therefore, the FDI policy in the host country does affect the extent of positive effects generated by inward FDI.

### LIBERALIZATION OF FDI POLICY

FDI laws in most countries have been liberalized in the past few years. In the 1960s and 1970s, only seven countries had enacted FDI legislation; in the 1980s, there were 29; in the

1990s, more than 77 countries; today, almost all countries have investment laws or codes organizing the investment framework for foreign investors (Hamdani 2001).

As countries continue to liberalize, MNCs are attracted to locations that offer the most appropriate conditions. Moreover, with an expected downturn in the global flows of FDI in the coming years, from a record level of $1.3 billion in 2000, the competition among various locations for FDI is likely to intensify even further. Countries are likely to step up efforts to attract FDI flows in 2001 through, for example, further efforts to liberalize FDI entry by opening up new sectors to foreign investment and more proactive investment promotion measures (UNCTAD 2005).

Based on the data provided by UNCTAD, Kobrin (2005) employed a cross-sectional regression methodology to analyse the determinants of liberalization of FDI policies in 116 countries from 1992 to 2001. He found that 95 per cent of the changes in such polices over the decade were liberalizing. The results support the explanation of liberalization as more determined by policymakers who believe that the country will get benefits from FDI, rather than due to external pressure from World Bank or IMF. Moreover, this paper found that country size, level of human resource capabilities, and trade openness are the primary determinants of the propensity to liberalize. Further, it argues that countries with larger markets are more likely to believe that the net benefits from additional inflows of FDI are likely to be positive.

Moran et al. (2005) reported that few restrictions on MNCs will be favourable for host country development but FDI in protected host country markets leads to an inefficient use of local resources and subtracts from local economic welfare. Investment restrictions and trade restrictions affect foreign investors' backward linkages into the host economy.

## Determinants of FDI inflows

The factors that create the investment climate in one country and determine its attractiveness for FDI are numerous and complex. The literature examining the determinants of (and

Table 13.1: Liberalizing FDI Policy Changes—116 Developing Countries and Economies in Transition, 1992–2001

*(number)*

| Region | Liberalization of Regulation | Promotion and guarantees | Total changes |
|---|---|---|---|
| Africa | 77 | 77 | 154 |
| Latin America and Caribbean | 77 | 70 | 147 |
| West Asia | 57 | 43 | 100 |
| Central Asia | 32 | 22 | 54 |
| South, East, and South East Asia and Pacific | 230 | 138 | 368 |
| Central and Eastern Europe | 102 | 104 | 206 |
| Total | 575 | 454 | 1029 |

*Source*: UNCTAD.

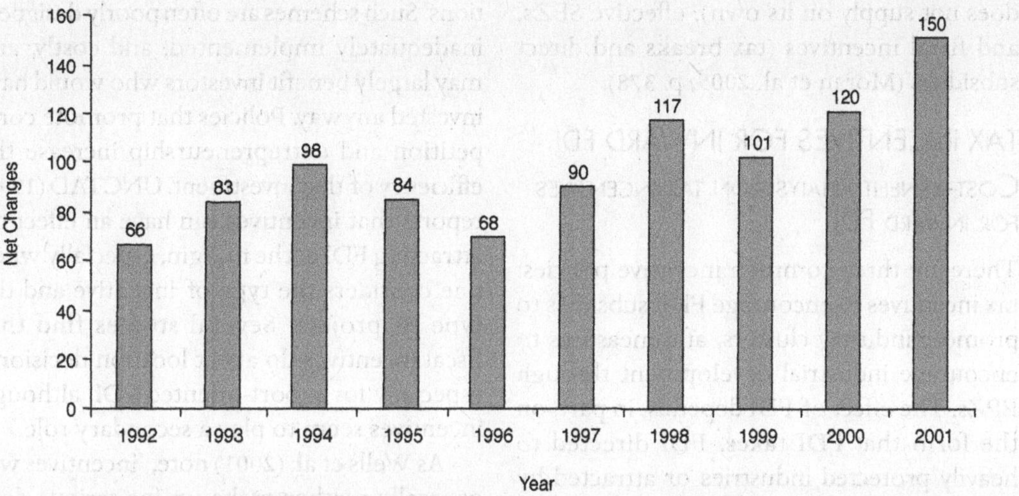


Figure 13.1: Liberalizing FDI Policy—Total Net FDI Regulatory Changes, 1992–2001 (number)

*Note*: The number of net changes is the number of liberalizing changes minus the non-liberalizing changes.
*Source*: Based on data from UNCTAD.

constraints on) FDI inflows in huge. The most important factors have been identified as a country's political and economic stability, geographic location, market size, membership and status in regional integration, legislation, infrastructure and telecommunications, availability of skilled labour, fiscal incentives, and FDI promotion. Obviously, many factors other than market size, particularly the policy and institutional framework, are important in determining a country's attractiveness to FDI.

The quality of the policy regime is an important determinant of the allocation of FDI flows among developing counties. Macroeconomic stability, corruption, rule of law, and effectiveness of the regulatory regime have been shown to be significant determinants of the location of foreign investment, after controlling for other variable. Time series analysis underlines the importance of governance and institutional quality for the allocation of FDI. Countries with better investment climates—indicated by the level of corruption, voice (political openness), rule of law, quality of the regulatory regime, government effectiveness, and political stability—tended to receive an increasing share of total FDI over the 1990s (OECD 2003).

Investment flows depend upon macro, micro, and institutional reforms—low inflation rates, realistic exchange rates, reasonably efficient legal and regulatory systems that protect low levels of corruption—that create favourable conditions for business operations in general. Beyond this, there are three categories of 'investment promotion' expenditures that are regularly associated with host efforts to attract foreign direct investors: providing information to MNCs (host country provides 'information externalities' that the market does not supply on its own), effective SEZs, and fiscal incentives (tax breaks and direct subsidies) (Moran et al. 2005, p. 378).

## TAX INCENTIVES FOR INWARD FDI

### COST–BENEFIT ANALYSIS ON TAX INCENTIVES FOR INWARD FDI

There are three common incentive policies: tax incentives to encourage FDI, subsidies to promote industry clusters, and measures to encourage industrial development through EPZs. The effect of FDI depends, in part, on the form that FDI takes. FDI directed to heavily protected industries or attracted by very costly incentives may have a low, or even negative, effect on growth and productivity.

Attitudinal and empirical research on the effect of tax incentives on FDI has been inconclusive. Some studies (for example, Fortune 1977; Root & Ahmed 1978; Hartman 1984; Boskin and Gale 1986; Papke 1987; Young 1988; Slemrod 1990; Grubert and Mutti 1991; He & Guisinger 1993; Swenson 1994; Hines 1996) have found tax incentives to be an important factor in attracting FDI and in the making of regional investment decisions, whereas others (for example Forsyth 1971; Carlton 1983; Lim 1983; Yelpaala 1984; Moore et al. 1987; Ernst and Young 1994) have come to the opposite conclusion.[3]

Many countries try to use specific investment policies such as tax incentives to attract investment or to channel it in particular directions. Such schemes are often poorly designed, inadequately implemented, and costly, and may largely benefit investors who would have invested anyway. Policies that promote competition and entrepreneurship increase the efficiency of that investment. UNCTAD (1996) reports that incentives can have an effect on attracting FDI at the margin, especially when one considers the type of incentive and the type of project. Several studies find that fiscal incentives do affect location decisions, especially for export-oriented FDI, although incentives seem to play a secondary role.

As Wells et al. (2001) note, 'incentives will generally neither make up for serious deficiencies in the investment environment nor generate the desired long-run strategies'. The Government may hope to make up for an unfriendly investment environment through incentive mechanisms. But while there are clearly examples in which targeted interventions (such as fiscal incentives, EPZs, or support for clusters) may indeed lead to higher investment levels and the jobs and related spillovers that go along with such levels; there is unfortunately little evidence that such initiatives can be systematically successful.

The important result is that higher tax rates do not seem to drive away investors, but the myriad and often arbitrary array of obstacles to starting and running a business do. A World Bank survey found—in a larger sample of 69 developing countries—that there is a significant negative correlation between the amount of management time spent on obtaining the necessary paperwork and the levels of FDI (OECD 2003).

In a world where an increasing number of governments compete hard to attract multinational companies, fiscal incentives have become a global phenomenon. A research by

[3]Part of this inconsistency may be the result of the different tax measurements employed in these studies. Several investigators, including Hartman (1984), Boskin and Gale (1986), and Young (1988) measured the effect of the effective tax rate on FDI. Grubert and Mutti's (1991) empirical estimates show that the statutory tax rate is a better determinant of income shifting than the effective tax rate.

Morisset and Pirnia (1999) reviewed the existing literature on tax policy and FDI. They draw the conclusion that incentives will generally neither make up for serious deficiencies in the investment, nor generate the desired externalities. They found that when other factors such as political and economic stability, infrastructure, and transport costs are more or less equal between potential locations, taxes may exert a significant impact. Based on a survey by FIAS, they conclude that if tax policy matters it is not the most influential factor in the site selection of multinationals. Most econometric studies have tended to confirm the results of surveys; that investors are mostly influenced in their decision by market and political factors and that tax policies appear to have little effect on the location of FDI.

For many reasons, a number of governments rely on tax incentive schemes to lure foreign investors. This selective approach, in contrast to a generalized tax reduction, is attractive to many countries because it may minimize the initial effect on fiscal revenues and, in principle, should help to target specific industries or activities that would bring the greater benefits to the country. Here, once a locational decision is narrowed down to a handful of alternative sites, incentives can play a decisive role in the final locational choice. Blonigen and Slaughter (1999) suggested that tax policies influence the magnitude of use of skilled labour and transfer of new technologies by foreign affiliates in the host country. These studies indicate that tax policy can be used not only to attract foreign investors but also to regulate some of their activities in the host economy. Additional evidence is required to study the possible effects at the country and enterprise levels. Tung and Cho (2000) indicate that tax incentives are effective in attracting FDI to China, and also that they influence the selection of a particular form of FDI.

Since tax policy seems to have a greater impact on the location decision within regional markets, the argument is that it can push governments to 'race to the bottom' with competitive tax reductions. The main concern is that various countries may end up in a bidding war that results in a 'prisoner's dilemma' which benefits the foreign firms at the expense of the winning State and the welfare of its citizens. The debate about the effectiveness of incentives in attracting investment—the potential benefit side—has diverted the attention from the cost side. Even if tax incentives were quite effective in increasing investment flows, the costs might well outweigh the benefits. This issue has become critical in view of the increase in tax competition around the world. This competition is not only taking place in relatively wealthy industrial countries but also in emerging markets where governments generally face severe budgetary constrains.

The broad-based survey studies provide mixed evidence on the effect of host-country incentives and inducement policies on the FDI decisions of transnational corporations. The survey evidence indicates that tax incentives rarely play a front-line role in determining whether or not particular overseas investment projects are implemented. However, the evidence does suggest that after such a project is decided upon, and some leeway is left in the determination of its precise location, such incentives become more relevant. Several studies have suggested that whilst these incentives are not one of the key influences on decision making, they are often considered as supplementary 'rewards' for investing. Both these points indicate that such incentives may involve unnecessary, expensive, and inefficient competition between host countries (UNCTAD 1992).

In sum, although many governments use tax incentives to lure foreign investors, attitudinal and empirical research on the effect of tax incentives on FDI has been inconclusive. Fiscal incentives, EPZs, or support for clusters may indeed lead to higher investment levels, jobs, and related spillovers, but such schemes are often poorly designed, inadequately implemented, and costly, and may largely benefit the investors who would have invested in the host country anyway.

## The Case for China

### *FDI inflows in China: 1979–2004*

As shown in Figure 13.2, in the early period of 1979–83, FDI was a modest amount of a few hundred million dollars annually. During the period 1984–91, FDI inflows grew steadily with an annual growth rate of nearly 20 per cent and reached US$4.37 billion in 1991. In 1992, the inflow of FDI into China was US$ 11.01 billion, double the 1991 figure. In 1998, this rapid growth trend continued, reaching US$ 45.46 billion. There were three years of stagnation from 1998 to 2000. Compared with 1998, China saw the first decline (by nearly 8 per cent) in 1999. In 2000, there was a slightly increase and in 2001 FDI inflows reached a peak of US$ 46.88 billion. The accumulated FDI inflows in China were US$ 560.16 billion from 1979 to 2004. The momentum continued in the first half of 2002, when inflows increased by 19 per cent over those in the same period in 2001.

The dramatic increases in FDI in the first half of the 1990s appear to be caused by four factors. First, the amount of aggregate FDI flowing to developing countries increased significantly in the 1990s. Second, China was deemed a less risky political and economic environment by risk assessment organizations such as the Economist Intelligence Unit.[4] Third, China is now becoming the world's fastest growing emerging market. An investigation by the American magazine Fortune shows that 92 per cent of MNCs have plans to set up business in China. Fourth, China systematically liberalized its foreign investment regime. Fifth, FDI flows increased in part because of the phenomenon of 'round-tripping' inward FDI. One estimate, by Harrold and Lall (1993) suggested that 'round-tripping inward FDI accounted for 25 per cent of China's FDI inflows in 1992.

### *Gradually liberalized FDI policy in China: 1979 to 2004*

After 30 years of isolation, in 1979, China decided to open up again for FDI. Since then it has gradually taken a number of measures to improve its investment climate and its attractiveness to existing and potential foreign investors. Since 1979, the FDI regime has been liberalized gradually, and a series of policies and laws for FDI have been implemented, aimed at attracting a high level of FDI inflows and accelerating the transfer of technology and modern management skills, as well as providing foreign exchange. Following the adoption of the 'Open Door policy' in late 1978 and the issue of the Joint Venture Law in 1979, China established four Special Economic Zones (SEZs), Shenzhen, Zhuhai, Xiamen, and Shantou, located in Guangdong and Fujian Provinces in 1980 (Liu et al. 1993, p. 864).

In 1992, during his famous tour to the southern, coastal, economically opened areas and SEZs, Deng Xiaoping explicitly declared

[4]On a scale in which 100 is the riskiest rating, China rated 15 in 1988, one of the EIU's lowest risk ratings. This jumped to 35 in 1989 but by 1992 had fallen back to 25 (*The Economist*, 21 May 1994, p. 120).

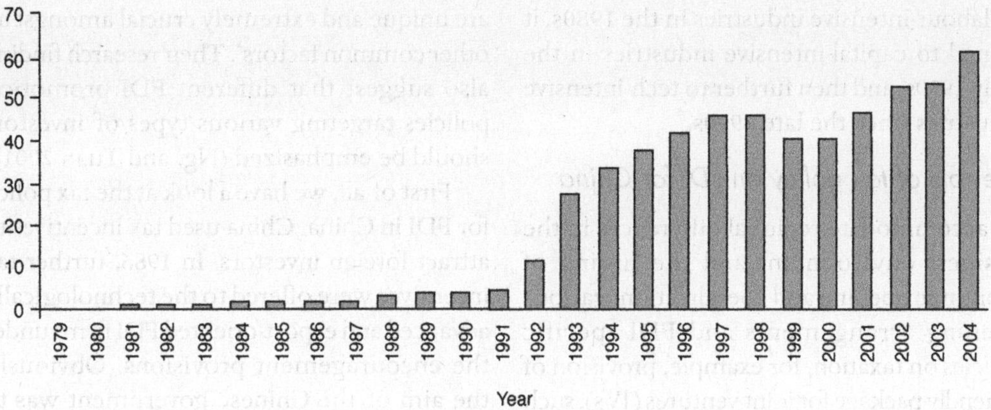


Figure 13.2: Actually used FDI in China, 1979–2004 (*Billion US$ at current price*)

*Source*: Data for 1979–82 are from Chen, Chang, and Zhang (1995), 'The Role of Foreign Direct Investment in China's Post-1978 Economic Development', *World Development*, Vol. 23, No. 4, pp. 691–703;
Data for 1983–9 are from the *Chinese Statistical Yearbook 1994;*
Data for 1990–2004 are from the *Chinese Statistical Yearbook 2005*.

his support for the successful economic development assisted by FDI and expressed a desire to see the pace of liberalization quickened. Deng Xiaoping's landmark visit set the scene not only for a decisive move away from a command economy in favour of a market-oriented economy, but also for a move from the uneven regional priority towards nationwide implementation of open policies to FDI. Consequently, the Chinese government reaffirmed the adherence of the open door policy and launched another massive drive to attract FDI (Liu et al. 1993, pp. 866, 869).

From 1979 to 1986, the bulk of attracted FDI was in *labour-intensive processing activities*, mainly of Hong Kong and Macau origin. From 1987 to 1991, more 'preferential' treatments aimed at the attraction of *export-oriented manufacturing firms and advanced technology JVs* were encouraged by refinement of existing laws, regulations, and the passing of the Regulations on Encouraging Foreign Investment and confirmation of its constitutional status (Article 22). The design of policy measures to attract targeted industries was considered in this stage. From 1992 to 1994, the types of FDI extended from manufacturing to some tertiary sectors, such as finance, insurance, and foreign trade, on a trial basis. From 2000, vast efforts were extensively extended to the service sectors in retailing, insurance, banking and finance, telecommunications, transportation, and trade, and as well as on much broader bases following the agreements reached during the WTO accession negotiations. Five major areas of business opportunities for foreign investment were announced in September 2000, regarding China's policy aimed at increasing aggregate demand, development of the great western region, modernization of state-owned enterprise systems, advancement of hi-tech industries, and expansion of the service sector.

According to UNCTAD (2001), China's FDI has experienced changes during the past 20 years. FDI in China was mostly concentrated on labour-intensive industries in the 1980s, it turned to capital-intensive industries in the early 1990s, and then further to tech-intensive industries since the late 1990s.[5]

### *The role of tax policy on FDI for China*

To accommodate regional differences in the business environment and the timing of economic opening and liberalization, various opening arrangements and FDI specific policies on taxation, for example, provision of a friendly package for joint ventures (JVs), such as 'preferential' taxation rate or tax holidays to foreign enterprises and JVs, were adopted by the local Chinese government (Ng. and Tuan 2001).

Ng. and Tuan (2001) report the empirical results from a survey in Guandong province states and show that 'preferential tax policy provision' is considered the most effective policy among the instruments by all classifications (25 items). From their analysis, all JVs in Guangdong considered 'high autonomy for business enterprises' the prime factor for making investment decisions and the 'provision of preferential tax policy' the most effective in meeting investment expectations. Furthermore, the survey findings also illustrate that sources of investment by country origin may reveal different expectations while specific policies designed to cater to special needs of investors form various countries may be necessary. Different types of FDI and FDI-related policies to meet expectations of foreign investors of different origins are essential.

The conclusion of this survey is, 'the building up of a healthy/sound legal system and the provisions of preferential tax policy are unique and extremely crucial amongst all other common factors'. Their research finding also suggest that different FDI promotion policies targeting various types of investors should be emphasized (Ng. and Tuan 2001).

First of all, we have a look at the tax policy for FDI in China. China used tax incentives to attract foreign investors. In 1986, further tax incentives were offered to the technologically advanced and export-oriented FDI firms under the encouragement provisions. Obviously, the aim of the Chinese government was to incorporate the tax incentives in its regional economic development and industrial development strategies. This reflected the government's growing concern over the relationship between FDI inflows into some economic sectors and industries and the overall goals of national economic and technological development.

However, the 'tax concession war' proved to be ineffective in influencing foreign investors' location decisions. Conversely, it created the impression that China had unstable and inconsistent tax policies. This was detrimental to the Chinese Government's persistent efforts to create a sound tax climate. As a result, the State Administration of Taxation (SAT) had to order the local governments to delete or to revise all tax provisions not mandated by national legislation, in order to provide a consistent and sound tax climate for FDI.

In general, from the early 1980s' initial offer of tax concessions[6] to the adoption of the

[5]See *http://english.people.com.cn/english/200109/28/eng20010928_81288.html*

[6]In the 1980s, two different income tax laws determined the tax rates and incentives for the different forms of FDI: Sino–foreign equity JVs paid taxes in accordance with one set of income tax laws (The Income Tax Law Concerning Joint Ventures with Chinese and Foreign Investment 1980), whereas Sino-foreign contractual JVs and wholly foreign-owned

Foreign Investment Enterprise and Foreign Enterprise Income Tax Law in the early 1990s, China has continuously and selectively used tax incentives as 'economic levers' to guide FDI into its designated regions, economic sectors, and manufacturing industries. However, the question is, how effective are these tax incentives in attracting FDI?

Admittedly, these tax incentives have, in general, had a certain positive impact on attracting FDI inflows into China. However, some tax incentives are more effective than others, some have more impact on one group of investors than on another while some are, in fact, ineffective. First, the tax incentives granted to technologically advanced and export-oriented enterprises, and the tax concessions offered to FDI firms engaged in low-profit operations or located in remote and poor areas, are undoubtedly rational not only from the perspective of China's needs to introduce advanced technology, expand international exports, and encourage the inflows of capital and technology into targeted regions and sectors, but also from the perspective of foreign investors' preferences to utilize their comparative advantages and to diversify their foreign operations.

The tax incentive package of the two years' exemption plus three years 50 per cent reduction on income tax to JVs operating for at least ten years has a stronger impact on cheap labour-seeking, export-oriented FDI (a group of resource-seeking FDI) than on market-seeking or strategic-seeking FDI.

The tax incentive package offered in the form of tax holidays has greater impact on investors from Hong Kong, Macao, Taiwan, and other East and South East Asian countries (mainly the overseas Chinese investors) than on investors from developed countries.

In 1993, China announced two important decisions relating to FDI firms. First, combined with China's efforts to get into the WTO, China decided to introduce national treatment for FDI firms in order to establish a level playing field for both domestic and FDI firms and also to meet the requirements of WTO regulations (*People's Daily*, Overseas Edition, 26 April 1993, p. 1). Second, China decided to change fundamentally its old taxation system and adopt a new taxation system. These two major policy changes marked the beginning of the third period of taxation policy development.[7]

At present, taxes applicable to foreign-invested enterprises as well as foreign individuals (including compatriots in Hong Kong, Macao, and Taiwan) include enterprise income tax, personal income tax, turnover linkage tax (including value added tax, consumption tax, and business tax), tariff, land value added tax, resource tax, and city real estate tax etc. China adopts low-tax policy towards foreign invested enterprises and at the same time grants preferential tax to the industries and regions,

enterprises paid in accordance with another set of laws (The Income Tax Law Concerning Foreign Enterprises 1981). In 1991, the laws were simplified and all forms of FDI were granted the same tax benefits (The Income Tax Law for Foreign Investment Enterprises and Foreign Enterprises 1991). In addition, since 1984, the Chinese government has sought to attract FDI to designated special tax incentive zones and has done so by providing additional tax incentives to FDI in these areas. China has secured a relatively large amount of FDI and offered to a variety of tax incentives attract FDI during the past two decades.

[7]Chen (1997), 'The evolution and main features of China's foreign direct investment policies, Working paper', Chinese Economies Research Centre, The University of Adelaide.

which are encouraged by the nation to receive investments.

## BEST PRACTICE OF TARGETED FDI PROMOTION STRATEGY

### The role of FDI promotion

There is intense competition for attracting FDI. Both theoretical and empirical evidence shows that investment promotion has played an important role in deciding the amount and orientation of inward FDI.

Investment promotion is defined to include only certain marketing activities through which governments try to attract foreign direct investment. Promotion excludes the granting of incentives to foreign investors, the screening of foreign investment, and negotiation with foreign investors, even though many of the organizations responsible for conducting investment promotion activities may also conduct these other activities. Investment promotion covers a range of activities, including investment generation (for example, image-building, general marketing, investor targeting), investment facilitation, aftercare services, and policy advocacy to enhance the competitiveness of a location (Wells and Wint 1990; Wells 1999; Loewendahl 2001).

Wells and Wint (1990) found that for industrial countries, promotion was the most significant variable, whereas in the sample of developing countries, the income and political stability variables were more important. They also found the net present value of proactive investment promotion to be almost $4 for every $1 expended. Specially, they found that investment promotion was most effective when it: (i) overcame information asymmetries; (ii) compensated for the imperfect functioning of international markets, which makes parent companies reluctant in considering new production sites; and (iii) led to product differentiation of the host country as a location for targeted activities.

There are some countries which have dramatically increased their FDI inflows with little or no investment promotion. China is the best example supporting this fact, mainly due to its large market opportunities and cheap and productive labour. Indonesia is a case where significant amounts of FDI have followed policy reforms without investment promotion. Thailand and Mexico are some other examples that raise the question of the necessity of investment promotion, keeping in mind the expenses involved. However, for some small countries without scale economy advantages, it is very hard to attract large amounts of FDI. But there are examples such as Singapore and Hong Kong which have attracted significant inward FDI.

Some governments have used targeted FDI attraction and incentives[8] to promote affiliate R&D, as in Singapore (Lall 2001). Although our main objective is not concerned with incentives as the best tools to attract FDI, we cannot refute their role in directing certain types of investment according to a country's economic development objectives. Therefore, we try to analyse the role of fiscal incentives and its pitfalls in the next sub-section.

[8] According to Wells and Wint (1990), investment promotion is not the only marketing technique that a government can use to attract investors. Organizations seeking to develop competitive marketing strategies can, to some extent, manipulate three variables: (i) Product, or, if the marketer is a country, the intrinsic advantages and disadvantages of the investment site; (ii) Price, or the cost to the investor of locating and operating within the investment site. For governments, this usually means tax incentives, grants, tariff protection, entry and exit costs, as well as the costs of instruments associated with 'one-stop shops'; (iii) Promotion, or activities that disseminate information, or attempt to create an image of the investment site and provide investment services for a prospective investor.

### INVESTMENT PROMOTION AS A SIGNIFICANT FACTOR ON ATTRACTING INWARD FDI

There has also been research on the costs and benefits of promotional programmes. Wells and Wint (1990) concluded that an efficient investment promotion programme can attract certain types of investors to a country at a cost that is significantly less than the value of the direct benefits that the country receives from the investment. They draw the conclusion that an investment promotion programme appears to be most successful in attracting investors to a country if it is focused on export-oriented investment, whether for export to the world market or to regional markets. They mention that investment promotion should also be effective in attracting domestic-oriented investment because promotion is capable of reducing the information costs associated with investing in certain locations, especially in countries, such as China, with complex investment climates. The empirical findings of their study suggest that, similar to the industrial buying decision promotion is a significant factor in the investment decision only in instances where governments use appropriate promotional techniques to attract investors in different stages of the investment decision process. In their research, an appropriate organization for investment promotion is provided.

### THREE STAGES OF FDI PROMOTION—OPENING, MARKETING, AND TARGETING

As of today, the majority of countries have already moved from the first generation of investment promotion—which mainly involves opening up of an economy to FDI—to the second generation, in which a government decides to 'market' its location actively, notably by setting up an investment promotion agency (IPA) (WIR 2001). To increase the efficiency of investment generation and, in particular, to enhance the chances of attracting export-oriented FDI, a number of IPAs go further and utilize at least part of their FDI promotion resources for investor targeting. This is the third generation of more focused promotion strategies, with special emphasis on attracting export-oriented FDI.

Promotional strategies are evolving against the background of a changing global environment for FDI, including increasing competition for such FDI. More and more countries are adopting a focused approach to investment promotion, inspired by the success of countries such as Costa Rica, Ireland, and Singapore. The role of IPAs in targeted investment promotion is an integral component of broader development strategies. The goal is to attract FDI that maximizes the advantages of a given location and contributes to carefully defined development objectives (WIR 2002).

### FDI PROMOTION ACTIVITIES AND AGENCIES IN CHINA

At present in China, governments both at the national and regional levels, are in charge of the investment promotion activities. Most promotion activities are taken up by branches of the Ministry of Foreign Trade and Economic Co-operation or Bureau of Foreign Trade and Economic Co-operation in each province. Most of them are poorly designed and operated. Their functions are confined to introducing the investment environment and giving potential investors information on preferential policies. There is no investment promotion agency at the national level.[9]

[9]Until the paper drafted in 2002, thee was no investment promotion agency at the agency level. However, Investment Promotion Agency of the Chinese Ministry of Commerce (CIPA/MOFCOM) was

### *FDI Management Institutions*

China has adopted a policy of management at different levels towards foreign investment, in which the State Council is the highest managing department, the Ministry of Foreign Trade and Economic Co-operation is the responsible department whose scope of responsibilities mainly covers the formulation of corresponding laws and regulations, approval of setting up and managing the FDI, etc. The State Development Planning Commission is in charge of the approval of the book of projects recommendation concerning newly-built foreign invested enterprises; the State Economic and Trade Commission is responsible for the projects concerning reform of outmoded enterprises, and the trade competent departments are in charge of formulating as well as approving trade planning of the key trade and trial trade. Provinces, municipalities, autonomous regions as well as municipalities with independent budgetary status own the power of examination and approval of projects with total investment value under US $ 30 million. Corresponding departments in local governments can approve and set up non-restricted projects within the limitation of their power; restricted projects and the projects above the restricted value are approved by the Ministry of Foreign Trade and Economic Co-operation.[10]

### *FDI Promotion Agencies*

There is no national level Investment Promotion Agency in China, the only nationwide promotion event is the China International Fair for Investment and Trade (CIFIT) which focuses on attracting FDI. The 'International Investment Forum' simultaneously held to support CIFIT, is China's most authoritative forum on foreign investment policies and international investment strategies and a significant place to be acquainted with information on hot investment issues and capital flows at home and abroad.[11] There are some IPAs (for example, Xiamen) established by municipal governments. Their functions, in general, include providing investors with all-round services including consultation, field surveys, negotiation, packaging, etc; and assisting investors in solving relevant problems and difficulties. They also act as a bridge between investors and various organs in local governments. Local IPAs operate according to international practices. They take all the needs of investors into full consideration and provide free of charge 'One Shop' Service all the year round—a more convenient and speedy gateway towards investment.[12, 13]

There are some provinces and cities in China that have set up promotion agencies to attract FDI and most of them have their own websites. Most of these are divisions of the regional Commission of Foreign Trade and Economic Co-operation, and the promotion

established in February 2003 as an investment promotion agency at the national level.

[10]Now changed to be the Ministry of Commerce.

[11]*http://www.chinafair.org.cn.*

[12]*http://www.xipa.org.*

[13]Many countries eager to attract foreign investment have created 'one-stop shops'—agencies charged with issuing all the permits required for a foreign investor or with assisting the investor in obtaining those permits from other authorities. Despite good intentions of governments', in the vast majority of cases the agencies have quickly become just another barrier to foreign investment. Without the solid backing of the country's top leaders, one-stop shops quickly lose their ability to issue permits that are be honoured by the implementing agencies, and investors find it better to negotiate directly with the responsible agencies (from 'Marketing sub-Saharan Africa as a Location for Foreign Investment' by Louis T. Wells).

activities are part of the function of the Foreign Investment Bureau. There is no doubt that they are financed by the local government and provide services to foreign investors. Their functions are different due to the extent of the openness of this region and the market and management experience that they have. For example, some regions which opened earlier than others have more mature institutions as well as administration skills on how to attract foreign investors. Tianjin Foreign Investment Service Centre was established in June 1987—the first in China. It has its own authorized website on investment (*http://www.tjinvest.gov.cn*).

Fujain and Guangdong provinces were the first two areas opened to foreign investors. They have more experience on attracting foreign investors. There is an IPA in Xiamen (Fujian province) and the Xiamen Foreign Investment Bureau is a functional institution under the Xiamen Municipal Government. It is in charge of organizing and coordinating foreign investment promotion activities in accordance with the national trade and economic policies as well as the industrial plan set out by the Xiamen Municipal Planning Committee. It is authorized by the Ministry of Foreign Trade and Economic Co-operation to examine and approve foreign investment projects; encourage research on industrial orientations and foreign investment promotion; organize the research, text-drafting, and feasibility studies on policies, law, and regulations relating FDI.It takes care of complaints filed by foreign-invested enterprises and collects statistics on FDI in Xiamen.

Another region which has greater advantage in FDI promotion is Guangdong province. There is a conducive investment environment in every small city within this province. It organizes many business fairs, investment promotion meetings overseas, and many exhibitions, for example, the electric technology and equipment exhibition (machinery and electrics) and the international automobile exhibition.

*Main functions of IPAs in China are as follows:* consultation; approval/procedure for foreign investment; services after the start of the operation; information service networks; investment conditions and environment; laws, regulations, and preferential policies; helping local companies to find their overseas co-operator; and assessment of various governmental departments and officials.

*The practice on the use of the internet.* There is an authority website at the national level: *http://chinafdi.org*. Some provinces and cities have their own websites for investment promotion. Not all regions have set up their own websites, some provinces have website that are far more sophisticated than those of others. Usually, accurate data are not available and the information is, in general, other than investor-related. The quality of the websites is different due to the differing experience of local governments in attracting FDI and the economic development level of the various regions. However, there are some common weaknesses: the websites have no sectoral information, some information seems untrue, many of them have no information on existing investors, and the English used is poor. Even worse, some regions have no website on investment promotion and some of them do not have an English version. The names of most websites are *invest++.gov.cn*, implying that it is a governmental website site.[14] The

[14]In June 2000, the (The Invest in Britain Bureau (IBB)) changed its name to Invest.uk in a swift attempt to both break away from the image of a government 'bureau' and to adjust to the 'new economy'. Invest.

information is not updated and is confined to information on preferential policies offered by the local government as well as the basic investment environment.

## RECOMMENDATIONS FOR DEVELOPING COUNTRIES

### A Targeted Approach Integrated with the Economic Development Strategy is Crucial

According to sources from the national planning meeting, China will guide foreign investment into areas such as electronic information, bio-technology, new materials, chemical industry, and construction materials. China will give priority to the introduction of high and advanced technologies that are of strategic importance and are most needed in the country. It will also encourage learning from advanced international management expertise and hiring of overseas of specialists. China will invite MNCs to help with the reform of SOEs and the disposal of bad loans of asset management companies. Further, foreign investors will be encouraged to participate in development of Western China. The country will provide the necessary assistance to MNCs to establish research and development centres.

The objective of all these efforts is to integrate FDI into China's economic development strategy. But it is not an easy task in practice. Therefore, 'best' practices in other countries' targeting strategies have implications for that in China. However, there is no one approach fits all.

Competitive positioning and sector/activity/region targeting is a complex process and requires: a detailed knowledge of industry sectors and trends, cluster development, FDI trends, company strategy, typical project requirements and parameters, and best-practice IPA activities. The strategy on targeting sector and company is important. After-care and supply chain development are also important. Effective co-ordination between industrial policy and investment promotion is also essential at the central and regional levels.

It is a crucial task to develop a practical targeting approach at the national and sub-national levels based on the analysis of locational competitiveness and trends of MNC investment, in order to attract investment most effectively and to prioritize the limited resources to where they are the most useful. It is important to identify sectors in which the host country has an existing competitive strength, or one that can be realistically developed.

### Need for Efficient IPAs

IPAs need to be sufficiently independent from the government, giving them greater credibility with investors. They need to operate along business lines if they are to achieve results in a competitive, commercial environment. A significant degree of autonomy and sufficient resources are, therefore, required. At the same time, IPAs need to have excellent links with government and private sector actors and a direct influence on policy. The agency must be strong enough to influence decisions that affect individual investments, as well as investment policy, and should have a voice in the policymaking process.

Investment promotion needs to be co-ordinated at the national and regional levels. Regional agencies within a country often compete for the same investment projects, and it is essential that there is effective co-ordination between agencies to avoid wasteful competition and a duplication of effort and resources. The national IPA, therefore, needs to be clear

---

UK conveys better the image of a market-focused, commercial organization.

on the type of FDI projects that it is aiming to attract, and when a possible project is in the officing there should be clarity on the most suitable region for that project. Getting the relationship right between national and regional IPAs is also of particular importance in China.

Better design of IPA websites is crucial in China. It is important to create an IPA website to develop the awareness and brand image of the IPA, provide information, gain market intelligence, and reduce costs and time in delivering marketing materials and brochures. Website are also important vehicles for generating leads, especially from companies in the information technology sector.

A best practice IPA website should combine the following features: (i) a clear, easy-to-use structure, with a site map and search function; (ii) speed, with simple, but effective graphics; (iii) links to regions, government departments, and other important stakeholders, as well as to IPA contacts; (iv) sector-specific options, with tailored information on target sectors, industries, and activities; (v) regularly updated (perhaps weekly) news reports, data etc; (vi) registration, for example, to e-bulletins, to gather market intelligence and deliver tailored marketing to users; (vii) good quality foreign language options, especially for key FDI source countries; (viii) a strong sales message with unique and distinctive selling points; (ix) the use of reliable, up-to-date, and comparative data supporting information and arguments; (x) a 'contact us' feature for potential investors to generate leads.

### An Integrated Promotion Approach is Important

Loewendahl (2001) argued that the most successful investment promotion agencies have developed an integrated investment strategy that combines marketing and company targeting with after-care and product development. It is important for China to design an investment promotion framework from setting the national policy context, economic development objectives, and the structure of investment promotion, to competitive positioning, sector/company targeting, marketing, and even project handling, after-care and product improvement.

## DISCUSSIONS FOR FURTHER STUDIES

First, for developing countries the most important problem is not to discuss if FDI is good or bad for the economy but to find out how to derive the maximum benefits from FDI at least costs. In this paper, the developing countries take the role of host countries of FDI although, at the same time, some developing countries are also beginning to invest in other countries and they are now encouraging their domestic firms to invest in other countries, which is an interesting topic for further study.

Second, there is no 'one for all' policy for all developing countries. The development path of each developing country depends on its resource endowment. Therefore, it is an urgent task for governments of developing countries to make an appropriate FDI policy framework based on its general development objective in order to better utilize inward FDI.

Third, some other questions are being raised now: what kind of FDI policy is the best policy? There are many successful cases in the developing world: Singapore, Taiwan, South Korea, Ireland, China, and Vietnam. Some countries have extremely restrictive regulatory framework on FDI, others seem much more liberal. FDI accounts for a large part of the economy in some countries, not so much in others. How much FDI is suitable for a certain country? Is a restrictive FDI policy good for the host country? From empirical evidence, we can see something in common: that is, a good FDI policy for developing countries is one which helps to achieve their development objectives based on its own resource endowment or comparative advantage. Thus, the FDI policy should match the regional development, industry development, and trade development strategies the country intends to achieve.

Fourth, what kind of FDI is good for the host economy? We can classify FDI in terms of forms: Greenfield and Brownfield investment; in terms of industries; in terms of technology type; in terms of source countries. The forms of FDI in China are SanZi: JV, foreign owned, and co-operative. Actually, the core criterion for most countries when they attract FDI is the quality of FDI. The higher the quality of FDI, the more benefits the host countries may get. But a fundamental problem is how to assess the quality of FDI?

Fifth, what kind of policy instruments can be used to attract FDI and better utilize FDI inflows. There are many studies on the determinants of location decision of MNCs. It is really necessary for host countries to study the decision making process of MNCs. Actually it is the starting point to understand what kind of policy will be effective in attracting the most beneficial FDI. Most studies, based on theoretical and empirical analysis, show that the most important determinants of FDI inflows are economic and policy stability, market size, and the growth of the market. Those factors are essentially important for big multinationals. However, some middle and small investors may be attracted by the financial incentives in order to obtain short-run profits. For example, at the beginning of China's FDI inflow, the incentives offered to investors had great effects on attracting FDI from overseas Chinese based in Hong Kong, Taiwan, and Macao. There are two dimensions of FDI policy: short-term incentives policy and long-term improvement policy. The short-term incentive policy concludes a series of preferential policies to investors, while the long-term improvement policy is the package that improves the investment climate through more transparency, rule of law (especially the law of Intellectual Property Rights, etc.).

Finally, there is demand for theories on appropriate policy in developing countries from the point of view of the countries themselves. Many regional governments are competing to attract high-quality FDI as an important part of the political performance. Meanwhile, many studies show that the competition for attracting FDI across regions is a zero-sum game, it may not be good for the economy. Based on the hypothesis of full competition, traditional theory cannot explain why in some circumstances, investors prefer FDI more to other methods, such as exports, licensing, and technology transfer, etc. Though modern FDI theories handle these questions successfully, they pay major attention to the investors and neglect the analysis for the other partition, that is the host country. It is, therefore, quite difficult for the FDI theory to explain the questions that arises from the practice of policymakers in developing countries. From an analysis of China's FDI policy, we know that there should be a substitute relationship between incentives and the investment climate. While offering incentives is a short-time policy, building a good investment climate is a long-run task. From our analysis, the incentives to foreign investors show greater negative effects on the economy. However, there is no doubt that the incentives, that is, tax incentives have played an important role in attracting FDI in the beginning stage of utilization of FDI. With China's significant economic growth in the last two decades, the business and investment climates have improved. The incentives would play a smaller role in attracting FDI and other policy tools may be more important in the new stage of development. This point enhanced the argument that there is no 'one for all' and 'one for always' policy for different countries at different times. In this paper, FDI promotion as an effective development tool is introduced with 'best practices' in developed and developing countries. If China needs to change its current FDI policy, the most effective way in the short term is to strategically design the targeted FDI promotion policy. Some Chinese scholars intend to study this issue using game theory from the perspective of the host country, so as to maximize the benefits from FDI. It is a valuable try in this field.

## BIBLIOGRAPHY

Blonigen, B. and M. Slaughter (1999), 'Foreign—Affiliate Activity and US Skill Upgrading', NBER Working Paper No. 7040, National Bureau of Economic Research, Cambridge, Massachusetts.

Boskin, M. and W. Gale (1986), 'New Results on the Effects of Tax Policy on the International Location of Investment', NBER Working Paper No. 1862, National Bureau of Economic Research, Cambridge, Massachusetts.

Carlton, D.W. (1983), 'Why New Firms Locate Where They Do: An Econometric Model with Discrete and Continuous Endogenous Variables', *Review of Economics and Statistics*, Vol. 65, MIT Press, Cambridge, Massachusetts. pp. 440–49.

Chang, H. and I. Grabel (2004), *Reclaiming Development*, AED Books, London and New York.

Chen, C. L. (1997), 'The Evolution and Main Features of China's Foreign Direct Investment Policies', Chinese Economies Research Center, Working Paper No. 15, The University of Adelaide.

Chu, B. (2002), 'Investment market of Mainland China after entry into the world trade organization', at www.ChinaFdi.org.cn.

Ernst & Young (1994), *Investment in Emerging Markets: A Survey of the Strategic Investment of Global 1000 Companies*, Ernst & Young International Ltd., New York.

Forsyth, D. (1972), *US Investment in Scotland*, Praeger, New York.

Fortune (1977), *Facility Location Decisions*, Fortune Inc., New York.

Grubert, H. and J. Mutti (1991), 'Taxes, Tariffs and Transfer Pricing in Multinational Corporation Decision Making', *Review of Economics and Statistics*, Vol. 33, pp. 285–93, MIT Press, Cambridge, Massachusetts.

Gore, C. (2000), 'The Rise and All of the Washington Consensus as a Paradigm for Developing Countries', *World Development*, Vol. 28, No. 5, pp. 789–804, Great Britain.

Hamdani (2001), 'FDI Policy and Upgrading', Presentation at ODI Conference on Making Openness Work, 16 March, London.

Harrold, P. and R. Lall (1993), 'China Reform and Development: 1992–1993', World Bank Discussion Paper No. 215, The World Bank, Washington.

Hartman, D.G. (1984), 'Tax Policy and Foreign Direct Investment in the United States', *National Tax Journal*, Vol. 37, No. 4, pp. 475–87, The National Tax Association, United States.

He, X. and S. Guisinger (1993), 'Taxation of U. S. Foreign Direct Investment Abroad: Effective Tax Rates and Tax Policy Competition in Developed and Developing Countries', *Journal of International Accounting Auditing & Taxation*, Vol. 2, No. 2, pp. 215–29, Elsevier, Netherlands.

Hines, James R., Jr. (1996), 'Tax Policy and the Activities of Multinational Corporations', NBER Working Paper No. 5589, National Bureau of Economic Research, Cambridge, Massachusetts.

Hou, J. W. (2002), 'China's FDI Policy and Taiwanese Direct Investment (TDI) in China', Center for Economic Development, Working

Paper No. 0216, Hong Kong University of Science & Technology.

Kobrin, S. J. (2005), 'The Determinants of Liberalization of FDI Policy in Developing Countries: A Cross-section Analysis, 1992–2001', *Transnational Corporations*, Vol. 14, No. 1, New York, pp. 67–101.

Lall, S. (2001), *Competitiveness, Technology and Skills*, Edward Elgar, Cheltenham.

Lim, D. (1983), 'Fiscal Incentives and Direct Foreign Investment in Less Developed Countries', *Journal of Development Studies*, Vol. 19, No. 2, Routledge, London, pp. 207–12.

Liu, Z. (1998), 'China's Tax Incentives for Foreign Investment Enterprises—Case Study of Developing Countries' Application of Tax Incentives for Attracting Foreign Direct Investment', A thesis for the degree of Master of Laws, Queen's University Kingston, Ontario, Canada

Liu, X., C. He, Z. Lu, B. Fan, and J. Zhou (eds), (1993), *A Guide to China's Foreign Economic and Trade Policies*, Jingji Guanli Chuncanshe, Beijing.

Loewendahl, H. (2001), 'A Framework for FDI Promotion', *Transnational Corporations*, Vol. 10, No. 1, New York, pp. 1–42.

Madani, D. (1999), 'The review of the role and impact of export processing zones', Policy Research Working Paper No. 2238, The World Bank, Washington.

Markusen, J. R. and A. J. Venables (2000), 'The Theory of Endowment, Intra-industry and Multi-national Trade', *Journal of International Economics*, Vol. 52, No. 2, pp. 209–34, Elsevier, Netherlands.

Moore, M., B. Steece, and C. Swenson (1987), 'An Analysis of the Impact of State Income Rates and Bases on Foreign Investment', *Accounting Review*, Vol. 62, No. 4, American Accounting Association, The United States, pp. 671–685.

Moran, T. H., E. M. Graham, and M. Blomstrom (2005), 'Conclusions and Implications for FDI Policy in Developing Countries, New Methods of Research, and a Future Research Agenda', *Does Foreign Direct Investment Promote Development? New Methods, Outcomes and Policy Approaches*, Center for Global Development and Institute for International Economics, Washington, pp. 275–376.

Morisset, J. P. and N. Pirnia (1999), 'How Tax Policy and Incentives Affect Foreign Direct investment: A Review', World Bank Policy Research Working Paper No. 2509, Washington.

Ng, Linda F. Y. and C. Tuan (2001), 'FDI Promotion Policy in China: Governance and Effectiveness', *The World Economy*, Vol. 24, No. 8, Oxford, pp. 1051–74.

OECD (2003), *Global Economic Prospects and the Developing Countries 2003*, Organization for Economic Co-operation and Development, Washington.

Papke, L. E. (1987), 'Subnational Taxation and Capital Mobility, Estimates of Tax-price Elasticities', *National Tax Journal*, Vol. 40, No. 2, The National Tax Association, The United States, pp. 191–203.

Ramo, J. C. (2004), 'The Beijing Consensus', The Foreign Policy Centre Web: http://fpc.org.uk/publications/123.

Root and Ahmed (1978), 'The Influence of Policy Instruments on Manufacturing Direct Foreign Investment in Developing Countries', *Journal of International Business Studies*, Vol. 9, No. 3, Palgrave Publishers Ltd., UK, pp. 81–93.

Singh, H. and W. Kwang (1995), 'Some New Evidence on Determinants of Foreign Direct Investment in Developing Countries', World Bank Policy Research Working Paper No. 1531, The World Bank, Washington

Slemrod, J. (1990), 'The Impact of the Tax Reform Act of 1986 on Foreign Direct Investment to and from the United States', NBER Working Papers No. 3234, National Bureau of Economic Research, Cambridge, Massachusetts.

Swenson, D. L. (1994), 'The impact of U.S. Tax Reform on Foreign Direct Investment in the United States', *Journal of Public Economics*, Vol. 54, No. 2, Elsevier, Netherlands, pp. 243–66.

Tung, S. and S. Cho (2000), 'The impact of tax incentives on foreign direct investment in China', *Journal of International Accounting*

*Auditing & Taxation*, Vol. 9, No. 2, Elsevier, Netherlands, pp. 106–35.

UNCTAD (1992), *The Determinants of Foreign Direct Investment—A Survey of the Evidence*, United Nations, New York and Geneva.

____ (1996), *World Investment Report 1996: Investment, Trade and International Policy Arrangements*, United Nations, New York and Geneva.

____ (2001), 'The World of Investment Promotion at a Glance—a Survey of Investment Promotion Practices', ASIT Advisory Studies No. 17, Advisory Services on Investment and Training, United Nations, New York and Geneva.

____ (2002), *World Investment Report 2002: Transnational Corporations and Export Competitiveness*, United Nations, New York and Geneva.

Wells, J. (1999), 'Marketing Sub-Saharan Africa as a Location for Foreign Investment', *Economic Perspectives*, an Electronic Journal of the U.S. Information Agency.

Wells, J., N. J. Allen, J. Morisset, and N. Pirnia (2001), 'Using Tax Incentives to Compete for Foreign Investment: Are They Worth the Costs?', FIAS Occasional Paper No. 15, The International Finance Corporation and the World Bank, Washington.

Wells, Louis T. and Wint, Jr. Alvin G. (1990), 'Marketing a Country—Promotion as a Tool for Attracting Foreign Investment', FIAS Occasional Paper No. 1, Foreign Investment Advisory Service, Washington.

Williamson, J. (ed.) (1990), 'Latin American adjustment: How Much Has Happened?', Institute for International Economics, Washington.

____ (2000), 'What Should the World Bank Think about the Washington Consensus', *The World Bank Research Observer*, Vol. 15, No. 2, Washington, pp. 251–64.

____ (2004), 'The Washing Consensus as Policy Prescription for Development', a lecture in the series '*Practitioners of Development*', delivered at the World Bank, 13 January, Washington.

World Bank (1994), 'China—Foreign Trade Reform: A World Bank Country Study', The World Bank, Washington.

Yang, J.L. (2000), 'A Game Analysis of Foreign Investment and Foreign Investment Policy', Economic Science Press, Beijing.

Yelpaala, A. (1984), 'The Impact of Industrial Legislation on the Behavior of Multinational Enterprises and Labor in the Industrializing Countries of East and Southeast Asia', Michigan Yearbook of International Legal Studies, Vol. 6, University of Michigan Press, Ann Arbor. pp. 383–414.

Young, K.H. (1988), 'The Effect of Taxes and Rates of Return on Foreign Direct Investment in the United States', *National Tax Journal*, Vol. 41, No. 2, The National Tax Association, The United States, pp. 109–21.

Zhou, D. S., S. Li and D. K. Tse (2002), 'The Impact of FDI on the Productivity of Domestic Firms: The Case of China', *International Business Review*, Vol. 11, Elsevier, Netherlands, pp. 465–84.

# 14

# China in Perspective

# From Economic 'Miracle' to Human Development?

MARIO BIGGERI*

The aim of this chapter is to present a model that examines the economic and institutional mechanisms related to the outstanding Chinese economic growth on the one hand and to the lack of human development for a large part of its population on the other, and to draw the relevant policy implications.

Our framework of thinking is based on the human development paradigm and on the historical perspective on the Chinese development experience in the early 1980s. Theoretically, the study is based on the role of institutions and structural characteristics in shaping the path of economic development. Indeed, we think that structural characteristics, institutions, and history are three basic dimensions for analysing any process of economic development. 'On [the] one hand, institutions can influence both the level and pace of economic development; on the other hand, economic development can and frequently does trigger institutional change' (Lin and Nugent 1995, p. 2303).

Moreover, as asserted in Reinert (2003), we affirm that economic development and human development can occur at the same time only if a country is able to transmit part of the gain in productivity towards an increase in real wages and in the social protection of workers and vulnerable people. This turns economic growth into human development, and workers become a part of the 'virtuous circle of development' by positively influencing the domestic demand for products. Most of the developed countries have followed this path in their development process.

In this paper, we argue that in the People's Republic of China (PRC), the outstanding economic growth has not translated into human development—too large a part of the

Special thanks to Marco Bellandi and Franco Volpi for their useful comments on previous versions of the paper.

I also wish to thank the National Council of Research (CNR) of Italy and the Chinese Academy of Social Sciences (CASS), L'Institute (Institute for industrial Development Policy), and Consorzio Ferrara Ricerche. The paper has benefited from the comments of participants at the ACDC, Neemrana, India, December 2005 and the referee suggestions. I am extremely grateful to Giovanna Hirsch for her assistance and contribution to this research. I wish to thank very much Simone Bertoli for his help and suggestions. The author retains the responsibility for the opinions expressed in the paper.

*Department of Economics, University of Florence, Italy. *mario.biggeri@unifi.it*.

population is not benefiting from the 'economic miracle'. From the 1990s onwards, China has seen high rates of economic growth coupled with low human development for a large part of the rural population. This raises concerns about the desirability and sustainability of this process of growth and development.

## FROM THE FORBIDDEN LAND TO THE PROMISED LAND OF CAPITALISM

### THE BRIGHT AND DARK SIDES OF CHINESE CONTEMPORARY POLICY AND ECONOMIC DEVELOPMENT OUTCOMES

The PRC has recorded impressive economic growth since the beginning of the early 1980s when it began a transition from a planned economy to a 'socialist' market economy. The success of the Chinese reforms was connected to their gradual[1] and experimental implementation and to the initial general conditions[2] of the Chinese economy.

China chose a gradual transition as opposed to the shock therapy transition strategy (suggested by both the World Bank and the IMF). This gradual approach gave time to institutions, economic agents, and social networks to adapt to the changes. At the same time, a gradual opening up to industrial international competition gave an opportunity to protect the 'new national private' industrial sector. The key to the success in transition was thus to gradually create the marketization of the system through the creation of a new private sector (Bellandi and Biggeri 2005).

Today, China is fully integrated in the global economy and it will possibly become a central power in international relations in the near future. During the last 28 years, China maintained an average annual GDP growth rate of nearly 8 per cent per capita and registered a consistent reduction in the number of people living below the poverty line. According to National Statistical Bureau (NSB) estimates the benchmark is 0.67 US$ per day the number of people below the poverty line registered a marked decrease from 250 million in 1978 to 37 million in 1999—34 million of whom were rural dwellers. The under-five mortality rate (per 1000 live births) experienced a decline from 64 in 1980 to 31 in 2004 and life expectancy at birth from 66.8 to 71.4 years (World Bank 2006). These are remarkable outcomes and can be considered the 'bright side' of the Chinese economic growth and development experience, that is well documented in the literature.

[1]Policies implemented during transition in a rapid way—although aimed at positive results—can cause instability and produce negative outcomes (Agénor and Montiel 1999; Biggeri 2004; Cornia 2004). Rapidity does not give time to a large part of the society (enterprises, households, governments, ...) to adapt to the new changes. A relevant example is the negative impact caused by the rapid institutional changes of transition economies under the economic advice of International Financial Institutions. The 'shock therapy' or better 'a shock without a therapy' (Ellman 2003, pp. 191–196) determined an unprecedented reduction in output, income, well-being including health and a rise in inequality and poverty (Cornia 2004; Chang and Grabel 2004).

[2]The initial general conditions of the Chinese economy also played an important role. Despite its mistakes, during the Maoist period China achieved good results in economic development as well as in some important social issues. For instance, a base industrial sector was built up with the potential for further development and the agricultural infrastructure, such as irrigation schemes, was also put in place. The health care system and the education system were improved or introduced (especially in rural areas) and opened to all citizens. It is also important to remember that at the end of the 1970s the 'one child per family' demographic policy, introduced by Zhou Enlai in the early 1970s to stabilize the population, started to show its initial results. Indeed, the coercive population control partially reduced the labour supply.

However, inspite of such extraordinary economic growth, China is experiencing an increasing number of problems due to its ongoing internal structural changes as well as the globalization process. These are worsening inequalities within the country with highly unbalanced development and environmental degradation.[3]

The major problem is that the desired trickle-down effect from developed to less developed regions (that is, the transmission of development to the inland-border regions) has not been automatic and thus has failed to materialize for most of the provinces (Biggeri 2003) as demonstrated by the actual disparities in per capita GDP and Gini indices of income distribution (Kanbur and Zhang 2005). The income inequality has increased, reaching even higher levels than those in Western countries. The imbalances between, and within, provinces as well as the divergence between rural and urban areas and industry and agriculture are also increasing. The urban–rural disparity appears even more serious if it is calculated using social indicators. Such a disparity mainly overlaps with the existing differences between coastal and inland regions, as the western and central provinces are essentially rural. The disparity among rural–urban residents saw a strong reduction during the early stages of reform with the average income ratio falling from 2.3 in 1980–81 to 1.72 in 1985. This underlines the success of the initial great reforms of the 1980s with institutional changes in the agricultural sector (de-collectivization) and the upsurge of township and village enterprises (TVEs) (Biggeri et al. 1999). This was, however, eroded in the early 1990s and the ratio increased to 2.71 in 1995. The trend seems to increase with the entry into the WTO: the ratio was 3.11 in 2002 (NBS 2003). China's entry into the WTO has had strong positive impacts on the opening up and transformation of the economy, creating new opportunities (Chow 2002; OECD 2002), challenges, and also some difficulties. The prices of base products of poor farmers in inland China have experienced a contraction. Although only 17 per cent of the GDP is produced by the primary sector, nearly 50 per cent of the active population is still engaged in the agricultural sector.[4] Despite its outstanding economic performance, in terms of the socio-economic transition and structural transformations, the PRC remains predominantly a 'rural country'.

Further, it is important to note that poverty in China has been consistently reduced during the 1980s, and to a lesser extent in the 1990s. However, if considered in its multidimensional characteristics (UNDP 2003) the second tier of poverty reduction is questionable in terms of health, environment, and access to public social services. A large proportion of rural dwellers found themselves marginalized or, as migrant temporary workers, 'too engaged that is, exploited' in the Chinese 'rapid economic growth'. Strong regional inequalities led to a surge of the phenomenon of temporary migrant workers who moved from backward rural areas to the industrial and manufacturing sector in more advanced provinces (Zhao 2003; Liang and Ma 2004; Hirsch 2005). Tables

[3]The rapid industrialization has led to an increase in environmental pollution with an apparent damage to the health of the population and a reduction in the already scarce cultivable land.

[4]When 'Deng Xiaoping era' started in the late 1970s China was predominantly an agrarian economy with more than 70 per cent people employed in the agricultural sector and around 30 per cent of GDP coming from agriculture.

A14.1.1 and A14.1.2 show the dimensions of these internal migrations. These aspects are a part of the 'dark side' of the Chinese economic growth where certain categories of workers are probably paying the social costs of this outstanding economic growth.[5] This was, in part, caused by the relaxation of migration rules after 1992 (Zhao 2003). Migration was almost forbidden during the Maoist period by a system of residence—the so-called '*Hukou* System'.[6]

According to international development organizations, the migration of poor households has the potential to reduce poverty considerably, and thus, they include labour mobility-enhancement components in their rural development projects (World Bank 2001). However, according to some recent studies, the contribution of labour migration to poverty alleviation in China is quite limited.[7] Because of the disparities many people migrate from the central and western regions to the coastal region for 'better' jobs (Liang and White 1997; for a push–pull model on Chinese migration see Hirsch 2005).

In the 1990s, there has been an impressive movement of people. According to NSB estimates[8] for 2003, migrant temporary workers were around 150 million, with 90 million floating population (NBS 2004, pp. 102–103). Mass migration can create instability in the system. Instability generates winners and losers, resulting in a change in the distribution of welfare (on a multidimensional perspective) (Biggeri 2004). Rich people are able to cope better with changes rather than poor people. A combination of 'rapid change' and 'social

[5]'Since the mid-1990s we have witnessed a surge in the relocation of transnational corporations (TNCs) in China from all over the world, especially from Hong Kong, Taiwan, Japan, USA, and Western Europe. More than 100 million peasant-workers have been working either in TNCs, directly owned or joint-ventured by big brand-name American and European companies, or in their Chinese production contractors and subcontractors' (Pun 2005, p. 2). Millions of migrant workers, particularly young girls, are recruited by the TNCs in urban cities to race against the time of increasingly short turnover between the placement of orders and shipment. In 2001, for instance, it was estimated that 82.7 per cent of the over 7 million population in Shenzhen alone (Guangdong province) were peasant migrants from the countryside, of which about 80 per cent were female (Pun 2005, p. 1).

[6]The hukou system was the most relevant institutional constraint to labour mobility from rural to urban areas in China since the pre-reform era (Hirsch 2005). Many authors in both China and Western countries have started studying this subject in relation to internal migration flows, aware that 'any meaningful analysis of Chinese migration must start by making reference to the hukou system, which affects migration in many important ways' (Pieke and Mallee 2000, p. 51)

[7]For instance, Du, Park, and Wang find—using household panel data and prior village migration networks as an instrument—that having a household member migrate increases household income per capita by between 8.5 and 13.1 per cent. Somewhat disappointingly, the authors find that the impact of migration on the rural poverty headcount has been modest, primarily because migrants do not come from the very poorest households (Du et al. 2005). 'On the negative side, the overall impact of migration on the poverty headcount has been modest, mainly because most poor households do not have migrants. The poorest rural households with few laborers and poor human capital are unable to allow members to migrate. Even if all households had migrants, we find that many of them would remain poor. Thus, migration will not solve China's poverty problems by itself any time soon' (Du et al. 2005, p. 706).

[8]From a technical point of view it is important to underline that most household surveys do not include rural migrants to urban cities. However, if 'rural migrants are disproportionate in the lower end of the income distribution in urban China excluding them may result in underestimates of urban inequality and poverty incidence' (Meng et al. 2005, p. 712).

segmentation' has often led to a highly skewed distribution of income and health gains, affecting, for instance, specific groups of the population (Cornia 2003, 2004).[9] In China, the passage to a market system has reduced the basic social services to the population including, and in general the rights of the workers. Trade unions are not present in the private sector and as the share of the private sector increases, automatically the share of workers unprotected by trade unions increases as well.[10] This is not meant as a critique of private sector growth, but of the tacit exploitation of workers. Hukou prevents migrant workers from settling down permanently at destination of migration; although the hukou control over migration has become less tight, the differential treatment has remained unchanged till very recently. In certain prefectures, local governments and enterprises often collaborate in the attempt to attract investment and frequently collude, squeezing migrants' work (Yao 2001). As the job market among migrants is highly competitive, it is possible for employers to hire the less expensive and 'less troublesome' workers (Li 2004) generally women.[11] Migrant workers often suffer discrimination in terms of job opportunities as in some places they are not allowed to do certain types of jobs (Zhao 2003) and are often confined to the kinds of work that urban residents are not willing to engage in (Chan 2003; Li 2004). Migrant workers as well as other 'outsiders' without urban or non-agricultural hukou are in fact not eligible to basic social protection and services funded by local budgets (such as medical care, schooling) or to fringe benefits provided by enterprises (Chen and Chan 1999; Hirsch 2005) and to schools for their children.[12] Temporary migrants are subject to a paternalistic dormitory labour regime[13] that allows absolute lengthening of working hours and double

[9]For instance, by age group (adults, young, children), sex (male/female), pregnant women, ethnic groups, poor and better-off unemployment, skilled/unskilled labour force, educated and uneducated persons, different location, etc. For a study of migration impacts on the places of origin see among others, Pieke and Mallee (2003) who underline the high incidence of rural women's suicides. This is confirmed by an article in the China Daily 'Rural women suffer from a sad fate' 6 June 2005; at least two million women try to commit suicide each year, the suicides are 250,000 each year (55 per cent of all women suicides in the world) and first cause of death for women between the ages of 18 and 34.

[10]More than 53 per cent are in industry (including construction).

[11]Most enterprises 'recruit village women who hold unmarried-status certificates for export-led production. They are assumed and expected to be more hard-working, deferent, submissive, obedient and docile than their male counterparts. On assembly line, the women workers are reinforced a traditional gender role and subordinate female identities, and hence an inferior socio-economic status.... To the deskilled women workers, the assembly line seems never-stop and they have to live a precarious working life' (Pun 2005, p. 12).

[12]Migrants' children are in fact not eligible for compulsory education that is geographically bounded, either their parents pay private school fees which are usually unaffordable for them, or send their children to informal schools, in the worst case, migrants' children miss out on any educational system. On this topic see several articles on the following websites: *www.chinadaily.com; http://english.people.com.cn; www.chinalaborwatch.org.* 'Deprived of their rights to stay in the city, there is almost no long-term planning on education, training, housing, medical care and social welfare to accommodate the new working class'. (Pun 2005, pp. 3–4).

[13]As argued by Pun, with accommodation tied to employment, the employer has control over the non-working life of the worker. With extended working, the employer can inhibit the job search time for workers. 'Dormitories are predominantly owned by local authorities and rented to factory owners'. Increasingly however, foreign-invested firms are building their own dorms to suit their own particular needs and typically, these facilities are within compounds flanking the factory (Pun 2005, p. 12).

extraction of labour power through total control of labour time and living space as well as unfair payment (Pun 2005, p. 12). Several surveys report that when they work in the same position as a local worker, they usually receive a lower pay (Meng and Zhang 2001); that they face poor working conditions and long hours (according to a survey conducted by Chan in Guangdong (1998), migrant workers usually work between 11 to 14 hours per day), they seldom have labour contracts and usually lack trade union protection (Chan 1998; Li 2004). Further, 'Analysts and economists have attested that although the Chinese economy has been developing fast, in real terms, the minimum wages have remained at the same level throughout the 1990s' (Pun 2005, p. 13). Calculations by Chan (2003) and Hirsch (2005) confirm that between 1993 and 2002 this is common in many big coastal cities. For instance, in the last decade, on the one hand, Guangdong province experienced an impressive growth of GDP per capita of 11.5 per cent per year, and on the other, the real minimum wage was kept almost constant (in Figure 14.1 the cases of Guangzhou, Dongguan, and Shenzhen are reported as examples).

The most obvious problems in China from the standpoint of workers' well-being is the precarious work place and scarce social protection due to the quasi-absence of workers' unions. This should be urgently remedied in order to reduce the negative consequences for Chinese workers (in terms of well-being: income, leisure time, and health). Thus, freedom of movement has been translated into the freedom to serve or to be exploited by capitalism where the winners are domestic and overseas Chinese entrepreneurs and MNCs (especially those using a predatory strategy) and the losers are the migrant workers.

As already mentioned, what is 'positively' impressive in China from an entrepreneurial point of view (profits) is the capacity to maintain low wages for unskilled and partially skilled workers (the same cannot be said for managers and highly skilled workers) through legal (contract temporary migration) and illegal migration from the inland towards the coastal provinces. This allows firms to cut costs and to be internationally competitive and to maintain production in the coastal areas—postponing Chinese inland development.

From a global perspective, if Chinese entrepreneurs and foreign investors in China are highly competitive in running their profitable businesses, this competitiveness is also due to the increasing 'flexibility' of Chinese workers' contracts and to the reduction of their rights and benefits in terms of social protection and welfare. Indeed, the changes in the structure of the production process have tended to increase the role of migrant workers that are not benefiting from the production and export growth that they contribute to fuel.[14] This perverse mechanism of labour cost competition, has consequences not only at an internal level, but also at the international level with the risk of exacerbating a 'race to the bottom' circle (Rodrik 1997) in terms of workers' wages, labour standards, and human rights and according to Anita Chan, 'In the "race to the bottom", China is defining the bottom' (Chan 2003, p. 41). Indeed, as in China, the main problem concerning globalization is that the participation in global product markets and the geographical dispersal of economic activity through sub-contracting has not led to a concomitant spread in social and

[14] In an electronic Specialized Town of the Pearl River Delta (Guangdong Province), it has been surveyed that there are 30,000 of resident people, but almost 300,000 migrant workers (Hirsch 2005; Caloffi and Hirsch 2004).

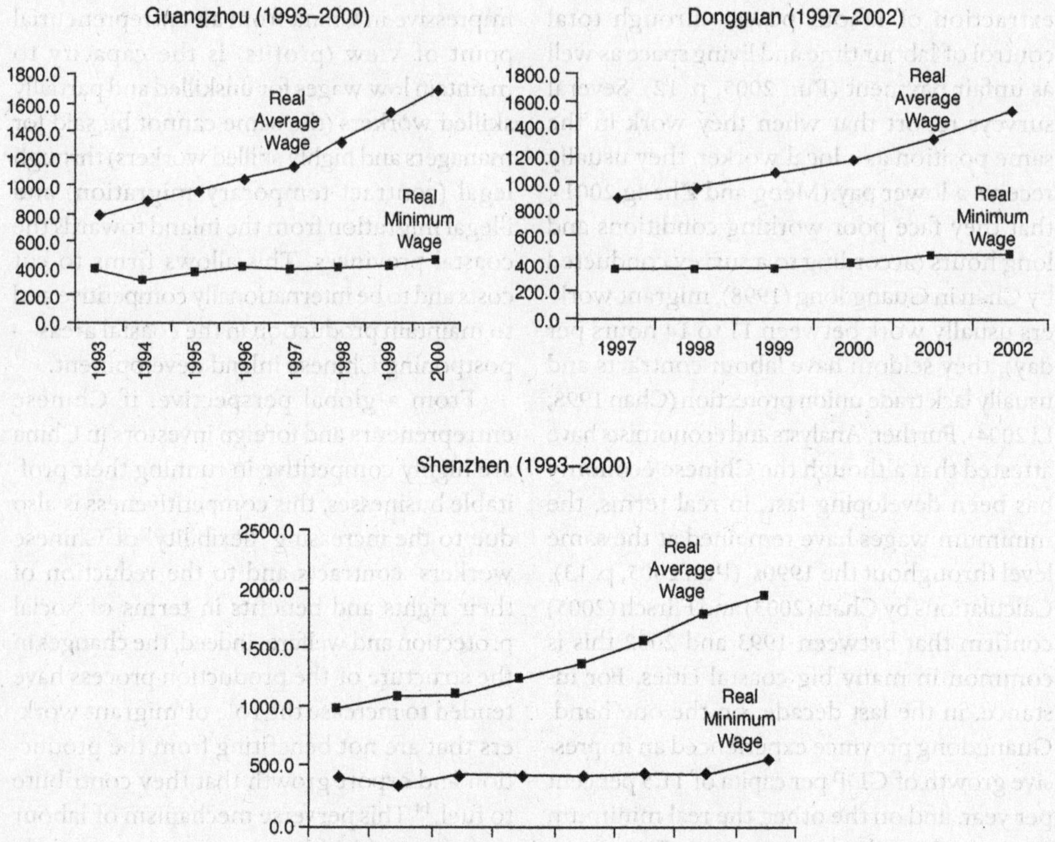


Figure 14.1: Income Gap between Migrant Workers (Real Minimum Wage as Proxy and Urban Workers Real Average Wage—including All Workers as Proxy (base year 1997)

*Source*: Hirsch (2005).

economic benefits for those newly integrated populations as it could have (Kaplinsky, Morris, and Readman 2001). This global competition to cut costs and to avoid tax determines the unclear location of profits since MNCs locate geographically using a 'predatory practice'. The competition between costly and cheap labour and between tax conditions (and the distribution of tax-monitoring) among states, or in the case of China between provinces and down to the county level, ends up ultimately undermining the workers' social protection. Also, international policies implemented by IFIs increase trade and financial liberalization and flexibilization of the labour market.[15] Governments under pressure from

[15] 'Labour market flexibility' is another term for weakening labour laws (including facilitation of 'flexible' contracts, limiting collective bargaining, increase in

local and foreign investors[16] (in China) and from IMF and World Bank loan conditionalities (in other developing countries) have too often allowed labour standards to be defined by the demand of supply chain flexibility: easier hiring and firing, short-term contracts, fewer benefits, and longer periods of overtime work.[17] It is relevant to highlight the issue that, the PRC in April 2006 released a Draft Labour Contract Law whose proclaimed purpose is to protect workers' rights and interest providing just minimal standards that are commonplace in many other countries, such as enforceable labour contracts, severance pay regulations, and negotiations over workplace policies and procedures. The Chinese Government is supporting these reforms in part as a response to rising labour discontent, while US-based global corporations such as Wal-Mart acting through US business organizations such as the American Chamber of Commerce in Shanghai and the US–China Business Council (and also the European Union Chamber of Commerce in China) are actively lobbying against this new legislation in favour of Chinese workers (Bello 2006). In other words, the process of 'informalization' can be seen as an international move on the part of the governments to 'weaken the rights of workers and unions...with the acquiescence of the State in the interest of renewed economic growth' (Rakowski 1994, p. 504 from Delahanty 1999, p. 13).

Nolan (2004, 2001) says that after almost 28 years of economic transition China is at the 'crossroads' since these emerging issues are relevant to the future well-being of the Chinese and, considering the 'size' of the country and its challenges in the globalized competition, of the rest of the world as well. Therefore, some basic questions should be of concern to Chinese policy makers: What are the goals of Chinese economic development? And what should be the strategy to achieve these goals?

As many other development economists have emphasized, we believe that there is a need to re-think the co-ordinate of development 'from per capita GDP growth[18] to human development and local well-being' (Mehrotra and Biggeri 2007). Indeed, in our view poverty reduction and human development[19] are the

overtime hours, cut in overtime pay, reducion of gender-sensitive benefits) (OXFAM 2004, p. 42).

[16]'Through the WTO and regional and bilateral trade agreements, corporations now enjoy global protection for many newly introduced rights. As investors, the same companies are legally protected against a wide range of governments' actions. Workers' rights have moved in the opposite direction. And it is no coincidence that the rise of the 'flexible' worker has been accompanied by the rise of the female, often migrant, worker. The result is that corporate rights are becoming ever stronger, while poor people's rights and protections at work are being weakened, and women are paying the social costs' (OXFAM 2004, p. 4).

[17]'Throughout the 1980s and 1990s, the IMF and the World Bank recommended and required, through loan conditionality, that governments make their labour laws more 'flexible' (OXFAM 2004, p. 42). 'For any single country, this advice from international financial institutions may seem necessary to stay competitive with other cheap and 'flexible' countries. But the advice to 'flexibilise' has been given systematically to many developing countries. The result? Countries are still in tough competition over labour costs, but all at lower levels of labour protection. Workers' rights are simply being traded away' (OXFAM 2004, p. 43).

[18]The Human Development Report uses the term 'ruthless growth' for growth that does not reach the poor (UNDP 2003, p. 67). Even with economic growth, the gap between rich and poor can increase, hence 'the quality of growth matters' (UNDP 2003; Cornia 2006).

[19]Human development is regarded as 'an expansion of capabilities' or of 'positive freedoms' (Sen 1999).

social and economic goals towards which China should move since human beings are the ends of economic activity rather than its means.[20]

Our hypothesis is that there is—given the 'maintained condition' of 'unlimited' supply of labour from rural areas (Lewis 1954)—a Chinese internal institutional mechanism which along with the increasing globalization works towards what has been called 'high productivity poverty' in the literature.[21]

## A CONCEPTUAL FRAMEWORK FOR UNDERSTANDING THE MECHANISM BEHIND RAPID ECONOMIC GROWTH AND POOR HUMAN DEVELOPMENT IN CHINA

In this section we present a conceptual framework to understand the labour market structure in a hypothetical coastal province (migrants' destination province such as Guangdong) and the unique features and role that workers' internal migration assumes in the Chinese context.[22] The peculiarity of the economic and social implications that internal labour migration in China may produce, largely depends on the characteristics of the existing and evolving institutional framework. Institutional and non-institutional factors may influence workers' wage level, wage rigidities, the share of permanently resident and migrant workers in different economic activities and, ultimately, their social and working conditions.[23] Institutions can be both formal (such as the hukou, minimum wage standards, migration regulations) and informal (such as verbal agreements, verbal contracts, 'deposit' practice);[24] while non-institutional endowments are human capital, physical capital, infrastructures, and services (such as education, training, health care, and other facilities). In order to keep things simple, our analysis will take into account only the institutional factors.

The most important feature is revealed by the 'distortions' created by the household registration system or hukou, an enforcement that has been gradually relaxed but still has important consequences on the segregation of urban resident and rural migrant labour markets. As already mentioned, under this system, rural migrants are not eligible for the social safety net that is available to regular urban residents.

Our interpretation of the effects of rural labour migration in coastal provinces draws on the main insights from the dualistic models of Lewis (1954, 1958) and Todaro (1969) and the three-sector model of Meng (2000) in which the main 'push and pull' factors are synthesized in the expected rural–urban income differentials. However, in order to take into account some other complexities of the phenomenon, our approach also refers to

[20]These are also the central issues that emerged from the Party Plenum (*New Daily October* 2005).

[21]This refers to a mechanism in which the ability of mobile multinational capital combines high productivity manufacturing and services with efficient and disciplined labour force much cheaper than that found in the more advanced countries (Diamond 2003; for the case of China see Chan 2001, 2002).

[22]The initial part of this section is based on Biggeri and Hirsch (2004).

[23]Neither the efficiency wage theory nor the theory of insider controls are sufficient to explain the wage differentials between firms in China (Dong 2005, p. 666). But 'by analyzing the sources of wage variations across firms, we discover that the change in wage sensitivity to institutional factors, e.g., market power, access to credit markets, union representation, and workers' influence in decision-making, play a significant role in explaining the contrast in changing wage structures between the urban and the rural firms'. (Dong 2005, p. 685). See also Chan (1999).

[24]For a description of such common practices in Guangdong enterprises that here migrant workers see Hirsh (2005).

sociological theories of segmented markets and institutional economics (Bian 1994; Lin and Nugent, 1995; Biggeri 2004). In fact, it is worth highlighting that dualistic segmentation alone is not adequate to represent the Chinese labour market, and that rural and urban traditional dichotomy in China is necessarily evolving with the emergence of a non-agricultural sector in rural areas and the increase in internal migration flows. Moreover, even if economic reforms in both rural and urban sectors have reduced some divisions in the labour market and have opened more employment opportunities to rural migrants, we see that such opportunities are restricted to certain positions and that workers' migration, under the existing formal and informal institutional framework, creates new forms of segmentation.

Rural–urban dichotomy has traditionally been a crucial feature of the Chinese economy and labour market. However, even within the rural and urban sectors further segmentation can be identified, in part due to the presence of institutional barriers which influence the access to education, social benefits, and distribution of assets. Our analysis adds to the work on labour market segmentation in most typical developing countries and transition economies. In particular, this approach considers internal divisions within a particular sector or firm. For example, in a specific firm in a specialized town we can find both regular resident workers and migrant workers (see Bellandi and Biggeri 2005). This feature complicates basic models but describes the peculiarities of the Chinese case better.

Taking these elements into consideration, the analysis presents a stylized labour market structure to fit the description of a coastal province characterized as a destination of a large number of migrant workers. In a coastal province, such as Guangdong, a large part of the labour force employed in labour-intensive industries is composed of migrant workers coming from different areas of the same province as well as from other provinces (Hirsch 2005). For instance, 25 per cent of the total Guangdong population is composed of floating population and 44 per cent of the total residents of the observed specialized towns are temporary residents.

Thus, the economic activities of Chinese coastal provinces can be divided first, following the spatial location, between urban and rural areas. Another type of labour market segmentation in the Chinese context is captured by the ownership of enterprises (Biggeri et al. 1999; Dong and Bowles 2000; Biggeri 2003). In order to take these differences into consideration, we differentiate between SOE and non-SOE sectors in urban areas and between a non-agricultural sector (mainly composed by TVEs and specialized towns) and an agricultural subsistence sector in rural areas.[25] Thus, the labour force in both urban and rural areas can be split into two sub-sectors (or rather two subsets of labour force): the resident and the migrant labour force (which may work in the same firm). Indeed, according to the literature, 'rural–urban migration is likely to have had a moderating impact on the wages of urban residents having similar characteristics as, or working in similar sectors to, migrants' (Appleton et al. 2005, p. 647).[26] Therefore, a Chinese coastal province labour force stylized structure can be featured by the following four sub-sectors (two of which are divided into two subsets of the labour force):

[25]This means that effect is moderate, and it affects mainly urban workers an advanced agricultural sector can also be supposed to exist.

[26]The effect is greater on urban workers with less education than on migrants and those working in the small size service and commercial sectors (Appleton et al. 2005).

| *Urban areas* | | *Rural areas* | |
|---|---|---|---|
| • **SOEs** workers (SO) | | • **Agricultural** workers/households (A) | |
| • **Urban** | resident workers (UR) | • **Rural** | resident workers (RR) |
| | migrant workers (UM) | | migrant workers (RM) |

Therefore, differentiating according to the residence registration status, the urban economic labour force of a coastal province is divided into:

• SOEs (resident) workers (SO)[27] subsector is composed of SOE employees. They are urban resident workers and their wage is assumed to be slightly higher than the marginal productivity of this sector due to institutional factors such as the provision of certain benefits to workers (fringe benefits) and trade union action. The SO sector utilizes more workers than needed, and disguised unemployment is, therefore, a diffuse problem.

The urban workers sub-sector can be divided into:

—The urban resident workers (UR) subset is mainly composed of workers who possess an urban regular registration status and are mainly engaged in the non-SOE sector. In this sector, workers receive a wage which is often slightly higher than marginal productivity due to the presence of certain institutional endowments (such as certain social benefits for workers) as well as turnover costs.

—The urban migrant workers (UM) subset is mainly composed of non-local workers and workers who lack a regular urban registration status. This sub-sector utilizes similar technologies as UR (because UR and UM can be a segmentation between workers in the same enterprise or in the same specialized town). Urban migrant workers receive a wage which is often lower than than marginal productivity because of the presence of institutional constraints (which can be either formal, such as hukou and migration status which imply the lack of social benefits for workers; or informal, such as verbal contracts or 'deposit' practice) and the lack of trade union action. We suppose that the wage received by migrant workers is close to the minimum wage $w_m$.

The rural labour market also presents a segmented structure. In our framework, the rural labour force is divided into three subsectors. A dynamic component can be identified in the TVEs and specialised towns sector.[28] This, in turn, is divided into two parts: a rural resident workers subsector (RR) and a rural migrant workers subsector (RM). On the other hand, the non-dynamic or non-advanced subsector mainly employs individuals in subsistence agriculture (A).[29]

Agricultural/household workers (A) are engaged in agriculture activities such as subsistence and semi-subsistence farming or subsistence non-farm activities or both. In the case of non-farm activities, households can be seen as multi-sectoral (in the traditional sense, that is, agricultural, industrial, and services) micro-enterprises. The workers in this sub-sector constitute the key source of

[27] Even if legally possible, employment in the SOE sector is generally out of reach for rural–urban migrants (see, for example, Seeborg, Jin, and Zhu 2000).

[28] Seldom also by high value added agricultural sector.

[29] Including subsistence off-farm activities.

China's unlimited supply of labour (in Lewis' sense).[30] Marginal productivity is very low, there is extensive underemployment and the subsistence wage for all workers is reached because of income sharing within families (or through informal social safety networks) (Ray 1998). The average A wage can be taken as the subsistence wage in rural areas. Low marginal productivity is mainly due to the typical vicious circle of poverty for low-income households and individuals, for example, low investment, low demand (low income), low productivity because of low investment. Farm households often show a high risk adversity which is relevant in maintaining them within the vicious circle of poverty.

• The Rural workers sub-sector comprises the following:

—The Rural resident workers (RR) subset has local workers with a non-agricultural hukou who work mainly in medium and small sized (non-agricultural) enterprises (often linked to export and MNCs). The workers are supposed to have a relatively higher average wage than those in RM and A subsets.

—The Rural migrant workers (RM) subset is mainly composed of non-local workers or of rural workers with agricultural hukou. They mainly work in medium and small sized (non-agricultural) enterprises (often linked to export and MNCs). Their average wage as well as productivity are supposed to be relatively higher than A, but their wage is supposed to be lower than RR due to their lack of non-agricultural hukou status.

Figure 14.2 represents the stylized labour force structure. Migrant workers (both from rural areas within the province and those from other provinces) who enter the coastal labour market are restricted to working as UM or as RM because of their non-residential status.[31] This is one of the most important elements that differentiates the Chinese case from the traditional models and from other countries. The direction of migration depends on the different wage levels and is influenced by the assumptions reported here.

The provincial labour force is divided into the six subsets previously described. Our main assumptions are summarized in the following points.

1. The average wage differs among sub-sectors,[32] and we assume that it can be ordered in this way: $w_{UR} > w_{SO} > w_{UM} = w_m$ in the urban area, and $w_{RR} > w_{RM} > w_A = w_s$ in the rural area. Therefore, in urban areas, the UR and the SO sub-sector workers have a wage level ($w_{UR}$, $w_{SO}$) above the minimum wage $w_m$ while $w_{UM}$ is supposed to be close to the minimum wage. In rural areas, workers are supposed to have a lower wage than that in urban areas. However, RR sub-sector workers are supposed to have a higher wage than RM workers and obviously higher than that of A. The wage of rural agricultural workers A is equal (or near) the subsistence wage level of rural areas $w_s$.

2. Migration between rural and urban areas (and between different rural areas) depends on wage level differentials.[33]

[30]It is commonly reported that in China there are about 150 million redundant workers in this sector (Ash 2004).

[31]Following Meng's model, we suppose that unemployment among migrants is very low (according to some surveys, less than 2 per cent of migrants in Jinan, Dongguan, and Shanghai are unemployed) (Meng 2000).

[32]If wage per hour is taken into account, the difference between the subsets is even larger.

[33]In theory, in order to reach an equilibrium and stop incentives to migration, it would be necessary that

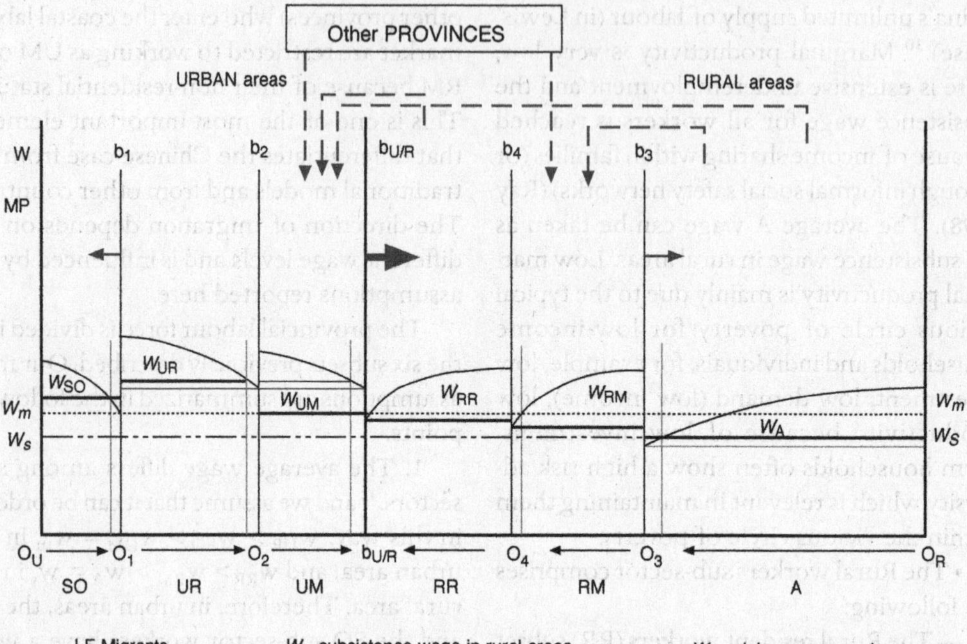


Figure 14.2: The Economic System of a Chinese Coastal Province and Migration Flows

3. Marginal productivity of labour (MP) differs across sub-sectors. In particular, $MP_{UR} >= MP_{UM} > MP_{SO}$ and $MP_{RR} >= MP_{RM} > MP_{A}$.

4. The average wages, because of the presence of institutions, are not equal to the respective marginal productivities of labour. For instance SO and UR workers are supposed to have MP lower than their average wage due to fringe benefits (and/ or trade union and political interventions); UM and RM workers are supposed to have MP higher than their average wage because of the lack of fringe benefits for these workers and the lack of trade union protection; while A workers are supposed to have an average wage higher than their MP due to income sharing.

5. Production techniques differ across urban and rural areas. The technical progress is neutral (Hicks).

6. The supply of labour (migrant workers) from other provinces is related to the demand for labour in the coastal province (minimum wage level $w_m$ in urban areas, and the subsistence wage in rural areas $w_s$) and by the level of the wage in the inland provinces (for example, minimum wage level $w_{mi}$, and the subsistence wage in rural areas $w_{si}$).

7. Everyone consumes and, therefore, forms part of the total demand, total demand is also composed by demand of consumers in other provinces and that of foreign consumers.[34]

RR and RM wage levels get closer to urban minimum wages, and A wage increases to RR new wage level.

[34]The importance of the demand in determining the production, in the earlier phase of development, is well emphasized in the literature. There is no sense in

Given the above assumptions, the model is represented in Figure 14.2. The horizontal axis represents the total labour force L of the province (including migrants). The economic activities are divided into urban and rural activities on the basis of their spatial location. Then, the urban economic labour force is further segmented into three urban subsectors. The same is done for the rural economy. Therefore, each sub-sector is represented by its own labour force.

On the *x* axis two main 'origins' are given, the one on the right is the origin of the urban areas activities, $o_U$, the other on the left is the origin of the rural areas activities, $o_R$. Urban and rural areas are divided by a barrier $b_{U/R}$. From the origin $o_U$ to the right upto $b_{U/R}$ the urban labour force is divided into sub-sectors. In particular, SO employees engaged are depicted up to the point $o_1$ from which the UR subsector starts, finishing at $o_2$. In the same direction it is followed by the UM subsector up to $b_{U/R}$. From the origin of the rural areas $o_R$ to the left, up to point $o_3$ is A, followed by the RM sub-sector upto point $o_4$ and by RR from this origin to the vertical axis $b_{U/R}$. The main barrier has been traced between urban and rural sectors, but other important 'border-lines' are traced within each sector—the four vertical lines ($b_1$, $b_2$, $b_3$, and $b_4$)—which divide the economy into segmented subsectors with different institutional endowments that influence the wage levels (and their rigidity) and the rate of employment. Moreover, they determine for each sub-sector a different 'economic environment'.

On the vertical axis *y*, the marginal productivity of labour (MP), and the wages (W) (average level for each subsector including benefits) are measured at constant prices. Let $w_s$ be the subsistence wage level in the rural economy and $w_m$ be the minimum wage level in the urban economy. Each sub-sector also has its own wage level—$w_{SO}$, $w_{UR}$, $w_{UM}$, $w_{RR}$, $w_{RM}$, $w_A$, with $w_{UM}$ close to the minimum wage $w_m$ and $w_A$ to the subsistence wage $w_s$. The wage bill of each sub-sector is given by the area under the wage horizontal lines. The dotted lines show that the average wage differs from the marginal productivity.

The marginal productivity curves are reported for each subsector. Therefore, the margin available for reinvestment (surplus on wage bill or profit) for each subsector(set) is given by the respective area under the marginal productivity curve minus the wage bill of the sub-sector(set). It is important to explain the consequences of the different institutional endowments on workers employed/unemployed, the wage level (including benefits and social protection), profits (and indirectly on capital accumulation) for each subsector.

The SO workers according to their marginal productivity should have a wage as the dotted line (that is, close to the minimum wage). However, for institutional reasons they receive a higher wage level (on average) $w_{SO}$ and the subsector employs a larger work force (from $A_1$ to $O_1$) at the same level of wage. This part of the labour force is hidden unemployment and may lead to a loss for the state sector.

The urban resident workers UR are employed till point $B_1$ and the wage level is slightly higher than the marginal productivity. The urban resident labour force $B_1$ $O_2$ is unemployed. The wage level of UR is under pressure because of the minimum wage and the unemployment in UR and the wage of RM.[35]

increasing production if there is no demand for the product since this creates an to over-production crisis. This occurred in China in the late 1980s.

[35]To understand the mechanism for urban areas only, UR subset can be further divided into categories of workers that are skilled or privileged workers and do

The urban migrant workers UM (similar to RM) have a marginal productivity as in the UR sub-sector (RR in rural areas). However, they have a wage level close to the minimum wage and they do not benefit from any social protection. This allows the firm to employ more workers according to the needs of production (in theory they can employ workers till the marginal productivity of the added migrant worker touches the minimum wage). The profits obtained are, therefore, much larger than in the UR subset.

The rural resident workers' (RR) marginal productivity is very close to the wage. The rural migrant workers (RM) conditions are the same as those of UM. The rural agricultural workers / households A have very low marginal productivity. As already mentioned there is disguised unemployment and the subsistence wage for all workers is reached only if there is sharing of income within families (or through informal social safety networks). The average A wage is supposed to be close to the subsistence wage in rural areas.

In Figure 14.2 we also consider the most relevant movements of the migrant workers who make up the floating population. We consider movements from rural to urban areas although the reverse could occur in some specific circumstances.[36] This kind of labour force migration follows the dotted arrows typically from A to RM or to UM, from RM to UM, from RR to UM. If floating migrants come from other provinces (inland provinces) they move to UM and RM subsets of the labour force. As already mentioned, labour force movements are even more complicated than those described in the figure as they may also include the structural passage from SOE sector to UR sector, or permanent migration flows from A or RM to RR or from A, RM, or UM to UR. However, we do not take these flows into account as they seem to be numerically less significant than those of the floating population and because their patterns and characteristics go beyond the scope of our model.

The mechanism of the model is the following. At the end of each period, profit is reinvested to respond to the potential demand for products.[37] Potential demand depends on the structure and income level of a society; on consumption pattern and on foreign demand for products. The expansion of capital leads, given the capital–labour ratio, to an expansion in the demand for labour. In other words, the potential demand must coincide with the real demand for products and with the demand anticipated by producers (economic activities) for their products. The pattern of production adjusts itself to the pattern of demand (Spaventa 1959, pp. 405–8).

This implies that after a period of time, each marginal revenue curve coincides with the respective new marginal productivity curve (which measures the increase in value of output at constant price) only if there is an increase in demand for the products that does not change the relative prices. In order to induce an increase in productivity, while maintaining the same conditions, demand must equal the expected demand for the products of the sub-sectors being considered; otherwise the change in relative price of factors and products

not have or do not do the same work as rural migrants (till point z in Figure 14.2) and the workers who have the same characteristics (the same MP) as rural migrants but do not do the same work.

[36]During recession (1989–90) people moved back from urban to rural areas thanks to the land use right (safety nets).

[37]The profit of a single enterprise depends on the composition of workers (migrant vs non migrant).

would nullifly the gain in productivity. Demand stimulus will lead to real income growth or to the choking-off of growth through rising relative prices of wages goods. The internal demand constraint in the case of the Chinese economy is overcome through exports.

Therefore, if the surplus on wages of each subsector is reinvested up to the right—shifting the marginal productivity curves of labour—employment will increase in the subsector, leading to economic growth and to the absorption of labour.[38] The new marginal productivity curves for labour in each subsector will be parallel to the respective old ones if the technical progress is neutral.[39]

This, given the rigidity of the wages and the downward pressure on labour costs, can determine the increase in total output just by an increase in profits. Such a mechanism may be described as growth of national income due to rise in capital accumulation, however, with low human development for certain categories of workers. In particular, in the UM and RM subsectors we attest to economic growth with high profits and low human development since migrant workers receive only part of the wage and no benefits or social protection.

From the conceptual framework sketched above we can draw some relevant observations on the mechanism produced by migration in a coastal province. The first is that it is likely that firms will continue to employ migrant workers as far as their wage is lower than their marginal productivity; increasing the subset of migrant workers UM. As already explained, this gap is likely because of their residential status which does not allow them to benefit from the social safety net provided to regular urban residents.

Chinese and foreign enterprises, in order to satisfy the increasing demand of products, tend to employ workers who generate higher marginal profits (as firms are not required to pay them social benefits) and create less 'trouble'. In other words, they are willing to employ the so-called 'temporary' migrant workers because of their lower costs. In fact, the number of migrant workers has significantly grown in coastal regions during the last decades meeting the increasing demand for workers in labour intensive industries.

Given the unique features of rural to urban migration in China, it is evident that it has a particular role to play in the economic growth that is quite different from other developing countries. Thus, migrant workers not only generate higher marginal profits, they also make the coastal economies flexible because working contracts are almost non-existent (migrants are hired and fired according to needs). Migrant workers offer a disciplined, flexible, and low-cost labour force to the growing labour intensive industry in the coastal regions. Migrant workers can, therefore, be considered as a labour reserve army. 'The workers are forced to leave the city once they lose their job in the urban factory, no matter how long they have been working there' (Pun 2005, p. 4). Indeed, 'they could dismiss workers at any time they want' (Pun 2005, p. 7).

[38]The process, in dualistic models at a constant capital–labour ratio, goes on until all the excess labour force is absorbed and disguised unemployment falls to zero.

[39]While, if the capital investment are not reinvested in neutral technology, but the capital labour ratio changes and it is biased to capital intensive techniques, as could be in the UR and UM subsectors, the marginal productivity curve of labour does not shift parallel to the right. Hence, over time there is the tendency to use more capital intensive techniques, instead of employment creation there could be a labour displacement which would aggravate problems of urban resident unemployment.

Certain institutions (legal barriers like the hukou) are set in a way that makes it possible, within certain limits, to control the flow of migrant workers from rural areas and from other provinces. According to Pun, the dormitory labour regime in China contributes to a specifically exploitative employment system in the post-socialist period (Pun, 2005).[40] That is, if there is an increase in migrant labour demand in a Coastal province it can be satisfied (if there is a wage incentive), not vice versa for supply of migrant labour.

In other words, we argue that the institutional framework influences the labour market structure. While on the one hand, it helps to create a boosting strategy for the economic growth process, on the other, it may impose severe costs to the system in terms of human development and social exclusion.

Even if labour migration could play an important potential positive role in both the places of origin and in the places of destination (quite limited in China according to some studies, see footnote 6), there are some aspects of this phenomenon that are worrisome from a human development point of view.

According to the assumptions just discussed and the hypothetical structure of a coastal province labour market reported here migrant workers can be considered as part of a new category of vulnerable people in China.[41] Not only do migrant workers get low wages, but they also face problems such as lack of enforceable civil and social rights, such as the right to voice their needs, social exclusion, unequal access to resources and opportunities, un-equal social welfare treatment (Li 2004).

There is another important aspect of the Chinese economic system that is worth mentioning again, which helps to explain the effects of migration on wages in the urban sector. It concerns the external and internal (among provinces) competition which induces implementation of strategies for cost reduction (for example to cuting labour costs) as well as the weakness of trade union action. Competition among local governments has led them to not only undertake investment for local infrastructure, to offer incentives for land use, fix local tax preferential arrangements but also to set the minimum wages as low as possible.

As already mentioned, the unlimited supply of labour due to demographic characteristics and the persisting labour surplus in the agricultural sector makes China a quasi-Lewisian economy (Chang 1993; Nolan 2004). The massive underemployment in Chinese agriculture deeply affects the character of development in other sectors (Nolan 2004). This is, in fact, one of the key migration push factors and it works as a powerful constraint on the rate of growth of real income for low-skilled occupations in the urban and rural non-farm sector.

The excess labour supply in A subsector in rural areas and in the inland provinces as well as the wage level differentials allow

[40]'This regime links with labour migration and reproduction cycles in the rural communities, serves global production, and generates hidden costs which are borne by female migrant workers. Local governments compete for foreign investment, openly neglecting the legal regulations and social provisions. The costs of labour reproduction such as education and general welfare, are entirely undertaken by the rural communities which subsidize wages, accommodation, and consumption. Wages of migrant workers are almost equal to that of ten years ago, if not declining. The lack of residential status in the city precludes the formation of a working class force, which could work for the labour rights of migrant workers in the industrial cities' (Pun 2005, p. 3, sic).

[41]See Cook (2002) for a discussion on social protection and the new forms of poverty and vulnerability.

Chinese coastal economies to have an unlimited supply of labour. This explains why after 28 years of outstanding economic growth, coastal provinces have still not exhausted their labour pool. As there is intense competition at national and international levels and minimum wage settings are decided at a decentralized level, these factors, in the presence of an unlimited supply of workers, put pressure on local governments to reduce minimum real wages.[42]

Moreover, the flexibility and poor conditions in which migrant workers work create a downward pressure on the unskilled workers in general. Some authors argue that some enterprises employ temporary migrant workers, while at the same time abolishing some jobs in the sectors that we have called RU and RR (Gu 2003). Others argue that migrant workers are more successful than laid-off workers in obtaining jobs, presumably because employers do not have to pay them any social benefits (Bhalla and Qiu 2004).[43]

The present analysis reveals an important policy dilemma concerning the reform of the hukou system that China will have to deal with in the near future. On the one hand, relaxing institutional barriers against free labour migration can be a further step towards the creation of a more market oriented labour market;[44] on the other hand, however, it is important to highlight that this will not create further segmentation and a race to the bottom in the entire urban labour sector, only if access to basic social rights is extended to migrant workers and a certain degree of restriction is maintained. The unlimited supply of labour from rural areas and directed towards urban and industrialized areas, at least as far as the unskilled labour market is concerned may, in theory, produce a downward pressure on resident unskilled labour force wages. The risk of an instantaneous removal of migration constraints creates an enormous pressure on labour cost and standards in the urban sector and an unsustainable stress on the already difficult process of creation of a comprehensive welfare system. As Meng (2000) argues, the wage gap between rural and urban sectors suggests the potential of migration to reduce urban labour costs. However, its effects greatly depend on the share of rural migrants in the total labour force employed in the urban sector, on the various forms of institutions which restrict migration, and on the rigidity of the urban resident labour market. The smaller the barriers to rural–urban migration, and the less rigid the urban formal sector, the lower will be the urban labour costs because of migrant pressure on wages.

## CHINA IN PERSPECTIVE: POLICY IMPLICATIONS FOR HUMAN DEVELOPMENT

In the previous section we described the economic and institutional mechanisms related to the outstanding Chinese economic growth as well as the poor human development of a large part of its population.

There are many factors that maintain the unlimited supply of labour, which is one of the causes of the high productivity and poor wages. First, there is surplus labour in the

[42]For an analysis of the available data on minimum wages in selected prefectures see the next section.

[43]It is very important to note the initial role that local governments had, and have, in shaping the types of industrial organizations (clusters), including the share of migrant workers and their labour/living conditions (Hirsch 2005, ch. 4; Di Tommaso and Bellandi 2006)

[44]From a social justice and human development point of view it is desirable that the discriminatory aspects linked to the possession of hukou are overcome. We want to emphasize that this can be done independently from maintaining restrictions to movement.

agricultural sector and in the rural areas in inland provinces which is augmented by: (i) internal policies favouring industry and urban areas, (ii) macro-regional policies tilting in favour of coastal macro-region, (iii) WTO rules (disadvantaging poor, small-scale household agriculture and TVEs or rural SMEs), and (iv) the reduction of cultivable land, the reduction of private and government investment in rural areas and especially in agriculture. These factors together tend to keep rural wages low. Also, the institutions that regulate migration and the wages of migrant workers are connected to the wages prevailing in rural areas. This helps to maintain the wages of migrants at very low levels. If rural wages increase migrant wages also have to increase. Entrepreneurs benefit from the low wages of migrants. Further, there is a growing demand for labour in the labour intensive sector for export (linked to the increase in FDI).[45] Also Organizations to protect workers (trade unions) are almost absent (see Pun 2005 on Chinese Working Women Network, CWWN).[46]

Under pressure of expectations of its people and IFIs, the government decided to sustain growth through exports and to upgrade technology through FDI to coastal areas, abandoning the ideas of equal growth across areas and disregarding the rights of workers outside the SOEs (in the early 1990s China faced some over-production crises). The engagement in WTO expels workers from agriculture and rural areas at a faster rate, hence, in order to absorb such labour surplus at a faster rate, the industrial sector needs to continue to expand. Since a very large share of the labour force in China consists of low productivity food farmers and migrant workers, with only a tiny surplus, the market for domestic manufactures is strictly limited. As the limits are approached, the pace of industrialization can be maintained only by manufacturing for export (that is, such rates of growth would not be sustained in a closed economy because of lack of demand).[47]

Further, the growth process in act may delay the development of coastal provinces in

[45]A good news is that because of shortages of labour, especially of skilled labour, some firms have started giving benefits and social protection to migrants.

[46]Here we report an important passage of John Sender on rural poverty and gender-related issues in economics and political attitudes: '...but any organization that has a realistic prospect of increasing the political and economic bargaining power of the lowest-paid wage workers is shunned, or dismissed as potentially "market distorting" and, *ipso facto*, harmful to the poor. There is, for example no support for, or even discussion of, the need to allocate resources to support the formation of trade unions by seasonal agricultural labourers. Nor is there support in the mainstream literature for effective legislation to monitor and enforce the rights of migrant domestic servants or women employed in garment sweat shops. Indeed, any State intervention that might create an "enabling environment" for more effective struggle by such workers is likely to be rejected on the grounds that it might compromise the viability of small enterprises. In fact, the voluminous literature on poverty published by the aid bureaucracy and its consultants studiously avoids mentioning the specific organizations, the legislation, or institutions that have historically been most significant in defending the human rights and living standards of the poor in capitalist labour markets.

At the same time, there is no discussion of the economic policies and the precise forms of State investment and intervention that might be capable of promoting the growth of female-wage labour-intensive enterprises' (Sender 2003, p. 419).

[47]This is one of the reasons why the Chinese economy is constantly looking to increase exports. Considering the limited internal demand, the international market is the main addressee of the continuous increasing production—thanks to WTO acceptance, FDI high profitability and expansion, and the increasing national reserves of foreign currencies. It also important to underline that FDI JV produce around 60 per cent of exports.

terms of quality and technological upgrade, maintaining labour industries there, which instead should have moved in the inland provinces. The possibility of manufacturing development in inland provinces does not seem very likely because of the fierce competition from coastal Chinese provinces with very similar labour costs and lower transportation costs (the only advantages in inland provinces are lower fixed costs for land and lower resident wages, but these are often overcome by higher transportation costs). It is evident that this leads to a 'race to the bottom'.

The question to be asked in relation to Chinese development is: Are human development and poverty reduction reconciliable with economic growth? We argue that these different goals can go together but the current path has to be changed so that human development and poverty reduction can take place in the long term (see also Nolan 2004). Recent Chinese economic history tells us that in the 1980s, China had the capacity to grow at high rates (Biggeri 2003) in a balanced way while increasing the levels of education, health of rural workers, and their income; at the same time maintaining the dignity of workers in the non-SOEs industrial sector (mainly collective TVEs).

China seems to be stuck in a system which is difficult to change.[48] In order to achieve human development and poverty reduction, policies must be changed. The policies proposed here are not very different from those that prevailed during the 1980s.

In the Chinese inland provinces, there is a need to overcome bottlenecks that are present because of a lack of appropriate infrastructure (such as 'space-serving' ones) and development human capital (education, health, research centres, and training programmes). This would facilitate economic growth and the multiplier effect of investment by producing positive externalities and reducing transaction costs. Indeed, these factors are fundamental for upgrading to new technology, improving productivity, and attracting private investment. Hence, in order to reduce the economic gap between the coastal region and the inland Chinese provinces, a redistribution policy has to be implemented at the central level in favour of inland provinces. At the same time, private investment and FDI should be encouraged, if social and environment-friendly. Higher taxes should be paid by profitable domestic and foreign firms to help the local governments and the central government to increase public expenditure on basic social services and infrastructure in rural areas.

Although the social costs are high, in order to enhance the level of GDP (and per capita GDP), the Chinese Government decided that the inefficient SOEs should be restructured, decentralized, or privatized. At the same time, there is a need to promote the development of non-SOEs, in both urban and rural areas. In particular, rural SMEs and TVEs—both private and collective—should be encouraged

[48] This would lead to the necessity for uncreasing internal demand through higher wages. If foreign demand is reduced, the Chinese economy will face a strong demand constraint. In this case, the crisis could be partially absorbed by withdrawing migrant workers and sending them back to rural areas or to inland provinces. The consequences will be dramatic for the income level crisis and for the increase in surplus of labour that is, unemployment and lower wages. However, according to experts, if there is no slowing down of production and an increase in internal demand, China's integration into the global economy could become a central cause of global capitalism's crisis of overproduction. The Chinese strategy / attitude is based on output maximization that is followed by profit maximization through cost reduction.

because they convert local savings into local investment. By providing new job opportunities in rural areas they help to control migration and reduce pressures of the agricultural labour force on land. Policymakers should enhance non-farm activities and TVEs which are fundamental in the evolution of local economic systems.

Although the agricultural sector in China is likely to play only a small part in driving 'economic growth' in the long run, it will remain crucial in determining the standard of living of many of the poor and vulnerable. First, at the end of 2000, according to the NSB, about 65 per cent of the total population lived in rural China most of whom were still related to agriculture, especially in the middle and west macro-regions (for a classification of the provinces into macro-regions see Table A14.1). According to the statistics, agricultural households are the closest to the Chinese national poverty line. Second, at the same time, a reduction of the income of agricultural households may lead to a reduction in the internal demand for goods and may create a destabilization effect in the country and also create political instability. Labour discontent has led to a huge upsurge in demonstrations, strikes, and other kinds of protests. According to the Ministry of Public Security, in 2005 there were 87,000 unrests mainly in rural areas—four times more than those that took place 10 years ago. Real growth in the income of farmers and rural workers is fundamental for poverty reduction and political stability and has the potential of creating higher internal demand that could contribute greatly to the development of the PRC economy.

China is a country characterized by small-sized, household agriculture (considering both the size and the number of persons engaged); and in the presence of agricultural labour surplus, poverty reduction can be obtained by an increase in agricultural productivity. This could be achieved though investment and by fostering institutions to increase incentives and to facilitate market access to all farmers. At the same time, in order to implement synergies in rural areas it is important to generate job opportunities in non-farm activities.

Agricultural development is related to investment in human and physical capital. The relationships among human and physical resources, the role of specialized education, of agricultural and non-agricultural infrastructure and of the centres for the diffusion of techniques are fundamental to the development of poor Chinese rural areas, including those where the national minorities live. For these reasons, Chinese policymakers should continue to enhance public education and research (for inputs—seeds, fertilizers—or techniques) and financial and infrastructural systems.

Another policy is to foster institutions to facilitate market access by the poor and to increase incentives. The bottom–up institutional reforms and agricultural policies were the major determinants of the success of the rural economic system in China in the 1980s.[49]

[49]They had a strong positive impact on the incentive system preserving, at the same time, the farm entitlements (access to land) and thus they were relevant in poverty reduction. A new co-operative system may be able to find solutions to the many problems faced by farmers without reducing their incentives, if incentive systems are suitable for different Chinese rural areas and type of products. The access to these markets is a matter of institutions and infrastructure. Although contrary to 'privatization mode', maintaining the right to land use is the most important way of preserving farmers entitlements. In China, land is still collectively owned—'all villagers are entitled to a plot of land, unless they have another source of fixed income'. The main problem for Chinese farmers is connected to the

The point is that the de-collectivization and marketization of the Chinese economy has led, in many parts of the country, to the closure of institutions rendering agricultural services which were fundamental for the adoption of new technologies by small-sized farm households. Farmers in the new system have, in theory, higher incentives, but in reality, in poor areas, they have had few opportunities to adopt new techniques and to become part of the market system. Indeed, the market system has been more suitable in areas where the agricultural system was already more advanced and non-farm activities quite well developed (Ghatak and Ingersent 1984).

Rural credit system and microfinance could be the answer to increase local savings and investment in farming and non-farm activities. It is important to stress that improper policies for the rural areas and especially for the poor, small-sized agricultural households may imply an increase in poverty and in migration towards the coastal macro-region and urban areas. The situation could also be exacerbated as a consequence of the SOE reform and the related rise in unemployment. It is relevant to take into account the fact that inland province farmers have been penalized by the Chinese entry into the WTO.

In conclusion, we affirm that a 'new' strategy, based on different social and economic policies, is needed for human development as well as long-term economic growth. We also believe that the Chinese government should not be worried about the decline in FDI. Foreign companies will not leave China. The Chinese economy is now quite advanced and in some aspects even more efficient and well-developed than western economies. Many MNCs are in China because of the facilities and capacity of the economic system, the competence and skills of the Chinese labour force or because they are producing for the Chinese market. However, many other investors are there to exploit the cheap and unprotected labour force and the environmental resources. The problem is obviously not related only to foreign MNCs and their JVs, which often behave well (especially USA and EU firms); the problem of worker protection is often worse in overseas Chinese and domestic Chinese firms operating as main firms or sub-contractors. Action should be taken by the Chinese government against these types of enterprises. Regulation, controls, and incentives to well-behaved entrepreneurs and penalties for the polluters and exploiters are the keys to reducing the exploitation by domestic as well as foreign firms.

marketization of the access to inputs market, to research-extension services, and product outlets.

## REFERENCES


Agénor, P. R. and P. Montiel (1999), *Development Macroeconomics*, second edition, Princeton University Press, Princeton.

Appleton, S., L. Song, and Q. Xia (2005), 'Has China Crossed the River? The Evolution of Wage Structure in Urban China during Reform and Retrenchment', *Journal of Comparative Economics*, Vol. 33, pp. 644–63

Ash, R. (2004), 'Rural Underemployment, Migration and Social Welfare in China', *DSG Asia*, 22 November 2004.

Bellandi, M. and Biggeri M. (2005) (eds), *La sfida industriale cinese vista dalla Toscana distrettuale*, L'institute, Toscana Promozione, Consorzio Ferrara Ricerche, Stibo, Urbania.

Bello, W. (2006), 'Chain-Gang Economics: China, The US, and the Global Economy', Paper for Nautilus Institute's China Project, Bangkok.

Bhalla, A. and S. Qiu (2004) (eds), *The Employment Impact of China's WTO Accession*, Routledge Curzon, London and New York.

Bian, Y. (1994), *Work and Inequality in Urban China*, State University of New York, Albany, N.Y.

Biggeri, M. (2003), 'Key Factors of Recent Chinese Provincial Economic Growth', *Journal of Chinese Economic and Business Studies*, Vol. 1, No. 2, pp. 159–183.

—— (2004), 'Has Economic and Social Instability Increased Over the Last Two Decades? Initial Evidence and Interpretations', mimeo.

Biggeri, M., D. Gambelli, and C. Phillips (1999), 'Small and Medium Enterprise Theory: Evidence for Chinese TVEs', *Journal of International Development*, Vol. II, No. 2, March-April, pp. 197–219.

Caloffi, A. and G. Hirsch (2004), 'Local Development Paths in Guangdong Province: Three case studies in comparison', Paper presented at the Annual conference of EUNIP, 15–17 December 2004, Birmingham.

Chan, A. (1998), 'Labor Standards and Human Rights: The Case of Chinese Workers Under Market Socialism', *Human Rights Quarterly*, Vol. 20, No. 4, pp. 886–904.

—— (2001), *China's Workers under Assault: The Exploitation of Labour in a Globalising Economy*, M.E. Sharpe, New York and London.

—— (2002), 'Labor in Waiting: The International Trade Union Movement and China', *New Labor Forum*, Fall/Winter, pp. 54–9.

—— (2003), 'Globalisation and China's "Race to the Bottom" in Labour Standards', *China Perspectives*, No. 46, March–April, pp. 41–50.

Chan, K. (1999), 'Internal Migration in China: A Dualistic Approach', in F. Pieke and H. Mallee (eds), *Internal and International Migration: Chinese Perspectives*, Curzon, London, pp. 49–71.

Chang, Ha-Joon and Ilene Grabel (2004), *Reclaiming Development: An Alternative Economic Policy Manual, Global Issues*, Zed Books, London.

Chang, K. (1993), 'The Peasant Family in Transition from Maoist to Lewisian Rural Industrialization', *The Journal of Development Studies*, Vol. 29, No. 2, pp. 220–44.

Chen, M. and A. Chan (1999), 'China's "Market Economics in Command": Footwear Workers' Health in Jeopardy', *International Journal of Health Services*, Vol. 29, No. 4, pp. 793–811.

Chow, G. (2002), *China's Economic Transformation*, Blackwell Pubblishers, Malden, Massachusetts.

Cook, S. (2002), 'From Rice Bowl to Safety Net: Insecurity and Social Protection during China's Transition', *Development Policy Review*, Vol. 20 No. 5, Blackwell Publishing Ltd, Oxford, pp. 615–33.

Cornia, G. A. (2003), 'Rapid Institutional Change Mortality Crises and Public Response', Paper presented at the seminar on 'Health and Social Upheavals', 13 and 14 March 2003, University of Florence.

—— (2004) (ed.), *Inequality, Growth, and Poverty in an Era of Liberalization and Globalization*, WIDER Studies in Development Economics, Oxford University Press, New York

—— (2006) (ed.), *Pro-Poor Macroeconomics, Potential and Limitations*, Palgrave, London.

Cornia, G. A. and V. Popov (2001), *Transition and Institutions*, OUP, Oxford.

Delahanty, J. (1999), 'A Common Thread: Issues for Women Workers in the Garment Sector', The North–South Institute, Ottawa, *www.wiego.org/publi4.ssi*.

Di Tommaso, M. and M. Bellandi (2006) (eds), *Il Fiume delle Perle: Luoghi e industria in Cina e il confronto con l'Italia*, Rosenberg and Sellier, Torino.

Diamond, S. (2003), 'The Race to the Bottom Returns: China's Challenge to the International Labor Movement', *University of California Davis Journal of International Law and Policy*, Vol. 10, No. 39.

Dong, X. (2005), 'Wage Inequality and Between-Firm Wage Dispersion in the 1990s: A Comparison of Rural and Urban Enterprises in China', *Journal of Comparative Economics*, Vol. 33, pp. 664–87.

Dong, X. and P. Bowles (2000), 'Segmentation and Discrimination in China's Emerging Industrial Labour Market', *http://www.cerdi.org/Colloque/IDREC2001/Dong_Bowles.pdf*, October.

Du, Y., A. Park, and S. Wang (2005), 'Migration and

Rural Poverty in China', *Journal of Comparative Economics*, Vol. 33, pp. 688–709

Ellman, M. (2003), 'Transition Economies', in Ha-Joon Chang (ed.), *Rethinking Development Economics*, London: Anthem Press, pp. 453–78.

FASC, NACO (1999), *'Abstract of the First National Agricultural Census in China'*, National Agricultural Census Office of China, Food and Agricultural Statistics Centre, China Statistics Press.

Ghatak, S. and K. Ingersent (1984), *Agriculture and Economic Development*, Wheatsheaf Books Ltd, Great Britain.

Gu, E. (2003), 'Labour Market Insecurities in China', ILO SES Working Paper, May.

Hirsch, G. (2005), 'Internal Labour Migration in China: Social and Economic Implications for the Guangdong Province', PhD Thesis, Doctorate in Politics and Economics of Developing Countries, University of Florence, Italy.

Kanbur, R. and X. Zhang (2005), 'Fifty Years of Regional Inequality in China Journey through Central Planning, Reform and Openness', *Review of Development Economics*, Vol. 9, No. 1, pp. 87–106.

Kaplinsky, R., M. Morris, and J. Readman, (2001), 'A Handbook for Value Chain Research', Mimeo, IDRC Institute of Development Studies, University of Sussex; School of Development Studies, University of Natal.

Lewis, W. (1954), 'Economic Development with Unlimited Supplies of Labour', *The Manchester School of Economic and Social Studies*, Vol. 12, No. 2, p. 139–191.

—— (1958), 'Unlimited Labour: Further Notes', *The Manchester School of Economic and Social Studies*, Vol. 26, No. 1, pp. 1–32.

Li, B. (2004), 'Urban Social Exclusion in Transitional China', LSE Centre for Analysis of Social Exclusion paper, No. 82.

Liang, Z. and Z. Ma (2004), 'China's Floating Population: New Evidence from the 2000 Census', *Population and Development Review*, London, Vol. 30, No. 3, pp. 467–88.

Liang, Z. and M. J. White (1997), 'Market Transition, Government Policies, and Interprovincial Migration in China: 1983–1988', *Economic Development and Cultural Change*, Vol. 45, pp. 321–39.

Lin, J. Y. and J. Nugent, J. B. (1995), 'Institutions and Economic Development', in J. Behrman and T. N. Srinivasan (eds), *Handbook of Development Economics*, Vol. 3, B, North Holland, Amsterdam, chap. 38.

Mehrotra, S. and M. Biggeri (2007), *Asian Informal Workers, Global Risk local Protection*, Routledge, London.

Meng, X. (2000), *Labour Market Reform in China*, Cambridge University Press, Cambridge.

Meng, X. and J. Zhang (2001), 'The Two-Tier Labor Market in Urban China: Occupational Segregation and Wage Differentials Between Urban Residents and Rural Migrants in Shanghai', *Journal of Comparative Economics*, No. 29, pp. 485–504.

Meng, X., R. Gregory, Y. Wang (2005), 'Poverty, Inequality, and Growth in Urban China 1986–2000', *Journal of Comparative Economics*, Vol. 33, pp., 710–29

NBS (National Bureau of Statistics of China), various years, Chinese Statistical Yearbook, Beijing: China Statistics Pr.

Nolan, P. (2001), *China and the Global Business Revolution*, Palgrave, Houndsmill.

—— (2004), *China at the Crossroads*, Polity Press, Cambridge, Blackwell Publishers Ltd, Oxford.

OECD (2002), *China in the World Economy: The Domestic Policy Challenges*, OECD Publications, Paris.

OXfam (2004), *Trading Away Our Rights: Women Working in Global Supply Chains*, Oxfam International, Information Press, Eynsham.

Pieke, F. and H. Mallee (1999) (eds), *Internal and International Migration: Chinese Perspectives*, Curzon, London.

Pun, N. (2005), 'A New Practice of Labor Organizing: Community-based Organization of Migrant Women Workers in South China', Paper presented at the International Conference on Membership Based Organizations of the

Poor: Theory, Experience and Poverty, Harvard University, WIEGO, the Cornell University and SEWA.

Ray, D. (1998), *Development Economics*, Princeton University Press, Princeton, New Jersey.

Reinert, E. (2003), 'Increasing Poverty in a Marshall Plans and Morgentau Plans as Mechanisms of Polarization of World Incomes', in H. Chang (ed.), *Rethinking Development Economics*, London: Anthem Press, pp. 453–78.

Rodrik, D. (1997), *Has Globalization Gone Too Far?* Institute for International Economics, Washington DC.

Seeborg, M., Z. Jin, and Y. Zhu (2000), 'The New Rural-Urban Labor Mobility in China: Causes and Implications', *The Journal of Socio-Economics*, No. 29, pp. 39–56.

Sen, A.K. (1999), Development as Freedom, Oxford University Press, Oxford.s

Sender, J., 2003 'Rural Poverty and Gender: Analytical Framework ad Policy Proposal', in Ha-Joon Chang (ed.) (2003), *Rethinking Development Economics*, Athem.

Spaventa, L. (1959), 'Dualism in Economic Growth', *Banca Nazionale del Lavoro Quarterly Review*, Vol. 51.

Todaro, M. (1969), 'A Model of Labor Migration and Urban Unemployment in Less Developed Countries', *American Economic Review*, Vol. 59, pp. 138–148.

UNDP (2003), (and previous years), *Human Development Report*, Oxford University Press, New York.

World Bank (2001), *China: Overcoming Rural Poverty*, The World Bank, Washington, DC.

—— (2006), (and previous years), *World Development Indicators*, World Bank, Washington.

Yao, Y. (2001), 'Social Exclusion and Economic Discrimination: The Status of Migrants in China's Coastal Rural Areas', China Center for Economic Research (CCER) Working Paper, No. E2001005.

Zhao, Z. (2003), 'Migration, Labor Market Flexibility, and Wage Determination in China—A Review', China Center for Economic Research (CCER), Beijing University, No. E2003007.

# Part VI

# Creating Policy Space

# 15

# India's Employment Guarantee Act
## Reclaiming Policy Space

Jean Drèze*

The draft National Rural Employment Guarantee Act entered national policy debates in India a few years ago like a wet dog at a glamorous party. The enactment of a national Employment Guarantee Act (EGA) was a long-standing demand of the labour movement, but it had never made much headway. In mid-2004, a series of unlikely events catapulted it to the top of the political agenda, at a time when privileged interests (notably those of the corporate sector and the so-called 'middle class') had an unprecedented hold on economic policy.[1] Within a year, employment on demand became a legal entitlement.

The enactment of the National Rural Employment Guarantee Act 2005 (hereafter NREGA, or just 'the Act'), right in the middle of a programme of neo-liberal economic reforms, can be seen as a useful illustration of the possibility of reclaiming 'policy space' in a democratic political system. As discussed in Ha-Joon Chang's contribution to this volume, there has been a significant shrinkage of 'policy space' in developing countries during the last twenty years or so. India's democratic institutions, however, present significant opportunities to resist this trend—opportunities that can be further expanded.

The extent of this achievement should not be exaggerated. The final version of the Act was significantly 'diluted', in some important respects, compared with the initial draft. And of course, the enactment of the law is only a first step, the real challenge is to ensure that it is adequately implemented on the ground. Nevertheless, the enactment of NREGA was a significant breakthrough, widely welcomed by workers' organizations. This chapter discusses some of the arguments and debates that have figured in this process.

## A BRIEF HISTORY OF THE ACT

Before moving on, it is worth recalling the major steps that led to the enactment of the NREGA. Though there is no obvious 'starting point' (as mentioned earlier, the demand for employment guarantee in India is far from

*This chapter is based on a series of articles published in Indian newspapers between 2004 and 2006, in the context of recent debates about the National Rural Employment Guarantee Act.

[1]On these events, and the campaign that led to the enactment of the NREGA 2005, see for example, McAuslan (2006) and Lakin and Ravishankar (2006).

new), an important prelude was the campaign for an EGA in Rajasthan, as an extension of the employment-based drought relief programmes undertaken in 2001 and 2003.[2] This was also an opportunity to create interest in a National EGA among leaders of opposition parties at the centre, notably Sonia Gandhi, who was Leader of the Opposition in the Lok Sabha ('lower house' of the Indian Parliament) at that time.

In early 2004, the promise of a National EGA was included in the electoral manifesto of the Congress Party. This promise seemed to be neither here nor there, as most people (including Congress leaders themselves) were quite sure that the Congress Party would lose the next election. As it turned out, however, the Congress came to power in May 2004 as the leading partner in the United Progressive Alliance (UPA) government. Apart from the Congress Party, the major partners in this alliance were the 'left parties', who were strong supporters of the EGA. Thus, EGA became one of the main planks of the National Common Minimum Programme (NCMP), on which the alliance was based. In fact, it was the first item in the NCMP's list of policy commitments.

In pursuance of this commitment, the National Advisory Council (NAC) drafted a National Rural Employment Guarantee Act in August 2004. The 'NAC draft', which was actually based on an earlier draft prepared by concerned citizens, set the framework for all subsequent discussions of the Act.[3] However, this draft went through numerous changes and revisions before it metamorphosed into the NREGA 2005. On 21 December 2004, the government tabled a severely diluted version of the NAC draft in Parliament. This draft (the 'National Rural Employment Guarantee Bill 2004') was so weak that it defeated the purpose of a legally enforceable employment guarantee.[4] For instance, the Bill left it to the Central Government to decide where and when the work guarantee would come into force. In other words, the government was offering an employment guarantee, but without any guarantee that the guarantee would come into effect! After being tabled in Parliament, the National Rural Employment Guarantee Bill 2004 was referred to the Parliamentary Standing Committee on Rural Development.

The National Rural Employment Guarantee Bill 2004 clearly fell short of the promise made in the NCMP. The response was a broad-based campaign to 'repair' the Bill and reinstate the crucial safeguards: irreversible guarantee, universal coverage, time-bound extension to the whole of rural India, assured minimum wages, full transparency, and others. The NAC, the left parties, and a wide range of organizations committed to the right to work played an active role in this campaign. This led to a series of amendments in the Bill in July and August 2005, largely based on the recommendations of the Standing Committee, which endorsed most of the campaign's demands. The most contentious issues were settled in August 2005, in a frantic round of

[2]There is a long history of the use of public works as a drought relief strategy in India (for further discussion, see Drèze 1990). On the employment guarantee campaign in Rajasthan, see Khera (2006).

[3]Both the NAC draft and the 'citizens' draft' are available at *www.righttofoodindia.org*, along with extensive documentation of the debate that led to the enactment of NREGA (including most of the papers cited in this chapter). Note that the NCMP policy commitment related not only to rural areas but also to 'urban poor and lower middle-class household[s]'. However, the extension of the Act to urban areas is yet to be considered seriously.

[4]For a critique, see Drèze (2004a).

bargaining between the constituent parties of the UPA alliance, and the left parties extracted some major last-minute concessions. Finally, the NREGA was passed in the Lok Sabha on 23 August 2005.

Interestingly, the Act was passed unanimously. Video recordings give an interesting glimpse of this moving event. The Minister of Rural Development, Raghuvansh Prasad Singh, made a spirited speech in Hindi, ending with *'rozgar guarantee zindabad'* (long live employment guarantee) and roaring applause. The Speaker of the House then proceeded to conduct the 'voice vote' on NREGA. When the time came for the opponents to say 'nay', there was pin-drop silence.

This political unanimity, however, was somewhat deceptive. While it would have been very difficult for any Member of Parliament to oppose the Act in public, there was a great deal of 'behind the scenes' opposition to the Act in the corridors of power, notably from the Finance Ministry.[5] Further, this opposition was organically linked to a powerful 'anti-NREGA' lobby, very vocal in the corporate-sponsored media and related forums. The fact that this small lobby nearly succeeded in derailing the Act (and did succeed in diluting it in some important respects), in spite of the tremendous popular appeal of the Act, is a telling symptom of the elitist nature of Indian democracy. In the end, the opposition was dispersed, and the demands of the working class prevailed. But this was something of an isolated victory, at a time when economic policy was overwhelmingly driven by privileged interests, and it was the outcome of a rather unlikely sequence of events.[6]

## EMPLOYMENT GUARANTEE AS A SOCIAL RESPONSIBILITY

The NREGA gives a legal guarantee of employment in rural areas to anyone who is willing to engage in casual manual labour at the statutory minimum wage. Any adult who applies for work under the Act is entitled to being employed on local public works within 15 days. Failing that, an unemployment allowance has to be paid. Guaranteed employment is subject to an initial limit of 100 days per household per year, which may be raised or removed over time. The Act applies in rural areas, and is to be extended to the whole of India within five years.[7]

[5]It is an open secret that the Finance Ministry opposed the Act (an 'expensive gravy train', in the words of a former Chief Economic Adviser) from the beginning. Indeed, it played a leading role in the attempted dilution of the draft Act prepared by the NAC. When this failed, the Finance Ministry insisted on the inclusion of a so-called 'anti-corruption clause', which gave sweeping powers to the Central Government to discontinue NREGA funding on the flimsiest suspicion of 'improper utilization of funds'. When the Act came into force in 200 districts in February 2006, the Finance Ministry restricted the financial allocation for administrative expenses to 2 per cent of total costs, making it very hard to implement the NREGA in states that did not have readymade arrangements for implementing large-scale public works. And in the run-up to the Union Budget 2007–8, the Finance Ministry opposed the demand by the Ministry of Rural Development for extension of the Act to another 200 districts. As the Rural Development Minister, Raghuvansh Prasad Singh, politely said in a recent interview to *Business Standard*, 'the Planning Commission and Finance Ministry are not showing interest in funding the programme'.

[6]There are interesting parallels between the NREGA 2005, the Right to Information Act 2005, and the Scheduled Tribes & Forest Dwellers (Recognition of Forest Rights) Act 2005. Each of these unusually progressive legislations has its roots in the NCMP. In each case, the government tried to get away with a 'diluted' version of the Act, but the loopholes were substantially removed through democratic opposition and public mobilization.

[7]For a reader-friendly introduction to the Act, see

The need for an EGA has often been questioned. Why is it not enough to initiate massive employment schemes? The main answer is that an Act places an enforceable obligation on the state, and gives bargaining power to the labourers—thus creating accountability. By contrast, a scheme leaves labourers at the mercy of government officials. There is another major difference between a scheme and an Act. Schemes come and go, but laws are more durable. A scheme can be trimmed or even cancelled by a bureaucrat, whereas changing a law requires an amendment in Parliament. Under the Act, labourers have durable legal entitlements. Over time, they are likely to become aware of their rights and learn how to defend them.

Opposition to the Act often arises from a failure to appreciate its far-reaching economic, social, and political significance. To start with, the Act can go a long way towards protecting rural households from poverty and hunger. One hundred days of employment at the statutory minimum wage is not the end of unemployment by any means, but for people living on the brink of starvation, it makes a big difference.[8] Second, NREGA is likely to lead to a substantial reduction in rural–urban migration: if work is available in the village, many rural families will stop heading for the cities during the slack season. Third, guaranteed employment contributes to the empowerment of women. A large proportion of labourers employed under NREGA are women, and guaranteed employment gives them some economic independence.[9] Fourth, the Act is an opportunity to create useful assets in rural areas. In particular, there is a massive potential for labour-intensive public works in the field of environmental protection: watershed development, land regeneration, prevention of soil erosion, restoration of tanks, protection of forests, and related activities. Fifth, the Act can help to activate and revitalize the institutions of local governance, including 'gram panchayats' (village councils) and 'gram sabhas' (village assemblies). It will give them a new purpose, as well as the backing of substantial financial resources.

Last but not the least, the Act is a means of strengthening the bargaining power of unorganized workers. This, in turn, could help them to struggle for other important entitlements, such as minimum wages and social security. The process of mobilizing for effective implementation of the Act also has much value in itself, as an opportunity for unorganized workers to organize.

Having said this, the Act involves substantial financial commitment. Even those who are otherwise sympathetic to the idea often wonder whether it is affordable. It is interesting that similar concerns have seldom been raised with respect to the 'interlinking of rivers' project.[10]

Dey, Drèze, and Khera (2006). For the full text of the Act, and related documents, see *www.nrega.nic.in*.

[8]In a note on the financial implications of NREGA, the National Advisory Council pointed out that a net income transfer equivalent to the earnings of 100 days of work at the statutory minimum wage would enable a large majority of poor rural households to cross the 'poverty line'. This should not be taken literally, since there are also second-round effects to consider, both negative (e.g. foregone earnings in other activities) and positive (e.g. multiplier effects). But it does give a useful indication of the potential impact of NREGA on rural poverty.

[9]According to recent data released by the Ministry of Rural Development, the proportion of women among NREGA labourers was above 40 per cent in 2006–7 (see *www.nrega.nic.in*).

[10]This is a heroic scheme aimed at linking India's major rivers through canals and other structures, to even out the surpluses and deficits of water between different basins.

The cost of that project is far greater, and its benefits (if any) far more speculative, than those of an EGA. Yet the project easily mustered support from some of the country's most prestigious institutions and personalities, based on the flimsiest possible arguments. It would be surprising if this had nothing to do with the fact that the interlinking project is a potential bonanza for the corporate sector.

Be that as it may, the economic viability of an EGA needs to be examined on its own terms, and not by comparison with extravagant projects. In a note on this issue prepared by the NAC, the cost of the Act was anticipated to rise from 0.5 per cent of GDP in 2005–6 to 1 per cent of GDP in 2008–9. This was based on the assumption that the Act would be gradually extended to the whole of India within four years, starting with the 150 poorest districts in 2005–6.[11]

The anticipated cost of 1 per cent of GDP is a financial cost. It is arguable that the 'real' cost would be much lower. For instance, the financial cost of employing a labourer on public works is the statutory minimum wage, but the economic cost (the real resources foregone) may not be so high, if the labourer is otherwise unemployed. However, even if the real cost of the Act is as high as 1 per cent of GDP, there is no cause for panic.

The challenge of financing the Act has to be seen in the light of the fact that India's tax–GDP ratio is quite low in an international perspective: about 15 per cent (for Centre and states combined) compared with, say, 37 per cent in OECD countries. Further, India's tax–GDP ratio has declined in recent years. For instance, the ratio of central taxes to GDP was only 9.3 per cent in 2003–4, compared with 10.6 per cent in 1987–8. These are some indications, among others, that there is much scope for raising India's tax–GDP ratio to finance the Act as well as related social programmes.

On the nuts and bolts of enhancing tax revenue, there are useful hints in the second 'Kelkar Committee' report recently submitted to the Ministry of Finance (Government of India 2004). Some aspects of this report are questionable, including its fixation with uniform taxes and its touching faith in the scope for raising revenue by lowering tax rates. Nevertheless, it also suggests many sensible ways of raising the tax–GDP ratio, such as introducing value-added taxes, extending taxation to most services, using information technology to broaden the tax net, eliminating arbitrary exemptions, and (last but not least) fighting tax evasion. If these opportunities are well utilized, public expenditure can be raised by much more than one per cent of India's GDP.

There are also other financing options, besides those recommended by the second Kelkar Committee. For instance, a recent World Bank study estimates that lifting the anachronic cap on the Professions Tax would enable state governments to collect additional tax revenue to the tune of 0.9 per cent of GDP. Similarly, revenue could be generated from 'green taxes' on environmentally harmful consumption, or more generally, on anti-social activities. There is also much scope for pruning unnecessary public expenditure, starting with military expenditure and subsidies for the rich. In short, the fundamental ability of the Indian economy to sustain an EGA is not in doubt; what is required is imagination and commitment for tapping that potential.

Some of these proposals are likely to be opposed by those who stand to gain from the

[11]In fact, the Act came into force in February 2006 in 200 districts, and is due to be extended to the whole of rural India within five years of its enactment, i.e. by mid-2010.

status quo, as happened recently with the introduction of value added taxes (VAT) as well as with the 'capital transactions' tax. One way to get around this is to link tax reforms more clearly with positive initiatives such as the EGA. Instead of piecemeal reforms, often derailed by vested interests, the need of the hour is for a comprehensive 'new deal', involving a higher tax–GDP ratio but also better use of tax revenue. A package of this kind has a greater chance of success than piecemeal reform.

'Tax the rich' would be a useful guiding principle for this package. During the last twenty years or so, India's so-called 'middle class' (read the top five per cent of the income scale) has become rich beyond its wildest dreams. It has literally transplanted itself to the first world without even applying for a visa. The time to share is long overdue.

To put it differently, the Indian economy badly needs a redistributive mechanism, in order to escape from the present situation where runaway growth co-exists with the stubborn persistence of mass deprivation. The EGA can play this role, among others. Viewed in this perspective, the Act need not be the object of a pitched battle between the working class and the privileged classes. It can also be seen as a national endeavour—a visionary initiative in which most citizens have a stake in one way or another. Better recognition of the wide-ranging social benefits of a National EGA could shed new light on the whole debate.

## EMPLOYMENT GUARANTEE AND ITS DISCONTENT

In *Manufacturing Consent* (Herman and Chomsky 1988) and other writings, Noam Chomsky presents an illuminating analysis of propaganda techniques in democratic societies. One of these techniques is 'flak'—a barrage of attacks on ideas that challenge the interests of established power.

The NREGA, no doubt a 'dangerous' idea, was the target of two waves of 'flak' before it was passed. The first wave occurred around December 2004, when the National Rural Employment Guarantee Bill was tabled in Parliament. The second occurred during the monsoon session of Parliament, in July–August 2005, just before the Bill was sent back to Parliament with a series of amendments based on the recommendations of the Standing Committee on Rural Development.

As Chomsky observes, flak often involves personal attacks, and that certainly applies in this case. To illustrate, Surjit Bhalla—one of the most vocal opponents of the Act—attacked the so-called 'leaders' of the pro-EGA campaign as 'liars' and accused them of being 'arrogant', 'ignorant', and 'brazen', among other colourful epithets (Bhalla 2004, 2005). In a more sober vein, the advocates of EGA were often called 'jholawala economists' (Dasgupta 2005), as if there was something indecent about an economist carrying a *jhola* instead of a corporate briefcase.[12] One commentator extended this term to the entire NAC, dismissing them as 'a bunch of jholewalas with their hearts in the right place but their worn out sandals walking the wrong way' (Singh 2005). Singh argued that instead of these jholawalas, the NAC needed 'people like Sam Pitroda', apparently forgetting that Sam Pitroda (a pioneer of the telecommunications revolution in India) was already a member of the NAC at that time.

Even fratricide figured in this merciless crusade. Jairam Ramesh, otherwise known as the 'poster boy of economic reforms', was called a 'turncoat' in the business media for supporting EGA and related ideas (*DNA* 7 August 2005). 'What is he smoking these days?', asked a dismayed member of

[12] A *jhola* is a cheap shoulder-bag, and a 'jholawala' is someone who goes around with a jhola.

the pro-reform brotherhood, quoted in the article.[13]

Apart from personal attacks, deceptive statistics played a major role in this propaganda operation. Surjit Bhalla deployed some of his most spectacular hat-tricks to rubbish the EGA. He even managed to show, based on a creative reading of National Sample Survey data, that 'poor agricultural workers had an unemployment rate of only 1 per cent' (Bhalla, 2004). Ergo, the EGA is not required. As the late Sudhir Mulji, who was otherwise on much the same side of the fence as Bhalla, soberly observed in *Business Standard*: 'That the magnitude of unemployment is substantially higher than one per cent inferred by analysts of NSS data is obvious to even casual observers if not to skilled statisticians' (Mulji 2005). It is worth adding that serious 'analysts of NSS data' were equally startled by this reading of the evidence.

In a related genre, statistical hyperbole was widely used to produce scary estimates of the cost of an EGA. One critic came up with a figure of Rs 208,000 crores per year (Debroy 2004a). In per capita terms, this is almost twenty times as much as the cost of Maharashtra's EGA, which is more liberal than the NREGA.[14]

It is also interesting to consider the 'alternatives' that were proposed by the opponents of the Act. One of India's leading economic columnists suggested dropping cash from helicopters instead of asking people to work for wages (Aiyar 2004). Another argued that 'the first best option would be to do nothing' (Acharya 2004). A third commentator tersely wrote that it would be 'better to have unemployment insurance alone, without the employment guarantee' (Debroy 2004a), without explaining how a universal unemployment insurance scheme could possibly work in rural India. A fourth proposal was to take refuge in Section 80G of the Income Tax Act, which allows donations to charity to be deducted from tax: 're-examine 80G, tighten it, and direct it for rural employment creation' (Srinivasa-Raghavan 2004).

The least unreasonable alternative was proposed by Surjit Bhalla. He suggested universal cash transfers as an alternative to guaranteed employment. I leave it to the reader to guess whether this was a serious proposal, or just another stick to beat the Act. Be that as it may, the proposal can easily be accommodated. All one has to do is to insert a clause in the Act stating that if the government prefers to pay the equivalent of 100 days' wages to every household in a particular district, instead of organizing public works, it is free to do so.

To avoid misunderstanding, let me clarify that I am not dismissing every critique of the Act as an act of propaganda or sabotage. Every version of the Act, from the first draft onwards (and including the final version), had some major flaws, and there was much scope for substantive disagreement on many aspects of the proposed employment guarantee. What is striking, however, is that reasoned critiques of the Act were few and far between.[15] Instead, a plethora of shallow arguments were invoked to deride it, often by influential economists with PhDs from world-class universities.

[13]Jairam Ramesh, economist turned politician (currently Minister of State for Commerce), is a leading member of the Congress Party, and played a key role in drafting the Congress Manifesto in early 2004, as well as the NCMP of the UPA government.

[14]Maharashtra, the pioneer in this field, enacted an EGA in the late 1970s. For further discussion, see for example, Mahendra Dev and Ranade (1997), and the literature cited there.

[15]For examples of insightful critiques of the proposed Act, see Banerjee and Bardhan (2004), Ramanathan (2004), Murgai and Ravallion (2005), Patnaik (2005), and Srinivasan (2005), among others.

There is an interesting message here about the smooth integration of the 'economics' profession with the structures of power.

Fireworks aside, was there any substance in this chorus of protest against the Act? I believe there was. As Rapoport (1960) pointed out in his pioneering work on 'ethical debate', even the most outlandish statements often have their 'domain of validity'. For instance, the statement 'black is white' makes sense in the limited circumstance where one is looking at the negative of a photograph. Similarly, there was an important message in these shrill interventions; this is discussed in further detail in the next section.

## EMPLOYMENT AND EMPOWERMENT

As the preceding section illustrates, opposition to the Act came chiefly from a small but powerful section of the corporate sector and its allies in the government.[16] This opposition was typically rooted in a 'minimalist' view of the role of the State in the social sector. In an article with a transparent title ('Can the State Really Help the Poor?'), T.C.A. Srinivasa-Raghavan clearly articulated the main argument of the minimalists: 'those who think that the money will reach the intended beneficiaries are living in a fool's paradise' (Srinivasa-Raghavan 2004). Similar statements can be found in most of the writings cited in the preceding section.

This argument should not be lightly dismissed. The record of anti-poverty programmes in India is far from encouraging. Recent studies of the National Food For Work Programme (NFFWP), the official 'precursor' of employment schemes to be initiated under the Act, are also sobering. They suggest that the Programme is a potential lifeline for the rural poor, and also has many other positive effects, from slowing down rural–urban migration to the creation of useful assets. However, much of this potential has been wasted due to the widespread corruption.

The issue is whether this situation is immutable, or whether corruption can be eradicated from public works programmes. The minimalists feel that corruption is an intrinsic feature of these programmes, but recent experience suggests otherwise.

One major achievement in this respect is the 'cleaning' of muster rolls in Rajasthan.[17] Fudging of muster rolls is the principal method through which public funds are siphoned off from rural employment programmes. For instance, unscrupulous officials enter fake names in the muster rolls and appropriate the wages of the fictitious labourers. This has been going on for decades all over India. In Rajasthan, however, this practice has been significantly curtailed, at least in areas where active use has been made of the state's Right to Information Act. This is largely a reflection not only of the accessibility of the muster rolls under the Act, but also of the culture of public vigilance and bureaucratic accountability that has started spreading in Rajasthan in the wake of the right to information movement.

A recent survey of the NFFWP, conducted in six states, confirms that Rajasthan is 'different' from other states in this respect. In each of the other five sample states (Chhattisgarh, Jharkhand, Madhya Pradesh, Uttar Pradesh, and West Bengal), the muster rolls were

[16]There were, of course, dissenting voices on this within the corporate sector. Indeed, some business leaders wrote lively defences of the Act (see, for example, Rao, 2004).

[17]'Muster rolls' are essentially work attendance registers, which are also used to claim money from the concerned authorities for the payment of wages.

virtually impossible to trace. In rare cases where they could be traced, simple verification exercises uncovered massive fudging. In Rajasthan, however, the muster rolls were easy to obtain and they were, by and large, accurate.[18]

There is much to learn from this experience. First and foremost, corruption is not an immutable feature of rural development programmes. Second, the best way to fight corruption in public works is to empower those who are at the receiving end of the system of fraud and embezzlement—starting with the labourers, for whom it is a matter of life and death. Third, the right to information is a powerful tool of empowerment. India's Right to Information Act, which came into force around the same time as the NREGA, is a major breakthrough in this respect. Fourth, a law is not enough—legal rights have to be combined with a process of public mobilization that enables people to exercise those rights.

The NREGA is an opportunity to take this process much further than it has gone in Rajasthan. Like the Right to Information Act, NREGA is an important tool of empowerment. It puts in place legal safeguards and accountability mechanisms that strengthen the bargaining power of labourers: job cards for all workers, pro-active disclosure of muster rolls, mandatory social audits by gram sabhas, penalties for any violation of the law, among others. The Act will also give labourers a new opportunity to become organized. Unlike a 'scheme', a law gives people durable entitlements that they can learn to fight for. This feature of Maharashtra's Employement Guarantee Scheme is well conveyed in a recent study by Anuradha Joshi. As Joshi points out, a strong National EGA is likely to lead to 'a flourishing of activist organizations that would help mobilize the poor in their interests' (Joshi forthcoming).

Thus, while the EGA is widely regarded as a potential fountain of corruption, it can also be seen (along with the Right to Information Act) as an integral part of the battle for restoring accountability in rural development programmes. There is a possible meeting ground here for the 'minimalists' and their opponents.

## THE EMPLOYMENT GUARANTEE ACT—ONE YEAR ON

The NREGA came into force on 2 February 2006 in 200 of India's poorest districts (about one-third of the country). Judging from early reports, the Act is not doing particularly well, whether we look at the levels of employment generation, or wage rates, or the persistence of corruption, or the quality of assets generated. However, this is not very surprising, since the implementation of the NREGA is a massive challenge, which is bound to require an extended 'learning phase'. Further, some bright spots have already emerged.[19]

First, the Act has led to a major refocusing of attention and energy towards rural employment. From village secretary to district collector, the main concern of the development administration in NREGA districts is how to meet the demand for work. That itself is a

[18]See Drèze (2005) for further discussion. Follow-up investigations in 2006 reinforced these findings. For instance, a massive 'social audit' conducted in Dungarpur District (Rajasthan) in April 2006 found little evidence of any significant fudging of muster rolls. In other states, the practice continues, but there are indications that it is beginning to fade away thanks to the transparency safeguards mandated by the NREGA are slowly taking root.

[19]For further discussion, see Dreze and Oldiges (2007).

breakthrough of sorts. Second, in the better-performing districts, NREGA has led to a surge in employment opportunities for the rural poor. To illustrate, in Rajasthan's six NREGA districts, almost every rural household has a 'job card', and the average job card holder had worked for more than 70 days under NREGA in 2006–7. This is an unprecedented achievement in the history of social security in India. Third, these positive experiences also lend support to the hopes that have been placed in other potential achievements of NREGA, such as enhancing food security, reducing distress migration, activating the gram sabhas, reviving the rural economy, and empowering disadvantaged groups. In particular, the Act is a powerful tool of social equity: women's share in NREGA employment in 2006–7 was above 40 per cent, and the share of 'scheduled caste' and 'scheduled tribe' workers was close to two-thirds.[20] Fourth, the possibility of preventing corruption in NREGA has been confirmed in some of the pioneer districts. This requires active exercise of the right to information, imaginative use of information technology and, most importantly, strict implementation of the transparency guidelines.

Last but not the least National Rural Employment Guarantee Act is releasing a great deal of creative energy in rural areas. A whole range of innovative activities can be linked with the NREGA: planning productive works, launching social security schemes, creating workers' associations, running effective worksite crèches, arranging work for persons with disabilities, conducting social audits, organizing literacy programmes, and much more. While these opportunities remain largely untapped, there have been a number of interesting initiatives across the country since February 2006, both in terms of state action as well as in terms of public action (in a wider sense).

One of the most creative initiatives in this respect is a recent 'social audit' of NREGA, conducted in Dungarpur District (Rajasthan) in April 2006.[21] This mass social audit involved more than 1000 participants from different parts of India. The volunteers spent a week walking from village to village across the district, inspecting every single NREGA worksite, verifying records, and holding public meetings. This experience gave them a many useful glimpse of NREGA's ability to bring about far-reaching economic, social, and political change in rural areas. Most rural households in the district had a job card, and on an average day, about half of them had a member employed on an NREGA project. New water-harvesting structures were springing up everywhere. The women of Dungarpur had cash in their hands and some economic independence. The muster rolls were available at the worksites, and extensive checks revealed that few of them were fudged. The entire administration was busy trying to meet the popular demand for employment. There were, of course, many lapses, notably relating to delayed wage payments and non-payment of minimum wages. Nevertheless, the overall picture of NREGA emerging from this exercise was overwhelmingly positive.

[20] Scheduled castes and scheduled tribes are disadvantaged social groups, entitled to special support from the state under the Indian Constitution. They account for 16 and 8 per cent of India's population, respectively.

[21] For an insightful account of this social audit, see Sivakumar (2006).

The need of the hour is to build on these positive experiences and to extend them across the country. In this respect, an important opportunity is that the EGA is becoming a matter of intense competition between political parties. As political parties become rival champions of the Act, there is a chance that NREGA will take off. This is another aspect of the role of democratic practice in reclaiming 'policy space'.

## REFERENCES

Acharya, Shankar (2004), 'Guaranteeing Jobs or a Fiscal Crisis?', *Business Standard*, 30 November.

Aiyar, Swaminathan S. Anklesaria (2004), 'Poverty Reduction by Helicopter', *Times of India*, 19 December.

Banerjee, Abhijit and Pranab Bardhan (2004), 'Food for Thought', *Hindustan Times*, 15 December.

Bhalla, Surjit S. (2004), 'Corruption with a Human Face', *Business Standard*, 11 December.

——— (2005), 'Ten Lies and an Act: III', *Business Standard*, 8 January.

Bhatty, Kiran (2006), 'Employment Guarantee and Child Rights', *Economic and Political Weekly*, May.

Dasgupta, Swapan (2005), 'Rename REGA as Corruption Guarantee Scheme', *Pioneer*, 14 August.

Debroy, Bibek (2004a), 'The Rs 208,000 Crore Puzzle', *Indian Express*, 23 October.

——— (2004b), 'Jobs, Not the Government's Job', *Indian Express*, 13 October.

Dey, N., J.P. Drèze, and R. Khera (2006), *Employment Guarantee Act: A Primer*, National Book Trust, New Delhi.

Drèze, Jean (1990), 'Famine Prevention in India', in Jean Dreze and A.K. Sen (eds), *The Political Economy of Hunger*', Clarendon, Oxford.

——— (2004a), 'Unemployment Guarantee Bill', *The Hindu*, 31 December.

——— (2004b), 'Democracy and the Right to Food', *Economic and Political Weekly*, 24 April.

——— (2005), 'Loot for Work Programme', *Times of India*, 1 July.

Drèze, J., and Oldiges, C. (2007), 'A Commandable Act', Frontline, 27 Junly.

Government of India (2004), *Report of the Task Force on Implementation of the Fiscal Responsibility and Budget Management Act, 2003*, Ministry of Finance, New Delhi.

Herman, Edward S. and N. Chomsky (1988), *Manufacturing Consent: The Political Economy of the Mass Media*, Pantheon Books, New York.

Joshi, Anuradha (forthcoming), 'Do Rights Work? Law, Activism and the Employment Guarantee Scheme', in M. Moore, S. Patel, and A. Joshi, (eds), *Employment Guarantee.*

Khera, Reetika (2006), 'Political Economy of State Response to Drought', *Economic and Political Weekly*, 16 December.

Lakin, J. and N. Ravishankar (2006), 'Working for Votes: The Politics of Employment Guarantee in India', mimeo, Department of Government, Harvard University.

Mahendra Dev, S. and A. Ranade (1997), 'Agricultural Growth, Employment and Poverty in Maharashtra with Emphasis on Employment Guarantee Scheme', in G.K. Chadha and A.N. Sharma (eds), *Growth, Employment and Poverty: Change and Continuity in Rural India*, Vikas, New Delhi.

McAuslan, Ian (2006), 'The Politics of Pro-poor Policy Change in India: The National Rural Employment Guarantee Act', mimeo, Institute of Development Studies, University of Sussex.

Mulji, Sudhir (2005), 'Employment Guarantee Scheme', *Business Standard*, 20 January.

Murgai, R. and M. Ravallion (2005), 'Employment Guarantee in Rural India: What Would it Cost and How Much Would it Reduce Poverty?', *Economic and Political Weekly*, 30 July.

Patnaik, Ila (2005), 'Will It Reduce Poverty or Fill Corrupt Pockets? A 7-item Reality Check', *Financial Express*, 19 August.

Ramanathan, Ramesh (2004), 'Time to Reflect on

the Rural Jobs Bill?', *Financial Express*, 17 December.

Rao, Jaithirth (2004), 'Forget Efficiency. Let's Do It', *Indian Express*, 10 December.

Rapoport, Anatol (1960), *Fights, Games and Debates*, University of Michigan Press, Ann Arbor.

Singh, Tavleen (2005), 'Why We Are a Poor Rich Country', *Indian Express*, 7 February.

Sivakumar, Sowmya (2006), 'Walking with a Purpose', *Frontline*, 6–19 May.

Srinivasa-Raghavan, T.C.A. (2004), 'Can the State Really Help the Poor?', *Business Standard*, 18 December.

Srinivasan, T.N. (2005), 'Guaranteeing Employment: A Palliative?', *The Hindu*, 3 January.

# Appendices

# Appendix A2

Table A2.1: Average Tariff Rates on Manufactured Products for Selected Developed Countries in Their Early Stages of Development

*(weighted average; in percentages of value)*†

| | 1820# | 1875# | 1913 | 1925 | 1931 | 1950 |
|---|---|---|---|---|---|---|
| Austria@ | R | 15–20 | 18 | 16 | 24 | 1 |
| Belgium* | 6–8 | 9–10 | 9 | 15 | 14 | 11 |
| Denmark | 25–35 | 15–20 | 14 | 10 | n.a. | 3 |
| France | R | 12–15 | 20 | 21 | 30 | 18 |
| Germany[a] | 8–12 | 4–6 | 13 | 20 | 21 | 26 |
| Italy | n.a. | 8–10 | 18 | 22 | 46 | 25 |
| Japan[b] | R | 5 | 30 | n.a. | n.a. | n.a. |
| Netherlands* | 6–8 | 3–5 | 4 | 6 | n.a. | 11 |
| Russia | R | 15–20 | 84 | R | R | R |
| Spain | R | 15–20 | 41 | 41 | 63 | n.a. |
| Sweden | R | 3–5 | 20 | 16 | 21 | 9 |
| Switzerland | 8–12 | 4–6 | 9 | 14 | 19 | n.a. |
| United Kingdom | 45–55 | 0 | 0 | 5 | n.a. | 23 |
| United States | 35–45 | 40–50 | 44 | 37 | 48 | 14 |

*Source*: Chang (2002), p. 17, Table 2.1.

*Notes*: R= Numerous and important restrictions on manufactured imports existed and, therefore, average tariff rates are not meaningful.

† World Bank (1991, p. 97, Box table 5.2) provides a similar table, partly drawing on Bairoch's own studies that form the basis of the above table. However, the World Bank figures, although in most cases very similar to Bairoch's figures, are *unweighted* averages, which are obviously less preferable to *weighted* average figures that Bairoch provides.

# These are very approximate rates, and give range of average rates, not extremes.

@ Austria–Hungary before 1925.

* In 1820, Belgium was united with the Netherlands.

[a] The 1820 figure is for Prussia only.

[b] Before 1911, Japan was obliged to keep low tariff rates (up to 5 per cent) through a series of 'unequal treaties' with the European countries and the USA. The World Bank Table cited above gives Japan's *unweighted* average tariff rate for *all goods* (and not just manufactured goods) for the years 1925, 1930, 1950 as 13 per cent, 19 per cent, 4 per cent, respectively.

Table A2.2: Average Tariff Rates (%) on Manufactured Products for Selected Developed Countries in the Early post-Second World War Period

| | 1950 | 1959 | 1962 | 1973 | 1979 |
|---|---|---|---|---|---|
| Europe | | | | | |
| Belgium | 11 | 14 | | | |
| France | 18 | 30 | | | |
| W. Germany | 26 | 7 | | | |
| Italy | 25 | 18 | | | |
| Netherlands | 11 | 7 | | | |
| EEC Average* | | 15 | 13 | 8 | 6 |
| Austria | 18 | | 20@ | 11 | 8 |
| Denmark | 3 | | | | |
| Finland | | | 20+# | 13 | 11 |
| Sweden | 9 | | 8 | 6 | 5 |
| Japan | n.a. | | 18 | 10 | 6 |
| United Kingdom | 23 | | 16 | | |
| United States | 14 | | 13 | 12 | 7 |

*Source*: Chang (2005), p. 54, table 5.

*Notes*:

* EEC average after 1973 includes Denmark and the UK.

@ 1960.

# Estimate by the author. The data on Finland's tariff rates are not readily available, but, according to the data reported in table 8.2 of Panić—(1988, p. 151), in 1965 tariff revenue as a percentage of all imports in Finland was 9.97%, which was considerably higher than that of Japan (7.55 per cent), which had 18 per cent average industrial tariff rate, or that of Austria (8.57 per cent), which had 20 per cent average industrial tariff rate. Given these, it would not be unreasonable to estimate that Finland's average industrial tariff rate in the mid-1960s was well over 20 per cent.

# Appendix A6

Table A6.1: INDEC 500's Sectoral Decomposition

| | 1995 | 1996 | 1997 | 1998 | 1999 | 2000 | 2001 |
|---|---|---|---|---|---|---|---|
| Domestic Firms | | | | | | | |
| Number of firms in panel | 317 | 301 | 268 | 267 | 258 | 244 | 240 |
| Firms in tradable sector | 195 | 180 | 172 | 174 | 164 | 153 | 148 |
| Gross Value of Production (as a % of Domestic firms' GVP) | 57% | 57% | 63% | 63% | 65% | 64% | 60% |
| Firms in non-tradable sector | 122 | 121 | 96 | 93 | 94 | 91 | 92 |
| Gross Value of Production (as a % of Domestic firms' GVP) | 43% | 43% | 37% | 37% | 35% | 36% | 40% |
| Foreign firms | | | | | | | |
| Number of firms in panel | 182 | 198 | 231 | 232 | 241 | 255 | 259 |
| Firms in tradable sector | 140 | 157 | 174 | 164 | 158 | 172 | 174 |
| Gross Value of Production (as a % of Foreign firms' GVP) | 80% | 80% | 73% | 68% | 61% | 66% | 67% |
| Firms in non-tradable sector | 42 | 41 | 57 | 68 | 83 | 83 | 85 |
| Gross Value of Production (as a % of Foreign firms' GVP) | 20% | 20% | 27% | 32% | 39% | 34% | 33% |

*Source*: Author's calculations based on INDEC.
*Note*: * Due to methodological reasons the number of firms adds up to 499 only.

Table A6.2: Leverage Ratios and Foreign Indebtedness, INDEC 500 (1995–2001)

| | 1995 | 1996 | 1997 | 1998 | 1999 | 2000 | 2001 |
|---|---|---|---|---|---|---|---|
| *Leverage ratio* (*) | | | | | | | |
| Indec 500 | 0.44 | 0.47 | 0.50 | 0.52 | 0.52 | 0.52 | 0.53 |
| Tradable sector | 0.45 | 0.47 | 0.50 | 0.51 | 0.50 | 0.49 | 0.51 |
| Non-tradable sector | 0.44 | 0.48 | 0.50 | 0.53 | 0.54 | 0.55 | 0.55 |
| *Foreign Liabilities / Total Liabilities* | | | | | | | |
| Indec 500 | 0.39 | 0.41 | 0.47 | 0.49 | 0.49 | 0.47 | 0.51 |

*(contd...)*

*(Table Appendix A6.2 continued)*

| | 1995 | 1996 | 1997 | 1998 | 1999 | 2000 | 2001 |
|---|---|---|---|---|---|---|---|
| Tradable sector | 0.42 | 0.44 | 0.51 | 0.55 | 0.54 | 0.53 | 0.56 |
| Non-tradable sector | 0.36 | 0.38 | 0.41 | 0.43 | 0.44 | 0.42 | 0.45 |
| *Foreign Liabilities / Total Assets* | | | | | | | |
| Indec 500 | 0.17 | 0.20 | 0.23 | 0.26 | 0.25 | 0.25 | 0.27 |
| Tradable sector | 0.19 | 0.21 | 0.25 | 0.28 | 0.27 | 0.26 | 0.29 |
| Non-tradable sector | 0.16 | 0.18 | 0.21 | 0.23 | 0.24 | 0.23 | 0.25 |

*Source*: Author's calculations based on INDEC.
*Note*: (*) Leverage ratio = Total Liabilities / Total Assets.

## Table A6.3: Retention Rates in Argentina's Corporate Sector, INDEC 500 (1995–2001)

*(per cent)*

| | 1995 | 1996 | 1997 | 1998 | 1999 | 2000 | 2001 |
|---|---|---|---|---|---|---|---|
| INDEC 500 | 59.8 | 55.6 | 66.7 | 41.7 | 1.4 | 2.3 | -252.5 |
| Domestic | 60 | 53 | 63 | 26 | –27(*) | –193(*) | –715(**) |
| Foreign | 60 | 58 | 69 | 50 | 9 | 18 | –171(*) |

*Source*: Author's calculations based on INDEC.
*Notes*: Retention rate = (Net Operating Profits—Interests—Dividends) / (Net Operating Profits—Interests);
(*) Negative retention rates result from dividend payments exceeding current net profits (after tax and interest payments);
(**) Negative retention rates result from negative net profits (after tax and interest payments).

## Table A6.4 Hedged, Speculative, and Ponzi Positions, INDEC 500 (1998–2001)

*(per cent)*

| | 1998 | 1999 | 2000 | 2001 |
|---|---|---|---|---|
| Hedged | 23 | 22 | 20 | 17 |
| Speculative | 49 | 41 | 40 | 36 |
| Ponzi | 28 | 38 | 40 | 47 |
| Total | 100 | 100 | 100 | 100 |

*Source*: Author's calculations based on INDEC.

Table A6.5: Rate of Growth of Investment Flows—INDEC 500 (1996–2001)

*(per cent)*

| | 1996 | 1997 | 1998 | 1999 | 2000 | 2001 |
|---|---|---|---|---|---|---|
| *Investment* (*) | | | | | | |
| Indec 500 | 3.5 | 12.6 | 6.4 | 5.1 | 3.9 | –0.4 |
| Tradable sector | 7.8 | 14.6 | 4.7 | –0.8 | 3.1 | 1.0 |
| Non-tradable sector | –1.4 | 10.1 | 8.7 | 12.4 | 4.8 | –1.9 |
| *Productive Investment* (**) | | | | | | |
| Indec 500 | –0.4 | 12.6 | 6.5 | 4.9 | 2.3 | –0.4 |
| Tradable sector | 5.7 | 15.5 | 3.8 | –1.2 | 2.1 | –0.1 |
| Non-tradable sector | –5.7 | 9.6 | 9.4 | 10.8 | 2.4 | -0.6 |

*Source*: Author's calculations based on INDEC.
*Notes*: (*) Annual rate of increase in firms' total assets;
(**) Annual rate of increase in firms' productive assets;

Table A6.6: Hedged, Speculative, and Ponzi Units, Tradable vis-à-vis Non-tradable Sector, INDEC 500 (1998–2001)

| | 1998 | | 1999 | | 2000 | | 2001 | |
|---|---|---|---|---|---|---|---|---|
| | Units | Per cent | Units | Per cent | Units | Per cent | Units | Per cent |
| Tradable sector | 304 | 100 | 292 | 100 | 294 | 100 | 297 | 100 |
| Hedged | 72 | 24 | 60 | 21 | 54 | 18 | 47 | 16 |
| Speculative | 138 | 45 | 122 | 42 | 116 | 39 | 110 | 37 |
| Ponzi | 94 | 31 | 110 | 38 | 124 | 42 | 140 | 47 |
| Non-tradable sector | 131 | 100 | 140 | 100 | 161 | 100 | 160 | 100 |
| Hedged | 26 | 20 | 34 | 24 | 38 | 24 | 32 | 20 |
| Speculative | 76 | 58 | 54 | 39 | 65 | 40 | 55 | 34 |
| Ponzi | 29 | 22 | 52 | 37 | 58 | 36 | 73 | 46 |

*Source*: Author's calculations based on INDEC.

Table A6.7: Hedged, Speculative, and Ponzi Units, Domestic vis-à-vis Foreign Firms, INDEC 500 (1998–2001)

| | 1998 | | 1999 | | 2000 | | 2001 | |
|---|---|---|---|---|---|---|---|---|
| | Units | Per cent | Units | Per cent | Units | Per cent | Units | Per cent |
| Domestic firms | 173 | 100 | 157 | 100 | 164 | 100 | 160 | 100 |
| Hedged | 39 | 23 | 40 | 25 | 35 | 21 | 27 | 17 |
| Speculative | 81 | 47 | 61 | 39 | 63 | 38 | 64 | 40 |
| Ponzi | 53 | 31 | 56 | 36 | 66 | 40 | 69 | 4 |
| Foreign firms | 262 | 100 | 275 | 100 | 291 | 100 | 297 | 100 |
| Hedged | 59 | 23 | 54 | 20 | 57 | 20 | 52 | 18 |
| Speculative | 133 | 51 | 115 | 42 | 118 | 41 | 101 | 34 |
| Ponzi | 70 | 27 | 106 | 39 | 116 | 40 | 144 | 48 |

*Source*: Author's calculations based on INDEC.

Table A6.8: Financial Positions before and after Dividend Payments, INDEC 500 (1998–2001)

(*per cent*)

| | 1998 | 1999 | 2000 | 2001 |
|---|---|---|---|---|
| Hedged units | | | | |
| *Before* Dividend Payments | 23 | 22 | 20 | 17 |
| *After* Dividend Payments | 18 | 18 | 16 | 15 |
| Speculative units | | | | |
| *Before* Dividend Payments | 49 | 41 | 40 | 36 |
| *After* Dividend Payments | 42 | 34 | 32 | 28 |
| Ponzi units | | | | |
| *Before* Dividend Payments | 28 | 38 | 40 | 47 |
| *After* Dividend Payments | 40 | 48 | 52 | 57 |

*Source*: Author's calculations based on INDEC.

Table A6.9: Hedged, Speculative, and Ponzi Units, Tradable vis-à-vis Non-tradable Sector Firms after Dividend Payments, INDEC 500 (1995–2001)

| | 1998 | | 1999 | | 2000 | | 2001 | |
|---|---|---|---|---|---|---|---|---|
| | Units | Per cent | Units | Per cent | Units | Per cent | Units | Per cent |
| Tradable sector | 305 | 100 | 293 | 100 | 295 | 100 | 298 | 100 |
| Hedged | 56 | 18 | 53 | 18 | 44 | 15 | 42 | 14 |
| Speculative | 119 | 39 | 101 | 34 | 86 | 29 | 83 | 28 |
| Ponzi | 130 | 43 | 139 | 47 | 165 | 56 | 173 | 58 |
| Non-tradable sector | 132 | 100 | 141 | 100 | 161 | 100 | 161 | 100 |
| Hedged | 22 | 17 | 27 | 19 | 29 | 18 | 26 | 16 |
| Speculative | 65 | 49 | 46 | 33 | 61 | 38 | 45 | 28 |
| Ponzi | 45 | 34 | 68 | 48 | 71 | 44 | 90 | 56 |

*Source*: Author's calculations based on INDEC.

Table A6.10: Hedged, Speculative, and Ponzi Units, Domestic vis-à-vis Foreign Firms after Dividend Payments, INDEC 500 (1998–2001)

| | 1998 | | 1999 | | 2000 | | 2001 | |
|---|---|---|---|---|---|---|---|---|
| | Units | Per cent | Units | Per cent | Units | Per cent | Units | Per cent |
| Domestic firms | 175 | 100 | 159 | 100 | 165 | 100 | 161 | 100 |
| Hedged | 31 | 18 | 35 | 22 | 27 | 16 | 26 | 16 |
| Speculative | 67 | 38 | 55 | 35 | 57 | 35 | 51 | 32 |
| Ponzi | 77 | 44 | 69 | 43 | 81 | 49 | 84 | 52 |
| Foreign firms | 262 | 100 | 275 | 100 | 291 | 100 | 298 | 100 |
| Hedged | 47 | 18 | 45 | 16 | 46 | 16 | 42 | 14 |
| Speculative | 117 | 45 | 92 | 33% | 90 | 31 | 77 | 26 |
| Ponzi | 98 | 37 | 138 | 50 | 155 | 53 | 179 | 60 |

*Source*: Author's calculations based on INDEC.

Table A6.11: Dividend Repatriation and Retention Rates

*(Million pesos/dollars and per cent)*

| | 1995 | 1996 | 1997 | 1998 | 1999 | 2000 | 2001 | 1995–2001 |
|---|---|---|---|---|---|---|---|---|
| Domestic firms | | | | | | | | |
| (1) Net Profits (*) | 3,700 | 3,861 | 3,746 | 2,032 | 703 | 268 | –99 | 14,212 |
| (2) Dividend payments | 1488 | 1817 | 1402 | 1506 | 893 | 787 | 804 | 8697 |
| (3) Dividend repatriation | 520 | 430 | 289 | 278 | 226 | 130 | 111 | 1985 |
| (4) Repatriation rate (**) | 14% | 11% | 8% | 14% | 32% | 48% | –113% | 14% |
| (5) Retention rate (***) | 60% | 53% | 63% | 26% | –27% | –193% | –715% | 39% |
| Foreign firms | | | | | | | | |
| (1) Net Profits (*) | 2873 | 3476 | 5751 | 3970 | 2531 | 3358 | 1405 | 23365 |
| (2) Total Dividends paid | 1155 | 1443 | 1762 | 1994 | 2295 | 2755 | 3802 | 15206 |
| (3) Dividend repatriation | 1069 | 1246 | 996 | 1445 | 1684 | 2115 | 3375 | 11929 |
| (4) Repatriation rate (**) | 37% | 36% | 17% | 36% | 67% | 63% | 240% | 51% |
| (5) Retention rate (***) | 60% | 58% | 69% | 50% | 9% | 18% | –171% | 35% |

*Source*: Author's calculations based on INDEC.
*Notes*: (*) Profits after interest and tax payments;
(**) Repatriation rate = (3)/(1);
(***) Retention rate = [(1)—(2)]/(1).

# Appendix A8.1
# Results of the VAR model

Table A8.1.1: Testing for Pro-cyclical Monetary Policy (BRAZIL 1999–2005)

*(VAR regression output—controls: changes in oil prices and in US interest rates)*

| | RIR (1) | RIR (2) | RIR (3) |
|---|---|---|---|
| RIR(–1) | 0.7132 | 0.7108 | 0.8915 |
| | (35.0636) | (35.2276) | (25.1841) |
| DGDP(–1) | –0.1520 P* | –0.1459 P* | –0.1089 P |
| | (–2.3355) | (–2.25470) | (–0.78139) |
| C | 2.9908 | 2.9900 | 1.0899 |
| | (12.4857) | (12.4894) | (2.29614) |
| D_OIL(–1) | –0.0063 | –0.0029 | |
| | (–0.50028) | (–0.24378) | – |
| D_OIL(–2) | –0.0266 | –0.0235 | |
| | (–2.15834) | (–1.97780) | – |
| D(US_INTEREST) | 0.4767 | – | – |
| | (0.95941) | | |
| R-squared | 0.9539 | 0.9533 | 0.8981 |

*Notes*: P stands for pro-cyclical; C for countercyclical; * indicates significance at 10 per cent (at least); t-statistics are in parentheses; Data in all tables A8.1.1–A8.1.6 are monthly data.

Table A8.1.2: Testing for Asymmetrical Monetary Policy (BRAZIL 1999–2005)

*(VAR regression output—controls: changes in oil prices and in US interest rates)*

| | RIR (1) | RIR (2) | RIR (3) |
|---|---|---|---|
| RIR(–1) | 0.7175 | 0.7138 | 0.8919 |
| | ( 35.1660) | (35.2287) | (24.8457) |
| DGDP_GOOD(–1) | –0.0651 P | –0.0729 P | –0.0963 P |
| | (–0.7368) | (–0.8235) | (–0.4721) |
| DGDP_BAD(–1) | –0.2440 P* | –0.2201 P* | –0.1200 P |
| | (–2.6845) | (–2.4683) | (–0.6284) |
| C | 2.9378 | 2.9461 | 1.0837 |
| | (12.2159) | (12.2058) | (2.2419) |
| D_OIL(–1) | –0.0082 | –0.0036 | – |
| | (–0.6492) | (–0.2996) | |
| D_OIL(–2) | –0.0274 | –0.0234 | – |
| | (–2.2438) | (–1.9781) | |
| D(US_INTEREST) | 0.6250 | – | – |
| | (1.2411) | | |
| R-squared | 0.9553 | 0.9543 | 0.8980 |

Table A8.1.3: Testing for Pro-cyclical Monetary Policy (CHILE 1999–2005)

*(VAR regression output—controls: changes in oil prices and in US interest rates)*

| | RIR (1) | RIR (2) | RIR (3) |
|---|---|---|---|
| RIR(–1) | 0.9120 | 0.9132 | 0.8934 |
| | (20.2103) | (20.2975) | (20.1444) |
| DGDP(–1) | –0.0868 P | –0.0947 P | –0.0768 P |
| | (–1.1683) | (–1.28935) | (–1.02503) |
| C | 0.1116 | 0.1221 | 0.1038 |
| | (1.3237) | (1.47088) | (1.23120) |
| D_OIL(–1) | –0.0144 | –0.0160 | – |
| | (–1.9855) | (–2.28576) | |
| D(US_INTEREST) | –0.2338 | – | – |
| | (–0.7978) | | |
| R-squared | 0.8569 | 0.8556 | 0.8504 |

Table A8.1.4: Testing for Asymmetrical Monetary Policy (CHILE 1999–2005)

*(VAR regression output—controls: changes in oil prices and in US interest rates)*

| | RIR (1) | RIR (2) | RIR (3) |
|---|---|---|---|
| RIR(–1) | 0.9148 | 0.9159 | 0.8954 |
| | (20.3262) | (20.3939) | (20.1696) |
| DGDP_GOOD(–1) | 0.0270 C | 0.0137 C | 0.0169 C |
| | (0.2292) | (0.1174) | (0.1409) |
| DGDP_BAD(–1) | –0.1482 P* | –0.1542 P* | –0.1275 P |
| | (–1.6656) | (–1.7417) | (–1.4104) |
| C | 0.0928 | 0.1050 | 0.0883 |
| | (1.0875) | (1.2504) | (1.0304) |
| D_OIL(–1) | –0.0149 | –0.0166 | – |
| | (–2.0579) | (–2.3733) | |
| D(US_INTEREST) | –0.2552 | – | – |
| | (0.8729) | | |
| R-squared | 0.8601 | 0.8585 | 0.8525 |

Table A8.1.5: Testing for Pro-cyclical Monetary Policy (MEXICO 1999–2005)

*(VAR regression output—controls: changes in oil prices and in US interest rates)*

| | RIR (1) | RIR (2) | RIR (3) |
|---|---|---|---|
| RIR(–1) | 0.9261 | 0.9122 | 0.8245 |
| | (17.7921) | (18.0814) | (17.2164) |
| DGDP(–1) | 0.1256 C | 0.1583 C | 0.1095 C |
| | (0.8063) | (1.0355) | (0.6633) |
| C | 0.2986 | 0.3126 | 0.6062 |
| | (1.2300) | (1.2881) | (2.5088) |
| D_OIL(–1) | –0.0102 | –0.0067 | – |
| | (–0.6892) | (–0.4660) | |
| D_OIL(–2) | 0.0028 | 0.0069 | – |
| | (0.1855) | (0.4786) | |
| D(US_INTEREST) | 0.6979 | – | – |
| | (1.0691) | | |
| R-squared | 0.8320 | 0.8291 | 0.8046 |

Table A8.1.6: Testing for Asymmetrical Monetary Policy (MEXICO 1999–2005)

*(VAR regression output—controls: changes in oil prices and in US interest rates)*

| | RIR (1) | RIR (2) | RIR (3) |
|---|---|---|---|
| RIR(–1) | 0.9171 | 0.9040 | 0.8162 |
| | (17.4519) | (17.8346) | (16.8762) |
| DGDP_GOOD(–1) | 0.2544 C | 0.2942 C | 0.2461 C |
| | (1.3217) | (1.5668) | (1.2028) |
| DGDP_BAD(–1) | –0.0910 P | –0.0803 P | –0.1247 P |
| | (–0.3698) | (–0.3269) | (–0.4699) |
| C | 0.3303 | 0.3453 | 0.6430 |
| | (1.3545) | (1.4201) | (2.6417) |
| D_OIL(–1) | –0.0084 | –0.0052 | – |
| | (–0.5646) | (–0.35778) | |
| D_OIL(–2) | 0.0036 | 0.0073 | – |
| | (0.2441) | (0.5128) | |
| D(US_INTEREST) | 0.6234 | – | – |
| | (0.9522) | | |
| R-squared | 0.8352 | 0.8330 | 0.8080 |

# Appendix A8.2
# Impulse Response Functions

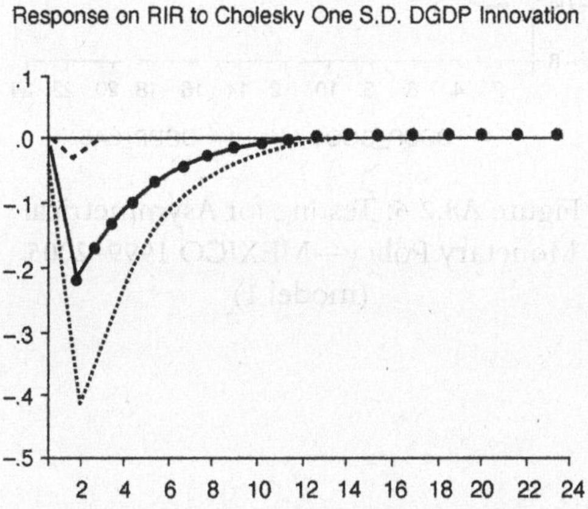


Figure A8.2.1: Testing for Pro-cyclical Monetary Policy—BRAZIL 1999–2005 (model 1)

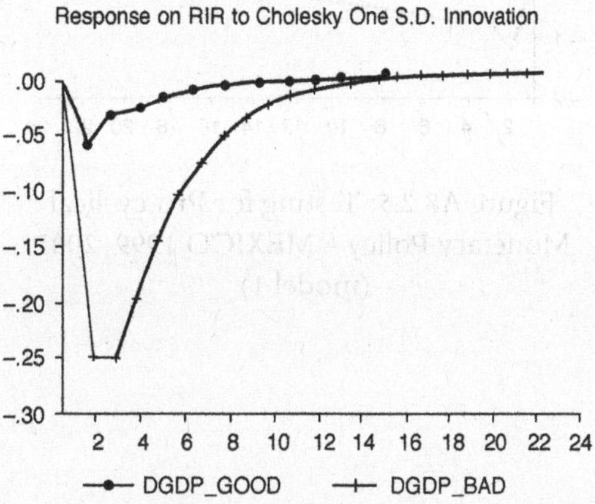


Figure A8.2.2: Testing for Asymmetrical Monetary Policy—BRAZIL 1999–2005 (model 1)

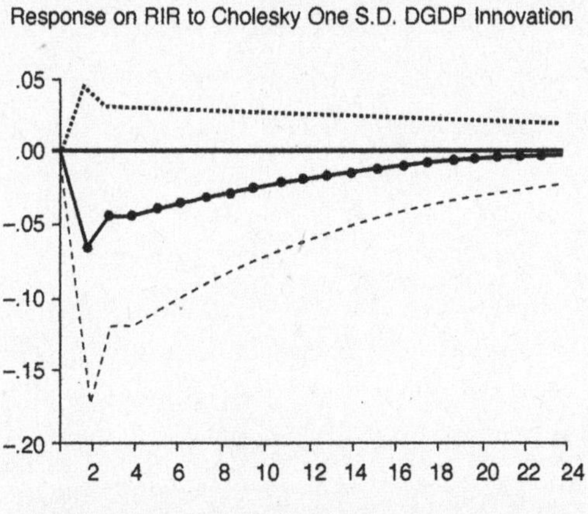


Figure A8.2.3: Testing for Pro-cyclical Monetary Policy—CHILE 1999–2005 (model 1)

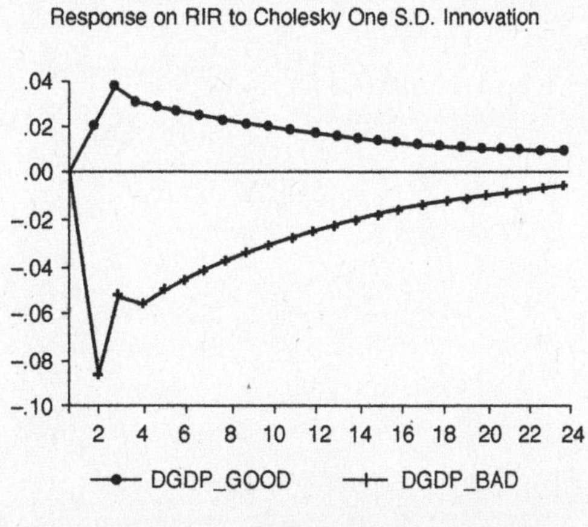


Figure A8.2.4: Testing for Asymmetrical Monetary Policy—CHILE 1999–2005 (model 1)

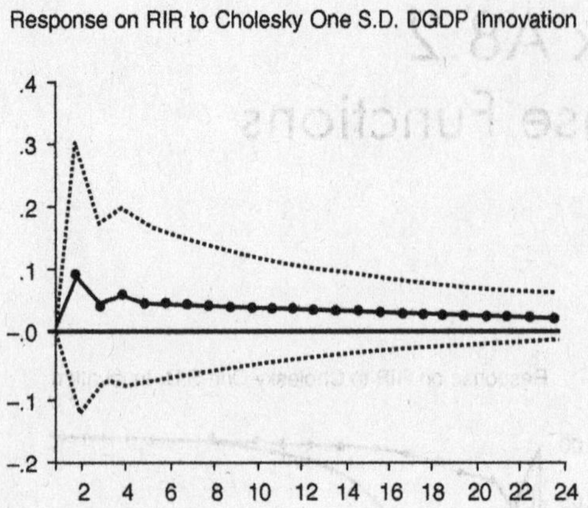


Figure A8.2.5: Testing for Pro-cyclical Monetary Policy—MEXICO 1999–2005 (model 1)

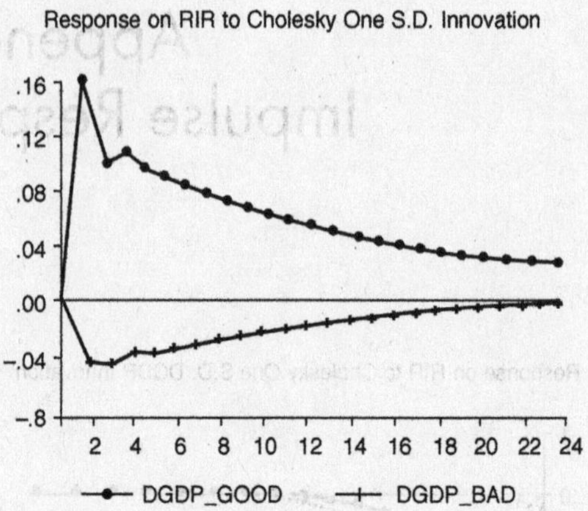


Figure A8.2.6: Testing for Asymmetrical Monetary Policy—MEXICO 1999–2005 (model 1)

# Appendix A10.1
# List of Industries

Cluster 1 Lowest wage

322 Manufacture of wearing apparel, except footwear

323 Manufacture of leather and products of leather, leather substitutes and fur, except footwear and wearing apparel

332 Manufacture of furniture and fixtures, except primarily of metal

Cluster 2 Low wage

321 Manufacture of textiles

324 Manufacture of footwear, except vulcanized or moulded rubber or plastic footwear

331 Manufacture of wood and wood and cork products, except furniture

356 Manufacture of plastic products not elsewhere classified

361 Manufacture of pottery, china, and earthenware

381 Manufacture of fabricated metal products, except machinery and equipment

385 Manufacture of professional and scientific, and measuring and controlling goods equipment not elsewhere classified, and of photographic and optical

390 Other manufacturing industries

Cluster 3 Average wage

311 Food manufacturing

312 Food manufacturing (not elsewhere classified and prepared animal feeds)

314 Tobacco manufactures

369 Manufacture of other non-metallic mineral products

Cluster 4 High wage

313 Beverage industries

341 Manufacture of paper and paper products

342 Printing, publishing, and allied industries

351 Manufacture of industrial chemicals

352 Manufacture of other chemical products

353 Petroleum refineries

354 Manufacture of miscellaneous products of petroleum and coal

355 Manufacture of rubber products

| | |
|---|---|
| 362 | Manufacture of glass and glass products |
| 371 | Iron and steel basic industries |
| 372 | Non-ferrous metal basic industries |
| 382 | Manufacture of machinery except electrical |
| 383 | Manufacture of electrical machinery apparatus, appliances, and supplies |
| 384 | Manufacture of transport equipment |

*Source*: OECD Stan Database: http: / / unstats.un.org / unsd / cr / registry / regest.asp? C1=2.

# Appendix A10.2

## A10.2.1: Cluster Shares in Value Added in Total Manufacturing

*(per cent)*

| | 1980 | 1981 | 1982 | 1983 | 1984 | 1985 | 1986 | 1987 | 1988 | 1989 | 1990 | 1991 | 1992 | 1993 | 1994 | 1995 | 1996 | 1997 | 1998 | 1999 | 2000 |
|---|---|---|---|---|---|---|---|---|---|---|---|---|---|---|---|---|---|---|---|---|---|
| Cluster 1 | 0.9 | 1.4 | 1.4 | 2.1 | 2.5 | 2.6 | 2.1 | 3.3 | 3.6 | 3.9 | 3.9 | 3.9 | 4.5 | 4.5 | 4.9 | 5.2 | 5.8 | 4.9 | 4.4 | 4.1 | 4.2 |
| Cluster 2 | 21.5 | 18.0 | 18.3 | 19.0 | 19.9 | 19.2 | 17.1 | 21.0 | 18.4 | 17.8 | 18.7 | 17.9 | 18.6 | 17.8 | 19.9 | 19.6 | 19.7 | 20.8 | 22.1 | 20.8 | 22.0 |
| Cluster 3 | 20.3 | 20.9 | 23.5 | 20.2 | 21.3 | 21.9 | 18.5 | 18.9 | 18.3 | 18.1 | 17.8 | 19.7 | 18.9 | 18.9 | 16.9 | 17.3 | 17.4 | 14.9 | 16.8 | 18.3 | 17.7 |
| Cluster 4 | 57.3 | 59.7 | 56.7 | 38.7 | 42.0 | 56.3 | 62.3 | 56.8 | 59.7 | 60.2 | 59.6 | 58.6 | 58.0 | 58.8 | 58.2 | 57.9 | 57.2 | 59.3 | 56.7 | 56.7 | 56.1 |

*Source:* Own calculations based on AMIS Database http://www.die.gov.tr/konularr/iy sanayi.htm.

## A10.2.2 Cluster Shares in Number of Hours Worked in Total Manufacturing

*(per cent)*

| | 1980 | 1981 | 1982 | 1983 | 1984 | 1985 | 1986 | 1987 | 1988 | 1989 | 1991 | 1992 | 1993 | 1994 | 1995 | 1996 | 1997 | 1998 | 1999 | 2000 |
|---|---|---|---|---|---|---|---|---|---|---|---|---|---|---|---|---|---|---|---|---|
| Cluster 1 | 2.7 | 3.1 | 4.2 | 4.2 | 4.3 | 5.8 | 5.7 | 6.9 | 8.4 | 9.4 | 9.7 | 11.1 | 11.6 | 12.3 | 13.6 | 14.3 | 11.6 | 11.3 | 11.3 | 11.3 |
| Cluster 2 | 31.8 | 35.5 | 31.6 | 33.9 | 34.1 | 33.3 | 33.1 | 32.8 | 32.8 | 32.4 | 31.7 | 32.4 | 33.2 | 33.2 | 34.4 | 36.2 | 39.4 | 39.5 | 38.8 | 39.7 |
| Cluster 3 | 28.7 | 25.6 | 25.9 | 24.2 | 24.2 | 23.2 | 22.4 | 21.7 | 21.1 | 21.6 | 20.6 | 20.3 | 19.5 | 20.2 | 19.3 | 18.4 | 17.5 | 17.4 | 18.7 | 17.9 |
| Cluster 4 | 36.8 | 35.8 | 38.3 | 36.8 | 36.6 | 37.7 | 38.8 | 38.6 | 37.7 | 36.6 | 38.0 | 36.2 | 35.7 | 34.3 | 32.8 | 31.2 | 31.5 | 31.7 | 31.2 | 31.1 |

*Source:* Own calculations based on AMIS Database http://www.die.gov.tr/konularr/iy sanayi.htm.

## A10.2.3: Manufacturing Share of Employment in Total Employment and Contribution of Manufacturing Sector to GNP

*(per cent)*

| | 1980 | 1981 | 1982 | 1983 | 1984 | 1985 | 1986 | 1987 | 1988 | 1989 | 1990 | 1991 | 1992 | 1993 | 1994 | 1995 | 1996 | 1997 | 1998 | 1999 | 2000 |
|---|---|---|---|---|---|---|---|---|---|---|---|---|---|---|---|---|---|---|---|---|---|
| Whole Manufacturing Share in Total Employment | – | – | – | – | – | – | – | – | 14.4 | 14.5 | 14.2 | 14.1 | 15.1 | 14.6 | 15.1 | 14.9 | 15.5 | 16.5 | 16.2 | 15.8 | 17.3 |
| Whole Manufacturing Share in GNP | 17.1 | 19.4 | 20 | 19.1 | 18.1 | 18.3 | 22.2 | 21.8 | 23 | 23.1 | 22 | 22.2 | 21.6 | 20.8 | 22.1 | 22.6 | 21.1 | 21.6 | 19.4 | 19.2 | 19.2 |

*Source*: State Planning Organization, Main Economic Indicators.

## A10.2.4: The Ratio of Private Sector Wage to Public Sector Wage Payments

*(per cent)*

| | 1980 | 1981 | 1982 | 1983 | 1984 | 1985 | 1986 | 1987 | 1988 | 1989 | 1990 | 1991 | 1992 | 1993 | 1994 | 1995 | 1995 |
|---|---|---|---|---|---|---|---|---|---|---|---|---|---|---|---|---|---|
| Cluster 1 | 33.8 | 70.8 | 46.5 | 63.3 | 56.9 | 41.5 | 54.7 | 68.3 | 53.7 | 61.8 | 42.9 | 4.2 | 37.4 | 36.9 | 27.1 | 28.7 | 46.1 |
| Cluster 2 | 70.2 | 66.9 | 60.2 | 76.3 | 84.1 | 84.2 | 88.0 | 81.0 | 75.1 | 63.0 | 65.7 | 61.2 | 51.4 | 50.1 | 43.5 | 46.8 | 55.3 |
| Cluster 3 | 73.2 | 62.2 | 74.7 | 65.4 | 82.3 | 79.9 | 82.9 | 79.7 | 89.0 | 61.1 | 70.4 | 53.5 | 47.4 | 48.5 | 44.6 | 49.0 | 56.7 |
| Cluster 4 | 63.8 | 61.2 | 63.3 | 75.6 | 81.6 | 86.4 | 94.8 | 97.7 | 99.1 | 78.3 | 83.7 | 71.1 | 67.6 | 63.3 | 59.4 | 77.1 | 77.3 |

*Source:* Own calculations based on AMIS Database http: / / www.die.gov.tr / konularr / iy sanayi.htm.

*Note*: Calculations are done by obtaining the percentage ratio of private sector hourly wages to public sector hourly wages for each cluster in each year.

## A10.2.5a: Correlations between Wage and Productivity Deviance Summary Table for 1980s

| | Clusters | Wage Deviations 1 | 2 | 3 | 4 | Productivity Deviation 1 | 2 | 3 | 4 |
|---|---|---|---|---|---|---|---|---|---|
| Wage Deviations | 1 | 1.00 | | | | | | | |
| | 2 | 0.44 | 1.00 | | | | | | |
| | 3 | 0.29 | –0.07 | 1.00 | | | | | |
| | 4 | –0.42 | –0.58 | –0.50 | 1.00 | | | | |
| Productivity Deviations | 1 | 0.42 | –0.03 | 0.56 | –.35 | 1.00 | | | |
| | 2 | –0.17 | –0.13 | –0.54 | 0.18 | –0.07 | 1.00 | | |
| | 3 | 0.16 | 0.65 | 0.49 | –0.57 | 0.36 | –0.28 | 1.00 | |
| | 4 | –0.06 | –0.24 | –0.18 | 0.64 | –0.44 | –0.50 | –0.40 | 1.00 |

## A10.2.5b. Summary Table for 1990s

| | Clusters | Wage Deviations 1 | 2 | 3 | 4 | Productivity Deviation 1 | 2 | 3 | 4 |
|---|---|---|---|---|---|---|---|---|---|
| Wage Deviations | 1 | 1.00 | | | | | | | |
| | 2 | 0.07 | 1.00 | | | | | | |
| | 3 | 0.04 | –0.85 | 1.00 | | | | | |
| | 4 | 0.57 | –0.54 | 0.34 | 1.00 | | | | |
| Productivity Deviations | 1 | 0.00 | 0.42 | –0.29 | –0.44 | 1.00 | | | |
| | 2 | –0.49 | –0.24 | –0.08 | 0.24 | –0.13 | 1.00 | | |
| | 3 | 0.03 | 0.02 | 0.08 | 0.13 | –0.67 | –0.42 | 1.00 | |
| | 4 | 0.75 | –0.32 | 0.26 | 0.91 | –0.21 | –0.46 | –0.08 | 1.00 |

*Source:* Own calculations based on AMIS Database http://www.die.gov.tr/konularr/iy sanayi.htm.

## A10.2.6: Share of Public Sector in Total Industry by Clusters

*(per cent)*

| | Cluster 1 | Cluster 2 | Cluster 3 | Cluster 4 |
|---|---|---|---|---|
| 1980 | 0.9 | 13.7 | 44.6 | 49.8 |
| 1981 | 6.8 | 12.6 | 50.5 | 55.4 |
| 1982 | 1.8 | 12.6 | 57.6 | 49.0 |
| 1983 | 1.9 | 12.6 | 51.2 | 62.5 |
| 1984 | 0.5 | 13.3 | 46.8 | 51.9 |
| 1985 | 12.2 | 10.7 | 50.7 | 43.6 |
| 1986 | 2.2 | 12.7 | 48.0 | 46.0 |
| 1987 | 2.3 | 10.4 | 42.5 | 37.0 |
| 1988 | 1.7 | 9.3 | 41.4 | 41.3 |
| 1989 | 1.6 | 9.0 | 37.7 | 44.2 |
| 1990 | 1.1 | 8.2 | 37.5 | 38.6 |
| 1991 | 1.7 | 7.3 | 39.8 | 37.9 |

*(contd...)*

*(Table Appendix 10.2.6 continued)*

| | Cluster 1 | Cluster 2 | Cluster 3 | Cluster 4 |
|---|---|---|---|---|
| 1992 | 1.2 | 7.2 | 36.4 | 36.1 |
| 1993 | 2.7 | 6.9 | 29.3 | 31.9 |
| 1994 | 2.7 | 4.7 | 21.4 | 33.9 |
| 1995 | 2.4 | 3.6 | 17.8 | 35.4 |
| 1996 | 0.7 | 4.4 | 12.6 | 35.8 |
| 1997 | 0.6 | 3.3 | 9.5 | 34.8 |
| 1998 | 0.6 | 2.7 | 14.2 | 37.1 |
| 1999 | 0.1 | 2.7 | 18.3 | 31.8 |
| 2000 | 0.4 | 1.7 | 21.7 | 25.5 |

*Source:* Own calculations based on AMIS Database http://www.die.gov.tr/konularr/iy sanayi.htm.

*Note:* Calculations are done by dividing the total public sector value added by the total value added produced for sub-industries within the clusters, for each year.

## A10.2.7: Ratio of Private Sector to Public Sector in Annual Number of Hours Worked by Clusters

*(per cent)*

| | Cluster 1 | Cluster 2 | Cluster 3 | Cluster 4 |
|---|---|---|---|---|
| 1980 | 1.2 | 16.9 | 55.1 | 39.2 |
| 1981 | 2.4 | 14.2 | 50.8 | 36.2 |
| 1982 | 1.1 | 14.6 | 50.6 | 33.5 |
| 1983 | 1.5 | 16.5 | 49.3 | 35.4 |
| 1984 | 0.6 | 16.4 | 48.8 | 34.7 |
| 1985 | 0.6 | 14.6 | 43.7 | 33.6 |
| 1986 | 1.7 | 16.3 | 41.7 | 33.7 |
| 1987 | 1.5 | 15.5 | 39.5 | 33.2 |
| 1988 | 2.9 | 14.5 | 38.2 | 31.8 |
| 1989 | 2.9 | 13.4 | 34.1 | 30.8 |
| 1990 | 2.7 | 13.0 | 35.0 | 30.5 |
| 1991 | 2.9 | 14.2 | 34.9 | 30.2 |
| 1992 | 2.1 | 12.0 | 33.3 | 28.4 |
| 1993 | 2.9 | 10.9 | 31.4 | 25.9 |
| 1994 | 4.9 | 9.8 | 30.8 | 27.2 |
| 1995 | 3.2 | 7.3 | 26.0 | 23.0 |
| 1996 | 1.7 | 6.3 | 22.5 | 20.4 |
| 1997 | 1.3 | 4.2 | 20.8 | 17.0 |
| 1998 | 1.2 | 3.2 | 20.5 | 16.1 |
| 1999 | 1.3 | 3.4 | 19.5 | 15.8 |
| 2000 | 1.5 | 2.5 | 18.7 | 14.2 |

*Source:* Own calculations based on AMIS Database http://www.die.gov.tr/konularr/iy sanayi.htm.

*Note:* Total annual number of hours worked in the private sector is divided by total number of hours worked in public sector in each cluster.

# Appendix A11

Table A11.1.1: Descriptive Statistics of Explanatory Variables

| | All | Non-participant | Self-employed | Temporary employee | Permanent employee |
|---|---|---|---|---|---|
| No. obs. | 13,896 | 12,362 | 182 | 367 | 985 |
| (%) | (100) | (89) | (1.3) | (2.6) | (7.1) |
| exper | 25 | 25 | 25 | 26 | 18 |
| | (10) | (10) | (9) | (8) | (8) |
| exper$^2$ | 705 | 729 | 698 | 713 | 404 |
| | (501) | (508) | (446) | (397) | (334) |
| no diploma (%) | 18 | 19 | 18 | 20 | 3 |
| element (%) | 54 | 56 | 45 | 68 | 22 |
| middle (%) | 8 | 9 | 8 | 5 | 6 |
| high (%) | 14 | 14 | 16 | 4 | 25 |
| univ (%) | 6 | 3 | 13 | 2 | 45 |
| nwinc | –0.48 | –0.48 | –0.55 | –0.92 | –0.36 |
| | (0.68) | (0.65) | (1.55) | (0.70) | (0.72) |
| kidun6 | 0.4 | 0.4 | 0.4 | 0.3 | 0.3 |
| | (0.7) | (0.7) | (0.7) | (0.5) | (0.5) |
| kidov6 | 1.2 | 1.2 | 1.6 | 1.6 | 1.0 |
| | (1.3) | (1.3) | (1.4) | (1.2) | (1.0) |
| unemp (%) | 3.4 | 3.2 | 1.1 | 7.6 | 4.3 |
| duration | 2.7 | 2.7 | 2.6 | 3.2 | 1.7 |
| | (4.7) | (4.8) | (4.6) | (4.7) | (3.9) |
| r_ist (%) | 14 | 14 | 8 | 11 | 16 |
| r_mar (%) | 15 | 15 | 14 | 18 | 20 |
| r_age (%) | 14 | 14 | 15 | 22 | 18 |
| r_cnt (%) | 17 | 18 | 14 | 18 | 14 |

*(contd...)*

*(Table Appendix A11.1 continued)*

| | All | Non-participant | Self-employed | Temporary employee | Permanent employee |
|---|---|---|---|---|---|
| r_md t(%) | 13 | 13 | 16 | 15 | 11 |
| r_blc (%) | 11 | 11 | 18 | 9 | 11 |
| r_est (%) | 7 | 7 | 8 | 4 | 6 |
| r_ste (%) | 9 | 10 | 6 | 3 | 4 |
| $pearn_s$ | 1.09 | 1.01 | 1.21 | 1.05 | 2.09 |
| | (0.74) | (0.65) | (0.96) | (0.57) | (1.02) |
| $pearn_t$ | 0.18 | 0.14 | 0.23 | 0.18 | 0.58 |
| | (0.43) | (0.39) | (0.52) | (0.34) | (0.67) |
| $pearn_p$ | 0.61 | 0.57 | 0.71 | 0.44 | 1.13 |
| | (0.40) | (0.36) | (0.51) | (0.30) | (0.53) |

*Note:* Sample means and standard deviations (in parentheses) of continuous variables, percentage distributions of dummy variables.

Table A11.1.2: Estimation Results of the Reduced Form Participation Equation

| | Non-participant | Self-employed | | Temporary employee | | Permanent employee | |
|---|---|---|---|---|---|---|---|
| | M | C | M | C | M | C | M |
| constant | 0.28 | –6.66** | –0.07 | –5.39** | –0.09 | –4.28** | –0.12 |
| | | (0.67) | | (0.57) | | (0.31) | |
| exper | –0.0068 | 0.0847** | 0.0009 | 0.1618** | 0.0027 | 0.1157** | 0.0032 |
| | | (0.0458) | | (0.0426) | | (0.0223) | |
| $exper^2$ | 0.00017 | –0.0013 | –0.00001 | –0.0036** | –0.00006 | –0.0036** | –0.00010 |
| | | (0.0009) | | (0.0008) | | (0.0005) | |
| element | –0.012 | –0.052 | –0.001 | –0.138 | –0.003 | 0.530** | 0.01 |
| | | (0.234) | | (0.147) | | (0.213) | |
| middle | –0.019 | 0.320 | 0.003 | –0.622** | –0.011 | 0.932** | 0.027 |
| | | (0.354) | | (0.269) | | (0.249) | |
| high | –0.048 | 0.833** | 0.009 | –1.109** | –0.021 | 2.068** | 0.059 |
| | | (0.315) | | (0.306) | | (0.223) | |
| univ | –0.157 | 2.465** | 0.026 | 0.224 | 0.001 | 4.570** | 0.130 |
| | | (0.346) | | (0.398) | | (0.232) | |
| nwinc | 0.040 | –0.491** | –0.005 | –0.900** | –0.015 | –0.696** | –0.019 |
| | | (0.129) | | (0.083) | | (0.065) | |
| kidun6 | 0.031 | –0.019 | 0.0002 | –0.667** | –0.011 | –0.692** | –0.019 |
| | | (0.142) | | (0.121) | | (0.079) | |
| kidov6 | –0.001 | 0.262** | 0.003 | 0.097* | 0.002 | –0.107** | –0.003 |
| | | (0.069) | | (0.052) | | (0.047) | |
| unemp | –0.007 | –1.257* | –0.015 | 0.351 | 0.006 | 0.531** | 0.015 |
| | | (0.726) | | (0.232) | | (0.213) | |
| duration | 0.0008 | 0.0010 | 0.00002 | 0.0059 | 0.0001 | –0.0310** | –0.0009 |
| | | (0.0190) | | (0.0133) | | (0.0117) | |
| r_mar | –0.017 | 0.501 | 0.006 | 0.269 | 0.004 | 0.240* | 0.007 |
| | | (0.329) | | (0.205) | | (0.133) | |
| r_age | –0.010 | 0.510 | 0.006 | 0.426** | 0.007 | –0.086 | –0.003 |
| | | (0.325) | | (0.199) | | (0.137) | |
| r_cnt | 0.016 | 0.104 | 0.001 | 0.023 | 0.001 | –0.643** | –0.018 |
| | | (0.331) | | (0.205) | | (0.143) | |
| r_mdt | –0.002 | 0.632** | 0.007 | 0.120 | 0.002 | –0.252* | –0.007 |
| | | (0.321) | | (0.212) | | (0.149) | |

*(contd...)*

*(Table Appendix A11.1.2 continued)*

| | Non-participant | Self-employed | | Temporary employee | | Permanent employee | |
|---|---|---|---|---|---|---|---|
| | M | C | M | C | M | C | M |
| r_blc | 0.001 | 0.850** | 0.010 | –0.219 | –0.004 | –0.228 | –0.007 |
| | | (0.319) | | (0.240) | | (0.152) | |
| r_est | 0.008 | 0.496 | 0.006 | –0.476 | –0.008 | –0.209 | –0.006 |
| | | (0.378) | | (0.312) | | (0.189) | |
| r_ste | 0.058 | –0.426 | –0.004 | –1.573** | –0.027 | –0.977** | –0.027 |
| | | (0.426) | | (0.369) | | (0.224) | |
| Number of observations | 13,896 | | | | | | |
| Log likelihood | –4891.1 | | | | | | |
| Chi-square | 2569.2 | | | | | | |

*Notes:* C and M denote coefficients and marginal effects of the explanatory variables respectively; Standard errors in parentheses; *statistically significant at 10 per cent, **at 5 per cent level. Significance levels of the marginal effects are similar to those of the coefficients;
Istanbul area and nodiploma are base categories for relevant dummies.

Table A11.1.3: Estimation Results of the Earnings Equations Corrected for Selectivity Bias

| Dependent Variable: ln(hourly earnings) | Self-employed | Temporary employee | Permanent employee |
|---|---|---|---|
| constant | 3.38* | –0.43 | –1.86** |
| | (2.00) | (0.69) | (0.28) |
| exper | –0.029 | 0.023 | 0.062** |
| | (0.047) | (0.038) | (0.011) |
| $exper^2$ | 0.0007 | –0.0007 | –0.0015** |
| | (0.0009) | (0.0007) | (0.0003) |
| element | 0.29 | 0.14 | 0.36** |
| | (0.25) | (0.12) | (0.10) |
| middle | 0.45 | 0.03 | 0.53** |
| | (0.38) | (0.23) | (0.12) |
| high | 0.77** | –0.47 | 1.43** |
| | (0.36) | (0.29) | (0.12) |

*(contd...)*

*(Table Appendix A11.1.3 continued)*

| Dependent Variable: ln(hourly earnings) | Self-employed | Temporary employee | Permanent employee |
|---|---|---|---|
| univ | 2.31** | 0.95** | 2.71** |
| | (0.46) | (0.34) | (0.20) |
| kidun6 | −0.09 | −0.29** | −0.16** |
| | (0.13) | (0.11) | (0.05) |
| kidov6 | 0.03 | 0.04 | −0.04** |
| | (0.10) | (0.05) | (0.02) |
| r_mar | −0.31 | −0.32* | 0.01 |
| | (0.35) | (0.17) | (0.06) |
| r_age | −0.72** | −0.52** | −0.12** |
| | (0.34) | (0.17) | (0.06) |
| r_cnt | −0.44 | −0.06 | −0.26** |
| | (0.33) | (0.17) | (0.07) |
| r_mdt | −0.93** | −0.37** | −0.26** |
| | (0.35) | (0.17) | (0.07) |
| r_blc | −1.50** | −0.28 | −0.23** |
| | (0.37) | (0.20) | (0.07) |
| r_est | −1.52** | −0.81** | −0.10 |
| | (0.40) | (0.26) | (0.09) |
| r_ste | −0.97** | −0.85** | −0.35** |
| | (0.48) | (0.32) | (0.11) |
| λ | −0.68 | 0.36* | 0.75** |
| | (0.56) | (0.20) | (0.11) |
| N | 182 | 367 | 985 |
| $R^2$ | 0.49 | 0.14 | 0.48 |
| F | 9.74 | 3.61 | 55.39 |

*Notes*: As for Table A11.1.2.

Table A11.1.4: Estimation Results of the Participation Equation with Predicted Wages

| | Non-participant | Self-employed | | Temporary employee | | Permanent employee | |
|---|---|---|---|---|---|---|---|
| | M | C | M | C | M | C | M |
| constant | 0.42 | -5.69** | -0.07 | -4.51** | -0.12 | -3.46** | -0.23 |
| | | (0.30) | | (0.21) | | (0.12) | |
| pearn | -0.017 | 0.062** | 0.001 | 0.088** | 0.002 | 0.217** | 0.014 |
| | | (0.007) | | (0.032) | | (0.006) | |
| nwinc | 0.076 | -0.449** | -0.006 | -1.028** | -0.026 | -0.671** | -0.044 |
| | | (0.126) | | (0.084) | | (0.063) | |
| kidun6 | 0.035 | -0.055 | -0.001 | -0.562** | -0.014 | -0.301** | -0.020 |
| | | (0.126) | | (0.110) | | (0.069) | |
| kidov6 | -0.001 | 0.186** | 0.002 | 0.229** | 0.006 | -0.118** | -0.008 |
| | | (0.06) | | (0.04) | | (0.04) | |
| unemp | -0.058 | -1.233* | -0.016 | 0.439* | 0.011 | 0.949** | 0.063 |
| | | (0.725) | | (0.231) | | (0.199) | |
| duration | 0.0057 | -0.0011 | -0.00001 | -0.0109 | -0.0003 | -0.0826** | -0.0054 |
| | | (0.0172) | | (0.0122) | | (0.0103) | |
| r_mar | -0.0446 | 0.2015 | 0.0026 | 0.3213 | 0.0083 | 0.5129** | 0.0338 |
| | | (0.3298) | | (0.2069) | | (0.1303) | |
| r_age | -0.0478 | 0.8139** | 0.0105 | 0.5202** | 0.0134 | 0.3637** | 0.0240 |
| | | (0.3254) | | (0.2017) | | (0.1350) | |
| r_cnt | 0.0518 | 0.0994 | 0.0013 | -0.0375 | -0.0010 | -0.7910** | -0.0521 |
| | | (0.3308) | | (0.2048) | | (0.1417) | |
| r_mdt | -0.0145 | 0.8683** | 0.0112 | 0.1668 | 0.0043 | -0.0157 | -0.0010 |
| | | (0.3210) | | (0.2131) | | (0.1462) | |
| r_blc | -0.0002 | 1.3547** | 0.0175 | -0.2257 | -0.0058 | -0.1742 | -0.0115 |
| | | (0.3211) | | (0.2403) | | (0.1495) | |
| r_est | 0.0004 | 1.1265** | 0.0146 | -0.4433 | -0.0114 | -0.0542 | -0.0036 |
| | | (0.3770) | | (0.3117) | | (0.1828) | |
| r_ste | 0.0976 | 0.1260 | 0.0016 | -1.5220** | -0.0391 | -0.9129** | -0.0601 |
| | | (0.4191) | | (0.3703) | | (0.2152) | |
| Number of observations | | 13,896 | | | | | |
| Log likelihood | | -5140.1 | | | | | |

*Notes:* As for Table A11.1.3.

# Appendix A14

Table A14.1: Size and Distribution of the Inter-country Floating Population by Macro Region and by Province, 2000

| | Total Population (1000) | Provincial Share of China's population (%) | Floating Population (1000) | Intra-province Floating Population (1000) | Inter-province Floating Population (1000) | Share of floating Popn over Total Provincial Popn (%) | Share of provincial floating popn over total floating popn (%) | Provincial share of inter-province floating popn (%) |
|---|---|---|---|---|---|---|---|---|
| China | 1,242,612 | 100.0 | 78,757 | 36,338 | 42,419 | 6.3 | 100.0 | 100.0 |
| East | | | | | | | | |
| Beijing | 13,569 | 1.1 | 2,604 | 140 | 2,463 | 19.2 | 3.3 | 5.8 |
| Tianjin | 9,849 | 0.8 | 791 | 56 | 735 | 8.0 | 1.0 | 1.7 |
| Hebei | 66,684 | 5.4 | 2,132 | 1,201 | 930 | 3.2 | 2.7 | 2.2 |
| Liaoning | 41,824 | 3.4 | 2,306 | 1,261 | 1,045 | 5.5 | 2.9 | 2.5 |
| Shanghai | 16,408 | 1.3 | 4,360 | 1,225 | 3,135 | 26.6 | 5.5 | 7.4 |
| Jiangsu | 73,044 | 5.9 | 5,007 | 2,470 | 2,537 | 6.9 | 6.4 | 6.0 |
| Zhejiang | 45,931 | 3.7 | 5,426 | 1,737 | 3,689 | 11.8 | 6.9 | 8.7 |
| Fujian | 34,098 | 2.7 | 3,807 | 1,662 | 2,145 | 11.2 | 4.8 | 5.1 |
| Shandong | 89,972 | 7.2 | 2,687 | 1,654 | 1,033 | 3.0 | 3.4 | 2.4 |
| Guangdong | 85,225 | 6.9 | 21,054 | 5,989 | 15,065 | 24.7 | 26.7 | 35.5 |
| Guangxi | 43,855 | 3.5 | 1,843 | 1,415 | 428 | 4.2 | 2.3 | 1.0 |
| Hainan | 7,559 | 0.6 | 654 | 272 | 382 | 8.7 | 0.8 | 0.9 |
| Middle | | | | | | | | |
| Shanxi | 32,471 | 2.6 | 1,459 | 792 | 667 | 4.5 | 1.9 | 1.6 |

*(contd...)*

*(Table Appendix A14.1 continued)*

| | Total Population (1000) | Provincial Share of China's population (%) | Floating Population (1000) | Intra-province Floating Population (1000) | Inter-province Floating Population (1000) | Share of floating Popn over Total Provincial Popn (%) | Share of provincial floating popn over total floating popn (%) | Provincial share of inter-province floating popn (%) |
|---|---|---|---|---|---|---|---|---|
| Inner Mongolia | 23,323 | 1.9 | 1,773 | 1,225 | 548 | 7.6 | 2.3 | 1.3 |
| Jilin | 26,802 | 2.2 | ,944 | 636 | 309 | 3.5 | 1.2 | 0.7 |
| Heilongjiang | 36,238 | 2.9 | 1,794 | 1,407 | 387 | 4.9 | 2.3 | 0.9 |
| Anhui | 59,000 | 4.7 | 1,184 | 954 | 230 | 2.0 | 1.5 | 0.5 |
| Jiangxi | 40,398 | 3.3 | 1,009 | 755 | 253 | 2.5 | 1.3 | 0.6 |
| Henan | 91,237 | 7.3 | 2,012 | 1,536 | 476 | 2.2 | 2.6 | 1.1 |
| Hubei | 59,509 | 4.8 | 2,239 | 1,629 | 610 | 3.8 | 2.8 | 1.4 |
| Hunan | 63,274 | 5.1 | 1,770 | 1,421 | 349 | 2.8 | 2.2 | 0.8 |
| West | | | | | | | | |
| Chongqing | 30,513 | 2.5 | 885 | 481 | 403 | 2.9 | 1.1 | 1.0 |
| Sichuan | 82,348 | 6.6 | 2,748 | 2,212 | 536 | 3.3 | 3.5 | 1.3 |
| Guizhou | 35,248 | 2.8 | 1,253 | 845 | 409 | 3.6 | 1.6 | 1.0 |
| Yunnan | 42,360 | 3.4 | 2,512 | 1,348 | 1,164 | 5.9 | 3.2 | 2.7 |
| Tibet | 2,616 | 0.2 | 153 | 44 | 109 | 5.9 | 0.2 | 0.3 |
| Shaanxi | 35,365 | 2.8 | 1,041 | 615 | 426 | 2.9 | 1.3 | 1.0 |
| Gansu | 25,124 | 2.0 | 717 | 489 | 228 | 2.9 | 0.9 | 0.5 |
| Qinghai | 4,823 | 0.4 | 308 | 184 | 124 | 6.4 | 0.4 | 0.3 |
| Ningxia | 5,486 | 0.4 | 366 | 175 | 192 | 6.7 | 0.5 | 0.5 |
| Xinjiang | 18,460 | 1.5 | 1917 | 506 | 1,411 | 10.4 | 2.4 | 3.3 |

*Source*: Author's elaboration on China Statistical Yearbook, NSB, 2002 (population census data).

Table A14.2. Rural Workers Migration in the PRC by Macro-region

| Macro-region | Total (1000) | Home country (1000) | Home province (1000) | Out of province (1000) | Regional share/tot (per cent) | Out of province/tot out province (per cent) | Home country (all in per cent) | Home province (all in per cent) | Out of province (all in per cent) | Total (all in per cent) |
|---|---|---|---|---|---|---|---|---|---|---|
| China | 72,006 | 27,133 | 21,262 | 23,611 | 100.0 | 100.0 | 37.7 | 29.5 | 32.8 | 100.0 |
| East | 34,108 | 15,149 | 12,518 | 6,441 | 47.4 | 27.3 | 44.4 | 36.7 | 18.9 | 100.0 |
| Middle | 23,221 | 7,350 | 5,202 | 10,669 | 32.2 | 45.2 | 31.7 | 22.4 | 45.9 | 100.0 |
| West | 14,677 | 4,634 | 3,542 | 6,501 | 20.4 | 27.5 | 31.6 | 24.1 | 44.3 | 100.0 |

*Source*: Author's elaboration on FASC, NACO, NBS (1999).